THE WAFFEN SS

Hitler's Elite Guard at War

1939–1945

THE WAFFEN SS

Hitler's Elite Guard at War

1939–1945

𝕾𝕾

By GEORGE H. STEIN

Columbia University

CORNELL UNIVERSITY PRESS

Ithaca, New York

CORNELL UNIVERSITY PRESS

First published 1966

Library of Congress Catalog Card Number: 66-11049

PRINTED IN THE UNITED STATES OF AMERICA

BY THE MAPLE PRESS COMPANY

TO MY PARENTS

Preface

THE complex and powerful SS organization headed by Heinrich Himmler has understandably received attention from those who have written about the Third Reich. Their focus has been mainly on such atrocious SS activities as racial extermination, medical experiments on the living, mass enslavement, and Gestapo tortures. These monstrous acts have been thoroughly and remorselessly exposed with the aid of the records collected for the trials of war criminals at Nuremberg. This is as it should be.

In the popular mind, both here and abroad, the letters *SS* have become a symbol for all that was most horrible in Hitler's Europe. Nonetheless, the doctrine of criminal conspiracy and collective guilt formulated during the Nuremberg era no longer satisfies serious investigators. Without minimizing the extent of the staggering crimes committed by Himmler's minions, recent research has shown that the SS was in fact more varied and complex than the monolithic criminal organization indicted before the International Military Tribunal. There appears to have been little uniformity among the various components of the SS at any time; and with the coming of war some components—like the concentration-camp system, the police system, and the Waffen SS—took on a life of their own and followed a course distinct from that of any of the others. Consequently, no sound interpretation or evaluation of the entire SS organization can be formulated until each of its more important elements has been subjected to a thorough investigation, based on the still largely unexploited SS records.

This book seeks to examine one of these elements; it is devoted to the Waffen SS, the military branch of the Nazi Elite Guard and the largest component of Himmler's wartime empire. Emphasis has been placed on the development of the Waffen SS: its purpose, the techniques by which it grew, its structure and organization, its utilization of foreign manpower, its relations with the Wehrmacht, the factors which set it apart from the Army, its successes and failures in battle, and the role it played in the military fortunes of the Third Reich. In addition, an attempt has been made to deal with the thorny and controversial problem of Waffen SS criminality.

It may be well to list some of the things the reader will not find in this book. First, although the more important campaigns and battles are given considerable attention, no attempt has been made to write anything like a complete campaign history of the Waffen SS. Such an endeavor would be a logical complement to the present study, but would require at least another volume to do it justice. Similarly, although a chapter has been devoted to a discussion of the effects of ideological indoctrination on the military performance of the Waffen SS, it has not been possible to treat in any detail the larger subject of SS ideology, which rightly belongs to the still larger subject of National Socialist ideology—a topic that falls outside the scope of this book.[1] Finally, a familiarity with the basic nature of the Nazi system and with the main outlines of the war in Europe has been taken for granted.

[1] Published literature on the ideology of the SS is almost nonexistent; anyone interested in the subject would do well to begin with the comprehensive survey article by Robert Koehl, "The Character of the Nazi SS," *The Journal of Modern History*, XXXIV (September 1962), 275–283. Some of the more important interpretations of the SS that discuss ideology are Karl O. Paetel, "Die SS: Ein Beitrag zur Soziologie des Nationalsozialismus," *Vierteljahrshefte für Zeitgeschichte*, II (January 1954), 1–33; Hans Buchheim, "Die SS in der Verfassung des Dritten Reiches," *ibid.*, III (April 1955), 127–157; Ermenhild Neusüss-Hunkel, *Die SS* ("Schriftenreihe des Instituts für wissenschaftliche Politik in Marburg/Lahn," No. 2; Hannover, 1956); Eugen Kogon, *Der SS-Staat* (Frankfurt am Main, 1946). Hans

The primary purpose of this book, then, is to trace the evolution of the Waffen SS and to ascertain the part it played in the history of the Third Reich. If, beyond this, it contributes a missing piece to the jigsaw puzzle which is the SS, my broader aim will have been achieved.

GEORGE H. STEIN

New York City
June 1965

Buchheim's suggestive essay, "Befehl und Gehorsam," Hans Buchheim *et al., Anatomie des SS-Staates* (Olten, 1965), I, 255ff., was published after the present book was already in press; I therefore could not take it into account.

Acknowledgments

I WOULD like to acknowledge my gratitude to Professor John H. Wuorinen for his advice, stimulation, and encouragement throughout the greater part of this project; to Professors Fritz Stern and Henry L. Roberts and Mr. Karl O. Paetel, who read an earlier version of the manuscript and made valuable suggestions for improving it; to Professor Harvey L. Dyck, my colleague, friend, and neighbor, for reading the completed manuscript and saving me from a number of solecisms, while at the same time making numerous suggestions for improving both its style and substance; and to my colleagues Professors Herman Ausubel and Norman F. Cantor for their wise counsel and encouragement.

To my friend William E. Shapiro for his assistance in the selection of photographs and maps.

To the staffs of the Exhibits and Publications Division of the National Archives, Washington, D.C.; the World War II Records Division of the National Archives, Alexandria, Virginia; the Wiener Library, London; the Institut für Zeitgeschichte, Munich; the Office of the Chief of Military History, Department of the Army, Washington, D.C.; and the Columbia University libraries for their courtesy and helpfulness.

To the William A. Dunning Fund of the Department of History, Columbia University, for financial assistance in preparing this book for the press.

To the editors of *The Wiener Library Bulletin,* London, and the *Military Review,* U.S. Army Command and General

Staff College, for permitting me to reprint portions of articles which I wrote initially for their publications.

To my wife, Dorothy Lahm Stein, to whom I am indebted above all others, not only for her inexhaustible patience and unfailing encouragement, but for the knowledge and skills that she so unstintingly contributed to ease the burdens of this work.

Author's Note on Sources and Style

NO serious study of the Waffen SS has ever before been published. Indeed, to my knowledge, there are only three works specifically devoted to the subject: the tendentious and superficial *Waffen-SS im Einsatz* (Göttingen, 1953) by former SS Oberstgruppenführer (Colonel General) Paul Hausser, the more sophisticated but no less tendentious *Die Armee der Geächteten* (Göttingen, 1963) by former SS Obergruppenführer (General) Felix Steiner, and the incisive but brief (twenty-nine pages) pamphlet entitled *Die Waffen-SS* ("Das Dritte Reich," No. 5; Berlin, 1960) by Walter Görlitz.

There are of course a number of good books and articles on the SS which also discuss the Waffen SS, although none has made use of the captured SS records recently made available to researchers. Gerald Reitlinger's authoritative study of the entire SS organization, *The SS: Alibi of a Nation* (New York, 1957), while not primarily concerned with the Waffen SS, provides an extremely valuable introduction to the subject. Also indispensable to students of the Waffen SS, especially for the period of its prewar development, are Ermenhild Neusüss-Hunkel's *Die SS* ("Schriftenreihe des Instituts für wissenschaftliche Politik in Marburg/Lahn," No. 2; Hannover, 1956) and the two studies by Hans Buchheim, *SS und Polizei im NS-Staat* ("Staatspolitische Schriftenreihe"; Bonn, 1964) and "Die SS in der Verfassung des Dritten Reiches," *Vierteljahrshefte für Zeitgeschichte,* III (April 1955), 127–157.

The many other books and articles upon which I have drawn (and to which I am indebted) are cited in footnotes and listed in the bibliography. My account, however, is based largely on original source materials, most of them captured German records formerly included in the collection of the World War II Records Division of the National Archives (previously the Adjutant General's Office, Departmental Records Branch, U.S. Army), at Alexandria, Virginia. Between 1956 and 1963, the major portion of this collection was microfilmed by the American Historical Association's Committee for the Study of War Documents in cooperation with the National Archives and the Department of the Army, and is now deposited in the National Archives, Washington, D.C.[1]

Two record groups contain the bulk of the materials relating to the Waffen SS. The first, and the most important single source from which this study is drawn, is the collection of Records of the Reich Leader of the SS and Chief of the German Police (*Reichsführer SS und Chef der Deutschen Polizei*). This is a vast collection which originally consisted of more than 1000 linear feet of files. The greater part of this material has been declassified and filmed; it is now available at the National Archives, where it is identified as Microcopy T–175.[2] Three mimeographed finding aids describe 536 rolls of microfilmed material from this record group.[3]

The second record group consists of operational records of Waffen SS units which served in Germany and Western Europe (those of units which were engaged along the eastern front have not yet been declassified). They are available on rolls 116–342 of National Archives Microcopy T–354.[4] I have examined some of the records of the Kommandoamt der Waffen SS (its operational headquarters) included in this collection, but they proved to be disappointingly routine. Nonetheless, anyone contemplat-

---

[1] Most of the original records have been returned to the Federal Republic of Germany.

[2] Cited as RFSS/T–175, followed by the roll and frame numbers.

[3] *Guides to German Records Microfilmed at Alexandria, Va.*, Nos. 32, 33, and 39 (Washington: National Archives, 1961–1963).

[4] A description of this material may be found in *ibid.*, No. 27.

ing a detailed campaign history of the Waffen SS or a study of units whose records are included in this collection would undoubtedly find this material of considerable value.

Small quantities of material relating to the Waffen SS may also be found in Records of Headquarters, German Armed Forces High Command *(Oberkommando der Wehrmacht)*, National Archives Microcopy T-77; Records of Headquarters, German Army High Command *(Oberkommando des Heeres)*, National Archives Microcopy T-78; Records of the National Socialist German Labor Party *(Nationalsozialistische Deutsche Arbeiterpartei)*, National Archives Microcopy T-81; and the huge collection of Records of German Field Commands, which covers a number of National Archives microcopies. Anyone desiring to locate Waffen SS records in these collections (other than those for which I have supplied specific references) has no option but to screen the relevant *Guides* item by item.

In addition to microfilmed German records, an invaluable source of documentary material for this narrative has been the material assembled for the various war-crimes trials at Nuremberg. Some of the documents used in the first Nuremberg trial have been published (in the original German text, although often in extract only) in the forty-two-volume *Trial of the Major War Criminals* (Nuremberg: International Military Tribunal, 1947–1949); all of the Nuremberg documents I have cited by initials (usually PS) and number (without further reference) may be found in this series simply by locating the letter-number combinations on the binding of the volumes.

Additional documents (in English translation) appear in the ten-volume compilation *Nazi Conspiracy and Aggression* (Washington: U.S. Government Printing Office, 1946).[5] However, most of the Nuremberg materials remain unpublished and are available only in mimeographed copy (usually in poor translation) at various depositories. The collection used in this study is located in the International Law Library, Columbia University, New York City. Most of the mimeographed documents I

---

[5] Cited as NCA, followed by volume and page numbers.

have used are from the twelve later Nuremberg trials (those held before the Nuremberg Military Tribunals) and bear the initials NG (Nazi Government), NO (Nazi Organization), or NOKW (Nazi Oberkommando der Wehrmacht). If the documents are bound, I have cited case number, document book (or other binding inscription), and page. Not surprisingly, I have found the originals of a number of mimeographed Nuremberg documents in the microfilmed SS records.

Finally, two sources that were invaluable in treating the combat role of the Waffen SS during the last two years of the war are *Hitlers Lagebesprechungen: Die Protokollfragmente seiner militärischen Konferenzen, 1942–1945* (Stuttgart: Deutsche Verlags-Anstalt, 1962) and *Kriegstagebuch des Oberkommandos der Wehrmacht (Wehrmachtführungsstab), 1940–1945* (Frankfurt am Main: Bernard & Graefe Verlag für Wehrwesen, 1961ff.), IV–V.

The abbreviated citations most frequently used in this book are:

IMT	*Trial of the Major War Criminals before the International Military Tribunal* (Nuremberg: International Military Tribunal, 1947–1949).
KTB/OKW	*Kriegstagebuch des Oberkommandos der Wehrmacht* (Frankfurt am Main: Bernard & Graefe Verlag, 1961ff.).
NCA	*Nazi Conspiracy and Aggression* (Washington: U.S. Government Printing Office, 1946).
NSDAP/T–81	Records of the National Socialist German Labor Party (Washington: National Archives, Microcopy T–81).
OKH/T–78	Records of Headquarters, German Army High Command (Washington: National Archives, Microcopy T–78).
OKW/T–77	Records of Headquarters, German Armed Forces High Command (Washington: National Archives, Microcopy T–77).

RFSS/T–175   Records of the Reich Leader of the SS and Chief of the German Police (Washington: National Archives, Microcopy T–175).

SHAEF Report *Report by the Supreme Commander to the Combined Chiefs of Staff on the Operations in Europe of the Allied Expeditionary Force, 6 June 1944 to 8 May 1945* (Washington: U.S. Government Printing Office, 1946).

TGMWC   *The Trial of German Major War Criminals: Proceedings of the International Military Tribunal Sitting at Nuremberg, Germany* (London: H.M. Stationery Office, 1949–1951).

In general, SS units, organizations, offices, and the like are rendered in the original German; where it seemed necessary (at least at first mention), I have supplied the English translation or equivalent in parentheses—e.g., Totenkopfverbände (Death's Head detachments). The most frequently used German terms are also defined in the glossary which begins on p. 300.

Similarly, SS ranks are given in the original German, with the equivalent German Army rank supplied in English translation in parentheses wherever it seemed desirable—e.g., SS Gruppenführer (Lieutenant General) Hans Schmidt. German Army ranks, on the other hand, have simply been translated—e.g., Generalleutnant Hans Schmidt would be rendered Lieutenant General Hans Schmidt. Since German Army ranks above colonel (Oberst) are not equivalent to those in the U.S. Army, a conversion table has been supplied on p. 295.

Contents

Preface vii

Acknowledgments xi

Author's Note on Sources and Style xiii

By Way of Introduction xxv

Chapter One—The Formative Years: 1933–1939 1
    Changing of the Guard
    The SS Verfügungstruppe: Organization, Selection, and
        Training
    Purpose of the Verfügungstruppe
    Wehrmacht and SS: The Führer Decree of August 17, 1938
    On the Eve of War

Chapter Two—From Verfügungstruppe to Waffen SS: The
First Months of War, 1939–1940 27
    The Polish Campaign, 1939
    Preparations for the Campaign in the West
    Struggle for Recognition and Manpower
    SS Recruiting Campaign of Early 1940
    The Title *Waffen SS* Becomes Official
    Fight for Arms
    The Waffen SS Joins the Army: Final Preparations for
        the Offensive

Chapter Three—Toward a Military Reputation: The
Waffen SS in the Western Campaign, 1940 60
Fall Gelb and the Role of the Waffen SS
The Waffen SS in the Netherlands
The Waffen SS in Flanders and Artois
Advance toward Dunkirk
The SS Totenkopfdivision and the Massacre at Le Paradis
Escape of the British Expeditionary Force
The Waffen SS and the Battle of France
The Waffen SS and the Western Campaign in Retrospect

Chapter Four—From West to East: The Development of the
Waffen SS between the Fall of France and the Invasion
of the Soviet Union 93
Struggle for Manpower: SS–Wehrmacht Relations, 1940–
1941
Reorganization and Expansion for a New Campaign
Balkan Interlude: The Waffen SS in Yugoslavia and
Greece, April 1941

Chapter Five—Some Military Consequences of an Ideology:
The Waffen SS in Russia 119
Operation Barbarossa
SS Ideology and the War in the East
A Waffen SS Defeat
A New Kind of War

Chapter Six—The West European SS: Mobilization of
Foreign Nationals, I 137
Myth of a European Army
The Germanic SS
Germanic Legions of the Waffen SS
The West European SS in 1942 and Thereafter

Chapter Seven—The East European SS: Mobilization of
Foreign Nationals, II 165
The Russian Winter Counteroffensive
Volksdeutsche in the Waffen SS

Baltic Legions of the SS, 1942–1945
The Eastern Waffen SS
Flights of Fancy: The British and Indian Legions
Conclusions

Chapter Eight—The Waffen SS Comes of Age: 1942–1943 197
Development of the Waffen SS in 1942
Organization and Development of the Waffen SS in 1943

Chapter Nine—To the Bitter End: The Waffen SS and the
Defense of the Third Reich, 1943–1945 212
Defensive Battles in the East, 1943–1944
Allied Invasion and the Battle for France, 1944
Last German Offensive in the West: The Ardennes, 1944–
1945
Last German Offensive in the Southeast: Hungary, 1945
Battle of Berlin and the Fall of the Third Reich

Chapter Ten—The Tarnished Shield: Waffen SS
Criminality 250
Waffen SS, Totenkopfverbände, and Concentration Camps
Waffen SS and Einsatzgruppen
The SS Sonderkommandos Dirlewanger and Kaminski
Military Atrocities of the Waffen SS

Chapter Eleven—Reprise and Assessment 282

Appendices 295
I Comparative Table of Waffen SS, German Army,
and U.S. Army Ranks
II List of Waffen SS Field Units, 1944–1945
III Glossary of Most Frequently Used German Terms
IV Chart of the SS Organization, 1943

Selected Bibliography 305

Index 315

Illustrations

facing page

SS Verfügungstruppen on review 28
Honor guard of Liebstandarte SS "Adolf Hitler" presents
   arms to Japanese Ambassador, Oshima 29
SS Division "Totenkopf" in Russia, 1941 60
Reichsführer SS Heinrich Himmler visiting SS troops in the
   East, 1941 60
SS panzer grenadiers in Russia, 1943 61
SS mountain troops hunt partisans in Serbia, 1942 61
SS Panzerkorps near Kharkov, March 1943 92
Commander of an SS panzer unit issues instructions, Russia,
   May 1943 93
SS noncommissioned officer, Kharkov, 1943 93
SS-Police unit along Slovenian border, February 1944 124
SS machine-gun post in Russian forest, 1943 124
SS Sturmbannführer Meyerdress, 1944 125
SS Kavalleriedivision "Florian Geyer" in Russia, 1944 156
Adolf Hitler, SS Obergruppenführer Felix Steiner, and
   SS Sturmbannführer Leon Degrelle, 1944 156
SS infantry in retreat, 1944 157
Reichsführer SS Heinrich Himmler, 1937 188
SS Oberführer Felix Steiner, 1940 188
SS Obergruppenführer Josef (Sepp) Dietrich, 1941 188
SS Obergruppenführer Paul Hausser, 1943 188
SS Obergruppenführer Theodor Eicke, 1943 189
SS Standartenführer Fritz Witt, 1942 189
SS Sturmbannführer Kurt Meyer, 1941 189
SS Obergruppenführer Hans Jüttner, probably 1943 or 1944 189

Maps

facing page

World War II in Europe, 1939–1941 62

World War II in Europe, 1942–1943 198

World War II in Europe, 1944–VE Day 214

All maps reprinted from Encyclopedia International, *by permission of the publishers, Grolier Incorporated, New York.*

By Way of Introduction

THE complexity of the SS organization defies brief exposition, but a series of short definitions tracing the main contours of the principal components of Himmler's empire can be offered here by way of introduction.[1]

The Allgemeine SS [2]

The revolutionary militia of the National Socialist movement during its early years was the brown-shirted Sturmabteilung (Storm Section), or SA. This Party army was, however, a mass organization, and Hitler felt a growing need for a small elite force that would be unconditionally responsive to his will. Accordingly, he ordered his personal bodyguards to recruit in each of Germany's major cities a small group of reliable

---

[1] For a schematic view of the SS organization during the war years see the chart on p. 304.

[2] The Allgemeine (General) SS remains one of the least-known components of the SS. Most of the information on which this summary is based may be found in NCA, II, 173ff.; TGMWC, XXII, 351, 477ff.; and the official history of the SS by Gunter d'Alquen, *Die SS: Geschichte, Aufgabe und Organisation der Schutzstaffeln der NSDAP,* reproduced in *Das Dritte Reich im Aüfbau* (Berlin, 1939), III, 201ff., and partly reproduced in English translation as Nuremberg Document 2284–PS. Vast and still unexploited records of the Allgemeine SS are scattered throughout RFSS/T–175. A large collection of records of the Oberabschnitte der Allgemeine SS may be found in rolls 343–602 of National Archives Microcopy T–354. For the strength of the Allgemeine SS (as well as the other branches of the SS) see the reports by Himmler's Inspekteur für Statistik, Dr. Korherr, in RFSS/T–175, 111/2635806ff.

Nazis who could be counted upon to spearhead a revolution and to provide protection for the Führer and his entourage as they traveled about the country. Altogether, some 200 men were selected for what was initially known as the Stosstrupp "Adolf Hitler." In time, these local shock troops became known collectively as the Schutzstaffel (Protection Squad), or SS.

After Hitler's abortive Munich putsch in 1923, the SA was outlawed. But the tiny SS, which had also participated, was overlooked by the authorities. When Hitler was released from prison at the end of 1924, the SA was still banned. Now more than ever he felt the need for a loyal bodyguard; by filling this role the small SS consolidated its position within the Nazi Party. In 1926, the ban on the SA was lifted, and the SS sank into the background for the next few years.

The real history of the SS begins on January 16, 1929, with Hitler's appointment of twenty-eight-year-old Heinrich Himmler as Reichsführer SS. At the time, the total strength of the SS was only 280 men. Hitler commissioned his "Ignatius Loyola" (as he called Himmler) to "form of this organization an elite troop of the Party, a troop dependable in every circumstance." Under Himmler's direction the SS, according to its official history, became a formation "composed of the best physically, the most dependable, and the most faithful men in the Nazi movement." [3] By the time Hitler became Chancellor in January 1933, the SS had some 52,000 members. The SA, of which the SS was still nominally a part, numbered in the neighborhood of 300,000 men.

By the end of the year, the SA had grown into an unwieldy organization of between two and three million members who, under the leadership of Ernst Röhm, were demanding a continuation of the revolution. Hitler, on the other hand, had already decided to stabilize his regime by coming to terms with the Army and the conservative elements in the nation. Tension increased until the summer of 1934, when Hitler was finally persuaded to purge the unruly SA; the SS provided the necessary gunmen and firing squads.

After the murder of Röhm and the emasculation of the SA, Himmler was made responsible only to Hitler, and the SS

[3] D'Alquen, *Die SS*, p. 7, quoted in Nuremberg Document 2284–PS.

became a separate formation of the Nazi Party (NSDAP). It grew during the course of the next decade into a powerful and highly complex organization with manifold activities.

Until 1933 there were no officially recognized branches of the SS; it was simply a group of part-time "volunteer political soldiers." Within the next few years, however, a number of specialized, full-time components developed out of this original nucleus. As a result, the main body was designated the Allgemeine (General) SS. It was composed of all SS men who did not belong to any of the special branches. In 1939 the strength of the General SS was about a quarter of a million men.

Although the General SS had no specific function other than to "remain on call as during the struggle for power [*Kampfzeit*]," individual members were utilized in many phases of SS activity. Above all, the General SS—with its racial selection, ideological teachings, rigorously enforced marriage code, smart black uniform, and shiny jackboots—was the backbone and spiritual fountainhead of the prewar SS. With the coming of the war, however, members of the General SS were drafted into the Wehrmacht or the Waffen SS in such numbers that the organization soon dwindled into insignificance. By the end of the war the strength of the General SS barely exceeded 40,000 men.

Of course the demise of the General SS was more than compensated for by the growth and development of other branches. The three main pillars of Himmler's wartime empire—Security Service, Police, and Waffen SS—were all established or brought under SS control between 1933 and the outbreak of the war.

The Security Service and the Police [4]

In 1931 Himmler established an unofficial SS security service, known as the Sicherheitsdienst, or SD. Under the direction of

[4] Much of the information on which this summary is based may be found in NCA, II, 196ff., 248ff.; TGMWC, XXII, 473ff.; and Reitlinger, *op. cit., passim.* An extensive index to the SS and Police documents received in evidence or referred to during the trial before the International Military Tribunal may be found in NCA, II, 237ff., 302ff.; 355 rolls of microfilmed records of the police and security agencies under the command of Reichsführer SS and Chef der Deutschen Polizei are described in *Guides to*

Reinhard Heydrich, the SD, on June 9, 1934, became the official intelligence and counterespionage agency of the Nazi Party. On November 11, 1938, a decree of the Reich Minister of the Interior appointed the SD the intelligence organization of the Reich. And finally, in the wake of the July 1944 attempt on Hitler's life, the SD absorbed the Abwehr, the intelligence department of the Armed Forces High Command. Such was the sequence of events by which the SS secured a virtual monopoly of intelligence and security activities in Nazi Germany.

Meanwhile, Himmler worked assiduously to gain control of the Third Reich's police system. His efforts were rewarded on June 17, 1936, when Hitler appointed him Chief of the German Police (Reichsführer SS und Chef der Deutschen Polizei im Reichsministerium des Innern).[5] Nine days later Himmler issued a decree dividing the German police system into two principal branches: the Ordnungspolizei (Regular Police), or Orpo, and the Sicherheitspolizei (Security Police), or Sipo. The Ordnungspolizei was uniformed and consisted of the Schutzpolizei (National Police), the Gendarmerie (Rural Police), and the Gemeindepolizei (Local Police). The Sicherheitspolizei usually wore mufti and was composed of the Reich Kriminalpolizei (State Criminal Police), or Kripo, and the Geheime Staatspolizei (State Secret Police), or Gestapo.

Himmler vested command of the Ordnungspolizei in SS Obergruppenführer (General) Kurt Daluege; the Sicherheitspolizei went to SS Obergruppenführer Reinhard Heydrich, who —in keeping with his dual responsibility—took the new title of Chief of the Security Police and SD. Heydrich was thus in control of an SS organization and two police organizations. To end this anomaly, on September 27, 1939, Himmler—acting in his

German Records Microfilmed at Alexandria, Va., No. 39 (Washington, 1963), and are available as RFSS/T–175.

[5] See "Erlass über die Einsetzung eines Chefs der Deutschen Polizei im Reichsministerium des Innern," June 17, 1936. _Reichsgesetzblatt,_ 1936, pp. 487 f., reproduced as Nuremberg Document 2073–PS. On the development of the political police in the first years of the Third Reich see "Die organisatorische Entwicklung der politischen Polizei in Deutschland in den Jahren 1933 und 1934," _Gutachten des Instituts für Zeitgeschichte_ (Munich, 1958), pp. 294ff.

capacity as Reichsführer SS und Chef der Deutschen Polizei—ordered the unification of the Gestapo, Kripo, and SD under a new main SS office called the Reichssicherheitshauptamt (Main Office of Reich Security), or RSHA.[6] Heydrich directed this organization until his assassination on June 4, 1942. After a short interregnum during which Himmler exercised personal control, SS Gruppenführer (Lieutenant General) Ernst Kaltenbrunner took over, holding the post until the end of the war.

It was the RSHA that was entrusted with the over-all administration of the "final solution" of the Jewish "problem," and members of the Gestapo, Kripo, and SD held the key positions in the murder squads (the so-called Einsatzgruppen, or Action Groups) which conducted the mass shootings of Jews and others behind the German armies advancing into the Soviet Union.[7] At its peak strength, during the last two years of the war, the RSHA and all of its subdepartments numbered fewer than 70,000 men.

As a result of Himmler's coordination of the Police, the officials of the Sicherheitspolizei and the Ordnungspolizei were given equivalent ranks in the SS.[8] Unlike the Security Police, the Ordnungspolizei was not integrated into the RSHA. It was, however, raised to the level of a separate main office (Hauptamt Ordnungspolizei) within the SS hierarchy. Few members of the Orpo were SS men, yet thousands were conscripted into Himmler's SS Police regiments. Some of these Police formations were sent into combat during emergencies, but most of them were employed to fight partisans and to assist the Einsatzgrup-

---

[6] The records dealing with evolution of the RSHA may be found in RFSS/T–175, rolls 232–233, 239. The evolution of the Gestapo is traced on rolls 422–432, and that of the SD on roll 239.

[7] A series of periodic reports on the genocidal and antipartisan activities of the Einsatzgruppen and their subformations in Eastern Europe between June 1941 and May 1943, entitled "Ereignismeldungen UdSSR, Meldungen aus den besetzten Ostgebieten," may be found in RFSS/T–175, rolls 233–235.

[8] See Hans Buchheim, *Die Aufnahme von Polizeiangehörigan in die SS und die Ausgleichung ihrer SS-Dienstgrade an ihre Beamtenränge (Dienstgradangleichung) in der Zeit des Dritten Reiches* (Munich, 1960), mimeographed.

xxx   *By Way of Introduction*

pen in their extermination operations. In fact, many of the worst atrocities attributed to the SS were actually committed by German policemen, not a few of whom had been walking a beat or directing traffic until the outbreak of the war.[9] Another 15,000 members of the Ordnungspolizei were drafted directly into the SS Polizeidivision, a field division of the Waffen SS created in October 1939.

To cap his integration scheme, Himmler appointed a Higher SS and Police Leader (Höhere SS- und Polizeiführer) in each military district (Wehrkreis) to serve as his personal representative and to coordinate the activities of the Orpo, Sipo, SD, and General SS in the area. With the coming of the war, this system was extended to the German-occupied areas as well, and the Higher SS and Police Leaders were the agents through whom Himmler transmitted many of his most notorious orders.[10]

The Waffen SS

At the beginning of World War II the term *Waffen SS* was unknown. Four years later, prefaced by such adjectives as elite and fanatical, it appeared regularly in Allied war communiqués. By 1940 *Waffen SS* had become the official designation for the combat units of the SS, which had grown from the handful of armed troops maintained by the Reichsführer SS, Heinrich Himmler, for security and ceremonial purposes. Originally known as SS Verfügungstruppen, the armed SS grew slowly in the prewar years. Hitler's bodyguard, the Leibstandarte SS "Adolf Hitler," provided the nucleus around which two regiments had grown by 1936. Two years later the armed SS consisted of four regiments. Although the SS Verfügungstruppen were described by their leaders as "political soldiers," "ideolog-

[9] On the Ordnungspolizei in general see Hans-Joachim Neufeldt, Jürgen Huck, and Georg Tessin, *Zur Geschichte der Ordnungspolizei 1936–1945* (Coblenz, 1957). Records of the Ordnungspolizei are scattered throughout RFSS/T–175, but rolls 229–231 contain a solid group of materials relating to the Ordnungspolizei and the SS Polizei Regimenter and Bataillonen.

[10] See Hans Buchheim, "Die Höheren SS- und Polizeiführer," *Vierteljahrshefte für Zeitgeschichte,* XI (1963), 362–391. Records of Höheren SS- und Polizeiführer and their subordinates in Germany and in the occupied countries may be found in RFSS/T–175, rolls 219–229.

ical troops," and the "spearhead of National Socialism," their actual purpose long remained unclear.

Then, on August 17, 1938, Hitler issued a decree which established the position of the SS Verfügungstruppe not as part of the Wehrmacht or of the Police but as a standing armed force at his own disposal. Selection of recruits was based on rigid racial and physical standards. Service was voluntary and counted as fulfillment of the national military obligation. In the event of mobilization, the SS troops were to serve under the operational control of the Army. In addition to regular military training, which was in some ways superior to that of the regular Army, the SS troops of the prewar period were subjected to intensive political and ideological indoctrination.

Combat-trained SS troops were represented in the military occupations of the Rhineland, Sudetenland, Austria, and Czechoslovakia. In the Polish campaign of 1939 the SS troops first distinguished themselves in action, and soon thereafter were increased to a strength of three divisions. By the end of the war the Waffen SS consisted of some thirty-eight divisions and had established an unrivaled reputation for toughness in battle. The better SS divisions were recognized as the elite of the German Army and were regarded by their opponents as most formidable adversaries.

By 1943, the exigencies of war had forced the Waffen SS to give up some of its exclusiveness. Large numbers of foreigners were recruited or conscripted, so that by the end of 1944 more than half the men wearing Waffen SS uniforms were not native Germans. Those foreigners who could meet SS racial standards (in general, west Europeans and *Volksdeutsche,* or ethnic Germans) were used as replacements in elite SS divisions or organized into so-called SS Volunteer Divisions (SS Freiwilligen Divisionen). The rest (mainly east Europeans) were segregated in special national formations labeled "Waffen-Grenadier Divisionen der SS." Only the elite armored and mechanized divisions retained any semblance of the old selection standards. It was these divisions, composed largely of Germans, that upheld the military reputation of the Waffen SS even during the last desperate months of the war.

The field formations of the Waffen SS spent the entire war under the tactical command of the Army and thus may be considered a *de facto* branch of the Wehrmacht. Generally speaking, Himmler's authority over the combat troops was limited to matters of administration, discipline, promotion, and ideological training. He did, however, exercise virtually complete control over noncombat formations such as reserve units, training detachments, and military schools.

Himmler adopted the practice of awarding nominal Waffen SS status to personnel in other branches of his appanage, either for administrative reasons or to protect them from conscription. In 1944, for example, some 40,000 of the 600,000 members of the Waffen SS were employed in other components of the SS organization.[11] More than half of them were assigned to the SS Economic and Administrative Main Office (SS-Wirtschafts-und Verwaltungshauptamt, or WVHA), which ran the concentration-camp system.[12] Although the concentration-camp personnel were not under the command of the Army or the Kommandoamt der Waffen SS, they wore Waffen SS uniforms and carried Waffen SS paybooks. Furthermore, there was a relatively limited but nevertheless continuous exchange of personnel between the concentration-camp staffs and the combat formations of the Waffen SS throughout the war. In short, the denials of SS apologists notwithstanding, there existed a connection between the Waffen SS and the concentration camps.[13]

The SS Totenkopfverbände

In addition to the Verfügungstruppe, there was another full-time armed SS formation in prewar Germany. It was composed of the so-called SS Totenkopfverbände, or SS Death's Head detachments, which guarded the concentration camps.

[11] Statistischewissenschaftliches Institut des Reichsführers-SS, "Stärke der SS am 30. 6. 1944," Geheime Kommandosache, RFSS/T–175, 111/2635907ff.

[12] On the concentration-camp system in general see Eugen Kogon, *Der SS-Staat* (Frankfurt am Main, 1946), and Rudolf Höss, *Kommandant in Auschwitz* (Stuttgart, 1958). Files of the WVHA and records of individual concentration camps may be found in RFSS/T–175, rolls 211–219.

[13] For a detailed discussion of this very important point see pp. 259ff.

The first of these units was established at Dachau late in 1933 by SS Standartenführer (Colonel) Theodor Eicke. Subsequently, Eicke was charged with the task of establishing and supervising similar guard detachments at other concentration camps. By mid-1934, Eicke (at the time an SS Brigadeführer [major general]) was semiofficial czar of Germany's burgeoning concentration-camp system. Following his role in the purge of the SA (June 30, 1934), in which the Dachau SS detachment shared with the Leibstandarte the dubious honor of manning the firing squads, Eicke was officially appointed Inspector of Concentration Camps and Commander of the SS Death's Head detachments (Inspekteur der Konzentrationslager und Führer der SS Totenkopfverbände). The new appointment carried with it a double bonus: the Totenkopfverbände were removed from the control of the General SS and Eicke was promoted to SS Gruppenführer (lieutenant general).

With his new Inspectorate firmly established at Oranienburg, near Berlin, Eicke reorganized and enlarged the Totenkopfverbände into five numbered Sturmbanne, or battalions: I "Oberbayern," II "Elbe," III "Sachsen," IV "Ostfriesland," and V "Brandenburg." In 1937 the five battalions were again reorganized, this time into three Standarten, or regiments, which carried the designations "Oberbayern," "Brandenburg," and "Thüringen." They were stationed in Dachau, Oranienburg (Sachsenhausen), and Frankenberg respectively. A few months later Standarte "Thüringen" was transferred from Frankenberg to the Buchenwald concentration camp in Weimar. After the occupation of Austria, a fourth regiment bearing the name "Ostmark" was established at Linz, later providing the guards for the nearby Mauthausen camp.

In addition to their guard duties, Totenkopf formations participated (along with the Verfügungstruppe) in the occupations of Austria, the Sudetenland, and Czechoslovakia. Totenkopf cadres also provided military training for members of the General SS who were to be mobilized as "police reinforcements" in the event of war. When war finally came, some 40,000 General SS reservists were called up to fill more than a dozen new Totenkopfstandarten. At the same time (October 1939), 6500 of the most experienced Totenkopf troops, reinforced by SS reservists, were formed into a new SS combat division (SS Totenkopfdivision) under the command of Theodor Eicke, who now gave up his concentration-camp duties for the more glamorous role of a Waffen SS field commander.

Throughout 1940 and well into 1941, the SS Totenkopfstandarten were employed to police the newly occupied areas and to carry out the deportations and executions that characterized Hitler's ethnic policy. Shortly before the invasion of the Soviet Union, however, some were disbanded, with their personnel used as Waffen SS replacements, while others were integrated directly into new or existing field formations of the Waffen SS. In this fashion, the SS Totenkopfverbände lost their anomalous position (while Himmler considered them part of the Waffen SS, the military authorities refused to recognize duty in the Totenkopfverbände as military service) and became an integral part of the Waffen SS.

In the meantime, the task of guarding the concentration camps was largely taken over by members of the General SS, who were given nominal Waffen SS status.[14] The wartime concentration-camp guards were organized into Totenkopfwachsturmbanne (Death's Head Guard Battalions), which, unlike the pre-1939 Totenkopf units, were under the direct command of the concentration-camp commanders. As of March 3, 1942, both the guard battalions and the camp administrations became part of the infamous Amtsgruppe D of the WVHA. As the war progressed and the manpower needs of the SS field formations increased, more and more able-bodied guards were transferred to the front. They were replaced by older members of such organizations as the SA, by wounded soldiers from all branches of the armed forces, and by members of the Waffen SS unfit for service in the field.

[14] On the nominal Waffen SS status of the wartime concentration-camp guards see Reitlinger, *op. cit.,* p. 265; Felix Kersten, *The Kersten Memoirs, 1940–45* (New York, 1957), pp. 250 f.; and the tendentious but useful evidence of Robert Brill, Paul Hausser, and Guenther Reinecke, TGMWC, XX, 291, 300, 339.

THE WAFFEN SS

Hitler's Elite Guard at War

1939–1945

CHAPTER ONE

The Formative Years:
1933-1939

SHORTLY before noon on Monday, January 30, 1933, Adolf Hitler took the oath of office administered by President Hindenburg and became the twenty-second Chancellor of the German Republic. Later that day, Hitler and his entourage vacated their headquarters in the Hotel Kaiserhof and moved across the street to the Reich Chancellery, the Palais Wilhelmstrasse 77. As he entered the inner courtyard, a detachment of the Reichswehr Chancellery Guard snapped to attention and presented arms to the new Chancellor, as they had to his predecessors; unlike his predecessors Hitler returned their salute with a partially raised arm—his version of the Nazi greeting.

Those Germans who may still not have known where Hitler's power lay were given a dramatic example that evening. Hitler's SA, SS, and Hitler Youth leaders had worked feverishly all afternoon to organize a demonstration befitting the Nazi assumption of power. Throughout Berlin and the surrounding countryside, company after company of the SA and SS were mobilized; in hastily commandeered trucks they were sped to assembly points along the Charlottenburger Chausee, until the broad avenue was filled with brown and black uniforms. As darkness settled over the capital thousands of torches were lighted, and like a blazing serpent the seemingly endless column of triumphant Nazis began to move through the Brandenburg Gate. With torches held high, the beat of drums and the pounding of boots almost drowning out the Horst Wessel song, the marchers paraded down the Wilhelmstrasse. As the aged President Hindenburg gazed in bewilderment from his residence, Hitler, leaning out a well-lighted window farther down the street, saluted each passing detachment and was answered with an ecstatic *"Sieg Heil"* and a circling of torches. So it went, hour after hour, through the night: SA, Hitler Youth, Stahlhelm, NSDAP, and—bringing up the rear—the black-uniformed SS.[1]

The burgeoning SS organization played an important role in the revolution Hitler now set in motion, which eventually culminated in his elevation to dictator and the complete Nazification of Germany. By February 22, fifteen thousand SS men and twenty-five thousand of their SA comrades had been appointed members of an auxiliary police force, which—under the guise of assisting the regular police—was assigned the task of crushing anti-Nazi elements and intimidating voters in the forthcoming election.[2]

Their first important task came in the wake of the Reichstag fire and the promulgation of the decree of February 28 "for the protection of the People and the State," [3] which gave the Nazis virtually unrestricted police power. Squads of SA and SS men went into action all over Germany, breaking into homes and hauling their victims off to makeshift prisons and concentration camps—all on the pretext of saving the nation from an imminent Communist uprising. Although the brown-shirted SA gangs were a ubiquitous manifestation of Nazi terror during this period, many of the organized arrests of those on the Nazi proscription lists were carried out by the better-disciplined and more efficient SS.

[1] The events of January 30, 1933, are fully described in Hans Otto Meissner and Harry Wilde, *Die Machtergreifung* (Stuttgart, 1958), pp. 190ff., and H. S. Hegner, *Die Reichskanzlei 1933–1945* (Frankfurt am Main, 1960), pp. 46ff.

[2] See Alan Bullock, *Hitler: A Study in Tyranny* (rev. ed.; New York, 1962), p. 261.

[3] "Verordnung des Reichspräsidenten von Hindenburg zum Schutz von Volk und Staat vom 28. 2. 1933." For full text see Hans-Adolf Jacobsen and Werner Jochmann (eds.), *Ausgewählte Dokumente zur Geschichte des Nationalsozialismus 1933–1945*, C, Dokument 3. II. 1933.

Despite the legalized violence that marked the election campaign, the Nazis were unable to achieve the majority they sought; with 43.9 per cent of the total vote, Hitler was forced to continue sharing the Government with his Nationalist allies.[4] But this situation was only temporary. During the following eighteen months Hitler dispensed with his allies, suppressed the opposition, gained control of the machinery of state, asserted his authority over the Party and the SA, and acquired the powers of Head of State and Commander-in-Chief of the Armed Forces. He emerged as dictator of Germany.

Looking back on the events of 1933–1934, one might assume that Hitler was confidently and systematically following a preconceived plan which led inexorably toward his seizure of absolute power. This, of course, was not so. Hitler, in 1933 as always, was a masterful opportunist with a ruthless will and a near-demoniac sense of mission. But he had not yet developed the blind faith in his own infallibility that marked his later years. The comparative ease with which he gained control of Germany came as a surprise to him. In mid-March, however, the passage of the so-called Enabling Act[5] and the process of *Gleichschaltung*, by which the whole life of Germany was to be brought under the control of the Nazi Party, still lay in the future.

True, Hitler was Chancellor, the Nazi Party was the largest in the nation, and the SA and SS were in control of the streets; but Hindenburg was still President, and the Reichswehr and—in many states—the Police were not yet under Nazi control. The powerful Communist Party (KPD), although cowed, had not been crushed; and the Nationalists, while friendly, still maintained a sizable and independent paramilitary force in the Stahlhelm (Steel Helmet) organization. It is therefore not surprising that Hitler was concerned about his personal security. Who, for instance, would protect him in the event of an Army putsch? Certainly not the Reichswehr troops who made up the Chancellery Guard. His immediate entourage? Of course the

[4] Bullock, *op. cit.*, p. 265.

[5] "Gesetz zur Behebung der Not von Volk und Reich vom 24. 3. 1933." Text in Jacobsen and Jochmann, *op. cit.*, C, Dokument 24. III. 1933.

watchdog-chauffeur Shreck, the adjutants Brückner and Schaub, and the faithful bodyguard Dietrich would give their lives for their Führer. But this ubiquitous SS "Chauffeureska" [6] which had guarded Hitler throughout the *Kampfzeit* was no longer enough. And so, for the third time in ten years, Hitler ordered the creation of a Stabswache, a headquarters guard composed of thoroughly reliable, full-time SS men who were to be under his personal command. On March 17, 1933, Josef (Sepp) Dietrich—the Bavarian ex-sergeant, former butcher, sometime waiter, and long-time bodyguard—established in Berlin an armed detachment of 120 specially selected SS men, creating the nucleus of what was later to become the Waffen SS.[7]

Changing of the Guard

The creation of the armed SS as a specialized formation alongside the General SS can be understood only if one bears in mind that the SS had originally been created to provide protection for the Führer and other prominent leaders of the Nazi movement during the struggle for power. Until 1932 the SS remained a relatively small and highly select branch of the SA. But during the last year of the *Kampfzeit* it grew enormously; and by January 1933 it numbered more than 50,000 men, with new members pouring in as quickly as they could be processed. Indeed, so rapidly was the SS growing in the early months of 1933 that Himmler was temporarily forced to bar further membership and to purge the thousands of "unqualified" opportunists who had clambered aboard the Nazi bandwagon since the *Machtergreifung*.[8] During this hectic period the SS seemed to be developing into a refined version of the SA, with individual units often more responsive to their local leaders than to either Himmler or Hitler. Under such circumstances the

[6] Ernst Hanfstaengl, *Hitler: The Missing Years* (London, 1957), p. 216. On Hitler's fear of assassination see Hermann Rauschning, *The Voice of Destruction* (New York, 1940), p. 61.

[7] "Ansprache des Reichsführers SS aus Anlass der Übergabe der Führerstandarte an die Leibstandarte 'Adolf Hitler,' Metz, Fort von Alvensleben, am 7. September 1940," RFSS/T–175, 90/2612641. See also Buchheim, "Die SS," p. 139.

[8] Neusüss-Hunkel, *op. cit.,* pp. 8, 18.

part-time volunteers of the General SS, despite their relative superiority to the SA in quality and discipline, no longer constituted the praetorian guard Hitler desired. Hence his decision to establish a new type of elite SS formation—the armed SS.

Soon after Sepp Dietrich's SS Stabswache moved into the former Imperial Cadet barracks on the outskirts of Berlin, the Reichswehr guards were restricted to the exterior of the Wilhelmstrasse complex and the black-uniformed SS men took over inside the Chancellery. Visitors now had to pass through three rings of SS guards to reach the Chancellor; and guests at Hitler's table were served by incongruously athletic-looking waiters wearing neat white jackets in place of their usual black SS blouses. When Hitler ventured out, his car was always accompanied by a number of open black limousines filled with armed young giants in full-dress SS uniforms. After the Chancellery had been rebuilt to Hitler's taste, the SS took over the exterior guard from the Army as well. In time, the two rifle-bearing, black-helmeted SS guards who stood like statues before the massive bronze door of the Chancellery became as familiar to Berliners as the Grenadier Guards at Buckingham Palace to Londoners.

During the Nazi Party rally in September 1933, Hitler awarded his Stabswache the official title Leibstandarte SS "Adolf Hitler" (SS Bodyguard Regiment "Adolf Hitler"). And on November 9, the tenth anniversary of the Munich beer-hall putsch, the men of the Leibstandarte swore a special oath which bound them unconditionally to the person of the Reich Chancellor, Adolf Hitler. The full significance of Hitler's action seems to have been grasped by few Germans at the time; not only had he withdrawn the Leibstandarte from the direct control of the Reichsführer SS and the NSDAP, but he had created —without any legal authority—an independent military force alongside the regular state security organs: the Armed Forces and Police. Although not yet dictator or even chief of state, Hitler had in fact established a praetorian guard which stood above both Party and State.[9]

[9] Buchheim, "Die SS," p. 139; Walter Görlitz, *Die Waffen-SS* (Berlin, 1960), pp. 9 f.

Concurrently with the creation of the Stabswache, a number of full-time SS "Political Purpose Squads" were established in such key cities as Hamburg, Dresden, Munich, Ellwangen, and Arolsen. During 1933 and 1934 they were reorganized and enlarged on the pattern of the Leibstandarte. In addition, members of the SS were selected to guard, on a full-time basis, the numerous political prisons and concentration camps which sprang up throughout Germany during 1933. These men, under the command of Theodor Eicke, became the nucleus of the SS Totenkopfverbände (Death's Head detachments) which by 1934 had become the official custodians of Germany's infamous concentration-camp system. The three militarized, full-time formations of the SS—the Leibstandarte SS "Adolf Hitler," the "Political Purpose Squads," and the Totenkopfverbände—were tributary streams that by the end of 1939 had merged to form the Waffen SS.[10]

In June 1934, the total strength of the armed SS was less than that of an infantry regiment. Its men were equipped with small arms only and were by military standards poorly trained. By no stretch of the imagination could this embryo Waffen SS be considered a threat to the regular Army. The SA, however, presented an entirely different picture. Under the leadership of the ambitious Ernst Röhm, the nearly three million dissatisfied Storm Troopers appeared to be threatening a "second revolution" in which the SA would absorb the regular Army and thus be in a position to challenge Hitler's political leadership. In the complex (and still not entirely clear) power struggle between the Röhm faction of the NSDAP and the Army chiefs and their allies, Hitler apparently became convinced that his sole chance of survival depended upon his ability to keep the Army on his side.[11] But the military leaders demanded as the price for their continued support of the Nazi regime the

[10] Paul Hausser, *Waffen SS im Einsatz* (Göttingen, 1953), p. 10; Buchheim, "Die SS," pp. 140ff.; Neusüss-Hunkel, *op. cit.*, pp. 36, 53; Görlitz, *op. cit.*, pp. 10ff.

[11] For details see Gerald Reitlinger, *The SS: Alibi of a Nation* (New York, 1957), pp. 54ff. On the role of the Army see John W. Wheeler-Bennett, *The Nemesis of Power: The German Army in Politics 1918–1945* (2nd ed.; London, 1964), pp. 304ff.

elimination of the SA threat. When Hitler was finally forced to sacrifice the revolutionaries in his own party, it was Himmler's SS—nominally still under the supervision of the Chief of Staff of the SA—which provided the armed force that decided the issue. Beginning on June 30, 1934, members of Sepp Dietrich's Leibstandarte and Theodor Eicke's Totenkopfverbände manned the firing squads that carried out the sentences imposed on the SA leaders and others by Göring and by Himmler and his sinister security chief, Reinhard Heydrich.[12]

In its first major undertaking, the armed SS demonstrated what were to become in Hitler's view its chief virtues: absolute loyalty and blind obedience. As Himmler later expressed it: "We did not hesitate on June 30, 1934, to do the duty we were bidden, and stand comrades who had lapsed, up against the wall and shoot them. . . . We have never discussed it among ourselves. . . . It appalled everyone, and yet everyone was certain that if it is necessary and such orders are issued he will do it again." [13] The SS' reward for its services was not long delayed. On July 26, the *Völkischer Beobachter,* the official Nazi organ, carried this message from the Führer: "In consideration of the very meritorious service of the SS, especially in connection with the events of 30 June 1934, I elevate it to the standing of an independent organization within the NSDAP." [14]

In conducting the "Blood Purge," the SS had in effect fought the Reichswehr's battle; and the generals were forced to repay the debt by acquiescing in the continued existence of Hitler's private army. In the words of Sir John W. Wheeler-Bennett:

[12] On the role of the SS in the Röhm affair see Neusüss-Hunkel, *op. cit.,* pp. 11ff. In the postwar German trials stemming from the purge of the SA, it was alleged that Eicke (killed in action in 1943) and one of his officers, former SS Standartenführer (Colonel) Michael Lippert, "aided and abetted" by Sepp Dietrich, had shot Röhm to death in his cell after he had refused to commit suicide. A précis of the trial held in Munich in 1957 is given in John Dornberg, *Schizophrenic Germany* (New York, 1961), pp. 34ff.

[13] "Rede des Reichsführers SS bei der SS Gruppenführertagung in Posen am 4. Oktober 1943," Nuremberg Document 1919–PS.

[14] The relevant portions of the newspaper announcement are reproduced in Nuremberg Document 1857–PS.

In order to rid themselves of their brown-shirted rivals they had made a temporary abdication of their proud position as the sole bearer of arms within the Reich, and had permitted an operation, which was clearly more than a police action, to be undertaken by an elite and fanatical force, the SS, which, though now in its infancy, was to challenge and humiliate the Army in its own field.[15]

On March 16, 1935, Hitler announced to his Reichstag and the world that Germany was reintroducing military conscription and intended to establish an army of thirty-six divisions. The same day he issued an order calling for the formation of the SS Verfügungstruppe, a fully militarized formation which was intended to serve as the nucleus of an SS division.[16] This development caused much misgiving in Army circles. Permitting the SS to maintain a few thousand militarized police troops and concentration-camp guards was one thing, but a full-strength SS division was quite another matter.[17] The generals, who had earlier conceded the existence of what they contemptuously described as Himmler's "asphalt soldiers," now went into opposition; and a silent but protracted struggle ensued between the High Command and the Reichsführer SS. Hitler was apparently content to allow neither side a complete victory: no SS division was actually established until after the outbreak of the war in 1939; on the other hand, the Army leaders were unable to check the slow but steady growth of the armed SS. It was perhaps symbolic of the growing importance of the armed SS that the first German troops to enter Saarbrücken during the remilitarization of the Rhineland, in March 1936, were members of the Leibstandarte SS "Adolf Hitler." [18]

[15] Wheeler-Bennett, *op. cit.*, p. 325.

[16] K. Kanis *et al.*, *Waffen SS im Bild* (Göttingen, 1957), pp. 13 f.

[17] By the end of May 1935 the total strength of the SS Verfügungstruppe was 8459. Of this number 2660 were members of the Leibstandarte SS "Adolf Hitler," 759 were attached to the two SS Führerschulen, and the remainder were members of the 1st and 2nd SS Regiments, whose six battalions were stationed in various parts of the Reich. See "Stärke der Verfügungstruppe der SS" May 31, 1935, RFSS/T–175 111/2635976. In addition there were 1338 full-time SS garrison troops and 2241 concentration-camp guards. See "Kasernierte SS" and "Stärke der Wachtruppen," *ibid.*, 111/2635974 f.

[18] Himmler's speech of September 7, 1940, RFSS/T–175, 90/2612641.

The SS Verfügungstruppe: Organization, Selection, and Training

By the beginning of 1936, the armed SS had crystallized into two clearly defined branches: the SS Verfügungstruppe (which included the Leibstandarte) and the SS Totenkopfverbände. The former, as Hitler's praetorian guard, developed an increasingly military complexion, while the latter attracted the bully-boys and sadists who made the term *concentration camp* synonymous with terror, brutality, and murder. Despite the differences in their daily duties, the two formations were regarded by Hitler as equally important elements in the Nazi machinery of terror and repression; and on April 1, 1936, the Verfügungstruppe and the Totenkopfverbände were both legitimized as "organizations in the service of the State" and placed on the Police budget of the Ministry of the Interior.[19]

On October 1, 1936, an Inspectorate of Verfügungstruppen was established within the SS Hauptamt to supervise the administration and military training of the field units of the SS.[20] To head the new organization, Himmler chose Paul Hausser, one of the few former professional soldiers of high rank in the prewar SS. Born in 1880, Hausser had been a career officer until his retirement from the Reichswehr as an acting lieutenant general early in 1932; subsequently he became regional leader of the Nationalist Stahlhelm in Berlin–Brandenburg, and after its absorption by the SA he served briefly as an SA Standartenführer (colonel), before transferring to the SS as head of the SS Junkerschule "Braunschweig," the first SS officer academy. During the war years, Hausser rose to become the Waffen SS' senior soldier—the first SS officer to command a corps, an army, and finally a full army group. In 1936, Hausser, newly promoted to SS Brigadeführer (major general) and Inspector of Verfügungstruppen, faced the exacting task of molding the ill-

---

[19] Görlitz, *op. cit.*, p. 13; Buchheim, "Die SS," p. 141. For a discussion of the character of the armed SS see Neusüss-Hunkel, *op. cit.*, pp. 21ff., 38ff., 55 f.

[20] Buchheim, "Die SS," p. 140.

trained formations of the armed SS into a full-fledged combat force.

As a first step, the scattered battalions of the Verfügungs-truppe were gathered together in two regiments: "Deutschland" in Munich, under the command of SS Standartenführer Felix Steiner, and "Germania" in Hamburg, under SS Standarten-führer Karl Demelhuber. Hausser's influence over the Leib-standarte, which remained in Berlin and was nominally a part of the Verfügungstruppe, was severely limited because Sepp Dietrich both outranked him and had direct access to Himmler and Hitler.[21] But after initial difficulties with the district leaders of the General SS, who fought to retain control over the Ver-fügungstruppen, and with the Army, which hindered the SS at every opportunity, Hausser at last succeeded in asserting his authority in the field of military training and organization.

In the prewar period, selection for the Verfügungstruppe was based on rigid physical and racial standards. Members of the Leibstandarte had to be at least five feet, eleven inches tall, while the other units required a minimum height of five feet, ten inches. So selective were the SS examiners in the early years that Himmler later stated: "Until 1936 we did not accept a man in the Leibstandarte or the Verfügungstruppe if he had even one filled tooth. We were able to assemble the most mag-nificent manhood in that early Waffen SS." [22]

Despite stringent entrance requirements and long periods of service (enlisted men four years, noncommissioned officers

[21] In 1942 Hitler described his former bodyguard, Dietrich, as "unique . . . a man who's simultaneously cunning, energetic and brutal. Under his swashbuckling appearance Dietrich is a serious, conscientious, scrupulous character. And what care he takes of his troops! He's a phenomenon in the class of people like Frundsberg, Ziethen, and Seydlitz. He's a Bavarian Wrangel, someone irreplaceable. For the German people Sepp Dietrich is a national institution. For me personally there is also the fact that he is one of my oldest companions in the struggle." *Hitler's Secret Conversations, 1941–1944*, translated by Norman Cameron and R. H. Stevens (New York, 1961), pp. 178 f.

[22] "Rede des Reichsführers SS auf der Tagung für Befehlshaber der Kriegsmarine in Weimer am 16. Dezember 1943," RFSS/T–175, 91/2613342.

twelve years, and officers twenty-five years), the prewar Verfügungstruppe seems to have had little difficulty attracting applicants. The opportunity of fulfilling the national military service obligation in an elite Nazi formation had a particularly strong appeal for members of the Hitler Youth, while many adventurous peasant lads were attracted by the promise of a career open to "talent." Too, the increasingly military character of the Verfügungstruppe served to blur its fundamental differences from the Army. Although the black SS dress uniform was retained until the war, the year 1937 saw the introduction of the Army's field-gray service uniform (with the *Hoheitszeichen,* the eagle and Swastika, worn on the left sleeve, and the SS runes and rank insignia on the collar tabs). The following year field-gray epaulets carrying Army branch-of-service pipings (different colors to denote infantry, engineers, etc.) were added. And as of August 26, 1938, the Verfügungstruppen received pay and allotments according to Wehrmacht pay regulations.[23]

By the end of 1937, the Verfügungstruppe had grown into three large infantry regiments, and a communications section and a combat engineer company had been established. Speaking to the assembled senior officers of the SS on November 8, 1937,[24] Himmler declared that "the Verfügungstruppe is, according to the present standards of the Wehrmacht, prepared for war." Regiment "Deutschland" was completely combat-ready, while the other two regiments were each prepared to field one battalion. Shortages of equipment and personnel were in the process of being remedied, and Himmler promised that "Germania" and the Leibstandarte "Adolf Hitler" would shortly be brought up to the same state of preparedness as "Deutschland." The biggest problem facing the armed SS was its lack of experi-

[23] Wolf Keilig, *Das Deutsche Heer 1939–1945* (Bad Nauheim, 1956), II, Section 141, p. 3; Buchheim, "Die SS," p. 148. For a compilation of the laws and regulations governing military service in the Third Reich see Rudolf Absolon, *Wehregesetz und Wehrdienst 1935–1945: Das Personalwesen in der Wehrmacht* ("Schriften des Bundesarchivs," 5; Boppard am Rhein, 1960), *passim.*

[24] "Rede des Reichsführers SS bei der Gruppenführerbesprechung in München im Führerheim des SS Standarte 'Deutschland' am 8. November 1937," RFSS/T–175, 90/2612393ff.

enced officers, and Himmler announced that his immediate goal was to make the officer corps of the Verfügungstruppe "as capable as the officer corps of the Wehrmacht."

In the prewar period SS officers were trained at two academies, the SS Junkerschule "Bad Tölz" and the SS Junkerschule "Braunschweig." [25] "Under the influence of Hausser's cadet schools," writes Gerald Reitlinger, "the Waffen SS was to develop the most efficient of all the military training systems of the Second World War, a cross between the Spartan Hoplites and the Guards Depot at Caterham." [26] But for Himmler the problem was one both of quality *and* quantity. The number of officers the SS was permitted to train was limited by the High Command and, although the quota was secretly exceeded, the expansion of the Waffen SS during the war continually outpaced the production of its cadet schools.[27]

On October 1, 1937, the Junkerschule at Bad Tölz moved into spacious new quarters, which had been built at state expense. The two academies were now able to produce a total of some 400 officers a year. But this figure included officers for the Police, and the number reaching the armed SS was sufficient only to fill adequately the needs of a force the size of the prewar SS Verfügungstruppe. The coming of war brought with it not only the demands of expansion but also the problem of battle losses. The type of aggressive leadership fostered by the SS officer-training program resulted in high casualties among commissioned personnel, which further aggravated the officer-supply problem.[28]

[25] "Rede des Reichsführers SS am 23. November 1942, SS Junkerschule Tölz," RFSS/T–175, 90/2612778. The officer academy at Bad Tölz was established in 1934, that at Braunschweig in 1935.

[26] Reitlinger, *op cit.*, p. 77.

[27] In 1938 Himmler informed his Gruppenführer that the SS had "illegally" trained "3 to 4 times as many officers as had been authorized." Himmler's "Gruppenführerbesprechung am 8. November 1938 im Führerheim der SS Standarte 'Deutschland,' " RFSS/T–175, 90/2612563.

[28] Nearly all of the 54 men who had, in 1934, constituted the first graduating class of Junkerschule "Tölz" were dead by 1942. Himmler's speech of November 23, 1942, RFSS/T–175, 90/2612778ff.

The entrance requirements of the SS cadet schools were exacting with respect to racial, physical, and political factors, but education and nonpolitical background were discounted. As a result, some 40 per cent of the officer candidates accepted before 1938 had only an elementary-school education.[29] In an effort to eliminate educational and social distinctions and open a career to talent, the SS in effect lowered its standards, and as a consequence the professional quality of many prewar SS officers was not on a par with that of their Army colleagues.

Nevertheless, under Hausser's expert guidance the young SS force steadily increased its military proficiency. With the advantages of small size and hand-picked manpower of the highest physical caliber, the Verfügungstruppe was able to introduce a number of innovations in the field of military training. In the Army, athletics was largely relegated to the sphere of after-duty recreation. In the SS, organized sports and physical conditioning were made an integral part of the training program. Officers and enlisted personnel were scheduled for daily athletic activities, such as long- and short-distance running, boxing, rowing, and various track and field events. This type of training, which resulted in a high degree of physical fitness, also fostered among officers, NCOs, and enlisted men a sense of fellowship and mutual respect generally unknown in the Army.[30]

The small size and elite nature of the Verfügungstruppe also made it possible to attain a level of individual training superior to that of the regular infantry units. Until 1939 nearly all SS infantrymen were trained as assault troops similar to British Commandos and United States Army Rangers. The time spent in the field and in the classroom was increased at the expense of the barracks-square routines so highly prized by the Prussianized German Army. The end product of SS training was a

[29] Himmler's speech of November 8, 1937, RFSS/T–175, 90/2612395ff.

[30] Kanis, *op. cit.*, p. 20. The SS emphasis on sports in military training bore a marked resemblance to the program instituted by General Hans von Seeckt in the 100,000-man Reichswehr during the Weimar period. See Gordon Craig, *The Politics of the Prussian Army* (New York, 1956), p. 495.

soldier who "was as much at home on the battlefield as on the athletic field." [31]

Never during his service in the Verfügungstruppe was the young SS trooper permitted to forget that he was part of an elite Nazi organization. Not only was every phase of his athletic and military preparation related to National Socialist ideology, but political and ideological indoctrination was given parity with the other phases of the training program. Until 1936 this training was conducted by special instructors who were under the direction of the SS Schulungsamt (SS Office of Education). But it soon became apparent that these instructors were developing into Soviet-style political commissars, thus creating a "dualism" in leadership. The authority of the line officer was being weakened by depriving him of "the most important part of his leadership function, . . . the indoctrination of his own men." [32] As a result, Himmler restricted the political officers to the task of preparing and supervising the ideological training program and turned over the instructional function to the individual unit commanders.

Before the end of 1938, the regiments of the SS Verfügungstruppe had reached such an advanced state of military proficiency that Himmler received permission from Hitler for the SS to use Army maneuver grounds without the usual safety precautions. Thereafter SS combat exercises were conducted with live ammunition and actual barrages of artillery "so that every man became accustomed to his weapons and also to being within 50 to 70 meters of the explosions of his own artillery fire." [33] Casualties were inevitable. Himmler agreed with his Army critics that it was "a shame to lose each good German lad," but he also believed that such losses had to be accepted because "every drop of blood spilled in peacetime saved streams of blood" in battle. In the sense that hard and realistic combat training increases a soldier's chances of surviving in battle, Himmler may have been correct; but the Waffen SS of the war

[31] Kanis, *op. cit.,* p. 26.

[32] "Rede des Reichsführers SS auf der Tagung der RPA-Leiter am 28. Januar 1944," RFSS/T–175, 94/2614803ff.

[33] Himmler's speech of December 16, 1943, RFSS/T–175, 91/2613342.

years never had low casualty rates. Nonetheless, the intensive training of the Verfügungstruppen paid handsome dividends of another kind: just as the 100,000-man Reichswehr served as the nucleus of an expanded Wehrmacht after 1935, so the 15,000 men of the Verfügungstruppe provided many experienced officers, commissioned and noncommissioned, for the greatly enlarged Waffen SS of the later war years.

Purpose of the Verfügungstruppe

For a number of years after its formation the exact mission of the SS Verfügungstruppe remained publicly unclear, but privately both Hitler and Himmler were explicit on the matter. The SS organization as a whole was first and foremost conceived by Hitler as a private army and personal police force. In the section dealing with the SS, the *Organization Book of the NSDAP* stated that "the original and most important duty of the SS is to serve as the protector of the Führer." But it went on to say that later "by decree of the Führer the sphere of duties has been enlarged to include the internal security of the Reich." [34] More vividly described by Himmler in 1936, the task of the SS was to "guarantee the security of Germany from the interior, just as the Wehrmacht guarantees the safety of the honor, the greatness, and the peace of the Reich from the exterior." [35]

In their public pronouncements the Nazi leaders generally pictured Jews and Bolsheviks as the main threat to the internal security of the Reich. In reality they feared larger segments of the German population, particularly in the event of complications abroad. Germany's foreign policy from 1935 onward made war a distinct possibility, and Hitler had grave misgivings about the attitude the German people and armed forces might adopt in the event of prolonged hostilities. Both Hitler and Himmler had lived through the turbulent days during the fall of 1918, when on all levels Germany's will to continue the war suddenly collapsed. Hitler's private conversations reveal a

[34] *Organisationsbuch der NSDAP* (Munich, 1943), p. 417.
[35] Nuremberg Document 1851–PS.

recurring preoccupation with the possibility that the revolutionary situation of 1918 might repeat itself. Early in 1942, after musing over the popular uprisings at the end of World War I, Hitler stated that "if the slightest attempt at a riot were to break out at this moment anywhere in the whole Reich," he would immediately have "all the leaders of the opposition, including the leaders of the Catholic Party, . . . arrested and executed." Within three days "all occupants of the concentration camps . . . [and] all the criminals . . . would be shot. The extermination of these few hundreds or thousands of men," Hitler felt, "would make other measures superfluous." [36]

Such an operation would have been carried out by Himmler's SS, and it was particularly for such a role that Hitler supported the establishment of the armed SS. For this purpose alone it need not have assumed proportions larger than those of a militarized police organization of moderate size. Yet by 1937 the Verfügungstruppe was well on the way to becoming a combat-ready infantry force, which, if not organized as such, was at least approaching the strength of an army division. This development can be traced to Hitler's and Himmler's conviction that the SS would find it difficult to carry out its internal-security role in wartime if it did not retain the respect of the populace and the armed forces by performing a fair share of front-line duty.

Thus Himmler stated to the assembled Gruppenführer of the SS on November 8, 1938, that "the Verfügungstruppe was organized to take its part in the war by going into the field." By sacrificing its "blood in battle at the front," the armed SS would retain "the moral right to shoot at malingerers and cowards on the home front." [37] Similarly, Hitler some years later described the armed SS as first and foremost "an elite

---

[36] *Hitler's Secret Conversations,* p. 388.

[37] Himmler's speech of November 8, 1938, RFSS/T–175, 90/2612546. Five years later Himmler pursued the same theme in somewhat greater detail during a secret gathering of Propaganda Ministry officials headed by Goebbels. See Himmler's speech of January 28, 1944, RFSS/T–175, 94/2614790ff.

police, capable of crushing any adversary." But "it was necessary that the SS should make war, otherwise its prestige would have been lowered." [38]

There was, however, a more compelling reason for the existence of the armed SS, which because of its delicate nature was not publicly expressed. This was that the SS should constitute the vanguard of a National Socialist army. "Every revolution," Himmler said privately, "tries to control the army and infuse the men with its own spirit. Only when that has been achieved is a revolution finally triumphant." Himmler saw "two ways of forming a Wehrmacht which would meet the demands of National Socialism." First, "the Führer could have scrapped the old officer corps entirely." That, Himmler felt, would have been the proper method, "but it would have taken far too long," and in the meantime Hitler could not afford to dispense with the experience and technical ability of the professionals. Yet Hitler knew that "these men were largely out of sympathy with National Socialism" and therefore had as an alternative created the Waffen SS, "an armed force to embody the views which National Socialism had to introduce into the Wehrmacht." [39]

In any event, the SS was not destined to succeed where the SA had failed, for it never became a serious rival to the Wehrmacht. Despite its rapid wartime expansion, the total strength of the Waffen SS remained less than 10 per cent that of the Wehrmacht, and SS officers never managed to invade the upper echelons of the German High Command. If the Waffen SS failed to convert the German armed forces to its ideology and methods, it did, as Himmler put it, "develop according to its own laws." And, judged by fighting ability alone, a case may be made for the efficacy of this "National Socialist revolution in the military field."

[38] *Hitler's Secret Conversations,* p. 178. See also the secret memorandum concerning the Führer's intentions regarding the future of the Waffen SS circulated by the OKH on March 21, 1941. Nuremberg Document D-665.

[39] Felix Kersten, *The Kersten Memoirs, 1940–1945* (New York, 1957), pp. 247 f.

Wehrmacht and SS: The Führer Decree
of August 17, 1938

Between 1935 and 1938, while the German armed forces grew at a prodigious rate, the formation of the promised SS field division was postponed from year to year. The military leaders defended their position by reminding their Party opponents that, while the NSDAP and the armed forces were the "twin pillars of the Third Reich," Hitler had promised that the only "bearer of arms" would be the Wehrmacht.

In the struggle between Himmler and the generals over the future of the armed SS, Hitler remained outwardly neutral. In the first place, he was not ready to risk a showdown with the High Command. Second, his conception of the armed SS was still that of an elite, militarized police force, a praetorian guard, and he was not yet particularly interested in its development beyond this stage. On the other hand, Hitler made it thoroughly clear that he would not tolerate any Army interference in the internal affairs of the NSDAP; under this protective mantle the armed SS was able to continue its slow but steady development.

Himmler, however, was more ambitious concerning the future of the SS. If the Army leaders refused to cooperate, their power would have to be broken. Himmler's golden opportunity to do precisely that came in January 1938, when it was discovered that the Minister of War, Field Marshal von Blomberg, had married a former prostitute. Outraged by this slur upon its honor, the Officer Corps demanded von Blomberg's resignation; and Hitler, who a few weeks earlier had attended the wedding, was forced to let the Field Marshal go. Since the logical successor to von Blomberg was the Commander-in-Chief of the Army, Colonel General von Fritsch, Himmler's security chief, Heydrich, had prepared a dossier which purported to prove him a homosexual. Though Hitler seems to have been genuinely shocked by the evidence against von Fritsch, he was quick to sense the advantages to be derived from the situation. Spurred on by Himmler and Göring—each of whom had his own reasons for wanting to block von Fritsch—Hitler decided to use the occasion to break the power of the generals and thus bring the Army under his own direct control.[40]

On February 4, 1938, he announced that there would be no successor to von Blomberg. Instead he decreed:

Henceforth I will personally exercise immediate command over all the armed forces. The former Wehrmachtamt in the War Ministry becomes the High Command of the Armed Forces [Oberkommando der Wehrmacht] and comes directly under my command as my military staff.[41]

The resignations of von Blomberg and von Fritsch were made public, and a tame general, Walther von Brauchitsch, was designated the new Commander-in-Chief of the Army. General Wilhelm Keitel, an ardent admirer of the Führer, was made Chief of Staff of the newly created OKW; and sixteen potentially dissident generals were retired, while another forty-four, together with many senior officers, were transferred to new duties. Göring was mollified with a field marshal's baton, Himmler had the satisfaction of seeing his hated rivals humbled, and Hitler had cleared the way for a more militant foreign policy. Above all, the Blomberg–Fritsch affair had resulted in the *Gleichschaltung* of the Army, the last stronghold of independent power with the capacity to challenge the Nazi regime.

On March 11, German troops marched into Austria. Among the leading elements of General Guderian's XVIth Army Corps was a motorized battalion of the Leibstandarte "Adolf Hitler" under the command of SS Obergruppenführer (General) Sepp Dietrich. In the wake of the *Anschluss* and the "coordination" of the Army High Command, Hitler became more amenable to a modest increase in the strength of the armed SS. In 1938 Himmler created for the SS Verfügungstruppe a new regiment named "Der Führer." The unit was composed largely of Austrians and was stationed in Vienna and Klagenfurt. Another

[40] Reitlinger, *op. cit.*, pp. 98ff.; Wheeler-Bennett, *op. cit.*, pp. 364ff.

[41] Hitler's decree appeared in the *Reichsgesetzblatt* of February 4, 1938. The portion quoted here may be found in Walther Hofer (ed.), *Der Nationalsozialismus: Dokumente 1933–1945* (Frankfurt am Main, 1957), p. 109.

SS Totenkopfstandarte was also established, bringing the strength of the Totenkopfverbände to some 8500 men.[42]

Now in firm control of the Wehrmacht, Hitler decided to put an end to the feud between Himmler and the Army by clarifying the anomalous position of the armed SS. On August 17, 1938, he therefore issued a highly important top-secret decree designed to regulate the police duties of the SS and to "delineate the common tasks of the SS and of the Wehrmacht." [43]

Hitler's decree began by stating that the Allgemeine (General) SS "being a political organization of the NSDAP . . . does not require military training and organization . . . nor is it to be armed." But "for special internal political tasks . . . or for use within the wartime army in the event of mobilization," the SS Verfügungstruppe, the SS Junkerschulen, the SS Totenkopfverbände, and the reserve units of the Totenkopfverbände (police reinforcement), were to be armed, trained, and organized as military formations. As to command authority, Hitler made it clear that in peacetime the armed SS was to be "under the Reichsführer SS and Chief of the German Police who . . . *alone* has the responsibility for the organization, training, arming and full use in regard to any internal political tasks which I may give him." The required "arms, ammunition, equipment, and military handbooks" were to be "procured from the Wehr-

---

[42] Himmler's speech of November 8, 1938, RFSS/T–175, 90/2612536.

[43] Nuremberg Document 647–PS. Apologists for the Waffen SS have claimed that only three copies of the decree were prepared and that its existence was not known within the SS Verfügungstruppe (Kanis, *op. cit.,* pp. 217 f.). There is some evidence to support this view. Although notations on the top of the original indicate that at least ten photocopies were made, these were probably circulated only among the top SS and Wehrmacht leaders. Such high-level documents were not generally passed down to the troop level; but the fact that "nonpolitical" SS leaders such as Hausser were unaware of the existence of the decree had no bearing on either its legality or its application. A number of references to the decree may be found in communications between the SS Hauptamt and various agencies of the OKW and OKH, and as late as 1940 it was the basis for negotiations between the SS and the OKW concerning the wartime status of the Waffen SS. See various communications and draft proposals regarding "Wehrdienstverhältnis und Wehrüberwachung der Waffen SS während des Krieges," February 1940, Geheim, RFSS/T–175, 104/2626508ff.

macht upon payment." But "in peacetime, no organizational connection with the Wehrmacht exists." [44]

Having established in its opening section the general position of the armed SS, the decree went on to define in detail the status and strength of the various armed formations of the SS. "The SS Verfügungstruppe," Hitler declared, "is neither a part of the Wehrmacht nor a part of the Police. It is a standing armed unit exclusively at my disposal." Regardless of its employment, the Verfügungstruppe was to remain "a unit of the NSDAP" and its members were "to be selected by the Reichsführer SS according to the ideological and political standards which I have ordered for the NSDAP and for the Schutzstaffeln." Service was voluntary, and recruits were to be selected "from those who are subject to serve in the Army and have finished their compulsory labor service." Duty in the SS Verfügungstruppe was counted toward fulfillment of the regular military service obligation. [45]

All armed units of the SS were to receive their "financial resources through the Ministry of the Interior." The OKW was, however, permitted to check the budget. The premobilization organization of the SS Verfügungstruppe was fixed at:

1 headquarters staff
Leibstandarte SS "Adolf Hitler" (motorized)
3 regiments ("Deutschland," "Germania," and "Der Führer")
2 motorcycle battalions under a regimental staff
1 combat engineer battalion (motorized)
1 communications battalion (motorized)
1 medical unit

In the event that the Verfügungstruppe was alerted "for use in the interior," the Leibstandarte was to be reinforced by

1 armored reconnaissance platoon
1 motorcycle company
1 combat engineer platoon (motorized)

Each of the other three regiments was to receive an extra

[44] Nuremberg Document 647–PS. Emphasis in the original.
[45] *Ibid.*

armored reconnaissance platoon, a light infantry motorcycle company, and a number of additional communications units.[46]

The peacetime strength of these units was to be the same as that of the equivalent units of the Army. "Personnel and equipment needs in excess of peacetime authorizations will be determined in cooperation with the High Command of the Wehrmacht and the Reichsführer SS and Chief of the German Police." But the final decision was Hitler's: "Any changes in the organization, strength and armament of the SS Verfügungstruppe require my approval." As a concession to the Army, Hitler gave its High Command (OKH) the authority to inspect units of the Verfügungstruppe and to report to him "about the state of combat training." But even this almost meaningless right could be exercised only "after prior consultation with the Reichsführer SS and Chief of the German Police." In an attempt to prevent a permanent schism between the armed SS and the regular Army, Hitler ordered that "as soon as the officer situation permits, a mutually agreed upon exchange of officers between the Army and the SS Verfügungstruppe is to be carried out." [47]

In the event of mobilization the SS Verfügungstruppe was to fulfill a dual mission. It might be ordered to serve under the command of the OKH, in which case it would be "completely under military laws and regulations, but [remain] a unit of the NSDAP politically." On the other hand, it might "in case of necessity" be placed under the operational command of the Reichsführer SS for use in the interior of the Reich. All decisions regarding "the time, strength, and manner of the incorporation of the SS Verfügungstruppe into the wartime Army" were to be made personally by Hitler on the basis of "the internal political situation at the time." [48]

----

[46] *Ibid.*

[47] *Ibid.* Although Himmler in his speech of November 8, 1938 (RFSS/T–175, 90/2612563), revealed that some 300 SS and Police officers had been temporarily transferred to the Army to fill gaps in units mobilized for the occupation of the Sudetenland, there is no evidence that any Army officers ever were seconded to the SS Verfügungstruppe.

[48] Nuremberg Document 647–PS.

Claims by apologists for the Waffen SS that no connection existed between the SS Verfügungstruppe and the SS Totenkopfverbände are supported by neither documentary evidence nor actual developments. The Führer Decree of August 17, 1938, clearly establishes such a connection in the event of mobilization. Although the peacetime SS Verfügungstruppe was a full-time formation, it had no replacement units; new recruits received their training within the active regiments. In the event of war, therefore, certain elements of the SS Totenkopfverbände were to "be transferred to the SS Verfügungstruppe" to ensure "a reserve which would meet the ideological and political spirit" of that formation.[49] By the end of 1940 all members of the SS Totenkopfverbände were part of the Waffen SS; and three entire regiments of Totenkopf troopers, some 6500 men, became the nucleus of a new SS field division.[50] Long before the end of the war former members of the SS Totenkopfverbände were to be found in the ranks of many field units of the Waffen SS.

The phenomenal growth of the Waffen SS after 1940 was not foreseen in the 1938 decree. In the event of war only a limited transfer of Totenkopf personnel to the Verfügungstruppe was envisioned. At the time, Hitler intended the SS Totenkopfverbände primarily as "a standing armed unit of the SS to clear up special tasks of a police nature." In peacetime this meant the guarding of concentration camps and political prisons. In the event of national mobilization, however, the SS Totenkopfverbände were to "be replaced in the guarding of the concentration camps by members of the General SS who are over 45 years of age and have had military training." Thus freed from their former duties, the Totenkopf formations, reinforced by a call-up of Totenkopf reservists, were to constitute a "police force" under the command of the Reichsführer SS.[51] Although the wartime tasks of the Totenkopfverbände were not spelled out in the Führer Decree of August 17, 1938, three months later Himmler stated that their mobilized strength would be in the range of "40–50,000" men and that they would

[49] *Ibid.*
[50] See p. 33.
[51] Nuremberg Document 647–PS. Cf. Neusüss-Hunkel, *op. cit.*, pp. 62ff.

be used to reinforce the Police, thus safeguarding the homeland while the Verfügungstruppe was at the front.[52]

Service in the SS Totenkopfverbände for noncommissioned officers and men was for twelve years. Since this duty did not count as military service, Hitler ordered that volunteers be chosen from among those "who, as a rule, have served their compulsory military duty in the Army." [53] The organization of the SS Totenkopfverbände as of April 1, 1938, was fixed at:

4 Standarten (regiments) of 3 Sturmbanne (battalions) with
3 infantry companies (each 148 men strong)
1 machine-gun company (150 men strong)
medical, transportation, and communications units

As in the case of the Verfügungstruppe, Hitler personally reserved the right to approve any changes in size, organization, and armament. With the exception of an advisory function in matters of armament and equipment, the Army had no voice in the affairs of the SS Totenkopfverbände.[54]

On the Eve of War

Hitler's painless experience in executing the *Anschluss* of Austria to Germany convinced him that he could safely move on to the next step in his plan of aggression—the annexation of Czechoslovakia. In this adventure, the armed SS was for the first time to be employed in a purely military role at more than token strength. During the German mobilization preceding the occupation of the Sudetenland in October 1938, four SS Totenkopf battalions and the entire SS Verfügungstruppe were, upon Hitler's orders, placed under the command of the Army. Three SS regiments—Leibstandarte "Adolf Hitler," "Germania," and "Deutschland"—actually participated in the occupation, while

[52] Himmler's speech of November 8, 1938, RFSS/T–175, 90/2612548.

[53] Most of the men recruited for the Totenkopfverbände before the issuance of the Führer Decree were youngsters between seventeen and nineteen, and this practice did not altogether cease after 1938. Cf. Himmler's speech of November 8, 1937, RFSS/T–175, 90/2612395; Neusüss-Hunkel, *op. cit.*, p. 55.

[54] Nuremberg Document 647–PS.

two battalions of the SS Totenkopf Regiment "Oberbayern," which had been operating on Czech soil in support of the SS-controlled Henlein Free Corps even before the invasion, were also incorporated into the occupation army.[55]

The first major commitment of the armed SS under the command of the Army seems to have been a success. Nevertheless, the basic antipathy of the High Command toward the SS remained. Only upon Hitler's insistence was a draft Order of the Day announcing the successful completion of the Sudetenland undertaking amended to include the SS and SA. The version prepared by Colonel Alfred Jodl of the OKW mentioned only the participation of "the Army, Air Force, and Police"; that signed by Hitler and released to the press stated that "the operation was carried out by units of the Army, the Air Force, the Police, the Armed SS (SS Verfügungstruppe), the SS and SA." [56] Thus in the end, the SS received the recognition the Army had attempted to deny it.

Late in the fall of 1938 it was decided to convert the SS Verfügungstruppe into a paratroop formation, but shortly after the first steps in that direction had been taken the decision was reversed and it was instead reorganized as a mobile assault force. Within three months the transformation was largely completed, and in the spring of 1939 the regiments of the SS Verfügungstruppe were used to fill gaps in a number of the Army panzer (armored) divisions that carried out the occupation of Czechoslovakia.[57]

During the early summer of 1939, Adolf Hitler, accompanied by Himmler and various high-ranking Army and SS officers, for the first time visited a combat exercise of the Verfügungstruppe. Conducted at the Münsterlager maneuver grounds, the operation featured a full-scale assault by SS Regiment "Deutschland" on a prepared defensive position. Supported by actual barrages from Army artillery batteries, the SS troopers, using live ammunition, demonstrated their unique assault tactics. Hitler, whose ability as a military strategist may

[55] Nuremberg Document 388–PS.
[56] *Ibid.*
[57] Kanis, *op. cit.,* p. 218.

be questioned but whose experience in front-line combat was as extensive as that of many of his generals, was impressed. His verdict: "Only with such soldiers can one do such a thing." [58]

As a result of the demonstration, permission was finally given to establish the first SS division. A few weeks later the OKH received orders from Hitler to provide the Verfügungs-truppe with the equipment necessary for the formation of an SS artillery regiment. But the conversion of the SS Verfügungs-truppe into the SS Verfügungsdivision was temporarily post-poned while its units, including the newly organized SS Artillery Regiment (SS Artillerie Standarte), were integrated once again with units of the Army in preparation for the opening operation of World War II.

On the morning of September 1, 1939, Hitler solemnly mounted the rostrum in the Kroll Opera House and announced to a hushed Reichstag that Germany was at war with Poland. Toward the end of his speech he declared: "From now on I am just the first soldier of the German Reich. I have once more put on that coat that was the most sacred and dear to me. I will not take it off again until victory is secured, or I will not survive the outcome." [59] Those in the audience who had not yet done so now noticed that Hitler had discarded his customary brown Party jacket for a field-gray uniform blouse resembling that of an officer in the Waffen SS.[60]

[58] *Ibid.*, pp. 38, 218.

[59] "Aus der Rede Hitlers am 1. September 1939 (Reichstag)," Jacobsen and Jochmann, *op. cit.*, G, Dokument I. IX. 1939.

[60] Hegner, *op. cit.*, p. 376 ("Hitler trägt einen feldgrauen Uniformrock der Waffen SS ohne Rangabzeichen"). In the matter of his wartime uniform Hitler was eclectic. If the blouse he chose to wear resembled that of the Waffen SS, his peaked cap resembled that of the Army, and the trousers he wore with this ensemble might be field-gray, brown, or black.

CHAPTER TWO

From Verfügungstruppe to Waffen SS: The First Months of War, 1939-1940

HEINRICH HIMMLER, speaking to the assembled senior officers of the SS in 1943,[1] described the expansion of the armed SS after the outbreak of World War II as "fantastic" and as having been carried out "at an absolutely terrific speed." In 1939, according to its chief, the armed SS had consisted of only "a few regiments, guard units, 8000 to 9000 strong—that is, not even a division; all in all 25,000 to 28,000 men at the most." Yet before the war was a year old its strength had risen to nearly 150,000 men. This sixfold increase marked the beginning of an expansion which was soon to establish the Waffen SS as "the fourth branch of the Wehrmacht."

The Polish Campaign, 1939

The short war against Poland, which began on September 1, 1939, did not seriously strain the German war machine. The contribution of the armed SS was modest but not negligible. The major portion of the SS Verfügungstruppe, shipped to East Prussia during the summer of 1939, was organized into regimental combat groups attached to larger Army formations.

The SS Regiment "Deutschland," the newly created SS Artillery Regiment, the SS Reconnaissance Battalion (SS Aufklärungs Sturmbann), and an Army tank regiment were

---

[1] "Rede des Reichsführers SS bei der SS Gruppenführertagung in Posen am 4. Oktober 1943," Nuremberg Document 1919–PS.

brought together to form the 4th Panzer Brigade under the command of an Army staff headed by Major General Werner Kempf. The SS Regiment "Germania" was attached to the 14th Army massing in the southern part of East Prussia. Another regimental battle group, composed of members of the Leibstandarte SS "Adolf Hitler" and supported by the SS Combat Engineer Battalion (SS Pionier Sturmbann), formed part of General Walter von Reichenau's 10th Army, which moved into Poland from Silesia. The SS Totenkopf Sturmbann "Götze," originally created to conduct operations of a "police nature" in and around Danzig, was reorganized into a reinforced infantry battalion with the name "Heimwehr Danzig" and was sent into battle under Army command.[2]

In the *Blitzkrieg* against Poland, the Verfügungstruppe received its baptism of fire.[3] The Army High Command, however, failed to commend the SS for its part in the campaign. On the contrary, the generals of the OKH expressed only negative views. The SS troops had suffered proportionally much heavier casualties than the Army, and the generals were quick to point out that this was because the SS—particularly its officer corps— had not been properly trained for the job. The SS leaders, on the other hand, argued that their troops were being forced to serve in strange units, under Army commanders, and were too often given difficult assignments without adequate support.[4]

Neither view was entirely devoid of truth. But while the

[2] "Truppenteile und Gliederung der SS-Verfügungstruppe im Feldzug gegen Polen (1939)," Keilig, *op. cit.,* II, Section 141, pp. 6ff. For battle details, see Hausser, *op. cit.,* pp. 28ff.; Kanis, *op. cit.,* pp. 40ff., 219. Information concerning "Heimwehr Danzig" may be found in RFSS/T–175, 104/2625579, and "Die Rede Himmlers vor den Gauleitern am 3. August 1944," *Vierteljahrshefte für Zeitgeschichte,* I (October 1953), 568.

[3] Only the SS Regiment "Der Führer" did not see action in Poland; its training still not completed, it spent September manning a section of Germany's West Wall.

[4] "Ansprache des Reichsführers SS aus Anlass der Übergabe der Führerstandarte an die Leibstandarte 'Adolf Hitler,' Metz, Fort von Alvensleben, am 7. September 1940," RFSS/T–175, 90/2612641ff. The pertinent portion of the speech is reproduced in Nuremberg Document 1918–PS. See also Hausser, *op. cit.,* p. 29.

A detachment of the prewar SS Verfügungstruppe presents arms. The black uniforms were later replaced by uniforms of Army field-gray. (Ullstein)

An honor guard of the Leibstandarte SS "Adolf Hitler" presents arms to the Japanese Ambassador, Oshima, as he arrives at the Berghof, Hitler's house on the Obersalzberg in Bavaria, to present his credentials on February 27, 1941. (U.S. Army Photograph)

generals seized upon the high casualty figures as an argument in favor of abolishing an independent SS army, Himmler and his associates used them to underscore demands for the formation of SS divisions entirely under the command of SS officers. In the end Hitler once again opted for a compromise, although one distinctly in favor of the SS. Himmler got his SS divisions; but they were divided among the larger armies and corps of the Wehrmacht, and they remained under the operational command of the OKH.

Preparations for the Campaign in the West

No sooner had Warsaw fallen than Hitler announced to his military chiefs his decision to attack in the West that same autumn. This announcement caused great consternation among the Army leaders, who felt that Germany was not ready for a decisive conflict with the western Allies. Throughout the early fall of 1939 a palace revolution raged within the Army High Command. Once again a plan to assassinate the Führer was considered; but, as in 1938, the generals, beaten and cowed, failed to act. Their chief, General von Brauchitsch, was not even permitted to resign. Ironically, the final offensive in the West was not launched until the following spring, the date advanced by the OKH in opposition to Hitler's demands for an immediate attack. But the various postponements were ordered by Hitler, not by the Army High Command, whose chief, in the words of Field Marshal von Manstein, "had been demoted from the status of military adviser to the Head of State to that of a subordinate commander pledged to unquestioning obedience." [5]

While Hitler was contending with his recalcitrant generals, Himmler—who missed no opportunity to accuse the Army of disloyalty—saw to it that reports of Army complaints concerning SS atrocities in occupied Poland reached the Führer's ears. Hitler had given the German military leaders notice before the Polish

[5] Field Marshal Erich von Manstein, *Lost Victories* (Chicago, 1958), pp. 73 f. See also Walter Warlimont, *Inside Hitler's Headquarters, 1939–45* (New York, 1964), pp. 50ff.; H. R. Trevor-Roper (ed.), *Blitzkrieg to Defeat: Hitler's War Directives 1939–1945* (New York, 1965), pp. 12ff.

campaign that activities would be conducted in the conquered area "which would not be to the taste of German generals," and he warned them that they "should not interfere in such matters but restrict themselves to their military duties." [6] But when, during the height of the campaign, a member of the SS Artillery Regiment and an Army military policeman shot fifty Jews who had been conscripted for forced labor, the local Army commander insisted on trying them by court-martial. Although the prosecuting officer demanded the death penalty, the murderers were sentenced to short prison terms for manslaughter, and even these were dropped as a result of strong pressure from Himmler.[7]

To prevent any further attempts by the military to prosecute SS personnel, Himmler prevailed on Hitler to amend those sections of his previous decrees which placed the armed SS under the jurisdiction of military courts during wartime. On October 17, 1939, the Ministerial Council for Defense of the Reich issued the "Decree relating to a Special Jurisdiction in Penal Matters for Members of the SS and for Members of Police Groups on Special Tasks." The net effect of the new decree was to free the armed SS from the legal jurisdiction of the Wehrmacht. Although members of the SS were still theoretically subject to the provisions of the military penal code, they were no longer tried by courts-martial but by special SS courts, whose members were appointed by the Führer at the suggestion of the Reichsführer SS.[8]

There were further complaints from Army commanders concerning the activities of the SS Totenkopf formations in Poland—perhaps not as many as might have been expected from men who claimed to be honorable, but just enough to provoke Hitler into speaking "very indignantly" to Keitel "about derogatory remarks made by senior officers concerning measures taken

[6] Fabian Schlabrendorff, *Offiziere gegen Hitler* (Zurich, 1946), pp. 34 f. See also Nuremberg Document 3047–PS.

[7] See p. 271.

[8] See *Reichsgesetzblatt* for 1939, Part I, p. 2107; *Reichsgesetzblatt* for 1940, Part I, p. 659. The pertinent portions of the decree and its amendments are reproduced in Nuremberg Documents 2946–PS and 2947–PS.

by us in Poland."⁹ The most persistent critic of Nazi policies in occupied Poland was Colonel General Johannes Blaskowitz, commander of the German Army in the area, who sent a memorandum to Berlin describing the behavior of the SS in Poland.¹⁰ This led to a conference between Himmler and Brauchitsch during which the Reichsführer SS admitted that "mistakes had been made" in carrying out the "ethnic policy" in Poland.¹¹ Himmler promised that he would take steps to see that in the future the task would be carried out "in as considerate a manner as possible and with a minimum of bloodshed." He also assured the Army chief that the SS wanted "good relations with the Army" and had no desire to "establish an [SS] army alongside the Army." Little of this reflected Himmler's true intentions; but during the early months of 1940 the Waffen SS was still in a precarious stage of development, and Himmler was not entirely certain that he could count on Hitler's support in the event of a showdown with the military leaders.

Despite the difficulties Hitler was having with his generals, there is no evidence that he was then considering an expansion of the Waffen SS at the expense of the Wehrmacht. His primary concern during the winter of 1939–1940 was the forthcoming campaign against France; the handful of SS troops available was of minor significance in an operation involving more than a hundred divisions. In addition, Hitler's attitude toward the armed SS during the early war years was still conditioned by his concept of its intended peacetime role. There was no reason to believe that the war would be a long one; it was expected that the armed SS would soon be able to return to its primary role of a "state police." In their temporary wartime role, Hitler regarded the Waffen SS troops as "guardsmen" while the Army constituted the "troops of the line"; he felt it "a good thing that the SS should constitute, in relation to the others, an absolutely distinct world." The duty of the Waffen SS was to "set

⁹ Jodl Diary, January 29, 1940, quoted in Telford Taylor, *The March of Conquest* (New York, 1958), p. 70.
¹⁰ Nuremberg Document NO–3011.
¹¹ Generaloberst Halder, *Kriegstagebuch* (Stuttgart, 1962), I, 183 f.

an example." But to maintain "a very high level . . . the SS shouldn't extend its recruiting too much." [12]

The ambitions of the SS leaders notwithstanding, Hitler approved only a modest increase in the strength of the armed SS. In the expansion of Germany's armed forces that followed the Polish campaign, the strength of the Waffen SS was limited to three field divisions and an enlarged Leibstandarte.

Immediately after the cease-fire in Poland, the combat elements of the SS were withdrawn to Germany for reorganization. The three regiments of SS Verfügungstruppen were brought together to form the SS Verfügungsdivision, and the SS Leibstandarte "Adolf Hitler" was brought up to the strength of a reinforced motorized regiment.[13] With the formation of these two units, Himmler had exhausted his supply of battle-trained SS personnel. He now had to face the problem of manning the two remaining divisions the SS had been allotted. The obvious solution was to launch a massive recruiting campaign. But this would mean that the new divisions would not be operational for at least six months, the time it would take to train the new recruits. Another possibility was to procure a supply of manpower that was already partially trained. It was at this point that Himmler and his recruiting chief, Gottlob Berger, decided on an ingenious plan—one that would, if successful, create two battleworthy divisions in time for the forthcoming western campaign and at the same stroke double the strength of the armed SS—without requiring the cooperation of the military authorities. The scheme was as simple as it was clever. Himmler, in his capacity as Reichsführer SS and Chief of the German Police, would simply transfer enough Totenkopf and Police personnel to the Waffen SS to man the two divisions. Then, under the existing decrees, the SS would recruit volunteers to bring the Totenkopf and Police formations back up to authorized strength.

The beauty of the plan was that it required only Hitler's approval. No additional decrees would have to be issued, there-

---

[12] *Hitler's Secret Conversations,* p. 178.
[13] Keilig, *op. cit.,* II, Section 141, pp. 7 f.

fore no negotiations with the military leaders would be necessary. The OKW and OKH were in any case preoccupied with weightier matters; and since the SS leaders intended to carry out their scheme in stages, the generals would be faced with a *fait accompli.*

The whole operation was based on two Führer Decrees: the decree of August 17, 1938,[14] which provided for the reinforcement of the SS Verfügungstruppe with members of the SS Totenkopfverbände; and the decree of May 18, 1939, which authorized the Reichsführer SS to increase the strength of the Totenkopf formations to between 40,000 and 50,000 men as "police reinforcements" *(Polizeiverstärkung)* in the event of war.[15] The latter decree was the key to the plan, and Berger later described it as having "broken the tight rein kept by the OKW on the further development of the SS." [16]

To what extent Hitler was party to Himmler's design is not clear; he did, however, approve the transfer of three Totenkopf regiments to a third SS division and the formation of a fourth SS division composed of members of the Ordnungspolizei. During October 1939 some 6500 members of the SS Totenkopfverbände,[17] a number of Verfügungstruppe veterans, and a sizable contingent of Police and General SS reservists were organized into the SS Totenkopfdivision.[18] At the same time

[14] See pp. 20ff.

[15] The relevant portion of the Führer Decree of May 18, 1939, was entitled "Regelung der Dienstverhältnisse der SS Totenkopfverbände." No copy of the decree was found in the SS records examined, but a number of references to it occur in communications between the SS and OKW. See, for example, Berger to Himmler, "Befehlsentwurf OKW," February 28, 1940, Geheim, RFSS/T–175, 104/2626511.

[16] Berger to Himmler, "Besprechung mit Major Ratke, Adjutant OBH," February 10, 1940, Geheime Kommandosache, RFSS/T–175, 104/2626613 f.

[17] The men were all members of Totenkopfstandarten 1, 2, and 3, the most experienced of the Death's Head units.

[18] According to SS Gruppenführer Eicke, the division's commander and former head of the concentration camps, a third of the men were active SS men with from two to four years of service; the rest were reservists with some military training. Eicke to AOK 2, "Ausbildungsstand," April 9, 1940, Geheim, RFSS/T–175, 107/2629888ff.

thousands of members of the Ordnungspolizei who, as Himmler admitted, were "neither National Socialists nor SS men" found themselves being conscripted to fill the ranks of a new division appropriately designated the SS Polizeidivision.[19]

By the end of November the Waffen SS consisted of three active divisions (Verfügungsdivision, Totenkopfdivision, and Polizeidivision), fourteen Totenkopfstandarten (composed mainly of General SS reservists called up as "police reinforcements"), and two Junkerschulen (Bad Tölz and Braunschweig). A force of this size required replacements, support units, and a reserve organization. In addition, the depleted Totenkopf and Police formations had to be brought back to authorized strength. In short, it became necessary for the SS to undertake a vastly intensified recruiting operation. The second phase of the Himmler–Berger plan was now to be put to the test; it remained to be seen whether the military leaders would acquiesce.

Struggle for Recognition and Manpower

In wartime Germany, military manpower was apportioned according to a flexible formula determined by the OKW (after consultation with the three service chiefs and the Reichsführer SS) and approved by Hitler. During 1940 recruits were assigned

---

[19] "Rede des Reichsführers SS am 19. Juni 1942 vor dem Führerkorps der SS Division 'Reich,' " RFSS/T–175, 90/2612906. The members of the SS Polizeidivision and the other SS Police units which were formed later did not have to meet the racial and physical requirements of the SS. Therefore, although these units were part of the Waffen SS, their members were not generally SS men, and they wore the uniform of the Ordnungspolizei. As late as April 24, 1943, Himmler—referring to the admission of Police officials into the SS—made clear that he approved such a step only in cases where "the man applies freely and voluntarily" and "if, by applying strict peacetime standards, the applicant is found racially and ideologically qualified." Those who could not meet these requirements "will have to wear the uniform of the Ordnungspolizei," and Himmler, referring "to the many thousands of reservists whom we inducted," pointed out that "due to present-day conditions not everybody in the Ordnungspolizei can be an SS man." Himmler to Kaltenbrunner, April 24, 1943, Geheim, Nuremberg Document 2768–PS. For the OKW's reaction to the formation of the Polizeidivision see Warlimont, *op. cit.*, p. 34.

to the Army, Navy, and Air Force in the proportion 66:9:25.[20] The Waffen SS was so small that it was not specifically included in the distribution scheme. Instead, Hitler simply allotted the SS a specific number of divisions (in the case of the Totenkopfstandarten, a maximum strength) and left the details to be worked out by those concerned.

All men of military age were registered with their local military headquarters (Wehrbezirkskommando or WBK) and could not be inducted into any branch of the armed forces or SS without an official WBK release.[21] The OKW and the OKH (in whose hands a good deal of authority in manpower matters still rested) could not refuse to allow the SS to recruit volunteers for its field units.[22] These were, after all, under Army command and as lineal descendants of the Verfügungstruppe had their status governed by the Führer Decree of August 17, 1938. The OKW therefore restricted itself to establishing an upper limit on the number of men the SS was authorized to recruit for its field formations.

The SS Totenkopfstandarten and Police formations were another matter. They were not under military jurisdiction, nor had duty in them been established as military service. In theory they were to be composed of veterans or members of older age groups. In practice, the SS had already enlisted predraft-age youths who had not yet registered with their Wehrbezirkskommandos. The OKW, reluctant to see any of its potential manpower diverted, hindered such SS efforts at every opportunity.

[20] Berger to Himmler, "Population Movement," August 7, 1940, Top Secret, Nuremberg Document NO–1825, Case XI, Document Book 65, pp. 1ff.

[21] For details see "Das Wehrersatz und Überwachungswesen," Absolon, *op. cit.*, pp. 126ff.

[22] The complex relationship between the Army High Command (OKH; Oberkommando des Heeres) and the Armed Forces High Command (OKW; Oberkommando der Wehrmacht) resulted in considerable stress within the German military establishment. Despite their disagreements, both organizations were equally hostile to the development and growth of the Waffen SS. For a detailed elaboration of the relationship between the OKH and the OKW, see Warlimont, *op. cit., passim.*

The High Command's natural antipathy to the existence of independent armed formations was, in this case, reinforced by the unenviable reputation won by the Totenkopf and Police units in carrying out "special tasks" in Poland.[23] But to Himmler these branches of the SS were perhaps even more important than the SS combat formations. They were in truth his private army, and he was determined to have them at maximum strength. The lines were being drawn for another clash between the SS and the Wehrmacht.

Recruiting for the SS had always been one of the functions of the district leaders of the General SS. But the coming of the war made it necessary to consolidate and centralize this increasingly important operation. To this task Himmler assigned Gottlob Berger, an SS Brigadeführer (major general) who had proved his organizational ability by directing the activities of the Henlein Freikorps during the 1938 Sudetenland crisis. To him, even more than to Himmler, must be attributed the remarkable growth of the Waffen SS. By a judicious mixture of diplomacy, threat, and duplicity, Berger was generally able to outwit and outmaneuver his military opponents: he thus not only fulfilled the desires of his Reichsführer but by his successes also encouraged him to undertake increasingly ambitious schemes to expand the wartime role of the SS.

Berger's first task was to establish a nationwide SS recruiting network which would be responsible to a central office in Berlin. On December 1, 1939, an order prepared by Berger and signed by Himmler created the Ergänzungsamt der Waffen SS (Waffen SS Recruiting Office) within the SS Hauptamt (SS Main Office), with Berger as its chief.[24] An SS Ergänzungsstelle (Recruiting Station) was then established in each of the seventeen SS

---

[23] For SS activities in Poland see Martin Broszat, *Nationalsozialistische Polenpolitik, 1939–1945* (Stuttgart, 1961), *passim*.

[24] Berger to Himmler, "Neuordnung des Ergänzungswesens," December 1, 1940, RFSS/T–175, 104/2626770ff. For detailed information concerning the new SS recruiting organization see the official 28-page handbook "Dienstanweisung für das Ergänzungsamt der Waffen SS und dessen Ergänzungsstellen," October 29, 1939, Geheime Kommandosache, RFSS/T–175, 104/2626776ff.

Oberabschnitte. Since these SS districts were coterminous with the Wehrkreise (military district equivalent to an Army corps area), Berger possessed a recruiting organization which geographically paralleled that of the Army. At the same time, the OKW issued an order to the commanders of the military districts explaining the function of the new bureaus and ordering them to deal directly with the Ergänzungsstellen in all SS personnel matters.[25]

The first overt opposition to Berger's new undertaking came not from the Army but from within the SS itself. The functions assigned to Berger's Ergänzungsamt had been previously handled by the district leaders of the General SS. One of these political satraps, Gruppenführer (Lieutenant General) Kaul, Chief of SS Oberabschnitt Südwest, refused to recognize the authority of the Ergänzungsstelle assigned to his district. In a series of bitter letters to Berlin,[26] Kaul argued that his headquarters had successfully conducted SS recruiting in the past and enjoyed the confidence of Army officials in the district. He did not therefore see why it was necessary to establish a new organization "headed by a lower-ranking empire builder" like Berger. Kaul was particularly angry at having been ordered to give up a large part of his own staff to man the new Ergänzungsstelle, in whose operations he was to have no authority.

While there was undoubtedly a good deal of sympathy for Kaul's position among the old-guard leaders of the General SS, the coming of war had drastically reduced their influence. Once the backbone of the SS, with a membership of over a quarter of a million men, the General SS was fast losing its significance. Its younger members were liable to conscription, and increasing numbers were being called up for military service. Others joined the Waffen SS or the Police, organizations which were now

---

[25] OKW Order, "Neuordnung des Ergänzungswesens der SS und Polizei," November 30, 1939, RFSS/T–175, 104/2626687. On the SS' organization parallel to the Army see Neusüss-Hunkel, *op. cit.*, pp. 34ff.

[26] Kaul's letters were written to SS Gruppenführer Wolff, Chief of Himmler's Personal Staff (Persönlicher Stab RFSS) and SS Gruppenführer Heissmeyer, Chief of the SS Main Office (SS Hauptamt). See RFSS/T–175, 104/262665ff.

Himmler's main interest. When, in a last desperate attempt to hold on to his crumbling power, Kaul threatened to arrest Berger's recruiting representative, Himmler intervened personally. In a wireless message, the Reichsführer angrily ordered the obstreperous Gruppenführer to cease all his obstructive activities and to support Berger or else suffer "the most unpleasant consequences." [27] Himmler's intervention was effective, and Berger's authority in recruiting matters was firmly established within the ranks of the SS.

The evolution of the Waffen SS is a tangled story, not only because of the complexity of the issues involved but also because of the dissension and intrigue these issues evoked within the higher levels of both the SS and the Wehrmacht. In the face of SS plans for large-scale recruiting, it was deemed advisable that the OKW issue a decree defining and regulating the wartime status of the Waffen SS. The prewar Führer Decrees, it was felt, had not adequately done this. So far as the OKW was concerned, the new decree was intended merely to bring order into a chaotic situation. But the SS leaders saw it as an opportunity to establish the Waffen SS as "the fourth branch of the Wehrmacht." [28]

Gottlob Berger, the chief negotiator for the SS, wanted a decree that would include five main points.[29] First and foremost, he wanted a clearly defined agreement governing relations between the SS Ergänzungsstellen and the military manpower agencies.

Second, Berger wanted the OKW to authorize the establishment of a peacetime reserve pool for the Waffen SS. The Führer Decrees of 1938 and 1939 had attempted to accomplish this by permitting personnel from the SS Totenkopfverbände to be

[27] Himmler to Kaul, Coded Wireless Message, February 2, 1940, RFSS/T–175, 104/2626664.

[28] For background information see Berger to Himmler, "Befehlsentwurf OKW 12. 1. 1210/AHA/(11C)," January 5, 1940, Geheime Reichsache, RFSS/T–175, 104/2626762ff.

[29] Berger's goals in the negotiations with the OKW were outlined in a long top-secret report submitted to Himmler on February 10, 1940. See RFSS/T–175, 104/2626604ff.

used as reinforcements for the field units in the event of mobilization. But Berger pointed out that in the Polish campaign this had proved impossible "because the Totenkopfstandarten were assigned duties within the framework of the campaign that were not foreseen at the time the Führer Decree was promulgated." And, although such a transfer had been effected after the campaign, only a reserve pool composed of men who had completed service in the Waffen SS could ensure a supply of trained manpower in the event the SS was "mobilized under circumstances where a mobilization of the Army is unnecessary." [30] As Berger was soon to discover, it was in just such circumstances that the military leaders feared a large and independent Waffen SS.

Third, Berger hoped to persuade the OKW of the justice of recognizing service in the SS Totenkopfstandarten as military duty *(Wehrdienst)*. It was grossly unfair, he argued, to deny these men such recognition, especially since many were older volunteers who "could still be playing the role of civilian breadwinner if they had not belonged to the SS and therefore willingly offered themselves for service." [31]

Fourth, the SS leader also wanted to have included in the new decree a clause firmly establishing the title *Waffen SS* "as the all-inclusive designation for the armed units of the SS." While the various branches of the SS were clear about the use of this term, Berger complained that the military authorities, particularly the manpower agencies with which he had to deal, were not.[32]

Berger's final goal was to persuade the OKW to allow the SS to recruit replacements for its field divisions from among men in the classes 1909–1912, most of whom had been reserved for the Army's newest divisions. Hitler had requested that youths between the ages of eighteen and twenty-two be permitted to remain free from military service as long as possible so they could complete a term of compulsory labor service in the Reichsarbeitsdienst (Reich Labor Corps). But the OKW's

---

[30] *Ibid.*   [31] *Ibid.*   [32] *Ibid.*

refusal to allow the SS a share of the older age groups had forced Berger to accept eighteen- and nineteen-year-old volunteers.[33]

Throughout the winter of 1939-1940, the SS leaders negotiated with military representatives in an attempt to reach agreement on a new decree. But two issues defied resolution: the High Command adamantly refused to recognize duty in the Totenkopfstandarten as military service, and it was equally unwilling to allow the SS an independent peacetime reserve. The reason for refusal was the same in both instances. Neither the Totenkopf formations nor the reserve components of the SS were subject to Wehrmacht control. Agreement to the SS demands, the OKW negotiators argued, would mean that "the Wehrmacht was no longer," as Hitler had promised it would be, "the only bearer of arms [*Waffenträger*] in the nation." [34]

Himmler's position as set forth by Berger was that "the full commitment of the Wehrmacht and the Police was possible only because of the internal security provided by the Totenkopfverbände." In addition, Berger again pointed out that the Totenkopf units were a source of reinforcements for the SS field divisions, without which the SS would be forced to fill all its future needs from volunteers of predraft age.[35]

After lengthy discussion, the OKW negotiators agreed to consider the formation of a peacetime SS reserve, but only if provision was made for joint SS–OKW administration of the program. A completely independent reserve was entirely out of the question. On the other hand, the OKW refused to make any concessions whatever concerning the status of the Totenkopf units. As Berger soon found out, the military leaders were in this case dealing from a position of strength. Keitel, the OKW chief, had discussed the matter with Hitler, who had agreed to postpone a decision until after the war. The SS leaders had been outmaneuvered—for neither the first time nor the

[33] *Ibid.* Classes and age groups are here used synonymously and refer to year of birth. The German military conscription procedure was based on a general call-up of classes—i.e., men born in a given year.

[34] Berger to Himmler, "Befehlsentwurf OKW 12. 1. 1210/AHA/(11C)," January 5, 1940, Geheime Reichsache, RFSS/T–175, 104/2626762ff.

[35] *Ibid.*

last. In the face of this decision, Himmler had to swallow his anger and content himself with a mild reproof delivered to Major General Hermann Reinecke by the head of Himmler's Personal Staff, Gruppenführer Wolff, for transmittal to Keitel. "The Reichsführer," Wolff told Reinecke, "was very surprised that Colonel General Keitel should negotiate with the Führer on SS matters without first contacting the Reichsführer SS." [36]

Himmler's reaction was mild compared to that of the generals when they discovered how rapidly the Totenkopf formations had grown. By June 1940 nearly 33,000 men were serving in these units, and it mattered little that the Death's Head troopers were classified as "civil servants" *(Beamten)* rather than as soldiers.[37] Of course in retrospect the whole controversy was inconsequential. Before the war was half over, most of the Totenkopf personnel, like their 6500 colleagues in the Totenkopfdivision, were serving in the field units of the Waffen SS; thus they too came under the tactical control of the Army. But during the first months of 1940 the issue was symptomatic of the basic antagonism between the SS and the Wehrmacht.

While Keitel and his associates in the OKW continued their efforts to curb or at least control the armed units of the SS, the Army leaders, who had had their fingers burned too often by meddling in political affairs, practiced the *Vogelstrausspolitik* which characterized so much of their attitude toward the SS: what they could not or would not alter they simply ignored.

Early in February 1940, Berger informed Himmler that, much to his surprise, the Army High Command (OKH) claimed to have no knowledge of the Führer Decree of May 18, 1939, which had authorized an increase in the number of SS Totenkopfstandarten; nor did it know the number, strength, and

---

[36] "Besprechung am 15. II. 40 mit General Reinecke," Geheime Kommandosache, RFSS/T-175, 104/2626596.

[37] On June 13, 1940, there were fourteen Totenkopfstandarten numbered 4 through 17 (Standarten 1–3 had been incorporated into the SS Totenkopfdivision), plus two Totenkopf Cavalry Standarten and a few support units, with a total strength of 32,822 men. For strength of the individual units and their locations during June, see "Stärkemeldung der SS Totenkopfstandarten," June 13, 1940, RFSS/T-175, 104/2625574 f.

disposition of these units.[38] And not until May, nearly nine months after the beginning of the war, did the military authorities file a formal complaint about the fact that Totenkopf personnel, who were not part of the Army, were wearing the Army's field-gray uniform. The SS replied that they were entitled to do so because they had been "committed by the Führer for special military duties" in German-occupied areas, and in any case, "it was too late to do anything about it now." [39] Himmler may have been unsuccessful in gaining military recognition for his Totenkopf formations, but he managed to dress them like soldiers. Small wonder that many of the early victims of Nazi racial policies died cursing the German Army.

It is difficult to avoid the conclusion that the generals were only feigning ignorance in matters concerning the Totenkopfstandarten. It is true that the SS leaders made every effort to keep secret the size of these formations, but it is hard to see how entire regiments of Death's Head troops stationed in Poland, Czechoslovakia, Norway, Denmark, and Holland could have escaped notice.[40]

[38] Berger to Himmler, "Besprechung mit Major Ratke, Adjutant OBH," February 10, 1940, Geheime Kommandosache, RFSS/T–175, 104/2626613 f. Himmler apparently insisted on secrecy in matters dealing with the Totenkopfstandarten, but Berger seems to have had doubts concerning the wisdom of this policy. During March he informed Himmler that "so far the Wehrmacht has not succeeded in finding out exactly how many men we have inducted and they won't be completely successful in the future . . . but to admit nothing is as foolish as admitting the figures immediately." The recruiting could not go on indefinitely without the knowledge of the OKW, and in any case the number of men authorized in the Führererlass had not yet been reached. (The strength of the Death's Head Corps was then a total of 30,487 men. "Stärkemeldung der verst. SS T. Standarten," March 1, 1940, RFSS/T–175, 104/2626524 f.) Berger expressed the opinion that "this kind of secrecy is hardly necessary and certainly dangerous since we must, in the end, go to the Reich authorities for the necessary means." Salaries, weapons, clothing, and the like would only be provided according to figures released by the SS; understating these would result in serious supply and administrative difficulties in the future. Berger to Himmler, March n.d., 1940, RFSS/T–175, 104/2626518ff.

[39] RFSS/T–175, 103/2626023 f.

[40] In June 1940 there was one SS Totenkopf regiment in each of these non-German cities: Oslo, Stavanger-Bergen, Radom, Brno, Cracow, Breda, Prague. Another was on the way to Copenhagen.

SS Recruiting Campaign of Early 1940

While negotiations for a decree governing the wartime status of the Waffen SS dragged on, SS recruiting moved rapidly ahead. The formation of the Totenkopf and Polizei Divisions had drastically thinned the ranks of the Totenkopfstandarten and the Police. The OKW's refusal to allow the SS to accept men of military age for these formations forced SS recruiters to turn their attention to older and younger men. In both directions lay difficulties. Men who were past the age of conscription had little incentive to volunteer for active service in the SS, while youths of predraft age had first to fulfill their compulsory labor-service obligation.

Berger attempted to solve the first problem by enlisting the support of the NSDAP. Various Party organizations were asked to urge their members to volunteer for service in the SS Totenkopf regiments. The drive was not especially successful; and the SA, which had reason to resent the SS, soon dropped entirely out of the program. As late as April 1940, the SS had been able to recruit only 1727 members of the NSDAP.[41]

The recruitment of youths met with better results. The SS succeeded in enlisting the support of Dr. Robert Ley, Chief of the German Labor Front (DAF), for a plan whereby youths between the ages of eighteen and twenty would be released from the compulsory labor service (RAD) if they volunteered and were accepted for long-term enlistments in the Totenkopf, Police, or field units of the SS.[42] On January 16, 1940, Keitel

---

[41] Berger to Himmler, "Übersichtsliste," April 2, 1940, Geheime Kommandosache, RFSS/T–175, 104/2626427 f. There also seem to have been a number of personal factors involved in the lack of SA support for Berger's drive to recruit Party members for the SS. Goebbels' diary entry for May 9, 1943, describes his conversation with Hitler concerning the appointment of a new chief of staff for the SA to replace Viktor Lutze, who had died in an air accident, and speaks of "the rather strained relationship of the SA with the SS," which he attributed to the fact that Lutze "permitted his wife and the family's friendship with Brauchitsch to maneuver him into excessive opposition to the SS." *The Goebbels Diaries*, edited by Louis P. Lochner (New York, 1948), p. 362.

[42] Memorandum by Berger, "Ersatz für die SS Totenkopfstandarten," January 12, 1940, Vertraulich, RFSS/T–175, 104/262672ff.

issued an OKW order confirming the authority of the SS to enlist twenty-year-olds for its field divisions.[43] The OKW made no mention of eighteen- and nineteen-year-olds for the Totenkopf and Police formations, and apparently had no authority to do so. A week later Reichsarbeitsführer (Reich Labor Leader) von Gönner notified Berger that the SS was authorized to recruit for the Totenkopfstandarten and the Police 6000 youths from age groups 1918, 1919, and 1920, and a further 2500 from the 1920 class for the SS field divisions. The SS was given until April 1, 1940, to complete the recruitment.[44]

The ever-alert Berger noticed that the OKW order of January 16 had failed to put a numerical restriction on the number of twenty-year-olds the SS was authorized to recruit. He immediately took advantage of the situation by issuing a secret order to all SS recruiting stations to disregard the 2500-man quota set by von Gönner and to enlist as many volunteers as possible from the 1920 class before the termination date of April 1.[45] This type of stratagem was typical of Berger's methods and in large part explains the success of the Waffen SS' independent recruiting policies. Such tactics did not, of course, make friends for the SS; but the more powerful Himmler's empire grew, the less it depended on the good will of others and the more it relied on coercion and intimidation to achieve its ends.

During the first months of 1940, Germany was flooded with leaflets, posters, and mailed circulars soliciting volunteers for the armed SS. "The SS Totenkopfstandarten," read one such announcement, "set up for the solution of special tasks, will immediately begin accepting volunteers." Men between the ages of twenty-eight and thirty-nine who could prove their Aryan ancestry, had no police or court record, were in good mental and

---

[43] The OKW order of January 16 apparently was only a partial concession to the SS, and Berger still had to negotiate with the RAD, which reserved the right to impose a numerical quota on the number of youths released from labor service. Not until June 28, 1940, did the OKW consent to the blanket release of all youths under twenty who enlisted in the Waffen SS for four and a half years or longer. RFSS/T–175, 104/2626226.

[44] Von Gönner to Berger, "Freiwillige der Polizei und der SS-VT," January 25, 1940, RFSS/T–175, 104/2626752. Cf. Absolon, *op. cit.*, p. 155.

[45] Berger Order, January 25, 1940, Geheim, RFSS/T–175, 104/2626745 f.

physical health, and stood at least 5 feet 7.5 inches tall were urged to enlist. A "special enlistment" was also offered to eighteen- and nineteen-year-olds if they volunteered for a twelve-year period. Such volunteers would be "freed from military service" and would be given the status of "civil servants" *(Beamten).*[46]

For the SS Verfügungsdivision and the Leibstandarte SS "Adolf Hitler" applicants had to be between seventeen and twenty-two, for the SS Totenkopfdivision the maximum age was twenty-six. The minimum height for these field divisions was 5 feet 7.5 inches (5 feet 6.7 inches "in special cases"), except for the elite Leibstandarte, which required no less than 6 feet 0.5 inches. The circulars ended with the reminder that "service in the Waffen SS counts as military service."[47]

Using the impressive communications facilities of the NSDAP and its affiliated organizations, the SS broadcast the message that its "active units are guard regiments in the finest tradition of the word" and that in an "ideological war it is a great honor to serve in a National Socialist corps."[48] The lure of elitism apparently had the desired effect; an increasing number of Germans volunteered for the Waffen SS. Indeed, there seemed to be little difficulty in securing sufficient applicants, especially for the field divisions.[49] The real problem was the reluctance of the military manpower agencies to release the men for induction into the Waffen SS. Throughout 1940 the SS leaders found cause to complain about the difficulties created by the military in this regard. On February 16, for example, Berger reported to Himmler that during the preceding month the SS had examined a total of 49,211 volunteers, of whom

[46] RFSS/T–175, 104/2626702. Halder noted in his diary on February 7, 1940, a report that the Waffen SS was mustering youths from classes 1920–1923 for service in Poland [Totenkopfstandarten]; "in this fashion [these age groups] will be tied down and picked through before we get to them." Halder, *Kriegstagebuch*, I, 186.

[47] "Merkblatt für den freiwilligen Eintritt in die Waffen SS," 1940, RFSS/T–175, 104/2626172. Cf. prewar standards, p. 10.

[48] Berger to all Ergänzungsstellen, February 1, 1940, Geheim, RFSS/T–175, 104/2626688ff.

[49] Some years later Himmler claimed that the Waffen SS received voluntary applications from 40 per cent of each age group that became subject to conscription. RFSS/T–175, 93/2613769.

only 19,087 were found qualified. On the basis of past experience, Berger cautioned that no more than a third of these were
likely to be released by the Wehrbezirkskommandos.[50]

The Totenkopfstandarten, however, were far less successful
than the SS field divisions in attracting volunteers. Consequently
toward the end of January, the SS, acting under the authority
of the existing Führer Decrees, issued an order calling for
the immediate induction into the Totenkopfstandarten of members of the General SS who belonged to age groups about to be
called up for military service.[51] The thousands of men thus conscripted could hardly be considered volunteers, yet the SS leaders
continued to maintain the fiction that the armed SS was a
volunteer formation.[52]

In the meantime the SS had discovered in the *Volksdeutsche*
(ethnic Germans) from German-controlled areas outside the
Reich a new source of manpower entirely free from Wehrmacht
restriction. By the end of January 1940, a total of 109 ethnic
Germans from Slovakia had been examined and 58 found
suitable for duty in the Waffen SS.[53] From then on an ever-
increasing number of *Volksdeutsche* volunteered or were conscripted into the ranks of the SS. Long before the end of the
war, they outnumbered native Germans in the Waffen SS.

To absorb the flood of new recruits, the SS established a

[50] Berger to Himmler, "Annahmeuntersuchungen im Monat Januar,"
February 16, 1940, RFSS/T—175, 104/2626592 f.

[51] During January 1940, the OKW had given the Wehrbezirkskommandos authority to induct immediately classes 1910—1918, the first two-
thirds of 1919, and all volunteers 1900—1923. Classes 1904—1909, 1920, 1921,
and the remaining third of 1919 remained under OKW control for later
use. "Übersicht über die Heranziehung der Geburtjahrgänge zum Wehrdienst," 103/2626103. Cf. Absolon, *op. cit.*, pp. 153ff.

[52] It is only fair to point out that these men would otherwise have been
conscripted into the Army. They had, in any case, voluntarily joined the
Allgemeine SS, and since Himmler made no distinction between the
various branches of the SS, he continued to think of them as volunteers.

[53] Berger to Himmler, "Slowaken-Deutsche," January 30, 1940, RFSS/T
—175, 104/2626692. Himmler's authority here stemmed from his position as
head of the Reich Commissariat for the Strengthening of Germandom
(RKFDV). For details see Robert Koehl, *RKFDV: German Resettlement
and Population Policy, 1939—1945* (Cambridge, Mass., 1957), *passim*.

replacement *(Ersatz)* regiment for each of its field divisions, and smaller *Ersatz* formations for specialized troops such as artillery, tank destroyers, and combat engineers. By the end of January 1940, the Waffen SS had more than 10,000 men in these replacement formations; [54] new recruits were constantly being added, while those who had completed their training were sent on to join the field divisions.

On January 23, the OKH issued a highly significant directive regulating the wartime status of the *Ersatz* formations of the Waffen SS. The Reichsführer SS was granted complete command authority over them regardless of their location, while the Commander-in-Chief of the Army retained only the right of inspection and had merely an advisory role in matters connected with military training.[55]

What appears on the surface a simple administrative agreement actually turned out to be a major concession to the SS. Himmler lost no time in scattering the SS replacement units all over German-occupied Europe; thus men who had been recruited for front-line service found themselves at times during their training period called upon to engage in "police activities." Waffen SS *Ersatz* battalions stationed in Amsterdam and Bergen were, on direct orders from Berlin, called out to put down strikes and demonstrations. Most of the German troops who carried out the destruction of the Warsaw Ghetto in 1943 were members of SS replacement units that happened to be quartered in the area. Of the daily average of 30 German officers and 1190 men involved in the month-long operation, 4 officers and 440 men were members of the Waffen SS Panzer Grenadier Training and Reserve Battalion 3, Warsaw; another 5 officers and 381 men were members of the Waffen SS Cavalry Training and Reserve Battalion, Warsaw. The extermination of the last 60,000 or so Jews remaining in the Ghetto cost the Waffen SS approximately a dozen dead and 60 wounded, many of whom were recruits with only a few weeks' training.[56]

[54] "Ersatzlage der SS-VT am 29. 1. 1940," RFSS/T–175, 104/2626754.
[55] OKH Order, "Ersatz-Einheiten für die SS-T. Div.," RFSS/T–175, 104/2626727.
[56] See Nuremberg Document 1061–PS.

The use of Waffen SS training and reserve units for police duties made it possible for Himmler eventually to integrate the SS Totenkopf regiments into the field units of the Waffen SS. SS Police regiments and various locally recruited security formations—reinforced when necessary by rear-area Waffen SS units—took their place.[57]

The Title Waffen SS Becomes Official

The rapid but haphazard growth of the armed SS made increasingly imperative a final agreement defining its wartime status. After months of negotiation the OKW had agreed to allow the SS to maintain an independent reserve under joint SS–OKW administration. But the military leaders still adamantly refused to recognize duty in the Totenkopfverbände as military service. A new draft proposal embodying the latest OKW concessions was prepared, and on February 28, 1940, Berger submitted a copy to Himmler with the suggestion that it be accepted.[58] Although he admitted that "the decree is no great advance," Berger felt it provided "a basis for an undisturbed build-up of the Totenkopfstandarten and for their later recognition." He regretted that the Reichsführer would not have a free hand in the administration of the peacetime Waffen SS reserve, but nevertheless felt that any attempt to seek further revisions "would only drag out the affair" to the point where "the whole thing may fall through." He reminded Himmler that "there are some gentlemen at the OKW who still earnestly maintain that the agreement represents too great a concession to us." The proposed decree, he concluded, provided "freedom of movement and points of departure" with which he could eventually make "the Waffen SS the fourth branch of the Wehrmacht." [59] On March 2 Himmler agreed to accept the OKW proposal.[60]

[57] For a detailed study of the SS Police formations during the war see Georg Tessin, "Die Stäbe und Truppeneinheiten der Ordnungspolizei," in Neufeldt, Huck, and Tessin, *op. cit.*, Part II, pp. 13ff.

[58] Berger to Himmler, "Befehlsentwurf OKW," February 28, 1940, Geheim, RFSS/T–175, 104/2626506 f.

[59] Berger to Brandt, "Besprechung mit SS Brigadeführer Petri," March 2, 1940, RFSS/T–175, 104/2626515 f.

[60] Himmler to Berger, March 2, 1940, RFSS/T–175, 104/2626505.

The title *Waffen SS* now became official. It applied to the SS Verfügungsdivision, the Leibstandarte SS "Adolf Hitler," the SS Totenkopfdivision, the SS Polizeidivision, the SS Junkerschulen, and all their replacement and training units. Service in these formations counted as active military duty. The SS Totenkopfverbände were also officially recognized as part of the Waffen SS, but "the decision as to whether this duty counts as military service is to be taken in the future." Their status during the war was to continue to be regulated by the Führer Decree of May 18, 1939.[61]

In addition to the armed formations, the OKW recognized as part of the Waffen SS seven administrative organizations handling recruitment, supply, administration, justice, welfare, weapons development, and medical services. It was agreed that duty in these bureaus was to be considered military service, but after April 1, 1940, their personnel were to be drawn only from the ranks of active Waffen SS units.[62]

Although the selection standards of the Waffen SS remained unaffected, the mechanics of mustering, acceptance, and induction of volunteers was to follow existing Wehrmacht procedure. On the controversial matter of a peacetime reserve for the Waffen SS, the OKW decree provided for the discharge, according to Army regulations, of Waffen SS personnel who had completed their active duty and for their enrollment in an SS reserve rather than in the Army reserve pool. But by a system of duplicate record-keeping, the program was in effect to be administered jointly by the Wehrmacht and the SS.[63]

The battle over reserve status and over recognition for the Totenkopfstandarten eventually became meaningless, for the quick victory envisioned by Germany's political leaders never materialized. Except for some older man and skilled workers demobilized after the fall of France, all Waffen SS personnel,

[61] OKW Order, "Wehrdienstverhältnis und Wehrüberwachung der Angehörigen der Waffen SS während des Krieges," February n.d., 1940, Geheim, RFSS/T–175, 104/2626508ff.

[62] The administrative organizations recognized as part of the Waffen SS were: Ergänzungsamt der Waffen SS; Personalamt der Waffen SS; Fürsorge und Versorgungsamt der Waffen SS; Sanitätsamt der Waffen SS; Verwaltungsamt der Waffen SS; SS-Gericht. *Ibid.*

[63] *Ibid.*

regardless of the conditions of their original enlistment, served
for the duration of the war or, as in the case of tens of thousands,
until death. As for the Totenkopfstandarten, they were eventually incorporated, unit by unit, into the larger field formations
of the Waffen SS.

Fight for Arms

In addition to manpower problems, the Waffen SS had to
face the task of equipping its new formations. Once again Wehrmacht cooperation left much to be desired. The basic problem,
as in recruiting, was the distinction made by the military between
the SS field formations and the Totenkopf units. The former,
with the exception of the Polizeidivision, had been designated
first-line divisions. On Hitler's personal orders they were to be
completely motorized and committed as part of the first attack
wave in the West. Apart from the Führer's desires, there was
the fact that the field SS was tactically part of the Army; the
OKW therefore had no choice but to order the OKH to provide the SS necessary weapons and equipment. But for the
Totenkopfstandarten there was little sympathy in the OKW,
and even less cooperation in the matter of arms and equipment.

Himmler had issued orders that the Totenkopf regiments
be equipped in the same fashion as regular infantry regiments.
But Oberführer [64] Gärtner, Chef des Beschaffungsamtes (SS
Procurement Office), who had been assigned the task, complained to his chief that a request to the OKH "under the
authority of the Decree of the Führer and Reichschancellor of
18 May 1939" for 84 light field pieces and 126 antitank guns
for the Totenkopfstandarten "had not even been answered."
At the end of January, therefore, "the 14 reinforced Totenkopf regiments still had no heavy weapons." [65]

---

[64] An SS rank with no exact Army equivalent; roughly halfway between
colonel (Standartenführer) and major general (Brigadeführer).

[65] Gärtner to Himmler, "Bedarf an Geschützen für die Waffen SS,"
January 11, 1940. Geheime Kommandosache, RFSS/T–175, 104/2626477.

The SS field formations were also short of artillery, particularly that of large caliber. Gärtner suggested to Himmler that the SS make itself "independent of the Wehrmacht in this respect" by securing the large stock at the Skoda works in occupied Czechoslovakia. The guns at Skoda had been manufactured for export to such countries as Iran, Lithuania, and Yugoslavia, but their "shipment was in question due to political developments." [66] The difficulty was that the OKW had already taken the equipment under its protection pending a decision on its final disposition; and for a number of reasons it opposed the supplying of heavy artillery to the SS. In the first place, given the shortage of modern artillery and related equipment, the Army wanted what there was for its own divisions. Further, the SS divisions were motorized; their heavy artillery would therefore have to be drawn by motor vehicles of a type that was in even shorter supply. The third and perhaps most important reason was the military's distrust of Himmler's motives. The Army felt that its possession of heavy weapons made it the final arbiter in any domestic situation which required the use of force. An SS similarly armed would be a serious threat in the event of a postwar clash between the Army and the National Socialists.

Perhaps the same considerations were responsible for the unusual energy which Himmler expended on securing heavy artillery for his Waffen SS. In any event, his efforts were successful; during March Hitler ordered the establishment of a new motorized heavy artillery regiment for the Waffen SS. [67] It was to consist of three battalions, one for each of the SS field divisions. An additional light artillery battalion was to be created for the Leibstandarte SS "Adolf Hitler." [68]

The military leaders had apparently not expected Hitler's action. Berger reported to Himmler that "the OKW, especially those gentlemen who do not wish us well, are at the moment in confusion. The approval of the four artillery battalions has

[66] *Ibid.*

[67] Himmler to Jüttner, March 23, 1940, RFSS/T–175, 104/2626468.

[68] For details see series of orders issued by Himmler to implement Hitler's decision. RFSS/T–175, 104/2626456ff.

deeply shaken them." [69] On March 26, in a personal letter to Himmler, Keitel rather ungracefully conceded that the SS could have a dozen 150-mm. howitzers from Skoda, but he warned that "it should be understood that the OKH will deliver the remaining equipment required only after the outfitting of the artillery formations of the divisions of the seventh and eighth wave has been completed." [70] In other words, the SS divisions which belonged to the first wave were accorded no better treatment than a third-rate Landwehr (reserve) division.

The Polizeidivision, which was not at this time considered a first-line unit and was therefore not motorized, was quickly outfitted with older models of horse-drawn artillery. [71] And Hitler's pet Leibstandarte received within a week the necessary guns, equipment, and motor vehicles for its new artillery battalion. [72] But for the Verfügungs and Totenkopf Divisions the required artillery—and indeed much else—was very slow in coming. The SS divisional staffs continually reported that the Army was not carrying out the orders issued by the OKW calling for the transfer of equipment, even though it was "lying in plain sight in Army field depots and motor pools." [73] A suggestion that perhaps the distribution could be expedited by allowing the SS to handle the transfer was abruptly dismissed with the observation that SS units under the command of the OKH would be supplied in the same fashion as Army formations. Part of the

[69] Berger to Himmler, "Anerkennung der Dienstzeit für die SS-T. St.," March 30, 1940, Geheim, RFSS/T–175, 104/2626430. Hitler, as early as January 21, 1940, had ordered the OKH to provide the Waffen SS with four heavy motorized infantry guns for a newly established heavy-weapons company. See OKH Order, "Aufstellung einer schw. I.G. Komp.," January 21, 1940, RFSS/T–175, 106/2629789.

[70] Keitel to Himmler, March 26, 1940, Geheime Kommandosache, RFSS/T–175, 104/2626453.

[71] This was done by temporarily attaching an entire Army artillery regiment (Art. Rgt. 300) to the Polizeidivision. A communications section and some other support units were also composed of Army personnel. See Neufeldt, Huck, and Tessin, *op. cit.*, Part II, pp. 24 f.; Keilig, *op. cit.*, II, Section 141, pp. 9 f.

[72] Jüttner to Himmler, April 2, 1940, Geheime Kommandosache, RFSS/T–175, 104/2626423ff.

[73] Undated report by Kommando der Waffen SS signed by Sturmbannführer Brandt to be placed before Himmler, RFSS/T–175, 104/2626279.

problem was undoubtedly rooted in hostility toward the SS. But the Army was also having great difficulty with its armament program. In many instances, particularly with regard to the Totenkopfstandarten, it was simply unable to fill SS needs without sacrificing a share of its own buildup.

By the beginning of May, with Denmark and Norway under German control and the main onslaught in the West only a day away, Oberführer Gärtner was forced to inform Himmler that "the Waffen und Geräteamt der Waffen SS no longer sees any possibility of obtaining the required weapons and equipment through the previously used Wehrmacht agencies in the time allotted." [74] But Gärtner had anticipated such a situation. Some months earlier, he had begun negotiations with the newly created Reich Ministry for Arms and Munitions [75] for the establishment of an independent SS procurement program.

In the preliminary talks Gärtner took the position that the German arms industry "could meet the requirements of the Waffen SS without disturbing the Wehrmacht's program." But in any case, the SS could no longer "go begging to the Wehrmacht." It was vital that the SS end its dependence and achieve "a position of equality." Moreover, dependence meant supervision; and Gärtner informed the Arms Ministry officials that "the Reichsführer SS had no intention of granting the Wehrmacht complete insight into the intended final structure, strength, and purpose of the Waffen SS formations, all the more so because the many-sided demands made on the Schutzstaffel encompass military, political, and police tasks." [76]

Gärtner's overtures were favorably received, and a meeting with Reichsminister Fritz Todt was arranged. After briefly restating the SS position, Gärtner presented Todt with a list of items the Waffen SS required immediately. It included 30,000

[74] Gärtner to Himmler, "Beschaffung von Waffen und Gerät für die Waffen SS," May 9, 1940, Geheime Kommandosache, RFSS/T–175, 104/2626361.
[75] Reichsministerium für Bewaffnung und Munition; as of September 2, 1943, Reichsministerium für Rüstung und Kriegsproduktion. Fritz Todt was Reichsminister until his death in February 1942; thereafter Albert Speer held the post until the end of the war.
[76] Gärtner to Himmler, May 9, 1940, Geheime Kommandosache, RFSS/T–175, 104/2626360 f.

carbines, 20,000 rifles, 50,000 bayonets, 10,000 pistols, 10,000 submachine guns, thousands of machine and antitank guns, hundreds of artillery pieces, millions of rounds of ammunition, and 250 field kitchens. Todt was sympathetic and agreed to do what he could for the SS. In return for his cooperation the German weapons czar requested a small favor. Could the SS provide him with 20,000 Polish workers for his munitions factories? Gärtner assured him that "the wish can be fulfilled." [77]

Gärtner, flushed with success, reported to Himmler that "the whole problem of armaments will be solved . . . with or without the Wehrmacht." A few days later the SS armaments chief notified the Army authorities that the Waffen SS intended to procure certain needed items on its own. Without waiting for approval, Gärtner placed an order for 30,000 smoke grenades with the firm of Hugo Schneider. By this time the western campaign was in full swing, and the OKW and OKH apparently had more urgent matters to consider. The SS challenge, however, was not to go unanswered.

On June 18, Brigadeführer (Major General) Max Jüttner, then acting as Himmler's chief of staff for Waffen SS affairs, received an official communication from General Friedrich (Fritz) Fromm, Chief of Army Ordnance and Commander of the Home Army, protesting the SS attempt at independent procurement and pointing out that it could "only create severe complications in the arms industry." The matter had been referred to the OKW, and Fromm had been authorized to inform Jüttner that "so long as the field formations of the Waffen SS are incorporated in the ranks of the Wehrmacht, they, like all such troops, will be supplied with weapons, munitions, and all similar needs by the supply organizations of the Army." After making it very clear that the OKW would tolerate "no private supply organization or procurement agency," Fromm's letter closed with the information that "the contract let to the firm of Hugo Schneider has been taken over by the Wehrmacht" and the Waffen SS' need for smoke grenades would be met "as far as possible" by the Army's supply organization.[78]

[77] *Ibid.*, 2626361 f.
[78] Fromm to Jüttner, June 18, 1940, Geheim, RFSS/T–175, 104/2626230.

It is not unreasonable to assume that the OKW's strong stand in the face of the SS challenge had Hitler's support. Certainly such an assumption would explain why the SS quickly dropped its plans for an independent armament program. But this was by no means the end of the matter. In 1940 Hitler had not yet completely broken with his generals, and neither Himmler nor his Waffen SS held the position they were to occupy in later years. By 1942, however, the situation was somewhat more favorable; following Todt's death and the appointment of Albert Speer as Minister for Armament, Himmler once more turned his attention to the problem of freeing the SS from dependence on the Wehrmacht for its armament. Speer was sympathetic to Himmler's arguments, and this time Hitler apparently supported the SS. An agreement was reached whereby the SS was to provide concentration-camp inmates for the war factories and in return receive 5 to 8 per cent of their output for the Waffen SS.[79]

But in 1940 the field divisions of the Waffen SS, with the exception of the Leibstandarte, received no special treatment in the matter of arms. Indeed, the Totenkopf and the Polizei Divisions were equipped almost entirely with captured Czech weapons; although they proved to be equal in performance to those of German manufacture,[80] their use was hardly in keeping with Himmler's concept of the elite and privileged nature of his Waffen SS. Moreover, the Army's lack of generosity forced the SS to go into battle with serious deficiencies in heavy weapons and with inadequate transport.

The Waffen SS Joins the Army: Final Preparations for the Offensive

Throughout the winter and spring of 1939–1940 Germany's military leaders worked feverishly to prepare the Wehrmacht for *Fall Gelb* (Case Yellow), the planned offensive in Western Europe. New recruits were trained and equipped, reserves were mobilized; and by April, forty-four fresh infantry divisions, one cavalry division, and a new mountain division had been

[79] See Reitlinger, *op. cit.*, pp. 262 f.
[80] See "Bericht über die tschechischen Waffen beim Kampfeinsatz," August 5, 1940, Geheim, RFSS/T–175, 104/2626129ff.

created.[81] For the vitally important mobile forces, the spearhead of *Blitzkrieg* operations, four new armored divisions were formed, giving the German Army a total of ten panzer divisions. But to support the armored forces the Wehrmacht still had only the four motorized infantry divisions with which it had begun the war the previous September. The deficiency was made up by the Waffen SS, which supplied the equivalent of three divisions of motorized infantry—the SS Verfügungsdivision, the Totenkopfdivision, and the reinforced regiment Leibstandarte SS "Adolf Hitler." Altogether, counting the nonmotorized Polizeidivision, replacements in training, and the personnel of the SS Totenkopf regiments, the armed SS had more than 125,000 men in uniform by the time the offensive in the West was launched.[82]

Like the Army, the Waffen SS spent the period of the so-called phony war building up its strength and training and equipping its formations. While the SS leaders in Berlin fought their policy battles with the mandarins of the High Command, SS field commanders were engaged in the practical task of preparing their units for the forthcoming offensive. For this purpose the SS field formations were assigned to various Army corps along Germany's western frontier. SS personnel under Army command were made subject to military regulations and, for the first time, were required to salute "according to military and not former SS or Police rank." As a concession to the political orientation of the Waffen SS, its members were granted permission to use the Nazi salute, and they were excused from church call and a number of other traditional military observances.[83]

The task of the SS field commanders, especially those of the

---

[81] Taylor, *op. cit.,* p. 17.

[82] SS divisions were larger than Army divisions, averaging 21,000 men each against 15,000 to 17,000 in a regular infantry division. For a statistical survey of the Waffen SS as of May 1, 1940, see "Übersichtsplan," May 4, 1940, RFSS/T–175, 104/2626381ff.

[83] OKW Order, "Anwendung der Standortdienstvorschrift . . . auf die in die Wehrmacht eingegliederten Teile der bewaffnenten SS und Polizei," April 26, 1940, Geheim, RFSS/T–175, 103/2626029 f.

two newest SS divisions, was complicated by a number of factors. First, much of the equipment supplied to the newly established Totenkopf and Polizei Divisions was of Czech manufacture, thus creating additional training and supply problems. Second, the attitude of individual Army commanders toward the SS formations in their midst was often less than cordial; again, this was most pronounced in the case of the newest SS formations. The older, established SS regiments—the Leibstandarte, "Deutschland," "Germania," and to a lesser extent "Der Führer"—had previously served under Army command and (except for "Der Führer") had fought in Poland. They were commanded by men like Paul Hausser, Felix Steiner, and Sepp Dietrich, who were respected or at least accepted by their Army colleagues.[84] But Himmler's two newest divisions and their commanding officers had yet to prove themselves. What little the Army field commanders had heard about them hardly seemed reassuring: The Polizeidivision, under the command of Karl von Pfeffer-Wildenbruch, a Police general, consisted of policemen armed with Czech weapons and vintage horse-drawn artillery; the Totenkopfdivision, led by SS Gruppenführer Theodor Eicke, Himmler's supervisor of concentration camps, included in its ranks a sizable number of former guards from those unsavory institutions.

Himmler had no pretensions about the Polizeidivision in 1940; it was not composed of SS men, and he did not object when it was assigned a passive defense role opposite the Maginot Line for *Fall Gelb.* The Totenkopfdivision, however, involved the prestige of the much-maligned concentration-camp guards. Here Himmler saw an opportunity to demonstrate that the dreaded Death's Head units were as capable of engaging in the honorable profession of soldiering as they were of brutalizing helpless prisoners. He therefore pressed strongly for the inclusion of the Totenkopfdivision in the crucial first-wave attack. However, Colonel General Franz Halder, Chief of the Army

---

[84] Dietrich had been a career soldier from 1911 to 1918, attaining the rank of senior noncommissioned officer. Hausser and Steiner had both been officers in the regular Army, the former retiring in 1932 with the rank of lieutenant general and the latter resigning in 1933 as a major.

General Staff, had already concluded that, while the division
"presented an orderly appearance," it would find "a battle of
combined weapons a difficult undertaking." [85] And in the end
the Totenkopfdivision was assigned to General von Weichs'
2nd Army, a part of the OKH reserve that was to move into
Belgium and Luxembourg in the wake of the lead divisions.

On April 4 the Totenkopfdivision received its first visit from
the commander of the 2nd Army. General Maximilian Freiherr von Weichs—one of the Army's senior field commanders,
an aristocrat, and a devout Catholic—was not favorably inclined
toward the SS and made no effort to hide the fact. The General's
manner upon arrival was described by SS Gruppenführer Eicke
as "cold and hostile." [86]

In their opening conversation with Eicke, Weichs and his
staff revealed their ignorance about the new division that had
been added to their command. They were under the impression
that the Totenkopfdivision was "organized and equipped like
a Czech foot division," and were very much surprised to discover it was really a modern, motorized infantry division. At a
time when only seven of the German Army's 139 infantry divisions were motorized this was indeed a command to be proud
of. And when Eicke added the information that a heavy artillery
section was being organized for the division, Weichs' professional interest was aroused and his coolness began to dissipate.
Weichs' inspection of the troops left him visibly impressed, and
he completed his visit in a frame of mind far different from that
in which he had arrived. When he returned for a second visit
some weeks later Weichs was "very friendly" and had nothing
but praise for the SS troops.[87]

The conversion of General von Weichs is a good example
of the manner in which SS–Army relations often worked out in
the field. Most of the ranking Army officers who had had no

[85] Halder, *Kriegstagebuch,* I, 179.
[86] Eicke to Kommando der Waffen SS, "Meldung," April 4, 1940,
Geheim, RFSS/T–175, 107/2629975ff.
[87] Eicke to Kommando der Waffen SS, "Besichtigung durch den Oberbefehlshaber der 2. Armee," April 29, 1940, Geheim, RFSS/T–175,
107/2629975ff.

contact with the Waffen SS expected SS divisions to be composed of Nazi street brawlers of the type that had made up the rank and file of the brown-shirted SA. They were therefore surprised and often pleased to find that they had been given command of a well-disciplined formation whose soldiers made an excellent impression. Von Weichs' most glowing praise, according to Eicke, was for the outstanding physical condition of the SS troops.

Whatever else may be said about it, there is no denying that the Waffen SS of the early war years was composed of men of exceptional physical fitness. Although the professionals continued to complain about the leadership and purpose of the Waffen SS, they had nothing but praise for the "human material" that made up the classic SS divisions. For example, Field Marshal Erich von Manstein, who had a great deal of experience with units of the Waffen SS, found the officers and noncommissioned officers of the Totenkopfdivision lacking in experience and leadership ability, but "as far as its discipline and soldierly bearing went, the division in question undoubtedly made a good impression." Throughout the war, the Totenkopfdivision "always showed great dash in the assault and was steadfast in defense," and Manstein was of the opinion that it "was probably the best Waffen SS division" he had ever come across.[88]

Elite military formations with high standards of physical selection, aggressive leadership, and an *esprit de corps* supplied by either tradition or ideological indoctrination make extremely formidable adversaries. The early SS divisions possessed all these qualities in abundance, and this fact is the key to an understanding of their combat performance.

[88] Manstein, *op. cit.*, pp. 187 f.

CHAPTER THREE

Toward a Military Reputation: The Waffen SS in the Western Campaign, 1940

THE western campaign of 1940 was a milestone in the development of the Waffen SS. For the first time SS troops fought in divisional formations under the command of their own officers, and by their performance assured the Waffen SS a permanent place as the *de facto* fourth branch of the Wehrmacht. There would be many more campaigns for the Waffen SS; its most glorious years still lay ahead. But it was in Holland and France during May and June 1940 that the Waffen SS began to acquire the reputation that in later years made it the hope of its Führer and the despair of its foes.

Fall Gelb and the Role of the Waffen SS

By the end of April 1940, the combat forces of the SS were at full strength; despite some shortages in artillery and transport, the Waffen SS stood ready for battle. The conquest of Denmark and Norway, begun on April 9, was virtually completed by the first week of May, and Hitler ordered the launching of *Fall Gelb*—the oft-delayed offensive in the West.[1]

The 136 divisions marshaled for the offensive were divided into three Army Groups—B, A, and C—spread in that order along a 400-mile front from northern Holland to the Swiss–French–German border. *Fall Gelb* was to be carried out entirely by Army Groups A and B, assisted by a division of airborne

[1] No units of the Waffen SS were involved in *Fall Weserübung*, the German invasion of Denmark and Norway.

A truck full of battle-weary SS infantry near Demiansk during the summer of 1941. The skull and crossbones on their collar patches in place of the SS runes identifies these men as members of the SS Division "Totenkopf." (Ullstein)

Reichsführer SS Heinrich Himmler greeting the officers of an SS cavalry regiment in the East, 1941. (Ullstein–Copress)

SS panzer grenadiers moving into new positions along the Russian front, 1943. The armored vehicle in the foreground is a Sturmgeschütz, a self-propelled assault gun with which SS panzergrenadier divisions were liberally equipped. (Ullstein)

A patrol of Waffen SS mountain troops (probably members of the 7th SS Gebirgsdivision "Prinz Eugen") hunts partisans in Serbia, 1942. (Ullstein)

troops. Army Group C, composed of nineteen static divisions, was to stand fast opposite the Maginot Line; with the exception of a feinting attack in the Saar area, it was given no active role in the first part of the campaign.

In its simplest form, the German plan called for three main attacks by about 75 divisions, with 45 held in reserve. The northernmost attack, to be delivered by a portion of Army Group B, was to smash the Dutch defenses and occupy Holland to deny the British Air Force the use of Dutch airfields for attacks on Germany. The remaining and much more powerful portion of Army Group B was to push into the heart of Belgium. The two attacks, it was hoped, would lure the Allies northward while the main German blow, delivered by Army Group A, thrust an armored wedge through southern Belgium and Luxembourg, into northern France. If all went according to plan, the Dutch and Belgian Armies would be swept aside, and the British Expeditionary Force and a portion of the French Army would be encircled and destroyed. There would then follow *Fall Rot*—a southward movement of all German forces into France to crush the remainder of the French Army.[2]

When the final dispositions were completed, the Leibstandarte SS "Adolf Hitler" and the 3rd SS Regiment "Der Führer" (detached from the SS Verfügungsdivision) stood poised on the Dutch frontier, the remainder of the Verfügungsdivision was on alert near Münster ready to move into Holland as soon as the border defenses had been breached, the SS Totenkopfdivision was held in OKH reserve near Kassel, and the Polizeidivision was in reserve at Tübingen, behind the upper Rhine front of Army Group C.[3]

The Waffen SS in the Netherlands

With an army too weak to defend their 200-mile-long frontier with Germany, the Dutch based their defense on a series of river and canal lines, lightly fortified near the border but growing

---

[2] For further details see Hans-Adolf Jacobsen, *Fall Gelb: Der Kampf um den deutschen Operationsplan zur Westoffensive, 1940* (Wiesbaden, 1957), *passim.*

[3] See situation map, "Lage West vom 10. 5. 1940," Halder, *Kriegstagebuch,* I, Appendix 4.

progressively stronger to the west; the last defense line surrounded "Fortress Holland" (including Rotterdam, Amsterdam, The Hague, Utrecht, and Leyden). Since it was known
that the Dutch defense relied heavily on the destruction of
bridges and the flooding of low-lying areas, the German plan
called for the seizure, by airborne troops and parachutists, of
the key bridges leading into "Fortress Holland" in order to
hold them open for the onrushing panzers and motorized SS
infantry.[4]

The success of the German attack depended essentially on
a force equal to about four divisions: 4000 Luftwaffe paratroops
and four regiments of Army airborne infantry to seize and hold
open the bridges behind the Dutch lines, and one Army panzer
division and four regiments of SS motorized infantry, heavily
supported by dive bombers and fighters, to smash through the
Dutch defenses, cross the German-held bridges, and occupy the
key cities within "Fortress Holland." The remaining German
forces assigned to the operation—a cavalry division and six
third-rate (Landwehr) infantry divisions—were of secondary
importance.

On May 9 Hitler finally decided that the attack would begin
the next day. The alert signal was flashed, and all along the
400-mile front German troops stood to arms. At nine o'clock
that evening the code word *Danzig* was released, signaling the
start of the offensive.[5]

One battle group of the Leibstandarte SS "Adolf Hitler,"
whose experiences have been recorded, took up a position at
the frontier bridge near the Dutch border town of De Poppe.
At exactly 5:30 A.M., as dawn was breaking, an assault squad
overpowered the Dutch border guards, cut the fuses to the
bridge-demolition charges, and raised the road barrier for the
waiting column of SS vehicles.[6] Similar scenes were enacted at

---

4 For a detailed discussion of the German plan for the invasion of the
Netherlands see Taylor, *op. cit.*, pp. 188ff.; Jacobsen, *Fall Gelb*, pp. 244ff.

5 "Das dienstliche Tagebuch des Chefs des Wehrmachtführungsamtes
im OKW, Generalmajor A. Jodl," entry for May 9, 1940. An English translation of this entry is reproduced in William Shirer, *The Rise and Fall of
the Third Reich* (New York, 1960), p. 720.

6 Kurt Meyer, *Grenadiere* (Munich, 1957), p. 19.

IRELAND

GREAT BRITAIN

NORTH SEA

GERMAN INVASION OF NORWAY APR. 9, 1940

NORWAY

SWEDEN

FINLAND

SOVIET ATTACK ON FINLAND NOV. 30, 1939

Lake Ladoga

Gulf of Finland

Leningrad

SIEGE OF LENINGRAD

ESTONIA

BALTIC SEA

LATVIA

SOVIET OCCUPATION OF BALTIC STATES, 1939

Moscow

LITHUANIA

Smolensk

U.   S.   S.   R.

Memel

GERMAN AIR RAIDS

Coventry

x BISMARCK SUNK, 1941

London

NETHER-LANDS

Danzig

EAST PRUSSIA

Warsaw

Brest-Litovsk

SOVIET INVASION OF POLAND SEPT. 17, 1939

EASTERN FRONT DEC., 1941

Stalingrad

English Channel

Dunkerque

Abbeville

BELG.

GERMAN INVASION MAY-JUNE, 1940

Berlin

GERMAN INVASION OF POLAND SEPT. 1, 1939

POLAND

Kiev

Kharkov

ATLANTIC OCEAN

Paris

Sedan

LUX.

GERMAN INVASION OF SOVIET UNION, 1941

MAGINOT LINE

FRANCE

Munich

CZECHOSLOVAKIA

Vichy

SWITZ.

AUSTRIA

HUNGARY

SEA OF AZOV

CASPIAN SEA

Bordeaux

UNOCCUPIED FRANCE

ITALIAN ATTACK ON FRANCE JUNE 10, 1940

GERMAN INVASION OF THE BALKANS APR. 6, 1941

RUMANIA

Odessa

CAUCASUS MTS.

Marseille

Nice

Toulon

YUGOSLAVIA

Bucharest

BLACK   SEA

Lisbon

Madrid

ADRIATIC SEA

BULGARIA

PORTUGAL

SPAIN

CORSICA

Rome

ALBANIA

Sofia

Teheran

Naples

Salerno

SARDINIA

GREECE

TURKEY

IRAN

OCCUPIED BY ALLIES, 1941

Strait of Gibraltar

M   E   D   I   T   E   R   R   A   N   E   A   N

Palermo

SICILY

AEGEAN SEA

Dardanelles

SP. MOROCCO

Oran

Algiers

Bône

Tunis

MALTA

GERMAN AIR-BORNE INVASION OF CRETE MAY, 1941

CYPRUS

SYRIA

OCCUPIED BY ALLIES, 1941

IRAQ

OCCUPIED BY ALLIES, 1941

Persian Gulf

FRENCH MOROCCO

ALGERIA

TUNISIA

S   E   A

CRETE

Tripoli

Benghazi

Derna

Tobruk

Bardia

Sidi Barrani

El-Alamein

PALESTINE

TRANSJORDAN

Suez Canal

Gulf of Aqaba

SAUDI ARABIA

L   I   B   Y   A

E   G   Y   P   T

Cairo

Gulf of Suez

RED SEA

WORLD WAR II IN EUROPE 1939-1941

Axis troop movements

Soviet troop movements

Extent of Axis domination at the end of 1941

| 0 | Miles | 500 |
| 0 | Kilometres | 500 |

other points along the front. As the vehicles of the SS spearhead moved across the bridge, swarms of Junkers–52 transports roared overhead on their way to drop German airborne troops deep inside the Dutch defenses.

By midday, after a breakneck advance of some seventy miles, the Leibstandarte had captured its objective—Zwolle, the provincial capital of Overyssel, and the two large bridges spanning the Yssel River nearby. Despite the spectacular and almost bloodless seizure of its objective, the Leibstandarte fell short of complete success; earlier in the morning, the Dutch, fearing a paratroop drop, had destroyed the bridges. Nevertheless the Leibstandarte's Third Battalion forced a crossing of the Yssel farther south near Zutphen and captured the town of Hooen and 200 of its defenders. A reinforced platoon of SS troops then pushed forward another forty-five miles, taking an additional 127 prisoners, and in the process winning for its commander, Obersturmführer (Captain) Krass, the first Iron Cross First Class to be awarded to an officer in the campaign.[7] Despite these achievements, the destruction of the Yssel bridges had effectively halted the Leibstandarte's lightning advance in that sector of the front; it was therefore withdrawn and sent south to join the 9th Panzer Division and the SS Verfügungsdivision in the main drive toward Rotterdam.[8]

Below the Leibstandarte another crossing of the Yssel was made on May 10. The 3rd SS Regiment "Der Führer," spearheading the advance of the 207th Infantry Division, went over near Arnhem and in the following days stormed the fortified Grebbe Line and advanced on Utrecht.[9]

Meanwhile the main assault on the Netherlands had been launched south of the Rhine. On the morning of May 11, the 9th Panzer Division and Paul Hausser's SS Verfügungsdivision were sent across the railroad bridge at Gennep (the only Maas

[7] *Ibid.,* pp. 20ff.

[8] The commander of Army Group B (Bock) withdrew the Leibstandarte because "it had gotten itself stuck." "Tagebuchaufzeichnungen des Oberbefehlshabers der Heeresgruppe B, Generaloberst F. v. Bock," entry for May 11, 1940, reproduced in Hans-Adolf Jacobsen, *Dokumente zum Westfeldzug 1940* (Göttingen, 1960), p. 15.

[9] Heeresgruppe B (Bock), May 15, 1940, *ibid.,* p. 34.

River bridge that had fallen intact into German hands).
Constantly exposed to air attack and possessing few antitank
weapons, the Dutch could do little to stop them. The German
tanks and SS motorized infantry sped through North Brabant,
encountering little opposition.[10]

As soon as the German offensive began, on May 10, the
Allies rushed the bulk of their mobile divisions into Belgium
to offer a continuous front to the advancing Wehrmacht. General Henri Giraud's Seventh Army on the far left of the Allied
line sped toward Antwerp and Breda. When word reached the
French that the Moerdijk bridges—which offered the only route
whereby Allied troops from Belgium could reach "Fortress
Holland"—were in the hands of German paratroopers, Giraud
was ordered to extend his advance and clear them.

On May 11 the French reached Breda and immediately sent
out two motorized groups: one northeast toward Moerdijk, the
other northwest to block the German advance through North
Brabant. Informed of the French move, the commander of the
9th Panzer Division divided his forces. Half of the German
armor and the SS Verfügungsdivision were peeled off to the
southwest to intercept the French. The rest of the division continued the advance toward Moerdijk, with the Leibstandarte
to follow in support upon its arrival from the north.[11]

The French force moving toward Moerdijk was spotted from
the air, subjected to attacks by Luftwaffe dive bombers, and
forced to retreat. The other French column reached Tilburg
during the afternoon of May 11 and ran head on into half of
the 9th Panzer Division and the SS Verfügungsdivision. The
panzers and motorized SS infantry, aided by the Luftwaffe, drove
the French back to Breda. The next day the tanks of the 9th
Panzer were sent north to rejoin their division, and the SS
Verfügungsdivision and Army infantry were left to finish off the
French forces in North Brabant. On May 13 the French
retreated to Rosendaal, and the next day they withdrew from
the Netherlands to Antwerp. Resistance in the province was
ended. The surviving Dutch troops retired to Zeeland, where

10 Taylor, *op. cit.*, p. 198.
11 *Ibid.*; Meyer, *op. cit.*, p. 22.

they joined French forces holding the area. It was against these that the SS Verfügungsdivision was now sent.[12]

Meanwhile, on the morning of May 12, the lead elements of the 9th Panzer Division's northern column had reached the German paratroops holding the bridges at Moerdijk, and immediately pushed across. By early afternoon contact had been established with the airborne troops holding the Rotterdam end of the bridgehead, but here the rapid German advance broke down. The Dutch had sealed the bridgehead and the Germans could not deploy their armor. On the morning of May 14, Rotterdam still held and "Fortress Holland" had not been breached. The OKH was anxious to pull the 9th Panzer Division and the motorized SS formations out of the Netherlands to help exploit the breakthrough in France. It was decided to force the defenders to their knees by a massive bombing attack.

Outside the city, the Leibstandarte was getting into position for the assault that was to follow the bombing. It had reached the headquarters of the 9th Panzer Division the preceding afternoon and had been ordered to attack behind the 9th Panzer "through or around Rotterdam in order to relieve the airborne troops encircled in the vicinity of Delft/Rotterdam and then to advance to Gravenhage (The Hague)." [13]

About 3:30 P.M. a large flight of Heinkel–111 bombers appeared and reduced the heart of the city to rubble; more than 800 civilians were killed, thousands wounded, and 78,000 made homeless. The last bombs fell about 3:45 P.M., and the Leibstandarte began to move in.[14]

The flames and wreckage-strewn streets delayed the advance. Some units became lost, and a number of columns were almost trapped by collapsing buildings and spreading flames. Perhaps this accounts for one of the more curious episodes of the day. The Dutch had finally accepted the surrender terms some two

[12] Taylor, *op. cit.*, pp. 198 f.; Jacques Benoist-Méchin, *Soixante Jours qui ébranlèrent L'Occident* (Paris, 1956), I, 115ff.

[13] Meyer, *op. cit.*, pp. 22 f.

[14] *Ibid.*, p. 24. The sequence of events during and before the bombing, as given by Meyer (who was an eyewitness), differs substantially from that offered by Taylor, *op. cit.*, pp. 200ff.

hours after the bombing. Accompanied by a column of their soldiers, General Kurt Student, commander of the airborne troops, and Lieutenant Colonel Dietrich von Choltitz proceeded to the Dutch military headquarters, which they intended to make their command post. While the Germans settled down in the building, several hundred Dutch troops gathered outside to surrender their weapons.

Suddenly there was a great roar of tanks and trucks. It was Sepp Dietrich's SS motorized regiment LAH, racing northward. . . . Trigger-happy and perhaps unaware of the surrender terms, the SS men were alarmed to see armed Dutch soldiers and cut loose at them with machine guns. Student and Choltitz ran to the window of the *Kommandantur* to see what was going on. A bullet clipped Student in the head, and he fell against Choltitz, seriously wounded and bleeding profusely.[15]

Apparently without knowing that they had nearly killed the founder and commander of Germany's paratroop corps, the men of the Leibstandarte swept on through Rotterdam.

The regiment reached Overschie, on the road between Rotterdam and Delft, and found only dead Germans and row upon row of destroyed Junkers transports. But the Dutch were still alive and greeted the SS troopers with heavy machine-gun and rifle fire. After some brisk fighting, the column reached Delft about 9 P.M. and established contact with survivors of the 22nd Luftlandedivision, which had been landed four days earlier. During the course of the day's fighting the regiment had taken 3536 Dutch prisoners.[16]

The next day the Leibstandarte arrived at The Hague. By then, the Dutch Army had capitulated. The War Ministry in

---

[15] Taylor, *op. cit.*, pp. 203 f. It should be noted that the Leibstandarte, contrary to many reports, had no tanks in 1940. If there were any tanks in the group that did the shooting, they belonged to the 9th Panzer Division, in whose wake the Leibstandarte was supposed to be advancing through the city. For strength and equipment of Leibstandarte, see "Verstärkung der Liebstandarte SS 'Adolf Hitler,' " August 28, 1940, Geheime Kommandosache, RFSS/T–175, 106/2629683ff. (Student survived and in 1941 led the airborne attack on Crete.)

[16] Meyer, *op. cit.*, pp. 24 f.

the capital was occupied and the garrison disarmed. The war in Holland was over for the Leibstandarte; it made a quick victory march north to Amsterdam, and then headed south to take part in the French campaign.

While the rest of the German mobile forces were on their way to France, SS Gruppenführer (Lieutenant General) Hausser led elements of his Verfügungsdivision and some Army infantry in a campaign to mop up the Franco-Dutch forces holding out in Zeeland and on the islands of Walcheren and South Beveland.[17] In short order, the SS Regiment "Deutschland," strongly supported by the Luftwaffe, smashed through to the coast. On May 17, French destroyers evacuated the survivors, and the SS troops captured the principal port of Vlissingen. The fighting in the Netherlands was over and the SS Verfügungsdivision was ordered to France.[18]

The Waffen SS in Flanders and Artois

By the time the Dutch capitulated the first two stages of the German offensive in Belgium and France had been completed: the outer Belgian defenses had been breached, the French and British armies drawn into Flanders, the French position on the Meuse cracked, and a rapid drive was under way to reach the English Channel and so divide the Allied forces.

On May 16, the SS Totenkopfdivision was pulled out of OKH reserve in Germany and ordered forward to help exploit the salient created by the German armored advance. By way of Namur-Charleville, the division raced through Belgium to join the XVth Army Corps (comprising the 5th and 7th Panzer Divisions), which formed the northern cutting edge of the Ger-

---

[17] On the first day of the German assault, the French had landed two infantry divisions (the 60th and 68th) on Walcheren and Beveland. The area was under naval command, and the Dutch forces, commanded by Admiral van der Stadt, were not included in the surrender of the Dutch Army. Benoist-Méchin, *op. cit.*, pp. 109 f., 145, 153.

[18] Fragmentary casualty reports sent to Himmler on May 17 indicate that the Verfügungsdivision paid a substantial price for its victories in Holland. See Kommando der Waffen SS to Reichsführer SS, "3. Meldung," May 17, 1940, Geheim, RFSS/T–175, 106/2629853ff.

man spearhead.[19] On May 17, General Erwin Rommel's 7th Panzer Division had reached Le Cateau and the next day pushed a tank battalion forward to capture Cambrai. Fearful of an Allied attack on the northern flank of the wedge, the XVth Army Corps halted at Cambrai to await infantry rein- forcements. On May 19 these arrived in the form of the SS Totenkopfdivision, which was immediately put to work clean- ing up the area and consolidating the German hold on Le Cateau and Cambrai. In the process the division got its first taste of battle and suffered its first casualties: 16 dead and 53 wounded during the period May 19–20.[20]

While the 7th Panzer Division and the SS Totenkopfdivi- sion were held up southwest of Arras, four other German armored divisions continued the drive westward. By the evening of May 20, the Germans had reached the Channel coast west of Abbeville, at the mouth of the Somme. A strip thirty to fifty miles long between the Scarpe and Somme rivers was in German hands, and more than forty French, British, and Belgian divi- sions—nearly one million men—were cut off from the main body of the French Army in the south.[21]

A desperate Allied effort to attack across the German salient in order to re-establish a common front with the main French forces south of the Somme fell victim to the general confusion, the chaotic communications, and the conflicting aims of the Allies. Only a limited offensive action south of Arras was launched by the British to ease the German pressure on their south flank. Nevertheless, this relatively weak counterattack turned out to be the most serious opposition the cocky Germans

[19] Kommando der Waffen SS to Reichsführer SS, "5. Meldung," May May 17, 1940, Geheim, RFSS/T–175, 106/2629853ff.

[20] See summary of Totenkopfdivision casualties for the period May 19–29, 1940, RFSS/T–175, 107/2630048ff.

[21] For details see excerpts from diaries of Jodl (OKW), Halder (OKH), Bock (Heeresgruppe B), and Kriegstagebuch der Heeresgruppe A for the period May 18–21 in Jacobsen, *Dokumente*, pp. 44ff. The official British account is given in Major L. F. Ellis, *The War in France and Flanders 1939–1940* (London, 1953), pp. 59ff., and a standard French version may be found in Benoist-Méchin, *op. cit.*, I, 196ff.

had yet encountered, and they were severely shaken by it.[22]

On the afternoon of May 21, the attacking Allied force—74 British tanks and two battalions of infantry, supported by an additional 60 tanks belonging to the French 3rd Light Mechanized Division—smashed into the flanks of the advancing 7th Panzer and SS Totenkopf Divisions. Before the attackers were finally stopped, they had thrown some of the Army and SS troops into a panic-stricken retreat, destroyed nine German medium tanks, a number of light tanks, and large amounts of motor transport. The battle cost the 7th Panzer Division 89 killed, 116 wounded, and 173 missing; the Totenkopfdivision lost 19 killed, 27 wounded, and 2 missing.[23]

The British counterattack was followed the next day by an attempted breakthrough by the trapped French forces in the east. The Leibstandarte SS "Adolf Hitler," on its way down from Holland, was rushed into the line to help the German infantry. Holding a sector nearly twenty miles wide in the vicinity of Valenciennes, the SS regiment beat back a number of weak French attacks.[24]

Advance toward Dunkirk

Meanwhile the OKH was pouring all its available mobile forces into the German salient to increase the pressure on the southern flank of the Allied forces trapped in Flanders. By May 24, the Allies had been compressed into a triangular area with its base on the Channel coast between Gravelines and Terneuzen and its apex near Valenciennes. The southern leg of the triangle ran along a series of canals behind which the British Expedi-

[22] For accounts of the battle of Arras see B. H. Liddell Hart (ed.), *The Rommel Papers* (New York, 1953), pp. 29ff.; Ellis, *op. cit.*, pp. 87ff.; Taylor, *op. cit.*, pp. 234ff. For the role of the SS Totenkopfdivision see series of letters and reports from its commander, Eicke, to the chief of Himmler's personal staff, Karl Wolff, RFSS/T–175, 107/2629895ff.

[23] The casualty figures for the 7th Panzer Division are given in *Rommel Papers*, p. 33; those of the Totenkopfdivision, in RFSS/T–175, 107/2630048ff.

[24] Meyer, *op. cit.*, pp. 25 f.: "Tagebuchaufzeichnungen, Herresgruppe B (Bock)", entry for May 23, 1940, Jacobsen, *Dokumente*, pp. 72 f.

tionary Force established a defensive line. The Germans now
massed the bulk of their forces in the salient to break it. All
three of the SS formations in France were committed to the task.

The Leibstandarte was moved in a forced night march from
Valenciennes toward the coast, and on May 24 stood poised to
force a crossing of the canal line opposite Watten.[25] Meanwhile,
farther to the southeast, the Totenkopf and Verfügungs Divisions
were fighting their way to the canal line against the stubborn
resistance of British rear-guard units.[26]

Having reached the vicinity of the canal line by May 24,
the Verfügungsdivision sent across a strong reconnaissance
platoon. The patrol of thirty-two men in armored cars penetrated to Merville—some five miles beyond the canal—where it
was engaged by enemy tanks and cut off. Still in touch with its
division by radio the next day, the patrol reported that only
eight of its members were still unwounded. Since their situation
was hopeless, the survivors were ordered to destroy their equipment and attempt to break out on foot during the night. None
of the thirty-two SS men returned.[27]

Farther south, elements of the Verfügungsdivision were busy
mopping up the British troops northeast of Arras, which was
still in British possession although surrounded by German divisions. During the night of May 23–24, most of the garrison
managed to withdraw behind the canal line, and the next day
British tanks covering the retreat of the rear guard clashed with
the SS troops. In the action, the Verfügungsdivision lost three
field guns and their crews, but claimed the destruction of most
of the attacking tanks.[28]

The unopposed advance of the SS patrol, which was later
cut off at Merville, indicated that a sector of the canal line was
not manned. A French unit holding the position had been
withdrawn before the arrival of the British force that was to
take over defense of the sector; the Verfügungsdivision took

25 Meyer, *op. cit.*, p. 26.
26 For details of the British defense see Ellis, *op. cit.*, pp. 121ff.
27 SS Verfügungsdivision to Kommando der Waffen SS, "Berichte der
SS-V.-Division," May 26, 1940, RFSS/T–175, 106/2629883 f.
28 *Ibid.*, 2629884.

advantage of the gap and made an unopposed crossing of the canal, its forward elements advancing to St. Venant. The British quickly sent a small force to hold the flank of the salient, but the canal line had been breached.[29]

For a variety of reasons, over which controversy continues to rage, a directive issued in the Führer's name during the afternoon of May 24 ordered the attacking German forces not to cross the canal line.[30] By the time the order reached the troops, the SS Verfügungsdivision was already across, and at least two other crossings had been made farther along the canal toward the coast. The Leibstandarte received the stop order just as it was about to launch its attack over the canal at Watten. The regiment was under heavy artillery fire in an exposed position; Sepp Dietrich chose to ignore the order and allowed his men to attack on schedule. Despite fierce opposition by the defending British and French troops, the Leibstandarte forced the canal and seized the height near Watten before halting.[31] There were now four breaches in the canal line. Only the southeastern third of the line remained unbroken.

Despite the relative calm along the Allied southern front following the German stop order, the Belgian Army, holding a wide sector along the other leg of the triangle, was in danger of crumbling; and the decision was reached in London to evacuate the British Expeditionary Force by sea from Dunkirk. The British therefore used the timely reprieve to redistribute their forces and to deploy three regular infantry divisions along the canal line to shield the retreat toward the coast.[32] The German motorized and armored divisions were also ordered to stabilize their sectors along the canal and to use the time for maintenance and repairs.[33]

For the SS units the stop order brought no period of rest.

---

[29] Ellis, *op. cit.,* p. 137.

[30] See "Dokumente zum 'Halt-Befehl' für die deutschen Panzertruppen vor Dünkirchen," Jacobsen, *Dokumente,* pp. 114 f.

[31] Meyer, *op. cit.,* pp. 26 f.

[32] For details see Ellis, *op. cit.,* pp. 139, 177ff.

[33] "Armeebefehl Nr. 5 für den 26. 5. 40," Jacobsen, *Dokumente,* pp. 128 f.

The Leibstandarte and the Verfügungsdivision had bridgeheads to defend. The Verfügungsdivision had gained a good bit of territory on the north bank of the canal line, including St. Venant, through which passed one of the British withdrawal routes to Dunkirk. The British wanted the town back. And on May 25 a brigade from one of the fresh divisions sent to the area mounted an attack which threw the SS out of St. Venant. The British thereupon rebuilt the bridge across the Lys, and the withdrawal continued behind a screen of outnumbered but determined infantrymen.[34] Although St. Venant remained in British hands for only two days, this was the first time in the campaign an SS unit had been forced to give up a major holding.

During the night of May 26–27, the stop order was lifted and the German troops all along the canal line resumed the advance. The SS Totenkopfdivision now also forced a crossing of the canal at Bethune and pushed north toward Merville. The British troops along the canal line knew that the fate of the BEF depended on their ability to delay the enemy advance long enough to permit a withdrawal to the Dunkirk perimeter, and they fought stubbornly for every foot of ground. But they were facing five panzer divisions, one Army motorized-infantry division, two SS motorized divisions, the Army's elite Regiment "Grossdeutschland," and the Leibstandarte SS "Adolf Hitler." [35] The fighting on May 27, 1940, was the bitterest of the entire campaign, and the SS units suffered accordingly.

The Verfügungsdivision was ordered to attack through the dense five-mile-deep Forêt de Nieppe with two of its three regiments. The remaining regiment—"Deutschland"—continued along the division's earlier route of advance through St. Venant toward Merville, with the 3rd Panzer Division on its right and the SS Totenkopfdivision on its left. The SS regiments advancing through the forest ran into extremely heavy resistance, and took "stiff losses" because "the division had no heavy artillery at its disposal and therefore could offer only a limited response to the enemy artillery which caused . . . those heavy cas-

[34] Ellis, *op. cit.*, p. 146.
[35] "Kriegstagebuch der Herresgruppe A," entry for May 27, 1940, Jacobsen, *Dokumente*, pp. 90 f.

ualties." The division appealed to SS headquarters "urgently, once again, to please send the heavy [artillery] detachment . . . as soon as possible." Especially severe casualties among the division's officers prompted an urgent request that "replacement officers be sent up . . . by motor transport as soon as possible because the division is once again attacking, and as a result of the resistance being encountered must count on an additional loss of officers." [36] Here may be seen the emergence of a problem that was to assume serious proportions during the later war years: the vigorous "follow-me" brand of leadership particularly characteristic of the Waffen SS resulted in a high level of combat achievement, but against a determined foe it also led to a high rate of casualties among SS officers.

While the bulk of the Verfügungsdivision was slowly fighting its way through the woods, the 3rd Panzer Division and the attached SS Regiment "Deutschland" (on the Verfügungsdivision's right flank) broke through the British line between St. Venant and Robecq. As the mass of the German panzer division gradually forced the defenders into the two towns, where they were besieged, its lead armored units rushed north toward Merville; and the SS regiment pushed forward on their right.[37]

The British had meanwhile established, along the Lys River between St. Venant–Merville–Estaires–Armentaires, a second defense line (the river was canalized along most of this line) which had to be held so that the main British and French forces could be withdrawn to the Lys during the coming night. The forward elements of the 3rd Panzer Division bogged down just short of Merville, but Regiment "Deutschland" managed to reach the Lys Canal between Merville and Estaires before noon on May 27. It was now far in advance of any other German unit along this sector of the front. Behind the regiment the remnants of the British 2nd Division were still resisting fiercely, thus delaying the advance of the other German forces. In front of the regiment lay the Lys Canal, which the British were deter-

[36] SS Verfügungsdivision to Kommando der Waffen SS, "Anforderung von Führer," May 27, 1940, RFSS/T–175, 106/2629881 f.
[37] Ellis, *op. cit.,* pp. 187ff.

mined to hold at all costs for at least twenty-four hours. SS
Oberführer [38] Felix Steiner, the regimental commander, ordered
an attack across the waterway.

What followed is recorded in a report prepared for SS headquarters by Steiner. It so impressed Himmler that he had it
presented to Hitler as an example of SS performance in combat.
This was an unusual step at the time, for Hitler was planning
strategy for the campaign and did not generally trouble himself
with the achievements of individual regiments. Nevertheless,
he read through the report and handed it back to Himmler's
adjutant with the comment: *"Sehr schön* [very nice]." [39]

The attack was launched by Steiner's Third Battalion, supported by two batteries of SS artillery. The assault overwhelmed
the "English infantry and machine-gun units which were defending the canal." By the afternoon of May 27, Steiner had two
battalions holding a bridgehead across the waterway. On the
left flank of the regiment, Estaires and Lestrem were still in
British hands. The SS Totenkopfdivision, which was supposed
to advance on Steiner's left, was still miles to the rear. The
situation on the right flank was not much better. Merville was
still occupied by the British; the lead elements of the 3rd Panzer
Division were pinned down south of the town, while the rest of
the division was fighting scattered survivors of the British 2nd
Division as far back as the canal line. Steiner therefore had to
stretch his slim forces to cover his own flanks while engineers
began to construct crossings over the Lys.[40]

About 7 P.M., Steiner and his adjutant were on the far side
of the canal inspecting the bridgehead when a group of tanks
suddenly emerged from a British-held village to the north and
attacked the First Battalion. The crossings were not yet ready
to accept even light vehicles, and therefore there were no antitank guns available. According to the battalion commander,

---

[38] An Oberführer held a rank for which there was no direct Army
equivalent; he was more than a colonel, but less than a major general.

[39] See handwritten comment by SS Gruppenführer Wolff on report by
Steiner, "Gefechtsbericht," May 31, 1940, RFSS/T–175, 106/2629848ff.

[40] *Ibid.,* 2629848.

some twenty British tanks broke into his position. The 3rd Company of the First Battalion was especially hard-hit, "and even though it is not customary," Steiner felt that "in this battle certain individual heroic acts must be mentioned." The report then went on to describe how a young officer in this company "felt duty-bound to set an example for his platoon when attacked at close range by an enemy tank. He defended himself with hand grenades, and was crushed by the English tank." One of his men, an SS private, thereupon "leapt onto the rear deck of an English tank in order to throw a grenade into its observation slit, but was shot off by another tank following behind." Many of the SS men refused to fall back in the face of the overwhelming attack and, according to their commander, "fired on the English tanks at a distance of under 15 feet with rifles, machine guns, and antitank rifles. The regiment is unfortunately unable to recommend these men for an award since they were killed in the process." But Steiner did recommend for the Iron Cross First Class three company commanders "who were the soul of the resistance." [41] Here we have one of the earliest recorded examples of the fanatically tenacious, almost suicidal behavior that characterized the combat performance of the Waffen SS throughout the war. This is not to say that other soldiers—both Axis and Allied—did not also at times display similar fighting qualities, but for the elite troops of the Waffen SS fanaticism (and often its corollary, brutality) was the rule rather than the exception.

The timely arrival of a tank-destroyer platoon belonging to the SS Totenkopfdivision forced the British tanks to withdraw before they had completely destroyed Steiner's bridgehead. They nevertheless continued to shell the SS troops from a distance, destroying five of the SS antitank guns and (more important) preventing the Germans from interfering with the retreat of the Allied forces. During the night of May 27, most of the British forces and a portion of the French First Army withdrew behind the Lys River.

[41] *Ibid.*, 2629850.

The SS Totenkopfdivision and the
Massacre at Le Paradis

While SS Regiment "Deutschland" was fighting along the Lys on May 27–28, the SS Totenkopfdivision had crossed the canal line at Bethune. The canal (called La Bassée Canal at this point) looped into the city, but a bypass cut straight across the loop. This is of importance only because it meant that the Totenkopfdivision had to cross two waterways in its advance. The first crossing was carried out on May 26 and resulted in heavy casualties, the division losing 44 killed, 144 wounded, and 11 missing.[42] The crossing the next day was no easier; indeed, all the German forces attacking the canal line south of Bethune found the going difficult and losses high.[43]

Across the canal things were no better. The British 2nd Division was sacrificing itself to keep open the line of retirement to the Lys. Less than a third of this division survived the day, but it exacted a heavy price from the advancing Germans. In concluding its account of the day's action, the official British history of the campaign records that "the German conduct of the day's fighting was stained by the shameful misconduct of one of the formations engaged"[44]—a reference to the SS Totenkopfdivision.

The British 4th Brigade (one of three in the 2nd Division), which was responsible for holding the canal line between Robecq and Bethune, had been forced bit by bit to fall back on Paradis and Locon in the face of the Totenkopfdivision's advance. There, the 1st Royal Scots, the 2nd Royal Norfolk, and the 1st/8th Lancashire Fusiliers made a final stand and were gradually overwhelmed.[45] About 100 men of the 2nd Royal Norfolk, surrounded at a farm near Paradis, refused to surrender; their orders had been to gain time for their comrades' withdrawal. The SS men besieging the farm were members of

---

[42] RFSS/T–175, 107/2630048ff.

[43] For details see Ellis, *op. cit.*, 183ff., particularly excerpt from war diary of German XXXIXth Corps, p. 192.

[44] Ellis, *op. cit.*, p. 192.

[45] *Ibid.*, p. 189.

the 4th Company of the First Battalion, 2nd SS Totenkopf Infantry Regiment, under the command of SS Obersturmführer (Captain) Fritz Knochlein. Finally, after having resisted as long as possible and having exacted a heavy toll from their opponents, the survivors, many of them wounded, surrendered.[46]

The twenty-eight-year-old SS officer had the prisoners searched, then marched in single file past a barn wall, where they were cut down by the fire of two machine guns. Those who still showed signs of life were shot or bayoneted. But two British soldiers remained alive; when the SS troops departed, the badly wounded men crawled out from under the heap of dead. They were later picked up by another German unit and sent to a hospital. Both men survived the war and gave evidence at the postwar trial of Knochlein. A British military court sentenced the ex-SS officer to death on October 25, 1948; he was hanged three months later.[47]

There is no reference to this incident in the SS records examined for this study. Reitlinger's account, however, states:

Knochlein was not liked by his fellow officers, who wanted to challenge him to a duel after this exhibition, which caused a considerable stir. From Hoeppner's [XVIth Corps commander] staff office came demands for an inquiry. As it happened, Colonel Gunter d'Alquen . . . arrived in Le Paradis next day as a war correspondent of the Wehrmacht propaganda section. He saw the bodies and was told the very lame story that dum-dum bullets had been used by the massacred men. But Eicke delayed the investigation. . . . There was no court-martial for Fritz Knochlein. He commanded a regiment of Norwegian volunteer SS men in Courland in December 1944 and received the Knight's Cross as a Lieutenant Colonel.[48]

The files of the Totenkopfdivision indicate that SS Gruppenführer Wolff, chief of Himmler's personal staff, inspected Le Paradis shortly after the massacre, but apparently his only com-

[46] The 2nd SS Totenkopf Infantry Regiment lost 1 officer and 16 men killed, 5 officers and 47 men wounded, and 3 men missing at Paradis on May 27, 1940. RFSS/T–175, 107/2630050.

[47] See Ellis, *op. cit.,* p. 192, and a fuller treatment of the massacre in Reitlinger, *op. cit.,* pp. 148 f.

[48] *Ibid.*

plaint was that a large number of SS dead in the area had not yet been buried.[49] However, it was not the habit of the SS to refer directly, especially in written communications, to atrocities.

There is evidence that SS reservists who were released from active duty in the Totenkopfdivision after the conclusion of the western campaign complained about "unsoldierly practices." All the men discharged from the division had been forced to sign an oath of silence, and therefore refused to discuss what they had witnessed. But some of them requested that they be assigned to a different formation in the event that they were ever recalled to active service; others went so far as to say that they intended to resign from the SS after the war. As a result Eicke came under heavy fire from Waffen SS headquarters, but he weathered the storm and the whole affair eventually blew over.[50]

The massacre at Le Paradis was, so far as is known, the first act of its kind perpetrated by the Waffen SS in the West. And as one commentator on the subject has stated, it "was sadly anticipatory of the Malmédy massacre of American troops in December 1944." [51] Similar behavior on the part of members of the Waffen SS in Poland has already been noted; it was to become increasingly evident on the eastern front after 1941.

While Knochlein's company was engaged at Le Paradis, other elements of the Totenkopfdivision, in the words of their commander, "thrust forward against English Guard regiments that fought magnificently and grimly to the death." The day cost the SS division "over 150 dead," while the British lost "more than 300 killed." [52]

49 Eicke to Wolff, June 4, 1940, RFSS/T–175, 107/2630062.

50 Kommando der Waffen SS to SS Totenkopfdivision, "Entlassung von Reservisten," August 27, 1940, RFSS/T–175, 107/2629935; Eicke to Jüttner, October 22, 1940, Persönlich, Geheim, RFSS/T–175, 107/2629927ff.; Jüttner to Eicke, October 24, 1940, RFSS/T–175, 107/2629921ff.

51 Taylor, op. cit., p. 265.

52 Eicke to Wolff, October 28, 1940, Persönlich, Geheim, RFSS/T–175, 104/2629896. If Eicke included the 100 men murdered at Le Paradis, the British, even in retreat, were giving as good as they got.

Escape of the British Expeditionary Force

Near the northern end of the front, the Leibstandarte SS "Adolf Hitler" resumed its drive toward the Dunkirk perimeter. On May 28, the regiment came very close to losing its commander. Dietrich, not satisfied with the information arriving at his command post, set out to visit his forward elements. On the way between his First and Second Battalions near Esquebeck, Dietrich's staff car unwittingly drew within fifty yards of a strong British position, was brought under heavy fire and immobilized.

The SS Obergruppenführer (general) and his aide took cover in a culvert while machine-gun fire set their car ablaze. As burning gasoline seeped into the culvert, the senior officer of the Waffen SS was forced to coat himself from head to foot with mud as protection against the intense heat. For the next five hours Dietrich and his aide lay helpless while a major battle was fought over them. As soon as word of Dietrich's plight reached regimental headquarters, two companies of SS troops were dispatched to assault the British position. They were driven back with heavy losses. An Army panzer company had no better luck, losing its commander and four tanks before giving up. Finally, five heavy tanks, a platoon of armored cars, and the entire Third Battalion of the Leibstandarte forced their way into Esquebeck from the rear, thus enabling an SS assault troop to extricate Dietrich and his aide from the culvert.[53]

After freeing its commander, the SS regiment continued toward Wormhoudt. The 2nd Warwickshire Regiment, defending the town, had been since early morning under severe attack by tanks and infantry, heavily supported by artillery and bombing attacks. It was under orders to hold till nightfall and then withdraw to the Dunkirk perimeter. The British managed to throw back the first attack, but with the arrival of the Leibstandarte their situation deteriorated. In house-to-house fighting the SS took prisoner 11 officers and 320 men. During the night

[53] Meyer, *op. cit.*, pp. 29 f.

The Waffen SS

the surviving British soldiers tried to withdraw, but the Germans pressed after them and the Leibstandarte captured another 6 officers and 430 men.[54]

By May 30, most of the BEF was safely inside the Dunkirk perimeter. The Leibstandarte harried the withdrawing flank guards as long as it could, but was soon ordered into reserve; a short time later it was pulled back to the area of Cambrai to refit for *Fall Rot*—the forthcoming offensive against the French armies south of the Somme–Aisne line. The SS Verfügungsdivision, which had never managed to get far beyond the woods of Forêt de Nieppe, was resting at Norbecque on May 30; soon after, it was sent back to join the Leibstandarte. The same day found the Totenkopfdivision at Bailleul. On May 31 the division was ordered to the Channel coast south of Dunkirk and, with its headquarters at Boulogne, put in a spell of coastal-defense duty before joining the drive into the heart of France.[55] Meanwhile the evacuation of the BEF by sea from Dunkirk was in full swing. By the time the rear guard surrendered on the morning of June 3, the greater part of the BEF—nearly 200,000 men—and an additional 140,000 French and Belgian troops had arrived safely in England. Against the British, the Germans had won the battle but lost the victory.

The Waffen SS and the Battle of France

The German plan for *Fall Rot* (Case Red) was issued by the OKH on May 31, 1940; its aim was to "annihilate the Allied forces still remaining in France . . . as soon as possible following the battle in Artois and Flanders."[56] Basically, it provided for the employment of all three army groups (A, B, and C) in an offensive in three main waves, rolling along the front from west to east: Army Group B was to attack on

---

[54] *Ibid.*, p. 30; Ellis, *op. cit.*, p. 206.

[55] SS Hauptsturmführer Grünwalder to Kommando der Waffen SS, "Bericht über meine Kurierfahrt zur V.- u. T.- Division," June 3, 1940, RFSS/T–175, 106/2629831ff.; "Kurier-Bericht für die Zeit vom 5.–6. 6. 1940," RFSS/T–175, 106/2629829 f.; SS Totenkopfdivision, "Schlachten- u. Gefechtsbezeichnungen," October 24, 1940, RFSS/T–175, 107/2629910.

[56] Oberkommando des Heeres, "Aufmarschanweisung Rot," May 31, 1940, Geheime Kommandosache, Jacobsen, *Dokumente*, pp. 152ff.

June 5 along a front stretching from the Channel coast to the Aisne north of Reims; Army Group A was to move forward on June 9 between the Aisne and the Franco-German border; and Army Group C was to assault the Maginot Line and the upper Rhine front about a week later. In all, the Germans marshaled 140 divisions for the operation, against which the French could pit barely 65 of their own.[57]

Meanwhile, the SS field formations prepared for their role in *Fall Rot.* To fill the gaps caused by battle losses, personnel replacements were sent from Germany: 270 to the Leibstandarte, 2020 to the Verfügungsdivision, and 1140 to the Totenkopfdivision. Casualties among officers had been so heavy that it was necessary to mobilize cadets from the SS Junkerschulen as replacements. During the first week of June, the two SS divisions in France finally received their heavy artillery battalions. Rested, fully manned and equipped, the Waffen SS was once again committed to battle. Before the fall of France the still unblooded Polizeidivision was also to see action.[58]

On June 4, the Verfügungsdivision's artillery regiment took part in the opening artillery duel with the French forces south of the Somme and suffered the first SS casualties of *Fall Rot:* 2 killed and 17 wounded. The next day elements of Army Group B pushed forward across the Somme in the first wave of the attack. As part of Panzergruppe Kleist, the Leibstandarte and Verfügungsdivision participated in the main drive toward Paris. In the meantime, the SS Totenkopfdivision was shifted from Boulogne to St. Pol, to be kept there on alert until needed.[59]

By June 6, the Verfügungsdivision was across the Somme and speeding south against only minor opposition. The next day, however, as the division approached the Avre River, its lead elements were pinned down by heavy fire from the south bank. Nevertheless, the SS Regiment "Der Führer," supported

---

[57] *Ibid.;* Taylor, *op. cit.,* pp. 281ff.

[58] Kommando der Waffen SS to RFSS, "12. Meldung," June 2, 1940, Geheim, RFSS/T–175, 106/2629877ff.

[59] SS Hauptsturmführer Barthelmess, "Kurier-Bericht für die Zeit vom 5.–6. 6. 1940," RFSS/T–175, 106/2629829 f.

by the division's artillery, managed to force a crossing and establish two bridgeheads on the other side.

The day the Verfügungsdivision crossed the Somme, it appeared that Kleist's panzer group had scored a major break-through. But by June 7 it became apparent that the armored attack was slowing down in the face of stiffening French resistance. The following day, Kleist's situation was the subject of an anxious discussion at the Führer's headquarters. In the end, it was decided to pull the entire panzer group out of the heavily defended sector north of Paris (it had lost 30 per cent of its tanks) and to reinsert it farther east, where German infantry had already broken through to the Aisne.[60] So the Verfügungs-division was ordered to give up its hard-earned bridgeheads. On June 9, the SS division was back across the Somme, out of the fight; it had lost 24 killed and 113 wounded in the three days of battle.[61]

The Leibstandarte SS "Adolf Hitler," which had also taken part in Kleist's abortive offensive, was pulled back across the Somme south of Bapaume, but unlike the Verfügungsdivision was given no rest. On June 9, the regiment was put under the command of the XLIVth Army Corps and immediately sent south to follow up the corps' rapid advance to the Marne near Château-Thierry. Back across the Somme, through Soissons, south toward Villers-Cotterets sped the "dog-tired" men of the Leibstandarte. On the way they encountered only sporadic resistance and "French stragglers . . . most of them from the French 11th Division . . . [who] willingly surrendered." Around 4 P.M. the SS regiment reached Villers-Cotterets and "captured a substantial number of surprised Frenchmen; the situation bore the stamp of an imminent collapse." [62]

By June 12, the Leibstandarte had reached the Marne near Château-Thierry and forced a number of crossings. The same

[60] Taylor, *op. cit.*, pp. 292ff.; Jacobsen, *Dokumente,* pp. 177ff.

[61] SS Verfügungsdivision, "Bericht Nr. 9 (Durch SS Obersturmführer Fetzer)," June 10, 1940, RFSS/T–175, 106/2629846 f.

[62] Meyer, *op. cit.*, pp. 32 f.; "Bericht des SS Obersturmführer Fetzer über die Kurierfahrt zur SS-V-Division und Leibstandarte SS 'Adolf Hitler' vom 8. bis einschliesslich 12. Juni 1940," RFSS/T–175, 106/2629822ff.

day, Kleist's panzer group, which had enjoyed a three-day rest, was reinserted along the Marne front between Château-Thierry and Epernay, and the Leibstandarte once more joined it. In the meantime, the SS Totenkopfdivision—which had been held in reserve—was ordered forward to join the advance. All three of the SS formations in France were now following in the wake of Kleist's panzer divisions as they swept through central France.[63]

On June 10, the French Government abandoned Paris; two days later the capital was declared an open city. On June 13, the French main line of resistance was dropped below Paris; and on the following day German troops entered the city. The German High Command, sensing the imminence of a French collapse, issued a directive on June 14 designed to conclude the campaign.[64] To prevent the French from forming a new front south of Paris, Hitler ordered "a sharp pursuit" in the direction of Orléans. Along the eastern front the Führer ordered the "annihilation" of the remaining French forces. To assist in this operation, Army Group C was ordered immediately to launch an assault against the Maginot Line and the Rhine front.[65]

In the operational orders issued in accordance with Hitler's directive, Kleist's panzer group (including the Leibstandarte, Totenkopfdivision, and Verfügungsdivision) was ordered to advance through Champagne toward Dijon in Burgundy to prevent the French forces in Alsace and Lorraine from retreating to the southwest.

While the Leibstandarte usually managed to be at the head of the advance (often without any authority other than Sepp Dietrich's), the much larger SS divisions generally followed well behind the rapidly advancing panzer divisions, guarding their exposed flanks, dealing with bypassed pockets of resistance, and picking up prisoners.

[63] See various Kriegstagebuch entries in Jacobsen, *Dokumente,* pp. 108ff.; Meyer, *op. cit.,* p. 34.

[64] Der Führer und Oberste Befehlshaber der Wehrmacht, "Weisung Nr. 15," June 14, 1940, Geheime Kommandosache, Jacobsen, *Dokumente,* pp. 163 f.

[65] *Ibid.*

The fifteenth of June found the SS Totenkopfdivision advancing through the department of Yonne as XIVth Army Corps reserve. At midnight the division received orders to follow behind the 10th Panzer Division, which had made contact with a retreating French force; the goal for the next day was Clamecy. During the next two days the Totenkopfdivision saw no action, but captured "some 4000 prisoners," and had two men injured in a motorcycle accident and two killed and three wounded by the attack of a French aircraft, "which was brought down." [66]

The experiences of the Totenkopfdivision during the days immediately following the fall of Paris were typical of the last days of the battle of France. "The greater part of this huge operation," writes Telford Taylor, "was more pursuit than battle." [67] But in isolated cases, individual French units resisted and sharp engagements resulted. One such battle figured in the otherwise uneventful advance by the SS Verfügungsdivision.

The division had been moving southward "over the Oise, Aisne, Marne, and Seine towards Dijon" since June 13. In "forced night marches [it] followed the panzer divisions of the XIVth and XVIth Corps . . . with the mission of securing their open left flank." [68] In the meantime, the assault on the Maginot Line had begun. To avoid encirclement, French forces in the Vosges area tried to escape to the southwest. A large French force tried to break through the Verfügungsdivision's sector, but "after intense fighting was thrown back with heavy losses; part of the [French] force was annihilated and the greater part was taken prisoner." [69]

During the night of June 16 and on the morning of June 17, further French counterattacks were warded off and "the towns

---

[66] SS Totenkopfdivision to Kommando der Waffen SS, "Kurier Meldung," June 18, 1940, RFSS/T–175, 107/2630040 f., and SS Hauptsturmführer Eugen Schlotter, "Bericht über meine Kurierfahrt zu den Feldeinheiten der Waffen SS vom 14.–21. Juni 1940," RFSS/T–175, 107/2630037ff.

[67] Taylor, *op. cit.,* p. 300.

[68] SS Verfügungsdivision to Kommando der Waffen SS, "Bericht Nr. 10 v. 11/6.–19/6.," June 19, 1940. Geheim, RFSS/T–175, 106/2629807ff.

[69] *Ibid.,* 2629808.

[of Channes and Bragelogne] which had been temporarily occupied by the [French] were retaken." At noon the Verfügungs-division continued its advance "on routes 80 and 71 on both sides of Chatillon." The retreating French troops, who had managed to insert themselves across this route, "offered a last, desperate resistance in the villages and heavily wooded areas; but at no point did they succeed in breaking through." By the evening of June 17, division commander Hausser considered "the enemy breakthrough attempt in front of the division fully shattered; more than 30,000 prisoners and endless amounts of matériel have fallen into our hands. In comparison to this great achievement our losses must be considered very small; during this day of battle 3 officers and 30 men were killed and 3 officers and 91 men were wounded." [70]

While the Verfügungsdivision was fighting its last major engagement of the western campaign, the Leibstandarte "disappeared." For three days none of the couriers from SS headquarters had been able to find the regiment; even panzer group headquarters had no idea where it was. Finally, on June 18, General von Kleist while out on an inspection trip found the regiment about fifteen miles south of Nevers on the road St. Pierre–Le Moutier–Moulins; he immediately ordered it to "establish a bridgehead across the Allier southwest of Moulins." [71]

Kleist had received orders to continue his thrust to the south to prevent a possible French stand along the Loire. In reality there was not much chance of this occurring. The French Government had collapsed, and the new regime under Marshal Pétain was already negotiating for an armistice; "The French had neither time, resources, nor . . . much inclination to organize a defensive line along this great river of central France." [72] Realizing this, Kleist now allowed his panzer

[70] *Ibid.;* SS Sturmbannführer Grezesch to Kommando der Waffen SS, "Fernschreiben Sonderzug-Heinrich Nr. 176, 22. 6. 40," RFSS/T–175, 106/2629810.

[71] SS Hauptsturmführer Eugen Schlotter, "Bericht über meine Kurier-fahrt zu den Feldeinheiten der Waffen SS vom 14.–21. Juni 1940," RFSS/T–175, 107/2630039.

[72] Taylor, *op. cit.,* p. 302.

divisions to slow down and sent some of his motorized forces ahead to lead the advance.

Following Kleist's orders, the Leibstandarte raced toward the Allier near Moulins. No sooner was the first German soldier on the bridge than the French blew it to pieces. But a crossing was effected over a burning railroad bridge nearby. Then, in a wild advance designed to "gain ground to the south," the Leibstandarte raced toward Vichy. Where the road was unblocked, the lead elements drove forward at top speed, engaging enemy forces along the way with massed automatic weapons fire from the moving vehicles. Barricades were smashed by armored cars and mortar fire; occupied towns were bypassed by the lead elements and then assaulted by the following SS infantry battalions. This was the kind of fighting at which Sepp Dietrich's men excelled.

In this helter-skelter fashion the Leibstandarte reached St. Pourcain on June 19. Gannat was taken the same day, the Allier recrossed over an undestroyed bridge, and a link-up effected with other German troops at Vichy. In the day's advance the regiment had captured nearly 1000 French soldiers. The next day, in the southward advance to Clermont-Ferrand, it captured an airfield, 242 aircraft, 8 tanks, a mass of vehicles, 287 officers (including a general), and 4075 soldiers. Then, in the deepest German penetration of the campaign, the Leibstandarte drove on toward St. Étienne, capturing the town and its garrison on June 24.[73]

While the Leibstandarte was ranging forward in the south, the SS Totenkopf and Verfügungs Divisions were still well to the rear guarding the flanks of the advance. The Verfügungsdivision, on the open left flank, had little to do after its success in beating off the French breakthrough attempt of June 16–17, and spent the rest of the week mopping up behind the Leibstandarte and the panzer divisions. The Totenkopfdivision, on the right flank, had even less to do, and since the beginning of

[73] Meyer, *op. cit.*, pp. 35ff. SS Obersturmführer Brandt, "Bericht," June 24, 1940, RFSS/T–175, 106/2629803ff., gives the same account with slight variation in detail.

Fall Rot had done no serious fighting of any kind. But finally, on June 19—much to Eicke's joy—the division "was at last committed with the forward elements of [Kleist's panzer group] and given the mission of advancing to Tarare (some 140 kilometers to the south) and then reconnoitering to Lyon." [74]

Even then, the Totenkopfdivision did not see much action. Its reconnaissance squadron did, however, fight a sharp engagement at Tarare with some French colonial troops, in which it took about 6000 prisoners with only light losses.[75] For Eicke's and Hausser's SS divisions, the Battle of France was, to all intents and purposes, finished.

While the motorized formations of the Waffen SS were racing through France, the horse-drawn Polizeidivision was finally permitted to engage in an offensive operation of its own. On June 9 and 10, the bulk of the division participated in the bitterly contested assault across the Aisne River and the Ardennes Canal. During the evening of June 10, the 1st Police Regiment and part of the 2nd stormed the wooded heights near Voncq; they gained their objective but the French counterattacked with tanks and drove the police troopers out of the woods. In his official account of the event, division commander Pfeffer-Wildenbruch wrote: "Three times the 1st Police Regiment attacked successfully, and three times it was forced back, always as a result of the fact that our antitank guns were powerless against the French medium tanks." During the night, elements of the 2nd Police Regiment finally succeeded in taking Voncq, and in the morning it was discovered that the French had withdrawn from the area.[76]

The Polizeidivision was then ordered to advance through

[74] SS Hauptsturmführer Eugen Schlotter, "Bericht über meine Kurierfahrt zu den Feldeinheiten der Waffen SS vom 14.–21. Juni 1940," RFSS/T–175, 107/2630038.

[75] SS Obersturmführer Brandt, "Bericht," June 24, 1940, RFSS/T–175, 106/2629805.

[76] SS Polizeidivision Kommandeur to RFSS, June 20, 1940, Geheime Kommandosache, RFSS/T–175, 107/2630506ff. Cf. Georg Tessin "Die Stäbe und Truppeneinheiten der Ordnungspolizei," in Neufeldt, Huck, and Tessin, *op. cit.*, Part II, p. 24.

the Argonne Forest. In its second (and last) major engagement, the division clashed with a French rear guard in the Argonne Pass near Les Islettes. The French, equipped with heavy artillery, "defended themselves here with the same toughness and skill as the French troops at Voncq." But in hand-to-hand combat, the 2nd Police Regiment broke through and captured the town of Les Islettes.[77]

For a time, the division continued to cover the left flank of the German advance, but it "had no more significant contact with the enemy." By June 20, the Polizeidivision had been taken out of the line and placed in reserve southwest of Bar le Duc. It had lost 7 officers and 125 men killed, 12 officers and 515 men wounded, and 45 men missing—a grand total of 704 casualties in only two comparatively minor engagements.[78] But Pfeffer-Wildenbruch, in a manner calculated to please his master, reported that his division was in "outstanding shape" and the "officers and men only regret that they have not been granted a greater opportunity to demonstrate their combat readiness and ability in battle with the enemy." [79]

Meanwhile, negotiations for an armistice continued. Since it had been agreed that the entire French coast, from Belguim to Spain, would come under German occupation, on June 19 the OKW ordered a portion of Kleist's panzer group to be prepared for transfer to the Atlantic seaboard. Shortly thereafter, the XIVth Corps—consisting of 9th and 10th Panzer Divisions, SS Totenkopfdivision, and SS Verfügungsdivision—was on its way west.[80]

On June 25, 1940—the day on which the cease-fire went into effect—the Verfügungs and Totenkopf Divisions were in the vicinity of Bordeaux, preparing to occupy the coastal sector south to the Spanish frontier; the Polizeidivision was in Army

[77] RFSS/T–175, 107/2630507.

[78] *Ibid.,* Jüttner to Himmler, "16. Meldung," Geheim, June 25, 1940, RFSS/T–175, 106/2629798.

[79] SS Polizeidivision Kommandeur to RFSS, June 20, 1940, Geheime Kommandosache, RFSS/T–175, 107/2630507 f.

[80] OKH (Halder), June 19, 1940; Heeresgruppe B (Bock), June 20, 1940, Jacobsen, *Dokumente,* pp. 228ff.

Group A reserve along the upper Maas near Rondilly; and the Leibstandarte was south of the demarcation line, near St. Étienne, preparing to move north to Paris to take part in a grand victory parade for the Führer.[81] The campaign in the West was over.

The Waffen SS and the Western Campaign in Retrospect

There would come a time during the course of the war when the success or failure of major military operations turned on the performance of the Waffen SS, but this was not the case in 1940. The German victory in the West would have been won in substantially the same manner without the participation of the three and a half SS divisions. The measure of the Waffen SS' contribution to the campaign was not quantity but quality.

From a purely tactical standpoint, the value of the SS units lay in the fact that they were large and—with the exception of the Polizeidivision—fully motorized. They were among the few infantry formations which the German Army possessed in 1940 that could keep pace with the fast-moving panzer divisions. In the invasion of the Netherlands, where only a comparatively small German force was committed, the Leibstandarte and Verfügungsdivision played major roles. In the rest of the campaign, the Waffen SS did its share of the fighting, but with a total of nearly 140 German divisions engaged it was a relatively modest share.

The official OKW communiqués, issued daily throughout the campaign, made mention of the Army, the Navy, the Air Force, but never the Waffen SS. In the end, however, the SS too received public recognition for its contribution, from the highest of all sources.

On July 19, 1940, the Führer spoke to his Reichstag and the

[81] OKH (Atlas zum Westfeldzug 1940), "Lage am 25. 6. 1940, 01.35 Uhr," *ibid.*, Map 3, following p. 340; Meyer, *op. cit.*, pp. 38ff.; Jüttner to Himmler, "16. Meldung," Geheim, RFF/T–175, 106/2629795ff. The grand victory parade was later canceled, and the Leibstandarte was sent on to Metz, where it remained until its next campaign.

world about the events of the preceding months.[82] After summarizing the campaign in the West, he praised the German forces involved, stating for the first time that "within the framework of these armies, fought the valiant divisions and regiments of the Waffen SS." In commenting on the performance of the "young units of our armored and motorized troops," Hitler declared: "As a result of this war, the German Armored Corps has inscribed for itself a place in the history of the world; the men of the Waffen SS have a share in this honor." He even praised the "reserve formations of the SS [Ersatz SS Formationen]," without which "the battle at the front could never have taken place." [83] In closing his tribute to the SS, Hitler thanked "Party Comrade Himmler, who organized the entire security system of our Reich as well as the units of the Waffen SS."

Present in the Kroll Opera House during Hitler's long address were all the leading generals of the Army (twelve of whom were publicly promoted to the rank of field marshal during the course of the speech) ; and the Führer's praise of the Waffen SS had the intended effect. The term *Waffen SS* now became the accepted designation for the field formations of the SS.

Even if Hitler had heard little mention of the Waffen SS through normal military channels, Himmler saw to it that SS combat reports were brought to his attention. And so the Waffen SS also shared in the promotions and medals Hitler distributed with such a lavish hand: six Knight's Crosses (*Ritterkreuze*), the highest basic order of the Iron Cross,[84] were awarded to SS officers. Predictably, one went to Sepp Dietrich for his leadership of the Leibstandarte; two of the others went to regimental commanders of the SS Verfügungsdivision: Felix

[82] "Aus der Rede des Führers vor dem Grossdeutschen Reichstag am 19. 7. 40 nach Beendigung des Feldzuges im Westen," Friedrich Heiss (ed.), *Der Sieg im Westen* (Prague, 1943), pp. 5ff.

[83] This was clearly a euphemistic reference to the SS Totenkopfstandarten and their "police duties."

[84] Technically, there was one higher order—the *Grosskreuz*—awarded for "deeds decisively influencing the course of the war"; Göring was its only recipient (also on July 19, 1940).

Steiner of the SS Regiment "Deutschland" and Georg Keppler of SS Regiment "Der Führer"; the remaining three were awarded to lower-ranking SS officers.[85]

In considering the military qualities of the Waffen SS as they were demonstrated in the six-week campaign of 1940, one finds, perhaps not surprisingly, that all the characteristics displayed by the organization in its heyday were already clearly in evidence during the first year of the war. In the first place, the SS troops, generally speaking, carried out their combat assignments with a toughness and determination that bordered on the reckless. They were, in Hitler's words, "inspired by a fierce will, troops with an unbeatable turn-out—the sense of superiority personified." But, as Hitler clearly realized, "troops like the SS have to pay the butcher's bill more heavily than anyone else." [86]

Elite soldiers in all armies are taught to be contemptuous of death; the regulars of the Waffen SS were no exception. Their special assault training stressed that speed and aggressiveness in the attack reduces casualties. This is of course true generally but not specifically; fewer soldiers will be killed in a battle that is won quickly, but more of the ones who rush forward to win it will die. Elite troops, however, have never been judged by the size of their losses, but rather by the glory of their achievements. Nevertheless, SS casualties need not have been so great had professional prudence replaced blind bellicosity.

In the hands of former regular Army officers like Paul Hausser, Felix Steiner, and Georg Keppler, the zeal of the SS troops—especially the relatively well-trained regulars of the prewar Verfügungstruppe—could be applied to produce a high level of military achievement at a tolerable cost in casualties, although even these commanders were not always able to restrain or control their less experienced junior officers. But the newer SS divisions—composed of reservists from the General SS, former concentration-camp guards, policemen, and raw recruits, and led by brave yet militarily inexperienced men like Theodor

---

[85] For details see Ernst-Günther Krätschmer, *Die Ritterkreuzträger der Waffen SS* (Göttingen, 1955), *passim*.

[86] *Hitler's Secret Conversations*, pp. 177 f.

Eicke and Karl von Pfeffer-Wildenbruch—paid a high price for their recklessness. Courage and ideological conviction are no substitutes for training, experience, and proper leadership. The rapid expansion of the Waffen SS during the war did not always allow for this fact. And many a young "black knight" was sent into the cauldron of battle with little more than ideological conviction or *esprit de corps* to sustain him.

In the Waffen SS, where loyalty, duty, and blind obedience were a way of life, the conduct of the troops depended to a large extent on the attitudes of their leaders. Despite the ideological indoctrination to which Waffen SS personnel were subjected (an indoctrination that preached, among other things, hatred for Germany's enemies, especially Jews, Slavs, Bolsheviks, and other "subhumans"), individual cases of misbehavior toward prisoners of war and noncombatants seem to have been relatively rare. But where such acts were ordered, encouraged, or simply condoned by unit leaders, large-scale atrocities occurred. It is difficult to imagine regular German Army troops who would not have hesitated at an order to shoot down 100 helpless prisoners of war; but when a junior SS officer gave such an order at Le Paradis it was obeyed without question or hesitation and members of the SS company went around with rifle and bayonet to finish off the survivors. This was not standard procedure, but similar incidents took place frequently enough—especially along the eastern front—for such behavior to become a hallmark of the Waffen SS.

Here, then, is the Waffen SS in 1940: small but well equipped; possessing an *esprit de corps* and motivated by an ideology, but lacking the traditions of an established military service; manned by men of exceptional physical fitness who are good soldiers yet are capable of committing unsoldierly acts; an elite force often indistinguishable from the best units of the German Army with which it serves, yet one which unmistakably bears the stamp of the SS organization and the National Socialist movement which spawned it.

Members of the SS Panzerkorps (SS Panzergrenadier Divisions "Leibstandarte Adolf Hitler," "Das Reich," and "Totenkopf") watching German dive bombers reduce a Russian defensive position near Kharkov, March 1943. (Ullstein)

The commander of an SS panzer unit in the East issuing final instructions before an attack, May 1943. The men in the picture are wearing the black Army tank uniform with Waffen SS insignia. (Ullstein)

An SS assault-group leader after his men have cleared the Russian defenders from a key street in the heart of Kharkov, March 1943. The piping on the man's collar identifies him as a noncommissioned officer; the object in his left hand is a hand grenade of a type known to American troops as a "potato masher." (Ullstein)

CHAPTER FOUR

From West to East:

The Development of the Waffen SS
between the Fall of France and
the Invasion of the Soviet Union

THE intensive recruiting campaign launched by the SS after the defeat of Poland continued throughout the spring and summer of 1940. By the end of May the authorized quota of new recruits for the Waffen SS had been filled. But Gottlob Berger's recruiters continued to accept volunteers in an effort to establish a reserve of young recruits that could be used to replace the many older reservists from the General (Allgemeine) SS serving in the field divisions. In addition, large numbers of young men were being recruited for the SS Totenkopf and Police regiments, which were still below the strength authorized by Hitler.[1] The seemingly limitless expansion of the armed SS and the attendant drain on the Wehrmacht's manpower pool led to another bitter clash between the military authorities and the SS high command.

Struggle for Manpower: SS–Wehrmacht Relations, 1940–1941

In its struggle for manpower, the SS followed two basic lines. First, it sought by various stratagems to siphon off volunteers from the younger age groups in the German manpower pool. Second, it intensified efforts to gain recruits from areas

---

[1] The SS Totenkopf and Police regiments (as distinguished from the field formations of the Waffen SS) were not under Army control, and Hitler set separate recruiting quotas for them.

outside the Reich, a source of manpower not subject to Wehrmacht control.

As early as 1938, Himmler had authorized the acceptance of qualified Germanics *(Germanen)* in the SS Verfügungstruppe.[2] He was not here referring to ethnic Germans, who had long been accepted in the armed SS. When Himmler spoke of *Germanen,* he meant non-Germans of "Nordic blood." Toward the end of 1938 there were only 20 such volunteers in the armed SS. By May 1940, there were 100, including 5 from the United States, 3 from Sweden, and 44 from Switzerland.[3] These men, who had been enlisted in the Waffen SS without any special effort on the part of Berger's recruiting office, served in regular units without regard for their foreign origins.

The German conquest of Denmark, Norway, Belgium, and the Netherlands, however, opened up an entirely new dimension in SS recruiting. On April 30, 1940, orders were issued for the establishment of SS Standarte (Regiment) "Nordland," to be composed of volunteers from Denmark and Norway.[4] This was followed in June by the establishment of SS Standarte "Westland," for volunteers from the Netherlands and the Flemish areas of Belgium. By July, enough volunteers were on hand to create a second battalion for "Westland." Concurrently with the Germanic recruiting campaign, the SS intensified its efforts to draw volunteers from among the millions of ethnic Germans living outside the Reich. During May, for example, more than 1000 *Volksdeutsche* from Romania were recruited, and by July they were beginning to arrive at the SS training center in Prague.[5]

---

[2] "Gruppenführerbesprechung am 8. Oktober 1938 im Führerheim der SS-Standarte 'Deutschland,' " RFSS/T–175, 90/2612561.

[3] See "Übersichtsplan," May 4, 1940, RFSS/T–175, 104/2626381ff. This document also includes figures on the number of *Volksdeutsche* serving in the Waffen SS and indicates their countries of origin.

[4] Deutsche Gesandtschaft Kopenhagen, "Aufstellung der SS-Standarte 'Nordland,' " May 20, 1940, Geheime Reichsache, RFSS/T–175, 104/2626350 f.

[5] Berger to Himmler, "Werbung für die SS-VT unter den Holländern," Geheim, May 15, 1940, RFSS/T–175, 104/2626355 f.; Berger to Himmler, June 4, 1940, Geheime Kommandosache, RFSS/T–175, 104/2626261; Kommando der Waffen SS, "Aufstellung der SS-VT-Standarte 'Westland,' "

By the end of the western campaign, the Waffen SS was receiving significant increments of foreign personnel, and future prospects in this direction appeared bright. Speaking to the officers of the Leibstandarte SS "Adolf Hitler" on September 7, 1940, Himmler declared: "We must attract all the Nordic blood in the world to us, depriving our enemies of it, so that never again . . . will Nordic or Germanic blood fight against us." [6] By the end of the war more than 100,000 west Europeans and perhaps four times as many other foreigners had passed through the ranks of the Waffen SS. But this is a story in itself, and will be treated in detail in subsequent chapters. In 1940, the SS still had to depend on native Germans (*Reichsdeutsche*) for the bulk of its manpower. And in this area the military authorities did their best to frustrate the overly ambitious efforts of the SS recruiting office.

Toward the middle of the year, the OKW apparently began to realize that the SS had far exceeded its authorized recruiting quotas. Major General Jodl, Chief of the Wehrmacht Operations Staff, noted in his diary on May 25: "The plan for an unlimited expansion of the SS is disturbing." [7] Consequently the OKW undertook an investigation of the SS recruiting operation.

During the first week of June, Berger reported to Himmler that 15,000 SS inductions were being held up because the military district headquarters (Wehrbezirkskommandos) refused to release the men. "The trouble," he complained, "is that the Führer's orders are never completely carried out, but are halted halfway." [8] In all probability, the military authorities had declared an unofficial moratorium on SS inductions until they

---

Geheime Kommandosache, June 6, 1940, RFSS/T–175, 104/2626256; Kommando der Waffen SS, "Aufstellung II./SS-Standarte 'Westland,' " July 11, 1940, Geheime Kommandosache, RFSS/T–175, 104/2626163ff.

[6] "Ansprache des Reichsführers SS an das Offizierskorps der Leibstandarte SS 'Adolf Hitler' am Abend des Tages von Metz (Überreichung der Führerstandarte)," September 7, 1940, Nuremberg Document 1918–PS.

[7] Jodl Diary, entry for May 25, 1940, Jacobsen, *Dokumente*, p. 77. Cf. Warlimont, *op. cit.*, p. 104.

[8] Berger to Himmler, "Zusammenstellung von Einberufungsvorgängen," June 4, 1940, Geheime Kommandosache, RFSS/T–175, 104/2626259.

could determine how many men the SS had actually recruited in the preceding months.

Berger soon discovered that his activities were being checked. He notified Himmler that "in June, for the first time, the gentlemen of the OKW managed to estimate the number of men we called up for the Police, Verfügungstruppe, and Totenkopfverbände. They were 'shocked' by their findings, and as a result a 'palace revolution' is raging in the OKW." The generals were "especially angry" that Berger had exceeded the authorized quota for the Totenkopfdivision by "900 men, with twelve-year service obligations." In fact, Berger impishly confided, he had called up 1164 men for the Totenkopfdivision during June. Furthermore, since the beginning of the recruiting campaign, he had accepted "approximately 15,000 men with twelve-year service obligations" for the Totenkopfdivision, a total of 11,000 more than Hitler had authorized.[9]

In the light of Berger's blatant disregard for the official recruitment quotas, it was not surprising that "once again, a very considerable wave of fear concerning the Waffen SS in general and the Reichsführer SS in particular is sweeping through the OKW."[10] In an attempt to justify his actions, Berger reminded the OKW that he needed the additional recruits to replace older General (Allgemeine) SS reservists scheduled for demobilization. There was a good deal of truth in this. Shortly before the fall of France, Hitler had ordered the Army to prepare for the demobilization of thirty-nine divisions and all noncareer soldiers in the classes 1896–1909. Although no SS divisions were scheduled for demobilization, over-age SS reservists were to be released from active service. Of the approximately 20,000 men in the SS Totenkopfdivision, 13,246 fell into this category. "For these," Berger insisted, "there must be replacements."[11]

But the OKW had little sympathy for the manpower problems of the SS during the summer of 1940. At the time, it was fighting another "small war" with the Oberkommando der Luft-

[9] Berger to Himmler, "Demobilmachung," July 3, 1940, Geheime Kommandosache, RFSS/T–175, 104/2626156.
[10] *Ibid.*   [11] *Ibid.*, 2626157.

waffe (OKL) over the apportioning of manpower. Göring, who wanted to establish a number of new airborne divisions, was demanding that the Luftwaffe be given one recruit for every three inducted by the Army. Facing a two-sided threat to the Army's manpower pool, the OKW (in Berger's words) reacted by "making it its chief duty to create difficulties for the SS in its replacement program." The SS recruiting chief concluded that "if it is not possible to arrive at an agreement in a friendly manner, then the Führer will have to decide again." [12]

Despite constant complaints to Himmler about his difficulties with the Army and the OKW, Berger had been remarkably successful in his recruiting campaign: between January 15, 1940, and June 30, 1940, a total of 59,526 men had been called up for service in the armed SS.[13] The reserve *(Ersatz)* formations of the Waffen SS were at full strength, and Himmler knew that there were sufficient young recruits in them to replace the older men about to be demobilized.[14]

On July 29, 1940, Himmler issued the Waffen SS' first (and last) demobilization order. It applied only to SS reservists in these categories: all those born before 1906, those born between 1906 and 1910 (inclusive) who requested release from active duty, and those born after 1918 who were farmers or workers in a vital industry. The order closed with a reminder that "every dischargee remains a reservist subject to recall." [15] Most of the men demobilized during the late summer of 1940 were eventually recalled to active duty.

Himmler did not share his recruiting chief's concern about the future of the Waffen SS, but of course he had the advantage of knowing some of Hitler's most recent thoughts on the

---

[12] *Ibid.*

[13] The figure includes men recruited for the Police and Totenkopf regiments. See Berger to Himmler, "Zusammenstellung von Einberufungen," July 2, 1940, Geheime Kommandosache, RFSS/T–175, 104/2626144ff.

[14] Kommando der Waffen SS to RFSS, "16. Meldung," June 25, 1940, Geheim, RFSS/T–175, 106/2629796.

[15] Kommando der Waffen SS, "Entlassung der Reservisten im Verlauf der Umorganisation," July 29, 1940, Geheime Kommandosache, RFSS/T–175, 104/2626188 f.

projected course of the war. For even while the SS divisions were training for the invasion of England (*Unternehmen Seelöwe*), the Führer was toying with the idea of invading the Soviet Union. Before the end of June, Colonel General Franz Halder, Chief of the Army General Staff, was informed that Hitler's "eyes were firmly directed toward the East." [16]

When, on July 11, Himmler responded to Berger's report concerning his difficulties with the OKW, he already knew that the services of his Waffen SS would be required in Hitler's newly conceived undertaking. In his note to Berger, Himmler confined himself to a reassurance that the Totenkopf and Polizei Divisions would not be demobilized; indeed, the Polizeidivision "will shortly be motorized." The memo ended with the cryptic comment: "Everything else verbally another time." [17] The "everything else" was surely Hitler's intention to attack Russia, a matter so delicate that it could not be referred to in writing even in a top-secret communication from the Reichsführer SS to one of his most trusted lieutenants.

Before the middle of July, Hitler had declared his intentions to the Army leaders, and by the end of the month preliminary plans were being prepared for war with the Soviet Union. One of the first concrete steps in this direction was the rescission of Hitler's demobilization order. Instead of being reduced from 160 to 120 divisions, the Army was to be enlarged to a strength of 180 divisions; of the twenty new divisions, ten were to be armored and five motorized.[18]

Reorganization and Expansion
for a New Campaign

The reorganization and strengthening of the Wehrmacht for war with the Soviet Union aggravated the existing disputes

[16] Halder, *Kriegstagebuch,* entry for June 30, 1940, p. 374. See also Alfred Philippi and Ferdinand Heim, *Der Feldzug gegen Sowjetrussland 1941–45* (Stuttgart, 1962), p. 27.

[17] Himmler to Berger, "Demobilmachung," July 11, 1940, Geheime Kommandosache, RFSS/T–175, 104/2626155.

[18] Philippi and Heim, *op. cit.,* p. 28.

between the armed services over the apportionment of manpower. At the beginning of the war the distribution of recruits had been fixed at: Army 66 per cent, Navy 9 per cent, and Luftwaffe 25 per cent. The requirements of the Waffen SS had not been fixed on a percentage basis, but were drawn from the Army's quota according to figures set by the Führer.[19] During August 1940, the OKW was convulsed by a bitter interservice fight over a new distribution formula. Berger reported to Himmler that the Luftwaffe was demanding 40 per cent and the Navy 10 per cent, leaving "only 50 per cent for the Army and the Waffen SS." [20]

By August, Hitler had apparently given Himmler some fairly concrete information about the role the Waffen SS was to play in the approaching campaign. Himmler in turn had discussed these plans with Brigadeführer (Major General) Jüttner, his chief of staff at the Kommando der Waffen SS; and Jüttner had passed the information on to Berger, who estimated that the Waffen SS would require a minimum of 18,000 new recruits a year to carry out its assigned role. On the basis of past experience, Berger predicted that the OKW would not permit the Waffen SS to recruit more than 2 per cent of the available manpower, which according to his figures would amount to only 12,000 men a year. Moreover, since Germany's birth rate had declined considerably during the late 1920s and early 1930s, the number of youths in the manpower pool would continue to decrease in forthcoming years so that, with only a 2 per cent share, the Waffen SS would have "to expect a low point of 9000 men in 1953." [21]

The only solution, as Berger saw it, was for the SS to intensify its recruitment in foreign lands. He pointed out that "no objections against a further expansion of the Waffen SS can be raised by the other armed services if we succeed in recruiting part of the German and Germanic population not at the disposal of the Wehrmacht. In this I see a special task

---

[19] Berger to Himmler, "Population Movement," August 7, 1940, Top Secret, Nuremberg Document NO–1825, Case XI, Document Book 65, pp. 1ff.

[20] *Ibid.*   [21] *Ibid.*

yet to be accomplished by the Reichsführer SS." [22] He asked Himmler "for an authorization to organize a recruitment office for foreign countries." Permission was soon granted.

But even with the use of foreign manpower, Hitler approved only a very moderate increase in the size of the Waffen SS during 1940. On August 6, 1940, he authorized the enlargement of the Leibstandarte SS "Adolf Hitler" from a regiment to a brigade; yet he used the occasion to issue a statement designed to reassure the Wehrmacht that he had no intention of permitting an unlimited expansion of the Waffen SS. According to an OKH memorandum distributed to all commanding generals on September 11, 1940 (and reissued for wider distribution on March 21, 1941), the Führer regarded the Waffen SS first and foremost as "a militarized state police [*Staatstruppen-Polizei*] capable of representing and imposing the authority of the Reich within the country in any situation." Such a task, Hitler believed, could "be carried out only by a state police that has within its ranks men of the best German blood and that identifies unreservedly with the ideology on which the Greater German Reich is based." Furthermore, "in our future Greater German Reich, a police force will have the necessary authority over its compatriots [*Volksgenossen*] only if it is established along military lines . . . [and] proves its worth and provides sacrifices of blood at the front in closed formations in the same way as every other unit of the Wehrmacht." However, "in order to ensure that the quality of the men in the units of the Waffen SS always remains high, the number of units must remain limited . . . [and] should, in general, not exceed 5 to 10 per cent of the peacetime strength of the Army." [23]

22 *Ibid.* Unfortunately, the author was unable to find a German copy of this very important document, and was forced to use a poor English translation that is part of a mimeographed collection prepared for the Nuremberg Trials. A number of infelicities have been corrected, without altering the sense of the passage.

23 Nuremberg Document D–665. In an effort to use Hitler's memorandum to clarify the relationship between the Wehrmacht and the Waffen SS and to prevent "the build-up of a military organization not under the command of the OKW," the National Defense Section (Section L) of the OKW submitted the following proposal (in the form of a memorandum) to General Jodl for transmission to Himmler:

In June, Hitler had set the peacetime strength of the German Army at sixty-four divisions. True to his word, he authorized only one new division for the Waffen SS. In the reorganized Wehrmacht (target date, May 1, 1941), the field component of the Waffen SS was to consist of four divisions and the Leibstandarte, the latter at brigade strength. Even the establishment of the one new SS division was made conditional on its being "recruited, for the most part, from foreign nationals." [24] As for the apportionment of German manpower during the expansion and reorganization, every branch of the service— including the Waffen SS—was to receive a share of the available age groups (1921, 1920, and the last third of 1919) proportional to its authorized strength within the Wehrmacht as of May 1, 1941.[25] Thus the field components of the Waffen SS, which would constitute approximately 3 per cent of the Wehrmacht on that date, were entitled to about 3 per cent of the recruits from these age groups.[26]

---

(1) Confirmation of the basic order which Hitler himself had given that the Waffen SS was a political organization of the National Socialist Party intended for internal tasks of a police nature.

(2) Confirmation of the fact already laid down by law that personnel replacement and equipment were the prerogative solely of the OKW.

(3) Waffen SS units temporarily incorporated in the Army to retain their military status only so long as they were so incorporated.

(4) Those parts of the SS organization which did not belong to the Waffen SS to have no military powers of command and not to have the right to wear military badges of rank or field-gray uniform.

According to General Walter Warlimont, Deputy Chief of the Operations Staff in the OKW, "this memorandum which had a suitable covering letter addressed to the Reichsführer SS was never heard of again." Warlimont, *op. cit.*, pp. 104 f.

[24] OKW to OKH/AHA/Ag/E, "Heranziehung der Rekruten," August 24, 1940, Geheim, RFSS/T–175, 103/2625971.

[25] *Ibid.*, 2625971 f.

[26] The armed SS (including the Police) had already accepted over 15,000 volunteers from the class of 1920 before the promulgation of the OKW directive. By the end of 1940, this figure had risen to 18,444. In addition, the SS had also dipped deeply into the classes of 1921 (W-SS: 10,400/Pol: 55), 1922 (W-SS: 9,254/Pol: 5), 1923 (W-SS: 5,229/Pol: 0). Even the sixteen-year-olds of the class of 1924 provided 168 recruits for the Waffen SS. For a complete list of inductions by age group see "Einberufung

The decision to attack the Soviet Union and the resulting prolongation of the war made it imperative for Himmler to seek a larger military role for his SS organization. The Waffen SS, according to Hitler, was to become the "state police force" of the Reich *after the war,* but in the meantime only its deeds at the front gained public recognition for the SS. Göring had his glamorous and—in 1940—highly successful Luftwaffe to boost his military and political prestige. Even Goebbels, who had no direct military function, found in the increased wartime role of his propaganda ministry a vehicle to inflate his power. What did the Reichsführer SS have to offer the German public? Certainly not the Gestapo, the concentration camps, the SD murder squads, or the cloak-and-dagger activities of the SS Reichssicherheitshauptamt. True, from a National Socialist viewpoint these were perhaps as important as the fighting at the front; but they were secret affairs, which gained little public recognition and even less glory for Himmler and his SS. Consequently, to gain a voice in military affairs and to enhance his public image, Himmler redoubled his efforts to enlarge the Waffen SS and thus increase its role in the forthcoming eastern campaign.

Himmler had nearly 40,000 men in the SS Totenkopf regiments.[27] If these troops could be integrated into the field component of the Waffen SS, an increase equal to two divisions would be achieved without further recruitment. Himmler had

bei der Polizei im Jahr 1940," and "Einberufung bei der Waffen-SS im Jahr 1940," February 23, 1941, Geheime Kommandosache, RFSS/T–175, 110/2635111ff.

27 The SS Totenkopf regiments (or Totenkopfstandarten, as they were often called) have been discussed in some detail in the section on definitions and also in Chapter Two. They should not be confused with the SS Totenkopfdivision, which was a field formation of the Waffen SS. The Totenkopf regiments (there were at one time as many as sixteen) were composed largely of youths below draft age and older SS reservists called up as "police reinforcements." Although technically part of the Waffen SS, the Totenkopf regiments were not under military control and were employed as militarized political police in German-occupied Europe, in which capacity they were unequivocally under Himmler's command. Totenkopf regiments were organized and equipped like regular Army infantry regiments, and their personnel wore the field-gray uniform, with a Death's Head on the collar tab in place of the usual SS runes.

already discovered that the security functions, for which the Totenkopf regiments had been established, could be handled effectively by Police formations composed of overage members of the Ordnungspolizei. Moreover, the reserve-training *(Ersatz)* formations of the Waffen SS, which had been scattered throughout German-occupied Europe, could also be called upon to carry out police tasks.

By deciding to make the SS Totenkopf regiments available for combat duty, Himmler had found a way to settle the long and acrimonious debate over their status. If they fought at the front, there would no longer be any excuse for the OKW's refusal to recognize duty with them as "military service." But the Wehrmacht authorities had made such recognition conditional on the Totenkopf units being placed under the tactical control of the Army. Although Himmler was willing to allow them to be used at the front, he was loath to give up his control over them, as he had done in the case of the field formations of the Waffen SS.

In the end (and a bit ahead of our story), a compromise was reached. By the start of the Russian campaign the SS Totenkopf regiments had been reorganized and redesignated SS infantry regiments.[28] Three of these were brought together to form SS Kampfgruppe (later SS Division) "Nord," and another was assigned to an existing SS division. These four regiments were unconditionally field formations of the Waffen SS and came under the tactical control of the OKH. The remaining five SS infantry regiments and two SS cavalry regiments were assigned to the Kommando Stab RFSS—a newly created SS organization which was responsible for antipartisan operations and similar assignments immediately behind the front. If used as reinforcements at the front, these regiments were to be under the temporary control of the Army, but Himmler retained the right to withdraw them for SS tasks at any time. As with so many other Wehrmacht–SS agreements,

[28] The title *Totenkopf* was henceforth restricted to the SS division of that name and to the infamous Totenkopfwachsturmbanne (Death's Head Guard Battalions), which held vigil over the concentration and extermination camps.

this one too fell victim to the demands of a long and costly war. In a relatively short time, all of the former SS Totenkopf-standarten became either cadres of new SS field divisions or replacements for losses in existing ones.[29]

The first tentative step toward the integration of the SS Totenkopf formations was taken during the western campaign, when Hitler—to spare Army manpower—ordered Himmler to prepare a fully equipped battalion for the occupation and defense of the Norwegian polar settlement of Kirkenes. By the end of June 1940, the battalion of specially selected Totenkopf regulars was on the way north. A year later it became part of the newly formed SS Division "Nord" and fought on the northern end of the Finnish front.[30]

A major step was taken on August 1, 1940, when Himmler, as part of a major reorganization of the Waffen SS, dissolved the Inspectorate of SS Totenkopfstandarten; thereafter these regiments were under the direct authority of the Kommando der Waffen SS.[31] A few weeks later, he approved a Wehrmacht request that the two SS Totenkopfstandarten in the Netherlands be placed under Army command in the event of a sudden enemy invasion.[32] This marked a fundamental departure; a year earlier Himmler had bitterly resisted any suggestion that Totenkopf units serve under Army command.

[29] The foregoing account is based on SS documents too numerous to cite individually. See particularly SS Führungshauptamt, "Zusammensetzung der Waffen SS," April 22, 1941, Geheim, RFSS/T–175, 104/2626944; SS Führungshaupamt, "Feldpostnummernverzeichnis der Einheiten der Waffen SS Stand vom 30. Dez. 1940," Geheim, RFSS/T–175, 104/2627061ff.; SS Führungshauptamt, "Unterstellungsverhältnis der Waffen SS," February 27, 1941, Geheim, RFSS/T–175, 104/2627078.

[30] Kommando der Waffen SS to Reichsführer SS, "16. Meldung," June 25, 1940, Geheime Kommandosache, RFSS/T–175, 106/2629796; Kommando der Waffen SS "Aufstellung eines verst. Bataillons," June 24, 1940, Geheime Kommandosache, RFSS/T–175, 107/2630321ff.

[31] Kommando der Waffen SS, "Auflösung der Inspektion der SS-T-Standarten," August 1, 1940, Geheime Kommandosache, RFSS/T–175, 107/2630267ff.

[32] Der Wehrmachtbefehlshaber in den Niederlanden to Höheren SS und Polizei Führer (Den Haag), "Abwehr von Feindlandungen," August 19, 1940, Geheim, RFSS/T–175, 107/2630239; Himmler's approval, September 4, 1940, 2630237.

In line with the general demobilization of older age groups, all Totenkopf reservists born in 1910 or earlier were offered their release from active duty. Apparently a sizable number of men accepted discharge, and during August three of the thirteen SS Totenkopfstandarten had to be dissolved.[33] By November the transfer of Death's Head troopers to the field units of the Waffen SS necessitated the deactivation of two more Totenkopf regiments.[34] Toward the end of the year the former duality of the Waffen SS—field formations and Totenkopfstandarten—was rapidly being broken down.

At the same time other phases of the reorganization and expansion of the Waffen SS were being carried out. One of the most important structural changes that Himmler decreed was the establishment, on August 15, 1940, of the SS Führungshauptamt (SSFHA) to act as "command headquarters for the military leadership of the Waffen SS (as far as its units are not under the command of the supreme commander of the Army) and for the pre- and postmilitary leadership and training of the Allgemeine SS."[35] The Kommando der Waffen SS (now redesignated Kommandoamt der Waffen SS) and all its subdepartments were transferred from the SS Hauptamt to the SS Führungshauptamt. Actually, the new organization was nothing more than a vehicle designed to elevate the military functions of the SS (which had all been gathered in the Kommando der Waffen SS) to a position of equality with the other *Hauptämter* or main branches of the multifaceted SS organization.[36] Himmler was personally in command of the new department, but the day-to-day operations were handled by SS Brigadeführer

[33] Kommando der Waffen SS, "Umorganisation und Entlassung von Reservisten," July 29, 1940, Geheime Kommandosache, RFSS/T–175, 107/2630309ff.; also separate order inactivating each regiment, "Auflösung der 12. Totenkopf Standarte," etc., 107/2630241ff.

[34] Kommando der Waffen SS, "Auflösung der 9. und 15. SS-T-Standarte," November 2, 1940, Geheime Kommandosache, RFSS/T–175, 107/2630137.

[35] See Befehl des Reichsführers SS, "Gliederung des SS-Führungshauptamtes," October 24, 1940, Geheim, RFSS/T–175, 103/2625794ff. The portion quoted is part of the original order issued on August 15, 1940, and may be found on frame 2625804.

[36] See diagram of the higher organization of the SS, p. 304.

Hans Jüttner, who "in personal union" exercised command of
the Kommandoamt der Waffen SS and was also "Chef des Stabes
des SS Führungshauptamtes." [37]

With the establishment of the SS Führungshauptamt,
Himmler had, in effect, created an SS high command which
could claim equality with the high commands of the other
armed services. After the middle of August, all high-level directives concerning the Waffen SS were issued by the SS Führungshauptamt. One of the first was an order calling for the reinforcement of the Leibstandarte to the strength of a brigade.[38]
Shortly thereafter, Field Marshal Keitel, chief of the OKW,
notified the Army High Command that "the Führer and
Supreme Commander of the Wehrmacht has ordered . . . the
establishment, within the framework of the Army, of a new
SS division . . . which shall utilize the manpower becoming
available from those countries inhabited by people of related
stock (Norway, Denmark, Holland)." In addition, Keitel
authorized the OKH to exchange all the foreign weapons still
in the possession of SS divisions for new ones of German manufacture and to provide them with new self-propelled assault
guns on the same basis as the motorized divisions of the Army.[39]

With the official authorization in hand, Jüttner began issuing the necessary directives to establish the new division.
Throughout the fall of 1940, the Waffen SS was convulsed by
the turmoil of expansion and reorganization. One by one, the
necessary components of the new and as yet nameless division
were created: a new artillery regiment, with personnel drawn
from the SS Verfügungs and Totenkopf Divisions; new battalions
of Germanic volunteers to bring Regiments "Westland" and
"Nordland" up to full strength; reserve-training (*Ersatz*) battalions to ensure replacements; and a division commander—

[37] RFSS/T–175, 103/2625795. For an organizational chart of the SS
Führungshauptamt see frame 2625796.

[38] SS Führungshauptamt, "Verstärkung der Leibstandarte SS 'Adolf
Hitler,' " August 28, 1940, Geheime Kommandosache, RFSS/T–175,
106/2629683ff. This directive implemented Hitler's authorization of August
6, 1940.

[39] OKW to OKH, "Ausbau der Waffen SS," September 19, 1940,
Geheim, RFSS/T–175, 106/2629681.

SS Brigadeführer (Major General) Steiner, formerly commander of Regiment "Deutschland." By December the various units destined to form the new division were ready. And on December 3, 1940, the SS Führungshauptamt, "on orders of the Führer," brought together the Regiments "Nordland," "Westland," "Germania" (taken from the SS Verfügungsdivision), and SS Artillery Regiment 5 to form the new SS division, which was named "Germania." [40]

The Verfügungsdivision was compensated for the loss of Regiment "Germania" by being given one of Himmler's extra Totenkopfstandarten. Redesignated SS Infantry Regiment 11, the former Totenkopf unit joined the veteran Waffen SS regiments "Deutschland" and "Der Führer." At the same time the division's name was changed from the rather unglamorous SS Verfügungsdivision to SS Division "Deutschland." [41] This name, however, and that of the new SS division ("Germania") were too easily confused with the regiments bearing the same names. By the end of the month, both divisions had been renamed: the Verfügungsdivision (alias "Deutschland") became SS Division "Reich" (later "Das Reich") and the new division became SS Division "Wiking"; both titles remained unchanged thereafter.

Out of the reshuffled SS Totenkopf regiments Himmler created another field formation for the Waffen SS; Totenkopfstandarten 6 and 7 (redesignated SS Infantry Regiments 6 and 7), with the addition of artillery and support units, became SS Kampfgruppe (Battle Group) "Nord." [42] But Himmler had to pay a price for this new addition to the Waffen SS: the Kampfgruppe was placed under the tactical command of the Army. The previously mentioned Totenkopf unit maintaining its

[40] SS Führungshauptamt, "Aufstellung der SS-Division (mot) 'Germania,'" December 3, 1940, Geheime Kommandosache, RFSS/T–175, 106/2629471ff.

[41] See Himmler's order of December 3, 1940, RFSS/T–175, 106/2629458.

[42] "Feldpostnummernverzeichnis der Einheiten der Waffen SS Stand vom 30. Dez. 1940, Geheim, RFSS/T–175, 104/2627061ff., and SS Führungshauptamt, "Aufstellung Kampfgruppe 'Nord,'" November 4, 1940, Geheime Kommandosache, RFSS/T–175, 106/2629670.

lonely vigil at Kirkenes above the Arctic Circle was reinforced and placed under Army command as SS Infantry Regiment 9.

Inevitably, the changes resulting from the reorganization and expansion caused a certain amount of confusion regarding the status of the various components of the Waffen SS. Toward the end of February, therefore, the SS Führungshauptamt issued a directive designed to clarify the situation.[43] It stated that "those portions of the Waffen SS and the Police that are integrated into the Army *are under* [*unterstehen*] the command authority of the Army, thus also under the territorial jurisdiction of the Wehrkreiskommandos.[44] The authority of the Reichsführer SS in the areas of ideological indoctrination, the appointment of officers and noncommissioned officers, as well as the assignment of replacements, remains unaffected." [45]

As listed in the directive, the SS units serving with the Army were:

> SS Division "Reich"
> SS Totenkopfdivision
> SS Polizeidivision
> SS Division "Wiking" (as of April 1, 1941)
> SS Kampfgruppe "Nord"
> Leibstandarte SS "Adolf Hitler"
> 9. SS Standarte [SS Infantry Regiment 9]

The *Feldtruppenteil* of the Waffen SS was now equivalent to six divisions. Despite the obstacles that had been placed in their path, Himmler and his aides had managed to double the size of the field component of the Waffen SS in a period of approximately six months.

Moreover, Himmler still retained a considerable armed force of his own. His directive of February 27 specified that "the reserve formations of the . . . [above-] mentioned units, as well as *the remaining portions of the Waffen SS* (SS Standarten etc.), do not come under the Army, not even in the

[43] SS Führungshauptamt, "Unterstellungsverhältnis der Waffen SS," February 27, 1941, Geheim, RFSS/T–175, 104/2627078ff.

[44] Headquarters of a military district within the Reich, equivalent to an Army corps area.

[45] *Ibid.*, 2627078. Emphasis in the original.

territorial jurisdiction of the Wehrkreiskommandos." [46] What were these "remaining portions of the Waffen SS"?

In addition to the reserve formations of the field units (there was one *Ersatz* battalion for each field regiment), Himmler retained control of the remaining five SS Totenkopfstandarten. These were withdrawn from their scattered European posts and gathered in Poland. There, at a newly established SS military reservation,[47] they were equipped with a full complement of infantry weapons, completely motorized, redesignated SS infantry regiments, and organized into combat brigades. SS Infantry Regiments 8 and 10 were brought together to form the motorized SS Brigade 1, and SS Infantry Regiments 4 and 14 became SS Brigade 2. The one odd SS Totenkopfstandarte remained independent as the motorized SS Infantry Regiment 5. The Totenkopf organization had also maintained two units of cavalry. These were reorganized so that they consisted of two squadrons of mounted troops, a squadron of bicycle troops, and a battery of horse-drawn artillery. Redesignated SS Cavalry (Kavallerie) Regiments 1 and 2, they completed the count of those combat-ready SS troops who were *not* under Army control.[48]

[46] The commanding general in each Wehrkreis was, however, "authorized to exercise inspection rights over all SS reserve units stationed in the area of his command, as well as to advise these units in matters of training." *Ibid.*, 2627079. The italicized phrase was underlined in the original directive.

[47] Since the beginning of the war, Himmler had been trying to secure a large reservation where the Waffen SS could conduct full-scale maneuvers, but all his efforts had broken down in the face of financial difficulties and the opposition of the Army. Finally, in view of the coming operation against the Soviet Union, Hitler added his weight to the side of the SS. Within a matter of months thousands of Poles were evicted from an area near Debica, and Himmler was given a number of square miles of Polish territory on which to train his troops. See Himmler's comments on Jüttner's "16. Meldung," June 25, 1940. RFSS/T–175, 106/2629795 f. For details on negotiations for the SS maneuver grounds at Debica see large file of correspondence in RFSS/T–175, 106/2629767ff.

[48] SS Führungshauptamt, "Verlegung der 8., 4. und 14. SS-Standarte," March 26, 1941, Geheime Kommandosache, RFSS/T–175, 104/2627031; SS Führungshauptamt, "Zusammensetzung der Waffen SS," April 22, 1941, Geheim, RFSS/T–175, 104/2626944ff.; SS Führungshauptamt, "Auf-

In short, until the demands of the front forced him to give
it up, Himmler retained complete control of a private army of
five infantry and two cavalry regiments. To eliminate any
distinction between these regiments and those SS formations
serving with the Army, Himmler ordered that "all armed units
of the SS are included in the Waffen SS; the designations 'SS
Verfügungstruppe' and 'SS Totenkopfverbände' are no longer
to be employed." [49]

In April, Himmler took a step that was to have fateful consequences for the Waffen SS. He issued a directive listing all the
SS organizations henceforth to be considered part of the Waffen
SS. The original list included 163 separate units, departments,
and installations. In addition to those already mentioned, it
embraced the two SS officer academies (SS Junkerschulen),
two new noncommissioned officers' schools,[50] various other military and technical training schools, and a host of administrative,
recruiting, supply, legal, and medical departments. All of these
were part of the apparatus necessary to maintain an armed
force. But Himmler also included all the concentration camps
(there were eight in April 1941), their staffs and guard detachments. Each camp had an SS Totenkopfsturmbann (battalion)
consisting of from three to seven guard companies—altogether
twenty-nine companies.[51]

During the course of the war, new camps were established
and the number of guards and staff members increased. By April
1945 approximately 30,000 to 35,000 Waffen SS personnel were
so employed. As far as can be determined, many of them seem to
have been former members of Totenkopfstandarten or older

stellung von 2 SS-Brigaden (mot)," April 24, 1941, Geheim, RFSS/T–175,
109/2633312ff.

[49] RFSS/T–175, 104/2626944.

[50] The first was established at Lauenburg on November 1, 1940, and
the second at Radolfzell during February 1941. SS Führungshauptamt,
"Aufstellung der SS-Unterführerschule," September 28, 1940, Geheime
Kommandosache, RFSS/T–175, 106/2629674ff.; SS Führungshauptamt,
"Errichtung einer SS-Unterführerschule in Radolfzell," January 29, 1941,
Geheime Kommandosache, RFSS/T–175, 104/2627169 f.

[51] SS Führungshauptamt, "Zusammensetzung der Waffen SS," April 22,
1941, Geheim, RFSS/T–175, 104/2626950.

reservists drawn from the General SS. But there is evidence that wounded Waffen SS soldiers were also assigned to these units, while some of the able-bodied Totenkopf personnel were sent to the front as replacements. All the guards wore Waffen SS uniforms and carried Waffen SS paybooks. Thus, in April 1941, Himmler established a link, however tenuous, between the field units of the Waffen SS and the concentration-camp staffs of the Waffen SS.[52]

Entirely outside the Waffen SS organization, Himmler established a sizable armed force made up of members of the Ordnungspolizei to handle the tasks for which the SS Totenkopf units had originally been conceived. To carry out "special tasks" behind the soon-to-be-opened Russian front, Himmler created three new Higher SS and Police Leaders (Höheren SS- und Polizei Führer) and assigned each a Police (Polizei) regiment consisting of two armored-car platoons, two antitank platoons, and three Police battalions. Three Police battalions and three squadrons of Police cavalry were held in reserve.

This Police "army" was entirely under the command of the Kommandostab Reichsführer SS, and the Higher SS and Police Leaders were responsible only to Himmler.[53] Some of these

---

[52] See pp. 259ff.

[53] On June 30, 1941, the Police forces on the Russian front were organized as follows:

Höh. SS- u. Pol. Führer A	*Höh. SS- u. Pol. Führer B*
Pol. Regt. Süd	Pol. Regt. Mitte
2 armored car platoons	2 armored car platoons
2 antitank platoons	2 antitank platoons
Pol. Btl. 314 (3 comp.)	Pol. Btl. 53 (3 comp.)
Pol. Btl. 45 "	Pol. Btl. 319 "
Pol. Btl. 303 "	Pol. Btl. 321 "
Höh. SS- u. Pol. Führer C	*Reserve*
Pol. Regt. Nord	Pol. Kav. Abt. (3 sqdns.)
2 armored car platoons	Pol. Btl. 254
2 antitank platoons	Pol. Btl. 304
Pol. Btl. 307 (3 comp.)	Pol. Btl. 315
Pol. Btl. 316 "	
Pol. Btl. 322 "	

Kommandostab RFSS, June 30, 1941, Geheim, RFSS/T–175, 106/2629064.

Police units were eventually thrown into the front lines during periods of crisis, but they were most often used in anti-partisan activities and mass executions of Jews and political prisoners. During the course of the war, Himmler established between twenty-five and thirty SS Police regiments for service in German-occupied areas. These units were composed largely of men over forty-five, a considerable number of youths of pre-draft age, and a few wounded war veterans no longer fit for front-line service. In addition, Himmler created numerous battalions of auxiliary-police troops composed of what he called "savage peoples" *(wilde Völker)*—mostly Latvians, Lithuanians, Estonians, Poles, and Ukrainians. These proved especially useful in the "cleanup" of Jews in the occupied areas.[54]

While major changes were being wrought in the organization and structure of the Waffen SS, its veteran formations—SS Division "Reich," SS Polizeidivision, SS Totenkopfdivision, and the Leibstandarte SS "Adolf Hitler"—remained in France, training for what was believed to be the forthcoming invasion of England (Operation Sea Lion). What the men of the Waffen SS did not know (although some may have suspected it) was that they were participating in an elaborate charade, for Hitler had long since given up his earlier intention to invade Britain and had decided to strike at Russia.

Accordingly, on December 18, 1940, Hitler issued his directive for "Case Barbarossa" *(Weisung Nr. 21—Fall Barbarossa)*: "The German Armed Forces must be prepared, even before the conclusion of the war against England, *to crush Soviet Russia in a rapid campaign.* . . . Preparations . . . will be con-

---

[54] For Himmler's comments on his Police formations see "Rede des Reichsführers SS auf der Tagung der RPA-Leiter am 28. Juni 1944," Geheim, RFSS/T–175, 94/2614737ff., and "Rede des Reichsführers SS bei der SS Gruppenführertagung in Posen am 4. Oktober 1943," Nuremberg Document 1919–PS. For wartime activities of the Ordnungspolizei, particularly in Russia, see RFSS/T–175, rolls 11 and 229–231. Records of the Höheren SS- und Polizeiführer and SS- und Polizeiführer in Germany and the occupied territories may be found in RFSS/T–175, rolls 219–229. Above all, see Neufeldt, Huck, and Tessin, *op. cit., passim.*

cluded by 15 May 1941." [55] Six weeks later, a draft order of battle was ready: all formations of the Waffen SS serving under Army command were included. To mask the purpose of the operation as long as possible, the OKH decided not to move the bulk of the German forces to the East until May and June. The motorized divisions of the Army and Waffen SS were to be the last to move. Of course, the growing intensity of the preparations soon made it obvious to the SS troops that something quite unusual was afoot, perhaps something bigger than the invasion of England. And so the spring of 1941 found the Waffen SS in France, Germany, and Poland getting ready for a campaign into the unknown.

When the first units of the Waffen SS finally received their marching orders they moved not against England or Russia but against Yugoslavia and Greece.

Balkan Interlude: The Waffen SS in Yugoslavia and Greece, April 1941

During the preceding October, Hitler's Italian allies, without warning, suddenly invaded Greece. Within a few weeks they were losing one battle after another against the tough Greek mountain troops. This "regrettable blunder," as Hitler put it, seriously endangered the Axis position in the Balkans. In view of the planned invasion of the Soviet Union, Hitler could not risk an uncertain military situation on his southern flank. He consequently directed the OKH to prepare a plan for a German attack on Greece. [56]

By mid-December, "Undertaking Marita" (the code name for the invasion of Greece) was beginning to take shape. Within the next three months sixteen German divisions were moved to

[55] An English translation of Hitler's entire directive is given in H. R. Trevor-Roper (ed.), *Blitzkrieg to Defeat: Hitler's War Directives 1939–1945* (New York, 1965), pp. 49ff. Plans for Barbarossa may be found in Nuremberg Documents 446–PS, 447–PS, C–35, C–78; OKW/T–77, rolls 778, 784, 792; and OKH/T–78, roll 335. The best published account of the preparations and planning is in Philippi and Heim, *op. cit.*, pp. 19ff.

[56] Hitler's Directive No. 18, November 12, 1940, Trevor-Roper, *Directives*, p. 42.

southern Romania. The Leibstandarte SS "Adolf Hitler" left Metz early in February to join them. As originally conceived, Marita called only for the seizure of the Greek mainland north of the Aegean Sea, but the landing of British troops in Greece early in March resulted in a decision to occupy the entire peninsula and the island of Crete.[57]

On March 25, 1941, after strong German pressure, Yugoslavia, following the example of Bulgaria, signed the Tripartite (Rome–Berlin–Tokyo) Pact. The way to the Greek border seemed open. But the next day a military revolt in Belgrade overthrew the Regency and the Government, proclaimed young Peter II king, and established a new, anti-German government under General Simović.

In a towering rage, Hitler ordered the invasion of Russia postponed for "up to four weeks" in order to "destroy Yugoslavia militarily and as a nation." For daring to oppose him, the south Slav state was to be crushed "with merciless brutality . . . in a lightning operation." Quickly, Marita was modified to encompass the destruction of Yugoslavia as well as Greece, and additional German divisions were diverted from the ongoing deployment for Barbarossa to the Balkans.[58]

On March 28 the SS Division "Reich" received orders to move by road from Vesoul in eastern France to Temesvar in southwestern Romania in order to take part in the invasion of Yugoslavia. Traveling day and night, the SS division made the trip in less than a week, during which time there occurred a number of incidents between SS and Army personnel serious enough in Army eyes to warrant a formal complaint from the

[57] Hitler's Directive No. 20, December 13, 1940, *ibid.*, pp. 46ff. The final decision to occupy Crete was not made until after Marita was launched. The operational plans for Marita may be found in OKH/T–78, rolls 329, 334, 346, and OKW/T–77, rolls 778, 781, 782.

[58] Hitler's Directive No. 25, March 27, 1941, Trevor-Roper, *Directives,* pp. 61 f. Hitler's angry statements concerning Yugoslavia were made at a meeting with the German military chiefs at the Chancellery in Berlin on March 27; see the OKW minutes of the meeting, Nuremberg Document 1746–PS.

Commander-in-Chief, Field Marshal von Brauchitsch, to Himmler.[59]

For a number of reasons, the SS division had trouble with its forced march: there were traffic snarls in the miles-long column, units ran out of fuel, vehicles broke down, and over-loaded trucks moved at a snail's pace over steep mountains. The proud SS troops were chagrined to find their struggling columns being overtaken by the convoys of the more experienced Army organizations. The newly assigned SS Infantry Regiment 11, formerly a Totenkopfstandarte, was extremely inexperienced in military road procedures, and it was commanded by an arrogant and volatile officer. When his floundering column was overtaken by a fast-moving Army formation, the SS commander halted it and prohibited any further movement until his regiment had passed the point. When the convoy leader protested, the SS officer had two Teller mines placed under the front wheels of the lead Army vehicle and ordered an SS man to stand guard over them with fixed bayonet.

In a similar incident the next day, an SS officer stopped an Army convoy attempting to pass his vehicles. In the dispute that followed (overheard and reported by a Munich traffic police-man) the SS officer angrily shouted at his Army counterpart: "If you drive on without my permission, I will order my men to fire on your column!"

Such was the inauspicious beginning of another chapter in the willy-nilly comradeship in arms between the Army and the Waffen SS. As usual, however, the elite SS formations proved their worth in combat. At dawn on April 6, 1941, the German armies moved into Yugoslavia and Greece. As part of General Georg-Hans Reinhardt's XLIst Panzerkorps, the SS Division "Reich" thrust toward Belgrade. Battered continuously by the Luftwaffe, the poorly equipped Yugoslav Army was quickly overrun. In typical SS style (although in this case without much risk), an assault group of the SS Division "Reich" raced toward

[59] See file beginning with Oberbefehlshaber des Heeres to Reichs-führer SS, "Marschbewegung der SS-Division 'Reich,'" May 23, 1941, RFSS/T–175, 107/2630630ff.

the capital. It reached the heavily bombed city on April 13 and accepted its surrender. For this exploit Hitler awarded the assault group's commander, SS Hauptsturmführer (Captain) Klingenberg, the Knight's Cross of the Iron Cross.[60] Four days later the Yugoslav Army capitulated.

Meanwhile, on the southern portion of the front, Wilhelm List's 12th Army, with eight infantry divisions, four panzer divisions, the Army's elite Regiment "Gross Deutschland," and the Leibstandarte SS "Adolf Hitler," attacked from Bulgaria through southern Yugoslavia, and on into Greece. Working closely with the 9th Panzer Division, the Leibstandarte advanced through Skoplje, and within three days had captured the stronghold of Monastir near the Yugoslav–Greek border. Since the beginning of the campaign, the Leibstandarte had suffered only five casualties, all wounded. But on April 10, the SS brigade was ordered to open the Klidi Pass—the gateway to Greece—for the German forces. Here the picnic ended. The vital pass was defended by veteran Australians and New Zealanders of the British Expeditionary Force. It took the Leibstandarte two days to force the defenders from their positions, at a cost of 53 dead, 153 wounded, and 3 missing.[61]

In another mountain engagement, this time against Greek troops, the Leibstandarte's reconnaissance battalion (*Aufklärungsabteilung*) stormed the heavily defended Klissura Pass, capturing more than 1000 of their opponents with a loss of only 6 men killed and 9 wounded. In describing the operation in his postwar memoir, Kurt Meyer, commander of the reconnaissance battalion at the time, offers a revealing glimpse of a type of unorthodox combat leadership that was, at least in the German armed forces, peculiar to the Waffen SS.

While two of his companies clambered up the cliffs to take the defenders in the flanks, Meyer and a small advance group began moving along the road through the pass. Suddenly a series of violent explosions tore huge craters in the road, sending portions of it hurtling into the valley below. The Greek

---

[60] Hausser, *op. cit.,* p. 41.

[61] SSFHA to RFSS, "Zahlenmässige tägliche Verlustmeldung LSSAH seit 6. 4.–18. 4. 41," April 26, 1941, RFSS/T–175, 108/2632356 f.

defenders had set off the main demolition charges. Through the clouds of dirt and smoke, intense machine-gun fire raked the pass.

We glue ourselves behind rocks and dare not move. A feeling of nausea tightens my throat. I yell to [Untersturmführer] Emil Wawrzinek to get the attack moving. But the good Emil just looks at me as if he has doubts about my sanity. Machine-gun fire smacks against the rocks in front of us. . . . How can I get Wawrzinek to take that first leap? In my distress, I feel the smooth roundness of an egg hand grenade in my hand. I shout at the group. Everybody looks thunderstruck at me as I brandish the hand grenade, pull the pin, and roll it precisely behind the last man. Never again did I witness such a concerted leap forward as at that second. As if bitten by tarantulas, we dive around the rock spur and into a fresh crater. The spell is broken. The hand grenade has cured our lameness. We grin at each other, and head forward toward the next cover.[62]

The next day Meyer's battalion took the key town of Kastoria and with it another 11,000 prisoners. For his unit's achievements during the previous twenty-four hours, Meyer was added to the growing list of SS men who had been awarded the Knight's Cross.[63]

In the days that followed, the Leibstandarte drove forward against crumbling resistance. By April 20, the SS unit had captured the Metzovon Pass, thus cutting through the withdrawal route of the Greek Epirus Army and forcing the surrender of its sixteen divisions. Three days later, the capitulation of the entire Greek Army was signed in Salonica.[64]

This left the British Expeditionary Force to fight on alone. On April 24, the Leibstandarte moved south in pursuit of the retreating British forces. Across the Gulf of Corinth and on through Peloponnesus the chase continued. Behind a screen of gallant rear guards, the British managed to evacuate most of their troops, just as they had done on a larger scale at Dunkirk less than a year earlier. On April 27, German troops entered

[62] Meyer, *op. cit.*, p. 64.
[63] *Ibid.*, p. 67.
[64] Hans-Adolf Jacobsen and Hans Dollinger, *Der Zweite Weltkrieg* (Munich, 1962), I, 298.

Athens. Three days later, the Germans were in complete control of the country. Altogether, 223,000 Greek and 21,900 British prisoners had been taken. German losses for the entire Balkan campaign were 2559 dead, 5820 wounded, and 3169 missing. Once again the Leibstandarte was ordered to participate in the victory parade, this time in Athens. The SS brigade was subsequently sent north to Prague, to be refitted for its next undertaking—the invasion of the Soviet Union.[65]

[65] *Ibid.;* Meyer, *op. cit.,* pp. 67ff. Between the start of the Balkan campaign and the end of the heavy fighting on April 18, the Leibstandarte lost 72 killed, 246 wounded, and 3 missing. By April 21, twenty-one of the wounded had died of their injuries, RFSS/T–175, 108/2632356 f.

CHAPTER FIVE

Some Military Consequences of an Ideology:
The Waffen SS in Russia

THE campaign in the Balkans had been a brilliant *Blitzkrieg,* but it had forced Hitler to postpone the opening of Barbarossa until June 22, 1941. Yugoslavia had deprived the Wehrmacht of nearly half of the best campaigning season in Russia. Thus the Yugoslavs, who had appealed to Stalin for protection against the Germans and been refused, unwittingly saved Russia from a fate even worse than the one that was to befall her.

Operation Barbarossa

By the beginning of June, 129 German divisions had been moved to the East, and the last-minute deployment of the armored and motorized divisions began.[1] When the alert signal *Dortmund* was flashed to the front commands on June 21, the German forces stood poised with seven armies, four panzer groups, and three air fleets—more than 3,000,000 men, 600,000 vehicles, 750,000 horses, 3580 armored combat vehicles, 7184 artillery pieces, and 2100 aircraft. From north to south along the main front, the German forces were divided into three army groups: Army Group North, under Field Marshal Ritter von Leeb, was to advance with two armies and one panzer group through the Baltic states and seize Leningrad; Army Group Center, under the command of Field Marshal von Bock, was ordered to attack with its two armies and two panzer groups

[1] Jacobsen and Dollinger, *op. cit.,* p. 358.

119

through White Russia toward Moscow; Army Group South, commanded by Field Marshal von Rundstedt, was to send its three armies and one panzer group through Galicia to capture Kiev and secure a bridgehead across the Dnieper River.[2]

Temporarily lost in this massive array of military might were the formations of the Waffen SS: Leibstandarte SS "Adolf Hitler" and SS Division "Wiking" with Army Group South; SS Division "Reich" with Army Group Center; SS Totenkopf-division and SS Polizeidivision (in reserve) with Army Group North; and far north of the main front, in Finland, SS Kampf-gruppe "Nord" and SS Infantry Regiment 9 with Colonel General von Falkenhorst's Norwegian Army Command.[3]

At 3:15 on the morning of June 22, 1941, as the sudden flash of thousands of guns brightened the pale dawn, the Wehrmacht

[2] Philippi and Heim, *op. cit.,* pp. 46, 52.

[3] The strength of the Waffen SS at the beginning of the Russian campaign was:

SS Division LSSAH	10,796	Administrative Department	4,007
SS Division "Wiking"	19,377	Reserve Units	29,809
SS Totenkopf Division	18,754	Inspectorate of Concentra-	
SS Division "Nord"	10,573	tion Camps	7,200
SS Division "Reich"	19,021	SS Guard Battalions	2,159
SS Polizei Division	17,347	SS Garrison Posts	992
Kommandostab RFSS	18,438	SS Officer and NCO Schools	1,028
		SS Volunteer Battalion	
		"Nordost"	904

The total strength of the Waffen SS amounted to 160,405 men. The report from which these figures were drawn was prepared some two months after the beginning of the campaign. By that time the Leibstandarte had been redesignated a division and is so labeled above. The same holds true for SS Division "Nord," which is simply a combination of the former SS Kampf-gruppe "Nord" and SS Infantry Regiment 9. The Kommandostab RFSS consisted of those previously discussed field formations which were not placed under Army control. The SS Volunteer Battalion "Nordost" consisted of Finns who had volunteered for service in the Waffen SS. It should also be noted that the introduction to the report states that "the figures are probably somewhat too low . . . since as a result of the present situation, the strength of the Waffen SS cannot be established with complete certainty." See report by Inspekteur für Statistik to Reichsführer SS, "Stärkemeldung der Schutzstaffel vom 30. Juni 1941," August 27, 1941, Geheim, RFSS/T–175, 111/2635846ff.

clashed with the Red Army in what was to become the greatest continuous land battle history had ever known. With the exception of the Polizeidivision, all the Waffen SS formations under Army command were in action within the first few days of the campaign. By early August, the Polizeidivision too was engaged, while immediately behind the front two brigades of Himmler's Kommandostab RFSS (SS Infantry Brigade 1 and SS Cavalry Brigade) were operating against Russian troops bypassed during the main advance.[4]

SS Ideology and the War in the East

Much has been written on the question why Hitler ordered the invasion of the Soviet Union. Nevertheless, there is agreement on three basic reasons, although scholars disagree on the weight to be assigned to each. Hitler, it may be said, invaded Russia first to crush Bolshevism, which he regarded as the inevitable ideological enemy of the Nazi "New Order" in Europe, second to destroy the USSR as a state (and thus also as a military threat), and third to gain for Germany *Lebensraum* and a vast new area for colonial exploitation. German power politics and designs on Eastern Europe (which had deep roots in German history) were thus inextricably entwined with the ideology and political immorality of National Socialism.[5]

The concomitant of Nazi-style colonialism was inevitably an irrational racism, which was symbolized by the reduction of the Slav, particularly the Russian, to the status of an *Untermensch*, a subhuman. The over-all consequences of this policy are too well known to require repeating here. Suffice it to say that in the military sphere too, the bloodiness and barbarity of

[4] The SS Cavalry Brigade was a last-minute merger of the SS Cavalry Regiments 1 and 2. For detailed day-by-day combat reports from the Waffen SS units engaged in Russia see "Tagesmeldungen der SS-Divisionen," July 6, 1941–March 12, 1942, Geheime Kommandosache, RFSS/T–175, 111/2635573ff.

[5] On German policy toward, and in, Russia during World War II see Alexander Dallin, *German Rule in Russia, 1941–1945* (New York, 1957); Alexander Werth, *Russia at War, 1941–1945* (New York, 1964); Gerald Reitlinger, *The House Built on Sand* (London, 1960). This last work will hereafter be cited by name.

the struggle (so reminiscent of crusades and religious wars) owed much to its ideological character.

Small wonder then that for the ideologically indoctrinated soldiers of the Waffen SS (much more so than for the rest of the Wehrmacht) the battle against the Red Army was a holy war, a crusade against Bolshevism and subhumanity. Although SS divisions fought in every theater of operations except Africa, it was in the East that they fought hardest, longest, and most fanatically. And it was there that the elite formations of the Waffen SS developed fully that blend of determination and ruthlessness which became their distinctive military style.[6]

To understand the character of that style, one must examine, if only briefly, the nature of SS ideology, keeping in mind that ideology was only one important factor contributing to the combat achievement of the elite SS divisions and that SS ideology in theory and Waffen SS ideology in practice were not always identical.

Despite the complexity of the SS organization and the variety of interpretations that have been offered to explain its character and significance, there can be little doubt that it possessed a distinct ideology—which in the case of the Waffen SS seems to have served more as a manipulative device than as a true ideology.[7]

SS ideology was rooted in the racist ideal known in Hitler's Germany as *Blut und Boden,* Blood and Soil. Out of it grew the concept of the SS as the living embodiment of the National Socialist doctrine of the superiority of Nordic blood.

[6] Although a detailed examination of the eastern campaign falls outside the scope of this study, some of the more important battles and their implications for the development of the Waffen SS will be noted. In addition to those already mentioned, two recent works that treat the eastern campaign are Alan Clark, *Barbarossa: The Russian–German Conflict, 1941–45* (New York, 1965), and Paul Carell, *Hitler Moves East 1941–1943* (Boston, 1964).

[7] As used here, a true ideology is defined as a reasonably systematic body of ideas combined with a passionate drive toward their execution. On the manipulative nature of SS ideology see Robert Koehl, "The Character of the Nazi SS," *The Journal of Modern History,* XXXIV (September 1962), 280.

In 1940, Himmler told the officers of the Leibstandarte SS "Adolf Hitler" that "the ultimate aim for these eleven years during which I have been the Reichsführer SS has remained unchanged: To create an order of good blood which is able to serve Germany." [8] Accordingly, the SS had two main functions; one positive, the other negative. In the positive sense, the SS was conceived as a racial and biological elite, a Nazi aristocracy, a new ruling class that would provide the leadership necessary to establish and maintain the "New Order" in a German-dominated Europe. In the negative sense, the SS accepted responsibility for the "elimination of all racially and biologically inferior elements and the radical removal of all incorrigible political opposition that refuses on principle to acknowledge the ideological basis of the National Socialist State and its essential institutions." [9] Until final victory was achieved in the racial struggle, the SS was to remain a "National Socialist Military Order of Nordic Men, a fighting force . . . bound by ideological oaths, whose fighters are selected from the best Aryan stock." [10]

To enable the SS to carry out its tasks, however difficult or distasteful, absolute obedience was demanded of all its members. Obedience must be unconditional. It corresponds to the conviction that National Socialist ideology must reign supreme. . . . Every SS man is therefore prepared to carry out blindly every order issued by the Führer or given by his superior, regardless of the sacrifice involved.[11]

Unquestioning submission to authority, then, was the second foundation stone of SS ideology.

In its role as the spearhead of the National Socialist revolution, the SS was prepared to combat any enemy of the Nazi Party or the Third Reich. But since its inception, the SS had

[8] This portion of the speech may be found in Nuremberg Document 1918–PS. For full text see RFSS/T–175, 90/2612641ff.

[9] Kogon, *op. cit.*, p. 20.

[10] *Organisationsbuch der NSDAP*, p. 416, Nuremberg Documents 1922–A–PS and 2640–PS.

[11] *Ibid.*

taught its members that the main enemy was "the Jewish–Bolshevik revolution of subhumans."[12] When this enemy was more or less eliminated in Germany, emphasis began to be placed on eliminating it from all of Europe. In particular, the ideological line of the SS began to stress the inevitability of decisive struggle between Nordic Germany (later enlarged to include Nordic Europe) and the breeding grounds of "the Jewish–Bolshevik revolution of subhumans," the Soviet Union. Even today this concept is the stock in trade of Germany's Waffen SS veterans' association (HIAG der Waffen SS). With the old racism barely concealed, the former SS men speak and write about the great service performed by the Waffen SS in saving western civilization from being overrun by "Asiatic Communism."[13]

Himmler constantly reiterated the theme of racial struggle in his speeches to his Waffen SS officers. In 1943, when the Waffen SS was taking in thousands of new recruits, many of them foreigners and youngsters who were not Nazis, he reminded the assembled officers of three SS divisions of the need for imbuing their men with the *Weltanschauung* of the SS:

I beg you as commanding officers, as chiefs and leaders, to instruct your men again and again in our ideological beliefs. . . . I ask you to look after them, and guide them, and not let them go before they are really saturated with our spirit and are fighting like the old guard fought. . . . We have only one task—to stand firm and carry on the racial struggle without mercy.[14]

Confronted with copies of Himmler's speeches, former members of the Waffen SS invariably claim that the fighting troops did not take his rantings seriously and regarded him as a rather

[12] Statement by Himmler in his pamphlet "The SS as an Anti-Bolshevik Fighting Organization," published in 1936 and partially reproduced as Nuremberg Document 1851–PS.

[13] The major outlet for SS apologetics is the Waffen SS veterans' magazine, a monthly called *Der Freiwillige: Kamaradschaftsblatt der HIAG* (Osnabrück). A periodical expressing similar views is *Nation Europa: Monatsschrift im Dienst der europäischen Erneuerung* (Coburg). A good example of the above view may be found in Felix Steiner, *Die Freiwilligen: Idee und Opfergang* (Göttingen, 1958), p. 57.

[14] See excerpts from Himmler's Kharkov speech of 1943 in NCA, II 192.

Members of an SS-Police unit ride an electric work-train into the mountains on an antipartisan drive along the Slovenian border, February 1944. These Police troops, not members of the Waffen SS, wear mountain uniforms with Police insignia. Note the number of relatively older men in the group. (Ullstein–Brauner)

A shivering SS soldier manning a heavy-machine-gun post on the edge of a Russian forest, 1943. (Ullstein–Brauner)

SS Sturmbannführer (Major) Meyerdress inspecting a defensive position, 1944. Meyerdress wears the black panzer uniform and the Knight's Cross with Oak Leaves. Behind the two SS officers lies the hulk of a Russian tank. (Ullstein)

comical figure out of touch with reality. This may have been true of some SS men, especially later in the war, when the Waffen SS had to resort to conscription. But in view of the amount of time devoted to ideological indoctrination in the prewar SS and the nature of the material presented, there can be little doubt that many of the men who made up the Waffen SS of 1941—particularly the officers and NCOs—subscribed to the basic views set forth in Himmler's statements on the racial struggle and similar matters.[15]

Moreover, before 1943 the new recruits coming into the Waffen SS were still overwhelmingly volunteers, who could hardly have failed to recognize the uniqueness of the formation they were joining. The official Waffen SS recruiting pamphlet issued to all potential volunteers told them that

if you answer the call of the Waffen SS and volunteer to join the ranks of the great front of SS divisions, you will belong to a corps which from the very beginning has been associated with outstanding achievements, and therefore has developed an especially deep feeling of comradeship. You will be bearing arms with a corps that embraces the most valuable elements of the young German generation. Above all, you will be especially bound to the National Socialist ideology.

The reader was reminded that the enlistment of so many young Germans in the Waffen SS was a "superb demonstration of the positive ideological commitment of Germany's youth, who understand the purpose of the SS' struggle, and who know exactly why the Waffen SS forms a brotherhood [*Gemeinschaft*] especially bound to the Führer." [16]

For the soldiers of the Waffen SS, the racial struggle did not take the form it did for the SS men who ran the extermination

[15] For samples of the type of material offered to members of the Waffen SS during their ideological training see folder containing instructional handbooks published by the SS Hauptamt, Schulungsamt, in the series entitled *Stoffsammlung für die weltanschauliche Erziehung der Waffen SS,* RFSS/T–175, 161/2693498ff. See also SS Hauptamt, Schulungsamt file containing instructional material and lecture slides for lessons on Jews, Communists, racial characteristics of various peoples, and the like, *ibid.,* 2694069ff.

[16] See *Dich ruft die SS* (Berlin, 194?), New York Public Library Microcopy Z–941.

camps or who staffed the execution squads of the Einsatzgruppen. According to Himmler, the Waffen SS would be playing a key role in the racial struggle by assisting in the military conquest of Russia, thus helping Germany secure vital *Lebensraum*, while at the same time destroying the "power of Bolshevism and the Jews."

On July 13, 1941, exactly three weeks after the invasion of the Soviet Union, Himmler traveled to Stettin to speak to a small group of Waffen SS men who were being sent as replacements to SS Kampfgruppe "Nord" on the Finnish front. The Kampfgruppe (battle group) had just suffered a devastating defeat in its first action, and Himmler thought it necessary to address a few words of encouragement to the new men. His impromptu address was transcribed, marked secret, and filed away. It is a remarkable indication of the perspective from which Himmler expected his Waffen SS to view the war with Russia.

To you SS men I need not say much. For years—over a decade—we old National Socialists have struggled in Germany with Bolshevism, with Communism. One thing we can be certain of today: what we predicted in our political battle was not exaggerated by one single word and sentence. On the contrary, it was too mild and too weak because we did not, at that time, yet have the insight we have today. It is a great heavenly blessing that, for the first time in a thousand years, fate has given us this Führer. It is a stroke of fate that the Führer, in his turn, decided, at the right moment, to upset Russia's plans, and thus prevent a Russian attack. This is an ideological battle and a struggle of races. Here in this struggle stands National Socialism: an ideology based on the value of our Germanic, Nordic blood. Here stands a world as we have conceived it: beautiful, decent, socially equal, that perhaps, in a few instances, is still burdened by shortcomings, but as a whole, a happy, beautiful world full of culture; this is what our Germany is like. On the other side stands a population of 180 million, a mixture of races, whose very names are unpronounceable, and whose physique is such that one can shoot them down without pity and compassion. These animals, that torture and ill-treat every prisoner from our side, every wounded man that they come across and do not treat them the way decent soldiers would, you will see for yourself. These people have been welded by the Jews into one religion, one ideology, that is called Bolshevism, with the task: now we have Russia, half of Asia, a part of Europe, now we will overwhelm Germany and the whole world.

When you, my men, fight over there in the East, you are carrying on the same struggle, against the same subhumanity, the same inferior races, that at one time appeared under the name of Huns, another time—1,000 years ago at the time of King Henry and Otto I—under the name of Magyars, another time under the name of Tartars, and still another time under the name of Genghis Khan and the Mongols. Today they appear as Russians under the political banner of Bolshevism.[17]

If the men of the Waffen SS shared even a measure of their Reichsführer's views (and many certainly did), it helps explain the zeal with which they pursued the war against Russia.

Since it has long been obvious that soldiers find it easier to kill (or risk being killed) when fighting an enemy they hate, all modern nations have attempted in one way or another to instill in their soldiers a picture of the enemy sufficiently repugnant or evil to inspire this hatred.[18] Two hate-inspiring images were deliberately fostered by the ideological indoctrination to which the men of the Waffen SS were subjected. The first was the old but persistent image of the enemy as subhuman. The second, closely related to the first and especially common to the modern soldier who (like the dedicated Nazi or Communist) is totalitarian in his thinking, was the image of the enemy as his ideological antithesis, or to use the obvious religious analogy, a devil who opposes "the truth" and must therefore be exterminated in a holy crusade. For the Waffen SS troops fighting on the eastern front, these two images of the enemy were inseparable.

When the enemy is regarded (as in the speech by Himmler quoted above) as a repulsive and evil animal, an *Untermensch*,

[17] "Der Reichsführer SS zu den Ersatzmannschaften für die Kampfgruppe 'Nord' am Sonntag, dem 13. Juli 1941, in Stettin," Geheim, RFSS/T–175, 109/2632683ff.

[18] For this aspect of the discussion I have drawn freely, both as to material and inspiration, on the perceptive book by J. Glenn Gray (*The Warriors: Reflections on Men in Battle* [New York, 1959]).

a subhuman, the result is an unmatched brutalization of warfare, for the soldier is generally set free from feelings of guilt or remorse for his grisly deeds. An obvious example, one uncomfortably close to home, is the attitude of American fighting men toward their Japanese enemies during World War II. A recent account of the Marine landing on the Japanese-held island of Tarawa in 1943 contains this passage:

> In war there is very little inclination for soldiers to consider an enemy as a feeling human being under any circumstances, and the Japanese made a perfect enemy. They had so many characteristics an American Marine could hate. Physically they were small, a strange color and, by some American standards, unattractive. With the fresh memory of Pearl Harbor in their minds and a few childhood memories of Japanese in bad motion pictures, Marines considered them "sneaky." Further, they did not understand and therefore hated this inscrutable Oriental for his "fanatical" willingness to die. Marines did not consider that they were killing men, their equals. They were wiping out dirty animals. . . . No matter how they might revise their opinion of the Japanese in later years, this blazing hatred was an effective and necessary stimulant at the time.[19]

The attitude of the American Marines toward the Japanese at Tarawa was by no means unique in the Pacific war, as anyone who experienced (or read about) it will surely admit. Unfortunately, an image of the enemy as something less than human is perhaps inevitable when soldiers are fighting a foe of another race or color. But clever and persistent indoctrination can achieve the same result even when there are few if any observable differences between antagonists. Thus, if Americans raised in a free society could react in this fashion toward the Japanese, it should scarcely be surprising that the men of the Waffen SS, products of systematic racial and political indoctrination, were at last equally "stimulated" in their struggle with the Russians.[20]

[19] Andrew A. Rooney, *The Fortunes of War* (Boston, 1962), p. 37.

[20] In addition to their formal ideological training, the men of the Waffen SS were fed a continuous diet of inspirational periodicals (*SS-Leithefte*) containing articles and stories that entertained while they indoctrinated. These publications were a means by which an SS man surfeited

In any case, the deplorable side effects that resulted from the artificial dehumanization of the eastern enemy are well known—the shooting of prisoners, the murder of civilians, the destruction of peaceful villages. The extent to which such acts were the result of ideological indoctrination *alone* is of course difficult to assess, and perhaps we shall have to be satisfied with the self-evident conclusion drawn by SS Obergruppenführer (General) Erich von dem Bach-Zelewski before the International Military Tribunal at Nuremberg. Asked whether Himmler's demand that thirty million Slavs be exterminated and the actual murder of ninety thousand Jews by one small Einsatzgruppe (composed in large part of Waffen SS men) were in keeping with National Socialist ideology, von dem Bach replied that "when, for years, for decades, the doctrine is preached that the Slav is a member of an inferior race and that the Jew is not even human, then such an explosion is inevitable." [21]

It is important not to forget the close connection between the *Untermensch* philosophy and that aspect of Nazi ideology which regarded the war against the Soviet Union as a crusade to save western civilization from the onslaught of "Asiatic Bolshevism." [22] All antagonists tend to differentiate between their own cause, which is "right and just," and that of the enemy, which is "wrong and evil"; but nowhere is this attitude so pronounced, so dogmatic, and so uncompromising as in a clash between ideologically antithetical totalitarian systems. Indeed, the war between Nazi Germany and Communist Russia was in many

---

with political and ideological propaganda could be lured into swallowing still more. "In these *Leithefte*," said Himmler, "we attempt to present, unnoticed, basic political information in every sentence." For a complete description of the use of *Leithefte,* see "Rede des Reichsführers SS auf der Tagung der RPA-Leiter am 28. Januar 1944," Geheim, RFSS/T–175, 94/2614803ff. A collection of *SS-Leithefte* covering a period of some eight years is on file at the Berlin Document Center Library and is now also available on National Archives Microcopy T–611, rolls 43, 44, 45.

[21] "Verhör in Nürnberg am 7. Januar 1946 (Nachmittagssitzung)," reproduced in Leon Poliakov and Josef Wulf, *Das Dritte Reich und Seine Diener* (Berlin, 1956), p. 152.

[22] On this point see Dallin, *op. cit.,* pp. 67ff.

ways reminiscent of the great religious wars of an earlier age. Although the majority of the soldiers involved were neither fanatic Communists nor dedicated Nazis,

when voluntary German SS troopers engaged fanatic Communists in Russia in World War II, a climax in enmity and hatred was reached in which all traces of chivalry vanished and all moderation was abandoned. Even to read about some of these battles with an attempt at imaginative understanding is sufficient to shake anyone to the depths.[23]

A Waffen SS Defeat

Depending on the source of the judgment, the men of the Waffen SS have been described as either fanatics or outstandingly courageous soldiers. Whatever the truth of the matter, they were undeniably determined soldiers. But determination, whether based on ideological conviction or some other factor, does not in itself explain the combat achievements of the elite SS divisions. Hand-picked personnel, good training, effective leadership, and first-class armament were also important. While the SS Divisions "Leibstandarte Adolf Hitler," "Reich," "Totenkopf," and "Wiking," which possessed these attributes, were distinguishing themselves in action during the first days of the Russian campaign, another SS formation, which lacked some of them, was suffering an ignominious defeat at the hands of the Soviet Army.

On July 2, along the northern sector of the Finnish front, SS Kampfgruppe "Nord," with a Finnish and a German Army division, assaulted the Russian stronghold at Salla. The five SS battalions employed in the attack were twice beaten back with heavy losses. On their third attempt, the Russians launched a counterattack that drove the SS units back beyond their starting line. By the end of the day the Kampfgruppe reported:

Situation serious. Signs of dissolution in the unit. Unrest carried to the rear by those retreating. Position can no longer be held in the

[23] Gray, *op. cit.*, pp. 156 f. The ferocity of some of the battles in which SS troops fought crack Red Army troops can be gauged from the accounts given in the previously cited works by Alexander Werth, Alan Clark, and Paul Carell.

face of continued armored attack. Russians attacking in great strength.[24]

According to eyewitness reports sent to Himmler, the SS men panicked in the face of the Russian attack; many threw away their weapons and ran from the battle, their eyes glazed with fear. Shouting in terror, "Russian tanks are coming!" the retreating SS troops ran right through the German artillery lines. Meanwhile, the Finns and the Army division had successfully assaulted their objectives; this forced the attacking Russians to fall back, and saved the SS combat group from being completely overrun. Its first battle cost the SS unit 73 killed (13 officers), 232 wounded (13 officers), and 147 missing.[25]

The rout of the Kampfgruppe was made even more distressing to Himmler and the SS leaders by the realization that most of the missing SS men had been taken prisoner by the Russians despite Himmler's repeated injunctions to the Waffen SS that they must fight to the death or kill themselves rather than surrender.[26] So little faith did General von Falkenhorst retain in the SS Kampfgruppe after its dismal showing that he added insult to injury by dividing its battalions among his Finnish and German Army formations.[27]

The fiasco at Salla clearly indicated that ideological conviction was no guarantee of success in battle. In the two former Totenkopfstandarten that had been brought together to create Kampfgruppe "Nord," there were undoubtedly many convinced

[24] Telegram from Hoh. SS- u. Pol. Führer Nord to SSFHA, July 2, 1941, RFSS/T–175, 111/2635801.

[25] SSFHA to RFSS, "Tagesmeldung der SS-Divisionen: 6. Meldung," July 19, 1941, Geheime Kommandosache, RFSS/T–175, 111/2635764.

[26] Long before the war Himmler had told his Gruppenführer that "there should never be such a thing as a captured SS man. He must first put an end to his life." (See "Gruppenführerbesprechung am 8. November 1938 im Führerheim der SS Standarte 'Deutschland,'" RFSS/T–175, 90/2612581.) During the period when the Germans were in retreat (especially after the beginning of 1943) SS men often committed suicide rather than surrender to the Russians. (See Werth, *op. cit.*, pp. 767, 782.)

[27] This was only a temporary situation, and some months later Himmler, having reinforced and overhauled the SS unit, reconstituted it as a division.

Nazis; but they were men trained for police duties, not war. Lacking sufficient combat training, led by incompetents whose "military" experience had been limited to the direction of concentration-camp guard detachments and the execution of helpless civilians, and composed in part of overage SS reservists, the SS Kampfgruppe was no match for the Russian veterans of the Finnish war.[28]

A New Kind of War

Despite Himmler's fears,[29] the setback suffered by the Waffen SS in the far north was successfully kept from the German public. At the same time, along the main front, the SS divisions were scoring one impressive victory after another. Yet from the very beginning, the fighting on the Russian front took on a character entirely different from anything they had yet experienced.

Like some prehistoric monster caught in a net, the Red Army struggled desperately and, as reflexes gradually activated the remoter parts of its body, with mounting effect. Until that day the Germans had always found that bodies of surrounded enemy lay down and died. . . . The speed and depth of a Panzer thrust; the tireless ubiquity of the Luftwaffe; above all, the brilliant coordination of all arms, had given the Germans an aura of invincibility that had not been enjoyed by any other army since the time of Napoleon. Yet the Russians seemed as ignorant of this as they were of the rules of the military textbooks.[30]

Despite great losses in territory, men, and equipment, the Rus-

[28] The foregoing account concerning the activities of SS Kampfgruppe "Nord" is based on a voluminous folder from the files of Persönlicher Stab RFSS which contains depositions, investigation reports, diaries, maps, combat reports, and directives pertaining to this unit during 1941. RFSS/T–175, 108/2632384ff.

[29] Speaking to a group of officers being sent as replacements to Kampfgruppe "Nord" after its defeat, Himmler said that he feared that "this setback could cloud . . . the reputation [of the Waffen SS] which was won at the cost of so much blood. For people do not speak about the victories of five [SS] divisions when they can talk about the defeat of a single one." See "Der Reichsführer SS zu den Führern der Ersatzmannschaften für die Kampfgruppe 'Nord' am Sonntag dem 13. Juli 1941, in Stettin," Geheim, RFSS/T–175, 109/2632686ff.

[30] Clark, *op. cit.*, p. 49.

sians continued to resist doggedly. And if their casualties were
astronomical, those suffered by the Germans were heavy too.
Also, both sides ignored the usual conventions of warfare.
Some German units (especially those of the Waffen SS) carried
out the infamous *Kommissarbefehl,* which ordered that all
political commissars of the Red Army captured in battle were to
be shot immediately. On the other hand, Field Marshal von
Manstein, in his postwar memoir, claims that on the very first
day of the offensive "our troops came across a German patrol
which had been cut off by the enemy earlier on. All of its
members were dead and horribly mutilated." [31] Similarly, two
weeks later, a company of combat engineers from the SS
Division "Reich" was temporarily cut off and partially overrun. When the survivors were finally extricated, it was found
that the Russians had shot "all those wounded or taken prisoner." [32] In still another incident, six members of the SS Division "Leibstandarte Adolf Hitler" were taken prisoner while on
patrol; some months later, when the Germans occupied the city
of Taganrog, their mutilated bodies were found in the courtyard well of the local GPU headquarters. Surviving civilian
prisoners described how the six SS men, who had been in the
custody of the Soviet secret police from the time of their capture, were led into the courtyard shortly before the arrival of
the German forces and beaten and hacked to death with axes,
shovels, bayonets, and rifle butts, after which their bodies were
thrown into the well.[33] In reprisal, the commander of the
Leibstandarte, Sepp Dietrich, ordered his men to shoot all
prisoners taken during the next three days. Some 4000 Russian
soldiers were therefore executed for a crime of which they were
innocent.[34]

[31] Manstein, *op. cit.,* p. 180.
[32] SS Division "Reich," report of July 10, 1941, in SSFHA to RFSS,
"Tagesmeldung der SS-Divisionen: 6. Meldung," July 19, 1941, Geheime
Kommandosache, RFSS/T–175, 111/2635762.
[33] With their usual efficiency, the Germans conducted a thorough and
seemingly dispassionate investigation of the incident (including autopsies).
See the voluminous report from Dietrich to Himmler, April 3, 1942,
RFSS/T–175, 108/2631518ff.
[34] Reitlinger, *op. cit.,* pp. 170 f.

Such was the hatred and barbarism generated by ideological war. Although both sides were guilty of war crimes, there can be little doubt that the greater opprobrium rests with the Germans, whose systematic and deliberate disregard for the conventions of war cost the lives of millions of Russian prisoners.[35] Although there are few records to prove it, the men of the Waffen SS are reputed to have killed a large number of their prisoners on the spot of surrender, and it is therefore not surprising that SS men fearing retribution often chose to commit suicide rather than give themselves up to the Russians.

In any event, the more savage the war became, the more the fighting qualities of the SS divisions stood out. As Himmler explained to Goebbels and his staff, the ideological conviction of the SS troops enabled them "to hold on in the instant that [they] would normally break down," and in "the hour of need permits [them] to transcend themselves." [36]

By mid-November, as Army Group Center lunged toward Moscow to deliver the *coup de grâce* to the dying Russian bear, the Waffen SS took stock of its losses. The figures were shocking. Since the beginning of Barbarossa, the Waffen SS had suffered 407 officers and 7930 men killed, 816 officers and 26,299 men wounded, 13 officers and 923 men missing, and 4 officers and 125 men killed in accidents.[37] But in the four months of bitter fighting, the Waffen SS had gained the military renown it was to retain among friends and foes for the rest of the war.

Some six weeks later, as the Germans were reeling back from the gates of Moscow in the face of a violent and unexpected Russian counterstroke, Reichsführer SS Heinrich Himmler received an unsolicited letter from the commander of the IIIrd Panzer Corps, General Eberhard von Mackensen.

It will perhaps be of some value to you to hear, from the mouth of that commanding general under whom the Leibstandarte has served during this long and difficult campaign and one who is a member

[35] See the figures in Clark, *op. cit.,* p. 207, and Werth, *op. cit.,* p. 708.
[36] "Rede des Reichführers-SS auf der Tagung der RPA-Leiter am 28. Januar 1944," Geheim, RFSS/T–175, 94/2614811.
[37] SSFHA to RFSS, "Tagesmeldung der SS-Divisionen: 31. Meldung," November 19, 1941, Geheime Kommandosache, RFSS/T–175, 111/2635589.

of the Army and not the SS, what he and the other divisions think about this unit.

Herr Reichsführer, I can assure you that the Leibstandarte enjoys an outstanding reputation not only with its superiors, but also among its Army comrades. Every division wishes it had the Leibstandarte as its neighbor, as much during the attack as in defense. Its inner discipline, its cool daredeviltry, its cheerful enterprise, its unshakable firmness in a crisis (even when things become difficult or serious), its exemplary toughness, its camaraderie (which deserves special praise)—all these are outstanding and cannot be surpassed. In spite of this, the officer corps maintains a pleasant degree of modesty. A genuine elite formation that I am happy and proud to have under my command and, furthermore, one that I sincerely and hopefully wish to retain! This unrestrained recognition was gained by the Leibstandarte entirely on the strength of its own achievements and moreover on the basis of its military ability against an enemy whose courage, toughness, numbers, and armament should not be slighted. The aura which naturally surrounds the Führer's Guard would not have sufficed, here at the front, to allow this recognition to fall into its lap.[38]

In the crucible of the eastern front, many of the generals who had regarded the Waffen SS as an unsavory band of *arrivistes* were forced to revise their opinions. Accordingly, Mackensen's tribute to the Leibstandarte was soon echoed by other generals in connection with the combat achievements of Waffen SS divisions.[39] Hence, from a strictly military point of view, his words might well serve as a eulogy—or epitaph—for the entire Waffen SS in the eastern campaign.

Of course, Mackensen and his Army colleagues chose to view only one side of the coin. The Leibstandarte and the other Waffen SS formations had already exhibited that brutality which little more than a year later would lead Himmler to boast to the assembled officers of three SS divisions: "We will

[38] Mackensen to Himmler, December 26, 1941, RFSS/T–175, 108/2632287 f.

[39] For example, Field Marshal von Manstein wrote: "In no circumstances must we forget, however, that the Waffen SS, like the good comrades they were, fought shoulder to shoulder with the army at the front and always showed themselves courageous and reliable." Manstein, *op. cit.*, p. 188.

never let that excellent weapon, the dread and terrible reputation which preceded us in the battles for Kharkov, fade, but will constantly add meaning to it." [40]

One of the first things the SS had done when it recaptured the city two weeks earlier was "to butcher 200 wounded in a hospital, and set fire to the building." [41] And if Russian claims may be believed, the Waffen SS also murdered some 20,000 civilians before being driven for the last time out of Kharkov in August 1943.[42]

[40] Speech by Reichsführer SS Heinrich Himmler at Kharkov, April 1943, Nuremberg Document 1919–PS (mimeographed). Kharkov had been liberated from the Germans in February 1943, but was recaptured the following month by a counterattack spearheaded by SS Divisions "Leibstandarte Adolf Hitler," "Das Reich," and "Totenkopf."

[41] Werth, *op. cit.,* p. 618.

[42] Closing speech on organizations by General R. A. Rudenko, Chief Prosecutor for the USSR, TGMWC, XXII, 352.

CHAPTER SIX

The West European SS:

Mobilization of Foreign Nationals, I

AT the outbreak of World War II the number of non-Germans serving in the Waffen SS was negligible; at the end, foreigners outnumbered native Germans. Of the thirty-eight SS divisions in existence in 1945, none was composed entirely of native Germans, and nineteen consisted largely of foreign personnel.[1]

Myth of a European Army

No serious study of the mobilization of non-German man-power for the German armed forces has yet appeared, although a good deal of tendentious literature has been published on the subject by former members of the Waffen SS.[2] As a result, a romantic legend has been created which, in its simplest form, portrays the Waffen SS of the later war years as a multinational European army composed of idealists fighting to preserve western civilization from the onslaught of "Asiatic Bolshevism." In recent years this theme has been elaborated by SS apologists to the point where the multinational Waffen SS has been depicted as a forerunner of NATO; and the punishment of Norwegian, Danish, Dutch, Belgian, and French SS veterans by their post-war governments has been decried as a miscarriage of justice.

The legend of "over a half million volunteers of foreign nationality" who "followed the dictates of their conscience" and

[1] See Appendix II, pp. 296ff.

[2] See the previously cited works by Hausser, Kanis, Steiner, Kersten, and also Leon Degrelle, *Die verlorene Legion* (Stuttgart, 1952).

voluntarily left their families and occupations to "offer their lives for a great concept" is patent nonsense.[3] It is true that some 500,000 foreigners served in the Waffen SS during World War II, but many of them were not volunteers and very few were idealists of the sort described.

The largest group of non-German SS men were eastern Europeans: Latvians, Estonians, Ukrainians, Bosnians, Croats, Serbs, Albanians, Hungarians, Romanians, Bulgarians, Russians, and the so-called *Volksdeutsche,* or ethnic Germans of Eastern Europe. A good many of these men were conscripted or coerced into the SS; others volunteered for strictly nationalistic reasons. For the Baltic peoples and the Ukrainians, the war against the Soviet Union was simply a struggle for national survival. Even Felix Steiner, an arch-propagator of the myth, has admitted that "the eastern volunteers fought primarily for the freedom and independence of their countries," [4] hoping that the Germans would grant some sort of autonomy to their homelands after the war.

Unlike those from Eastern Europe, the foreigners from Western Europe in the SS more nearly conform to the legend. Although exact figures are lacking, probably as many as 125,000 west Europeans served in the Waffen SS. Nearly half of these enlisted before the war turned irrevocably against Germany. Some pressure, mostly in the form of propaganda, was exerted by the Germans and native Nazi groups on potential recruits, but the majority seem to have been true volunteers.

The remaining 60,000 or so joined during the last year of the war. Some were Frenchmen and Walloons who automatically became SS men when their units were transferred from the German Army to the Waffen SS in 1943; [5] others were drawn from the thousands of collaborators who fled to Germany from their native lands in the face of the Allied invasion of the Continent; and still others were youths conscripted for labor service in the Reich who were persuaded to exchange the harsh life of the slave laborer for that of the SS soldier.

[3] Steiner, *Die Freiwilligen,* p. 9.
[4] *Ibid.,* p. 57.
[5] See p. 163.

The breakdown of the west European or "Germanic" SS was as follows: the largest single group, some 50,000 men, was Dutch; Belgium provided 40,000 SS men, almost evenly divided between Flemings and Walloons; 20,000 men came from France; Denmark and Norway each produced about 6000 men; and another 1200 came from such countries as Switzerland, Sweden, and Luxembourg. Moreover, for about two years, from 1941 to 1943, some 1000 Finns served in the Waffen SS; but as citizens of an independent and cobelligerent nation, they occupied a unique position in relation to the other foreign volunteers.[6]

The strange spectacle of people joining an army until lately that of a national enemy is frequently explained by the argument that they sought to save Europe, or at least their homelands, from "Bolshevism."[7] This may have been true of some, but almost certainly not of the majority. Indeed, the first group of west Europeans volunteered for the Waffen SS while the German–Soviet nonaggression pact was still in effect.

Steiner admits that most of the west European volunteers were youths who acquired their pan-European and anti-Communist convictions only after having "experienced war in the East."[8] Many of them at first suffered from conflicting feelings about their enlistment in the Waffen SS. According to Steiner, they lost their "mental reservations" only after "having witnessed in the fate of the Russian people the diabolical results of the Bolshevik dictatorship and recognized in the fanatical combat leadership of the Red soldier the pitiless determination of

---

[6] The Finns will be discussed more fully below. Official figures concerning west European volunteers (insofar as they were uncovered in the course of this study) do not extend beyond the beginning of 1942 (see SS Hauptamt, "Übersicht über die in der Waffen SS befindlichen germanischen Freiwilligen: Stand v. 15. Januar 1942," RFSS/T–175, 109/2633910), but those given in Steiner, *Die Freiwilligen,* pp. 373ff., are probably as accurate as any presently available.

[7] See, for example, Kanis, *op. cit.,* pp. 116 f., which shows a photograph taken in 1944 of the visitors' directory in a hospital for wounded foreign SS men; there are ten names representing nine different nationalities, and the caption (published in 1957) reads: "They fought for their Fatherlands against Bolshevism."

[8] Steiner, *Die Freiwilligen,* p. 50.

the wielders of power in Moscow to achieve victory over the free world without regard to the human sacrifice." [9]

Without relying on Steiner's view alone, it may safely be concluded that if the western volunteers ever had a strong idealistic conviction concerning the need for saving Europe from the onslaught of "Red Imperialism," they acquired it after their enlistment in the SS. The exceptions would, of course, be youths who were members of such political organizations as Mussert's Dutch Nazi Party (NSB), Quisling's Norwegian Nazi Party, and Degrelle's Belgian Rexists. Groups of this sort did provide a share of the volunteers, but until the great influx of refugee collaborators in the last year of the war the number was far smaller than might be expected.

It might be assumed that the youngsters were encouraged to volunteer by parents with pro-German sympathies. Some undoubtedly were. But Himmler himself admitted in 1943 that at least a third of them had been disowned by their families and that a number of married volunteers had even lost their wives as a result of their enlistment.[10] A graphic example of familial discord is found in a letter written in 1942 by a Norwegian SS volunteer to a friend and included in the official SS censor's report sent to Himmler: "My father has very little sympathy with my political beliefs. So little, that when I tried to visit him on Christmas Eve while on leave (I hadn't seen him for 7–8 months), he threw me out." [11]

In 1948 a Dutch psychologist, Dr. A. F. G. van Hoesel, published the results of a study he had made of 450 young Netherlanders who had been arrested for military collaboration with the Germans. Most of the men had served in the Waffen SS. After personally interrogating them, interviewing their parents and friends, and screening their court records, van

[9] *Ibid.* It is interesting to note that Steiner's statement would hardly be less meaningful if the word German were substituted for "Russian," Nazi for "Bolshevik," SS for "Red," and Berlin for "Moscow"—a point that surely escaped the self-righteous former SS general.

[10] "Rede des Reichsführers SS auf der Tagung für Befehlshaber der Kriegsmarine in Weimar am 16. 12. 1943," RFSS/T–175, 91/2613345.

[11] "Auszug aus einem Brief eines Norwegers zur Heimat (Soldat Leo Larsen)," RFSS/T–175, 22/2527277.

Hoesel concluded that the vast majority had been motivated to volunteer by such factors as a desire for adventure, better food, the prestige of wearing an SS uniform, sheer boredom, desire to avoid the unglamorous compulsory labor service, and a variety of personal factors which included, in some instances, a wish to avoid prosecution for juvenile delinquency or petty criminality. In any case, few of the youths who made up the bulk of the Dutch SS volunteers were motivated by any form of political or ideological idealism.[12] Berger, who handled foreign recruitment, certainly had no illusions about the idealism of his recruits, although he paid lip service to the myth. In a secret communication to the Höhere SS- und Polizeiführer Nordwest, SS Gruppenführer (Lieutenant General) Rauter, he admitted that many of the Dutch volunteers lacked moral integrity; some even had criminal records. But Berger felt that "many 'criminals' are quite outstanding soldiers if one knows how to handle them." And, in any event, "we will never be able to prevent men from joining the legions and the Waffen SS who are neither National Socialists nor idealists, and instead take this step for more materialistic reasons. That is the way it is everywhere in the world and it was no different in Germany during the *Kampfzeit*."[13]

It may be concluded that the majority of the west European volunteers enlisted in the Waffen SS for reasons other than those of political or ideological conviction. Steiner, in a semi-philosophical essay on the "political-intellectual background" of the volunteer movement, states that they did so neither because they were Nazis nor because they were opportunists, but rather as a result of deeper "psychological" factors related to the "intellectual despair of Europe's youth."[14]

As Steiner sees it, the world-wide depression of the 1930s adversely affected the career opportunities of a large segment

[12] See Dr. A. F. G. van Hoesel, *De Jeugd die wij vreisden* (Utrecht, 1948), quoted in Henry L. Mason, *The Purge of Dutch Quislings: Emergency Justice in the Netherlands* (The Hague, 1952), pp. 22ff.

[13] Berger to Rauter, "Freiwillige in der Niederländischen Legion," April 9, 1942, Geheim, RFSS/T–175, 111/2635463ff.

[14] See "Die supranationale Freiwilligen-Bewegung des 2. Weltkrieges und ihr politisch-geistiger Hintergrund," Steiner, *Die Freiwilligen*, pp. 41ff.

of Europe's youth. Disillusioned by the apparent helplessness and instability of their governments, many of them began to search for an ideal that would give meaning to their lives. According to Steiner, some were impressed by Germany's economic recovery after 1933 and, unlike their skeptical elders, tended to regard developments in the Third Reich with "idealistic hopefulness." All their sympathies, however, disappeared with the German invasion of their homelands. On top of this disillusionment came still another—"the quick collapse of the seemingly powerful army of the western world." This, Steiner claims, led to a strange reaction among many of these young people; instead of venting their anger on the Germans, they tended to blame their own governments for the debacle. In a state of shock and with a feeling of "inner helplessness," they were now exposed, for the first time, to a close view of their conquerors. "They observed the good behavior and discipline of the German troops and began to make comparisons that did not turn out to be unfavorable for the Germans." Steiner concludes that "all these psychological factors and their concern about the future destiny of their homelands combined at this time to lead a part of the youth to make the decision to enter the German Wehrmacht as volunteers."

Stripped of its romantic and subjective elements, Steiner's thesis appears to possess some validity; certainly it merits further investigation. But it does little more than explain the general psychological factors which made the west Europeans receptive to the solicitations of the SS recruiters.

A summary of the available evidence indicates that the largest group of western volunteers joined the SS for such non-idealistic reasons as a desire for adventure, status, glory, or material benefit (in addition to pay and allotments, volunteers were promised civil-service preference and grants of land after the war). Perhaps the next largest group was composed of adherents of political or nationalist organizations who hoped to improve the fortunes of their movement or to demonstrate their ideological commitment to National Socialism by serving in the SS. Among those that cannot be placed in either of these two broad categories, there were undoubtedly some who were motivated primarily by a genuine desire to participate in a war against the Soviet Union. Certainly the thousand Finns who served in the Waffen SS fit this description. But for them the war was no ideological crusade. The Finns were simply interested in carrying on the struggle against their nation's archenemy. They were fighting not "Bolshevism" but rather age-old Russian imperialism.

If many of the foreign SS men eventually came to speak the language of the myth, it was a result either of ideological indoctrination received after their enlistment or of a need to justify themselves to those of their countrymen who had not collaborated with the enemy.

It will be recalled that as early as 1938, Himmler had decided to recruit foreigners of "Germanic" blood for the armed SS. At that time Himmler was simply indulging a personal passion. Just as King Frederick William of Prussia sent his recruiting officers throughout Europe to hunt for exceptionally tall soldiers for his Potsdam Guards, so Himmler sought recruits from all the Germanic countries for a racial show regiment. With the German occupation of Denmark, Holland, Norway, and France, Himmler's dream became a reality. Through the efforts of Berger's SS recruiting office enough Danes, Alsatians, Norwegians, and Netherlanders were induced to volunteer for the Waffen SS to provide the basis for two regiments. These regiments ("Westland" and "Nordland"), with the addition of a veteran all-German SS Regiment ("Germania"), formed the heart of the new SS Division "Wiking." Nevertheless, despite a promising beginning, the foreign recruiting campaign was to encounter serious difficulty; and when the "Wiking" Division went into combat during the summer of 1941, fewer than one third of its men were west European volunteers.

Although Berger tried hard to recruit as many foreign volunteers as possible during the summer of 1940, the SS leaders were not yet seriously considering the formation of a European army. But the conclusion of the campaign in the West did not bring peace. The tight rein on its domestic recruiting and plans for the continuation of the war in new directions led the Waffen SS to undertake a massive recruitment of "Germanic" foreigners from the occupied western countries and *Volksdeutsche* from Central and Southeastern Europe. With Hitler's

approval, Berger established within his SS Hauptamt a new
department to handle foreign recruiting; and with a new fund
for the purpose, the campaign rolled into high gear.[15]
    The plan to recruit large numbers of foreigners for the
SS was purely a matter of expediency; Himmler needed young
men for his Waffen SS, and so long as the requirements of the
Wehrmacht were paramount inside Germany, he was forced to
turn elsewhere. But the steps had to be justified on ideological
grounds; after all the SS was a *weltanschauliche Truppe*.[16] Thus
was born another one of those curious Nazi manipulative
devices, neither cynical propaganda nor true ideology but
rather a series of factitious ideas that survives in the present-
day myth of the Waffen SS as a multinational army of volunteers
struggling to save Western Europe from Communism.
    Since early SS attempts to recruit foreigners were directed
at "Germanic" peoples only, the racial aspects of SS ideology
required no alteration. Toward the end of 1940, the SS Hauptamt established a camp at Sennheim in Alsace, where incoming
foreign volunteers from Western Europe were given premilitary
physical and ideological training. Volunteers who passed the
course and still desired to serve in the Waffen SS took the SS
oath and were sent on to join an active unit for further training.[17] Their ideological training was the same as that of the
regular SS recruits. But by 1943 the influx of non-Germanic
personnel forced the SS to give up its uniform ideological
indoctrination. The SS Hauptamt then prepared a specially
tailored program for each national or ethnic group.[18] The
Ukrainians, for example, were spared the lectures on the inferi-

---

[15] Berger became Chef des SS-Hauptamtes on August 15, 1940. See
RFSS/T-175, 103/2625795.
    [16] Ideological corps.
    [17] On Sennheim see Berger to SSFHA, "Freiwillige aus germanischen
Ländern," February 2, 1942, Geheime Kommandosache, RFSS/T-175,
109/2633660, and Berger to Rauter, 109/2635463. After January 30, 1941,
all foreign volunteers (but not *Volksdeutsche*) took the SS oath to Adolf
Hitler as "Führer" and not as "Führer und Kanzler des Reiches." For this
order and full text of the SS oath see RFSS/T-175, 107/2630599.
    [18] "Rede des Reichsführers-SS Reichsinnenminister Himmler auf der
Tagung der RPA-Leiter am 28. Januar 1944," Geheim, RFSS/T-175,
94/2614801ff.

ority of the Slav race, while the devoutly Moslem Bosnian recruits heard no criticism of organized religion.

Despite this tactical retreat from ideological uniformity, the Waffen SS maintained its basic racial and political teachings for German and "Germanic" recruits. As the war situation deteriorated, however, less training time was available, and therefore the indoctrination was much less thorough. Hausser in his postwar apologetic warns that the "intensity and range" of the *"weltanschauliche-politische Schulung"* in the combat formations of the Waffen SS "should not be overvalued." He insists that the attitudes of the troops reflected those of their commanders, who thought "primarily, if not entirely, in soldierly terms [*soldatisch*]." [19] This last statement may perhaps describe Hausser's own attitude and that of other SS leaders who had been Army officers; it need not, however, be accepted as an accurate appraisal of Waffen SS commanders in general.

While the basic racial beliefs of the SS were officially retained, another SS doctrine was gradually modified. Within the Waffen SS, especially in the Junkerschulen and among those connected with the foreign volunteer movement, the proposition of a Greater Germanic Reich gave way to the concept of a European union of free, self-governing states with a common army in which each state would be represented by a national contingent. The Waffen SS was viewed as the forerunner and eventual nucleus of this European army. Under this new concept, the unifying element of race was replaced by a common opposition to "Bolshevism." [20]

It is difficult to trace the exact origin of the new movement. Berger asserts in his postwar testimony that he had been in favor of a European union rather than a Greater Germanic Reich from the very beginning of the war. He has been supported by Felix Kersten's recollections.[21] But the documentary evidence fails to bear out this claim. Berger may have favored European union when speaking to foreigners whose support he was trying to win, but within the highest councils of the SS

[19] Hausser, *op. cit.*, p. 231.

[20] *Ibid.*, pp. 231ff.

[21] See Final Plea for Gottlob Berger, United States Military Tribunal IV, Case 11 (mimeographed); Kersten, *op. cit.*, pp. 251, 255ff.

he spoke otherwise. In 1942, presiding over a conference on Germanic matters, Berger said:

As a result of the Führer Decree . . . responsibility for the entire Germanic area has been transferred to the Reichsführer SS. In this connection it must be our duty to pave the way for the Führer, in order that he may later amalgamate the Germanic countries into the Germanic Reich. Without sacrificing their nationality and their culture these countries are to belong to the Germanic Reich.[22]

Himmler apparently found it expedient to allow his subordinates to voice support for a European union. But Hitler, and therefore Himmler, never gave up the goal of a Greater Germanic Reich ruled from Berlin. It could not have been otherwise: the Führer's racial and geopolitical beliefs militated against the idea of a Europe not completely dominated by Germany.

It is noteworthy that nowhere in the many secret speeches made by Himmler during the war does he advocate either a European political union or an independent European army. Indeed, Steiner in his postwar book on the subject says that the "Berlin dogmatists," and particularly Himmler, would not consent to a purely military training and orientation of the foreign volunteers but insisted on a pan-Germanic approach that conflicted with the concept of a European political union and an integrated European army that was advocated by many in the Waffen SS. Steiner claims that, from the very beginning, the field troops were generally skeptical of the Germanic concept "because historically and politically it was pure romanticism." It could, however, be accepted as a "connecting cultural bridge" so long as it "remained confined to this and did not slip off into a muddled, mystical or completely racial presentation." [23]

When the Germanic concept began to take on "imperialistic overtones," the Waffen SS, according to Steiner, "was the first, and perhaps the only institution that objected loudly." Apparently these objections fell on deaf ears, for Steiner tells us that

[22] Nuremberg Document NO–3026, United States Military Tribunal IV, Case 11, Prosecution Document Book 65 (mimeographed), p. 4.

[23] Steiner, *Die Freiwilligen*, p. 67.

not until vast numbers of non-Germanics came into the Waffen SS during the latter part of 1942 was "the Germanic idea buried." The way was then open for the "historically and politically correct idea of a Europe with a common destiny [*Schicksalsgemeinschaft*], which embraced all European volunteers and bound them together in spirit." [24]

Of course, this was just so much wishful thinking. Himmler was quite willing to allow such views to circulate so long as they proved useful as manipulative devices. But he never deviated from the orthodox National Socialist line set by Hitler, and he made sure that his combat officers were clear on the matter. In April 1943, Himmler made a secret speech to the assembled officers of three SS divisions ("Leibstandarte Adolf Hitler," "Das Reich," and "Totenkopf") at Kharkov, in which he gave his views on the future of Europe:

The result, the end of this war, regardless of how many months or even years it lasts, will be this: that the Reich, the German Reich or the Germanic Reich of the German nation, will with just title find confirmation of its evolution, that we have an outlet and a way open to us in the East, and that then, centuries later, a politically German—a Germanic World Empire will be formed. That will be the result, the fruit, of all the many, many sacrifices which have been made and which must still be made.[25]

Here we have the "imperialist tendencies" to which, Steiner claims, the Waffen SS objected. There is not a single word about a European union, only a Germanic Reich and eventually a Germanic World Empire. Further on in his speech, Himmler became more specific:

In the first operation, all those peoples who were at one time part of Germany, part of the German Empire (the Roman Empire of the German Nation) and belonged to us up to 1806 or only till 1648—that is Flanders, Wallonia, and the Netherlands—must and will be incorporated into the Germanic Reich. Over and above this we must have the power to bring into the fold, and make part of

[24] *Ibid.*, p. 68.

[25] Speech by Reichsführer SS Heinrich Himmler at Kharkov, April 1943, Nuremberg Document 1919–PS. The sections quoted are from a mimeographed transcript which, although not complete, is more extensive than the extract published in NCA, II.

our community in a second operation, also those Germanic peoples and states which have never been part and parcel of the German Reich—I mean Denmark and Norway, the Danish and Norwegian people.

Himmler's plan not only rejected a European union of "free states"; it also had no room for a European army. For Himmler the SS remained, at least in theory, a "Germanic" order. Referring to the recruitment of foreigners for the SS he observed:

It has not always been liked and is still not liked by many of the political leaders in these countries. From the beginning I have said to them: "You can do what you like . . . but you may be sure that an SS will be set up in your country, and there is but one SS in Europe, and that SS is the Germanic SS led by the Reichsführer SS. You can resist, or you can offer no resistance; it's all the same to me. We shall do it in any case!" We have told them this curtly, plainly, and clearly from the beginning.

As for the "great concept," the ideal for which the foreign SS man was asked to risk his life, Himmler had only this to offer:

We do not expect you to renounce your nation, or do anything which a proud and self-respecting fellow who loves his country cannot do. We do not expect you to become German out of opportunism. We do expect you to subordinate your national ideal to a greater racial and historical ideal, to the Germanic Reich.[26]

Nowhere, here or later, does Himmler advocate anything other than a Germanic Reich and a Germanic SS—both dominated by and operating for the benefit of Germany. Without Himmler's approval, the dreams of the visionaries in the SS were incapable of realization. Shortly before the end of the war the Waffen SS had indeed become an army of Europeans; it never was a European army.

The Germanic SS

Before the end of 1940 it became clear that the SS could not hope to secure a sizable number of volunteers from Den-

[26] *Ibid.*

mark, Holland, Belgium, and Norway without the support and assistance of local political groups. The pro-German circles in these countries were generally willing to cooperate; but, being for the most part strongly nationalistic, they insisted that their countrymen serve in exclusive national formations, under the command of their own officers.

At the time, Hitler was not favorably inclined toward such a plan, and Himmler ordered Berger to intensify efforts to gather foreign recruits for the integrated SS Division "Wiking." While negotiations with the pro-German groups in the occupied countries continued, Berger cast around for additional sources of foreign manpower. His eye fell on Finland, a nation that had recently fought a gallant but losing war against Russian aggression. In view of the increasing possibility of a German–Soviet conflict, Finland seemed a fertile field for SS recruitment. Acting on information obtained from a group of pro-German Finnish military men, Berger concluded that a battalion of Finns could readily be gathered. On February 13, 1941, he received Himmler's permission to begin recruiting.[27]

Despite serious difficulties with the German Foreign Office and the Finnish Government, Berger managed to establish a Finnish Volunteer Battalion in the Waffen SS. The first group of Finns (116 combat veterans) arrived in Germany during the second week of May, and by the beginning of the Russian campaign 400 Finns were serving with SS Division "Wiking." Additional recruitment during the second half of 1941 raised the number of Finns serving in the Waffen SS to over 1000. Until they were recalled by their government in mid-1943, the Finns constituted one of the most formidable of the foreign SS contingents.[28]

In order to achieve success in his Finnish endeavor, Berger had agreed to permit the Finns (with the temporary exception of the first 400) to serve in a closed battalion, under the command of their own officers. Although this agreement was later

[27] Berger to Himmler, "Finnland," March 6, 1941, Geheim, RFSS/T–175, 110/2634992.
[28] The Finnish volunteers in the Waffen SS are discussed by the present author in an article to appear in the *Vierteljahrshefte für Zeitgeschichte*.

broken, it set a precedent for similar arrangements with volunteers of other nationalities. The planned invasion of the Soviet Union was drawing closer, yet the SS Division "Wiking" was still short of the required Germanic volunteers. Indeed, the Waffen SS as a whole was desperately in need of manpower. Whether they liked it or not, the German leaders were being forced to consider the creation of closed foreign formations.

At the beginning of April, Hitler agreed to the establishment of the SS Freiwilligenstandarte "Nordwest." This regiment was authorized to accept up to 2500 volunteers from Flanders and the Netherlands. The men would not have to meet the usual SS racial requirements and would not be considered SS men; they would, however, be serving in the SS, with all the privileges and responsibilities this entailed.

By establishing a joint Dutch–Flemish formation, the SS was very cleverly catering to the political ambitions of Anton Mussert's NSB (Nationaal Socialistische Beweging) and Staf de Clerq's VNV (Vlaamsch Nationaal Verbond), both of which advocated a culturally autonomous Flemish–Dutch union within a Greater Germanic *(Grossgermanische)* Reich. On April 26, 1941, Berger informed Himmler that de Clerq had swallowed the bait and had promised to assist in the recruiting of VNV members for service in the SS Freiwilligenstandarte "Nordwest." [29]

No sooner had Yugoslavia fallen than the SS set to work recruiting members of the ethnic German community in the Banat. So badly were these men needed that SS Gruppenführer Hausser was ordered to induct racially acceptable volunteers directly into his "Reich" Division while it was still in Yugoslavia.[30] Nevertheless, Himmler was not yet prepared to

29 Berger, in line with Hitler's plans for Belgium, was actually working for the incorporation of Flanders (as well as Wallonia) into the Reich; not into the *Grossgermanische* Reich, but rather as part of the more limited *Grossdeutsche* Reich. Under this plan Flanders and Wallonia would simply be two *Gaue* (provinces) of Germany. Toward this end, the SS was operating through the pro-Nazi DEVLAG (Deutsche-Flämische Arbeitsgemeinschaft), which had been established in 1935 with German support. DEVLAG, under its leader Jef van de Wiele (who had been designated by Hitler the future Gauleiter of Flanders), stood opposed to de Clerq's VNV

cast aside the *Untermensch* philosophy. When Berger requested permission to organize "64 racially suitable and 615 racially unsuitable Ukrainians" into a nucleus for the eventual establishment of a Ukrainian volunteer formation, Himmler refused.[31] Two more years and a succession of German military reverses would be required before the Slav was to be accorded the privilege of dying in an SS uniform.

On April 30, 1941, Hitler set the final date for Operation Barbarossa. The invasion of the Soviet Union was scheduled to begin on June 22, 1941. Himmler immediately ordered his recruiting chief to procure 20,000 men for the Waffen SS within the next month. As a result of Hitler's intervention, the OKW reluctantly lifted the restrictions on recruitment; for the month of May, the Waffen SS was permitted to accept an unlimited number of enlistees. But to cut its losses, the OKW added the proviso that the volunteers must enlist for a twelve-year term; few, it was felt, would be willing to make such a sacrifice.

One would think that by 1941 the military authorities would have learned something from their previous dealings with the SS. Apparently they had not. Many Waffen SS recruiting officials simply assured potential volunteers that the twelve-year requirement was merely a formality, and that they would be released at the end of the war or in two years, whichever proved to be the longer period.[32] By May 29 Berger was able to report that "the order that was given has been carried out." A week later he informed Himmler that "altogether 22,361 men will have arrived in the barracks of the reserve units of the Waffen SS by

---

and its advocacy of an autonomous Flemish–Dutch union. *Hitlers Lagebesprechungen* (Stuttgart, 1962), p. 507, n. 2. See also SS Führungshauptamt, "Aufstellung der SS-Freiwilligenstandarte 'Nordwest,' " April 3, 1941, Geheim, RFSS/T–175, 110/2634951ff., and Berger to Himmler, "Flandern," April 26, 1941, Geheim, RFSS/T–175, 110/2634879 f.

[30] Berger to Himmler, "Werbung in Jugoslawien," April 26, 1941, Geheim, RFSS/T–175, 110/2634794.

[31] Berger to Himmler, "Ukrainer," April 28, 1941, Geheim, RFSS/T–175, 110/2634861. For the text of Himmler's refusal see 2634860.

[32] See various reports from Berger to Himmler entitled "20,000 Mann-Aktion," beginning on May 14, 1941, RFSS/T–175, 110/2634853, and running backward on this roll to frame 2634765.

June 9." The majority of these men were young volunteers, many from the still unmustered class of 1923. By the time the OKW discovered that the SS recruiters had by their promises negated the twelve-year enlistment requirement it was too late to do anything but complain.[33]

To help fill the required 20,000-man quota, Berger also had ordered the call-up of eligible members of the General SS and had intensified his efforts to enlist foreign volunteers, but in this latter area the pickings had again proved slim. Aside from the 400 Finnish veterans who had been sent to join SS Division "Wiking," the SS had managed to scrape together only about 2000 west European volunteers by June.[34]

It was at this point that Himmler decided to support the formation of national legions in order to tap the manpower resources of the pro-Nazi but strongly nationalistic groups in the German-occupied lands.

Germanic Legions of the Waffen SS

A few days after the German invasion of the Soviet Union the Führer approved the formation of national legions to take part in the "battle against Bolshevism." A legion was to be established for each of the German-occupied nations of Western Europe. In addition, Hitler suggested that similar legions be solicited from such ideologically friendly states as Italy, Spain, and Croatia.[35]

Hitler's original intention was to let the SS handle the entire foreign-legion movement. But Himmler was, at this time, interested only in legions composed of "Germanics." During the early days of July a number of high-level conferences were held between representatives of the Wehrmacht, SS, and Foreign Ministry to work out the details of Hitler's plan. It was finally

[33] See Berger to Himmler, "Beschwerde des OKW über Werbung Maiaktion," June 7, 1941, Geheim, RFSS/T–175, 110/2634753ff.

[34] Berger to Himmler, "20,000 Mann-Aktion," June 6, 1941, Geheim, RFSS/T–175, 110/2634766ff.

[35] Himmler, "Aktennotiz," Führerhauptquartier, June 29, 1941, RFSS/T–175, 106/2629090 f. This memorandum was reproduced as Nuremberg Document NO–1087.

decided that legions composed of Norwegians, Netherlanders, Swedes, Danes, and Flemings would be set up within the framework of the Waffen SS, while units of Croats, Spaniards, and Frenchmen were to be organized by the Wehrmacht.[36] During the time the details of the legion program were being debated in Berlin, Berger's agents were going ahead with the recruitment. The promise of national formations under the command of native officers had the desired effect. Hundreds of volunteers enlisted the first week. Despite the resistance of the Danish Government, 500 Danes—nearly half of them members of the armed forces—had volunteered by the time the SS Führungshauptamt officially established the Freiwilligenverband "Danemark" on July 12, 1941.[37] While recruiting was still under way in the lowlands, a group of Flemings serving in the recently created Freiwilligenstandarte "Nordwest" was transferred to form the nucleus of the Freiwilligen Legion "Flandern." Similarly, a handful of Netherlanders was taken from the same regiment to create a cadre for the Freiwilligen Legion "Niederlande." [38]

[36] Berger to Himmler, "Entwurf des Führererlasses über den Einsatz ausländischer Freiwilliger," July 9, 1941, Geheime Kommandosache, RFSS/T–175, 106/2629026ff. The Swedish legion never materialized, but the SS organized a Wallonian legion which it turned over to the Army for service; it was transferred back to the Waffen SS along with the French legion in 1943.

[37] SS Führungshauptamt, "Aufstellung des Freiwilligenverbandes 'Danemark,' " July 12, 1941, Geheim, RFSS/T–175, 110/2634700 f. In an attempt to prevent the formation of the legion, the Danish authorities branded as traitors all military personnel who enlisted and deprived them of their pension rights. Berger was forced to fly to Copenhagen to retrieve the situation. Himmler, furious at the Danish Government's action, ordered that the pensions be paid by the SS and that Denmark be forced to accept the bill. See Berger to Himmler, "Bericht der Dienstreise nach Danemark vom 17.–18. 7. 41," July 19, 1941, Geheim, RFSS/T–175, 110/2634671ff.; telegram from Copenhagen to Himmler, July 20, 1941, 106/2628961; Himmler to Berger, July 28, 1941, 110/2634668.

[38] SS Führungshauptamt, "Gliederung der SS-Freiwilligenstandarte 'Nordwest' und Aufstellung der Freiw. Legion 'Niederlande,' " July 26, 1941, Geheim, RFSS/T–175, 110/2634655 f.; "SS-Freiw. Standarte 'Nordwest' und Legion 'Niederlande,' " September 24, 1941, Geheim, 110/2634459ff.

By the end of July the first contingent of 480 Danes under the command of former Danish Army Colonel Krhyssing was undergoing training in Germany and some 600 men of the Legion "Flandern" were similarly engaged in Poland. The first Norwegian legionnaires arrived at Kiel on July 29 under the command of Captain Jörgen Bakke, and two days later the SSFHA issued an order establishing the Freiwilligen Legion "Norwegen." Toward the middle of August some 1000 volunteers for Legion "Niederlande," under the command of former Dutch Army Colonel Stroink, were on their way to Poland to join the unit's cadre in combat training.[39]

The Waffen SS had established four national legions in as many weeks. Despite this promising beginning, the legion movement did not fulfill the expectations of its founders. No sooner were the legions in training than serious friction developed between the volunteers and their German instructors. Within a few weeks, Colonel Stroink and five of the twenty-three Dutch officers in Legion "Niederlande" had resigned. The Flemings, who had no native commander to intercede for them, suffered grievous indignities at the hands of the German training personnel. Some months later, Staf de Clerq submitted a long complaint to Himmler about the mistreatment of his countrymen. Flemish volunteers had been beaten, threatened with pistols, and subjected to continual verbal abuse; they had been publicly called a "filthy people," a "nation of idiots," and a "race of Gypsies." [40] Such treatment was hardly conducive to the continued growth and development of the formation. It is therefore not surprising that Legion "Flandern" totaled a mere 875 men at the beginning of 1942. And of even this small number, the greater part had been tricked into enlisting. According to

[39] SS Führungshauptamt, "Aufstellung der Freiwilligenlegion 'Norwegen,'" July 30, 1941, Geheim, RFSS/T–175, 110/2634601ff. See also Steiner, *Die Freiwilligen,* pp. 125ff. By the end of July, the number of men in the legions was: Danemark 480, Niederlande 1100, Flandern 600. No figure is given for Norwegen. See SS Ergänzungsamt to Berger, "Einberufung zur Waffen-SS," August 1, 1941, RFSS/T–175, 110/2634571ff.

[40] Berger to Jüttner, "Vermerk v. Staf de Clerq," March 25, 1942, Geheim, RFSS/T–175, 111/2635480ff.

de Clerq, 500 Flemings working for the Germans in northern France had been induced by a promise of higher wages to volunteer for labor in Poland; upon their arrival, they discovered that they had actually "volunteered" for service in the Waffen SS.[41]

In Denmark, the Netherlands, and Norway, the initial interest shown by pro-German elements also waned as a result of the manner in which the volunteer program was being mismanaged. Although no attempt was made to apply the usual SS racial and physical standards (only the regular Wehrmacht requirements had to be met), none of the legions had reached regimental strength by year's end. The response had been greatest in the Netherlands, which had provided 2559 men for Legion "Niederlande." Far behind came Legion "Norwegen" with 1218 men and Freikorps "Danemark" (the designation *Legion* had been dropped in this case) with 1164. The thoroughly disillusioned Flemings brought up the rear with their 875 men.[42]

By November 1941, the Dutch and Flemish legions had completed a light training program in Poland and were preparing to join the 2nd SS Infantry Brigade behind the Leningrad front. Shortly before their departure, Himmler issued a comprehensive directive governing the status of the national legions. It placed the legionnaires under German military law and SS regulations, ordered that they be tendered the SS rank equivalent to that previously held in their national army, did not grant them German citizenship but bound them to Adolf Hitler by a personal oath, provided regular SS pay and compensation for dependents, specifically indicated that legionnaires were not SS men and were to wear the SS uniform with a national emblem in place of the SS runes, and stated that while they were normally to serve in an exclusive national formation under their own officers, they could, on request—and if qualified—be

---

[41] *Ibid.*

[42] SS Führungshauptamt, "Übersicht über die in der Waffen SS befindlichen germanischen Freiwilligen: Stand v. 15. Januar 1942," RFSS/T–175, 109/2633910.

transferred to a regular SS formation.[43] With slight modifications, this directive governed the legions as long as they existed. But, as we shall see, it was often disregarded in practice, and the consequences for the legion movement were manifold.

During the second week of January 1942, the Russians launched a surprise counteroffensive north of Novgorod in an attempt to envelop the German armies besieging Leningrad. In short order the Soviet forces had thrust a deep salient into the German line. To prevent a breakthrough along this thinly defended sector of the front, the Germans threw into the fray every formation at their disposal: engineers, artillerymen, construction units, Police formations, supply units—and the newly arrived Dutch and Flemish legions. Poorly trained, ill equipped, partially demoralized, and sent into action piecemeal, the legionnaires were badly mauled during the winter's fighting.

Meanwhile the two remaining SS legions were proving to be even greater disappointments. The two lowland legions, in spite of their shortcomings, were at least actively engaged in combat; but neither the Danes nor the Norwegians were even remotely combat-ready at the beginning of the year. Ordered by Himmler to investigate the delay, SS Gruppenführer Krüger reported that, in the case of the Freikorps "Danemark," the trouble was poor leadership. According to Krüger, the Danish commander, Legion-Obersturmbannführer (Lieutenant Colonel) Krhyssing, and his deputy, Sturmbannführer (Major) Jörgensen, were anti-Nazis and were doing nothing to prepare the Freikorps for combat. The discipline in the unit was poor and there was a great deal of friction between Danish Nazis and anti-Nazis. But Krüger felt that with the proper leadership the legion could be made ready for combat in a few weeks.

[43] Reichsführer SS, "Aufstellung und Einsatz ausländischer Freiwilligenverbände," November 6, 1941, Geheime Kommandosache, RFSS/T–175, 109/2633820ff. See also Berger's order of January 29, 1943, governing the acceptance of Germanic volunteers for the Waffen SS and the national legions, Nuremberg Document NO–1479, United States Military Tribunal IV, Case 11, Prosecution Document Book 66–G (mimeographed), pp. 40ff. Hereafter cited as Nuremberg Document NO–1479, USMT IV, Case 11, PDB 66–G, pp. 40ff.

A squadron of the 8th SS Kavalleriedivision "Florian Geyer" riding past a disabled Russian tank, 1944. (Ullstein–Copress)

After awarding the Swords to the Knight's Cross to SS Obergruppenführer (General) Felix Steiner (middle), Hitler presents the Oak Leaves to the Knight's Cross to SS Sturmbannführer (Major) Leon Degrelle, commander of the SS Freiwilligen-Panzerbrigade "Wallonien," 1944. (Ullstein–Copress)

Exhausted SS infantry take a brief rest while retreating to avoid encirclement by the Red Army, 1944. The camouflage jackets worn by these men were standard issue; although the Army developed a similar jacket, few Army personnel were supplied with them. Camouflage jackets were therefore a fairly reliable means of identifying troops of the Waffen SS. (Ullstein–Truöl)

In view of the national sensitivity of the Danes, Krüger ruled out the substitution of a German commander. He had, however, sounded out the Danes on the appointment of SS Sturmbannführer Christian von Schalburg, a former Danish officer then serving with the SS Division "Wiking," and found a majority of the legionnaires willing to accept him as a replacement for Krhyssing. Urging Himmler to approve the change, Krüger pointed out that Schalburg had an excellent combat record and was also a "reliable National Socialist." [44] Himmler eventually concurred, and under their new and energetic commander the Danes were quickly whipped into shape. In May 1942, Freikorps "Danemark" was sent as a replacement unit to the elite SS Division "Totenkopf."[45] For the next year, first with "Totenkopf" and later with the 1st SS Infantry Brigade, the Danes remained in action along the Russian front.[46]

The Norwegians had in the meantime been sent to the Leningrad front to gain some combat experience. Starting in late February, the legionnaires were sent out on patrols and small-scale raiding operations. Of all the legions, "Norwegen" suffered the fewest casualties during the first half of 1942. It also did the least amount of fighting. In the second half of the year, the Norwegians joined the Danes in the 1st SS Infantry Brigade.

Thus a year after the start of the movement, the Waffen SS had four legions—a matter of perhaps 5000 men—engaged in the "battle against Bolshevism."

The West European SS in 1942 and Thereafter

Although the original intention had been to maintain the legions separately from the Germanic SS, the two movements

[44] SS-Gruf. Krüger to Himmler, February 13, 1942, RFSS/T–175, 111/2635498ff., and telegram from SS-Brig. Hansen, February 22, 1942, Geheim, 2635496 f.

[45] Steiner, *Die Freiwilligen*, p. 137. Only parts of the Totenkopf Division were still in combat; some of its units had been withdrawn from the front for refitting.

[46] For a tendentious account of the combat achievements of "Danemark" (also spelled "Danmark") see "Zur Kriegsgeschichte des Freikorps 'Danmark,' " *Der Freiwillige* (September 1964), pp. 7ff.

tended to flow together after the beginning of 1942. Once the first flush of enthusiasm had passed, it became clear that future volunteers for the legions would have to be drawn from the same source as that used to maintain a flow of replacements for SS Division "Wiking"—the discontented, adventurous, and occasionally idealistic youth of German-occupied Western Europe. At first the standards for enlistment in the legions were somewhat lower than those for the SS. But this distinction became increasingly less noticeable as the need for manpower forced the Waffen SS to reduce its racial and physical requirements. By mid-1943 the legions and the Germanic SS had been merged.

Even before the end of 1941 it had become evident that the Germanic SS program was in trouble. The basic problem was that the original promises made to the volunteers by the SS were not being kept. Thus foreign officers, after six months with the SS, were in many cases still being forced to serve as enlisted men. Finnish NCOs, veterans of the Russo–Finnish war, were "unable to pass beyond the rank of private." Other foreign officers in the SS were abruptly discharged and sent home without any explanation. Men who had enlisted with the understanding that they would be assigned to closed national formations were indiscriminately sent as replacements to all-German SS units. Thus, in one instance, nine Danes with only four weeks' training were sent to the SS Division "Reich" and, shortly after their arrival, were killed in action. The fact was reported by enemy propagandists and, according to Berger, turned "all of Denmark" against the SS.[47]

A more serious grievance was that foreigners who had volunteered for one-year service in the Waffen SS, during the early stages of the foreign movement, were not being released at the end of their enlistments. This was especially true of the Danes and Norwegians serving in the SS Division "Wiking." As a result, some volunteers sent home on furlough or on convalescent leave had slipped across the Swedish border to avoid

[47] For a complete summary of the problems faced by the SS leaders in connection with the foreign volunteers' movement at the beginning of 1942, see the long report (with annexes) from Berger to SS Führungshauptamt, "Freiwillige aus germanischen Ländern," February 2, 1942, Geheime Kommandosache, RFSS/T–175, 109/2633657ff.

further service. A much more drastic step was taken by two foreign SS men (a Dane and a Norwegian) serving in Regiment "Nordland" of the SS Division "Wiking"; they left their advance outpost in the front line and deserted to the Russians. For the Waffen SS it was the first recorded case of its kind and touched off a reaction far out of proportion to the event's actual significance.[48]

Apart from the many broken promises, the foreign volunteers complained bitterly about the manner in which they were being treated by their German Waffenbrüder. The indignities suffered by the Flemings have already been mentioned. None of the other volunteer groups seems to have been subjected to such a concentrated dose of maltreatment. But many foreigners assigned to predominantly German units found it very difficult to make friends; moreover, no allowances were made for their inability to understand or speak German. As one volunteer put it: "Every tie, every connection, between German and Norwegian is lacking." Among other things, the Germans made the mistake of believing that all the volunteers were dedicated National Socialists and would therefore accept any treatment out of idealism. According to this same volunteer, however, most of his countrymen were not Nazis, but simply patriots who preferred "the protection of Germany to that of England." Many of the volunteers from Norway had been impressed by the superiority of Germany, its system, and its new ideas, but "this was before they knew it for what it really was." By 1942 they were so disillusioned that "even the old Norwegian Nazis could no longer deny it." [49]

Similar complaints by other volunteers caused their sponsors in the home country to file protests with Berger's SS Hauptamt. The reaction from Finland, the only truly independent nation with a significant contingent of its citizens serving in the Waffen SS, was of special concern to the SS leaders in Berlin. Reporting on a conversation with State Police Chief Aaltonen,

---

[48] See report by Wiking commander SS Gruppenführer Steiner, March 12, 1942, RFSS/T–175, 107/2631083 f.

[49] Secret affidavit by SS man Per Imerslund, a Norwegian volunteer in the Waffen SS; annex to report from Berger to SSFHA, February 2, 1942, RFSS/T–175, 109/2633669ff.

one of the sponsors of the Finnish SS battalion, Berger's deputy in Finland disclosed that returning Finnish SS men were angry that, contrary to agreement, their battalion was commanded by German officers. Moreover, these Germans had little or no combat experience, yet they persisted in treating veteran Finnish officers and NCOs "like recruits." The Finnish Police Chief believed that their attitude clearly indicated that the Germans "had not the slightest understanding of the Finnish mentality." The continuance of this sort of treatment, Aaltonen felt, would lead Finnish volunteers to "shoot their German officers the first time they go into combat," as indeed a group home on leave over Christmas had, in his presence, threatened to do.[50] Similar complaints by other Finnish notables finally resulted in the filing of a formal protest by the Finnish Foreign Minister.

To Gottlob Berger, the apostle of the foreign volunteer movement, the situation appeared critical. On February 2, 1942, after having collected sufficient evidence to support the claims of mistreatment, he sent his findings to Himmler. "The procurement of volunteers from Germanic and ethnically German areas," Berger reported, "is becoming increasingly difficult and will cease altogether unless basic changes are made." [51]

The major problem, Berger informed his chief, lay in the division of authority which existed between the SS Hauptamt and the SS Führungshauptamt. Recruitment and over-all responsibility for the foreign volunteer program were functions of Berger's SS Hauptamt; but once the volunteers took their service oaths, they came under the authority of Hans Jüttner's SS Führungshauptamt. To the practical soldiers in the operational headquarters of the Waffen SS, the foreigners were just so many bodies that had to be trained, equipped, and sent into battle as quickly and efficiently as possible. Inevitably, the foreign volunteers heard one tune from Berger's recruiters and quite another once they were firmly in the hands of the Waffen

---

[50] SS Obersturmführer Gerlinger to Berger, "Besprechung mit den Chef der Finnischen Staatspolizei Aaltonen," January 8, 1942, Geheim, RFSS/T–175, 109/2633666.
[51] Berger to SSFHA, "Freiwillige aus germanischen Ländern," February 2, 1942, Geheime Kommandosache, RFSS/T–175, 109/2633657.

SS. The failure to honor the promises made to the volunteers at the time of their enlistment, the mistreatment of individuals and groups, and the total lack of concern with the political implications of these acts had brought the whole foreign volunteer movement to the brink of complete collapse.

Acting on Berger's recommendation, Himmler issued a series of directives designed to correct the worst abuses in the treatment of the foreign volunteers. The men whose enlistments had expired were released from SS service, and the number of native officers in each foreign unit was increased. At the same time, a special effort was made to select qualified young foreigners for admittance to the SS officer academy at Bad Tölz. As a result of these steps, the foreign units were eventually led by young SS-trained foreign officers in the lower grades and by German officers in higher grades, with an added stiffening of experienced German NCOs and specialists. One of Himmler's directives required all responsible German personnel assigned to units composed of foreigners to undergo a two-week orientation course conducted by specialists from the Germanic Directorate of Berger's SS Hauptamt. To avoid any future leadership difficulties, Himmler personally reserved the right to appoint all the officers in the foreign units of the Waffen SS. In a final memorandum, he reminded the SS leaders of the importance of the foreign volunteer movement and the interest that the Führer himself had in the matter.[52]

These remedial measures were at best only partially suc-

[52] Despite his interest in the foreign volunteer program, Hitler had long remained skeptical of its practicability and had only been won over by Himmler's continuous urgings. The Führer's doubts seem never to have been entirely allayed, and as early as April 5, 1942, he expressed them once more to Himmler: "In any case, we must not commit the mistake of enlisting in the German Army foreigners who seem to us to be worthwhile fellows, unless they can prove that they're utterly steeped in the idea of a Germanic Reich. While we are on the subject, I'm skeptical about the participation of all those foreign legions in our struggle on the Eastern front. One mustn't forget that, unless he is convinced of his racial membership of the Germanic Reich, the foreign legionary is bound to feel that he's betraying his country. The fall of the Hapsburg monarch clearly shows the full size of this danger. On that occasion, too, it was thought the other peoples could be won over—Poles, Czechs, etc.—by giving them a military formation in the Austrian Army. Yet at the decisive moment it

cessful; but they saved the Germanic volunteer movement from disintegrating. With the correction of the worst abuses, the Finnish authorities permitted the 1180-man Finnish Volunteer Battalion to be sent to fight with the SS Division "Wiking" for a one-year period.[53] In other cases, however, irreparable damage had been done by the inept handling of the volunteers. According to Berger, "the unceremonious discharge of one [Swedish officer] . . . resulted in the closing off to us of the heretofore friendly Swedish officer corps," thus destroying a "new and promising recruiting effort." [54]

In any event, the Germanic-legion movement never recovered its initial momentum. Before long enlistments dwindled to the point where they no longer covered the losses the legions sustained in battle. By the end of 1942 the legions had become ineffective in the type of warfare being waged along the Russian front. It was therefore decided to regroup them into a larger formation.

The vehicle for this regroupment was the newly established SS Panzergrenadierdivision "Nordland," which Hitler had authorized at the end of 1942 as part of the first major expansion of the Waffen SS. The 650 survivors of Freikorps "Danemark" became the nucleus of Panzer-Grenadier-Regiment "Danmark" (the name was changed to reflect native spelling); the 1700 members of Legion "Niederlande" became part of Panzer-Grenadier-Regiment "Nederland" (here too the spelling of the name was changed): and the remaining 600 men of Legion "Norwegen" constituted the base for Panzer-Grenadier-Regi-

became obvious that precisely these men were the standard-bearers of rebellion."

Hitler's comment was an accurate prediction of the future of the foreign SS program, particularly in regard to the eastern SS. The warning was ignored by Himmler. Hitler's statement was made during his evening dinner on April 5, 1942, *Hitler's Secret Conversations,* p. 384.

[53] Steiner, *Die Freiwilligen,* pp. 76, 120. The number of Finns in the Waffen SS during this period is given in "Übersicht über die in der Waffen SS befindlichen germanischen Freiwilligen: Stand von 15. Januar 1942," RFSS/T–175, 109/2633910.

[54] Berger to SSFHA, "Freiwillige aus germanischen Ländern," February 2, 1942, Geheime Kommandosache, RFSS/T–175, 109/2633658.

ment "Norge." The three regiments of "Nordland" were filled out by transfers from SS Division "Wiking," new recruits (not legionnaires) from the "Germanic" lands, and large numbers of native Germans. "Flandern," the black sheep among the legions, was completely broken up and its personnel was used to fill gaps in a number of Waffen SS formations.[55] Thus the national legions were merged with the Germanic SS, and a new phase in the mobilization of west European manpower began.

The great expansion of the Waffen SS that took place during the last two years of the war was reflected in the growth of the west European SS. Paradoxically, German military reverses and the increasing danger of an Allied invasion of Western Europe worked to the advantage of SS recruitment in this area. Those who had collaborated with the Germans now found themselves in an extremely unpleasant position. They feared not only Allied retribution but also local resistance movements, which endangered the lives of the more active collaborators. For many of these men, the shadowy dangers of the eastern front seemed less frightening than the very real dangers at home. By drawing on these elements the Waffen SS was able to achieve a significant increase in the size of its west European formations.

Before the end of 1943 the Regiment "Nederland" had been taken out of SS Division "Nordland" (which now became a German–Scandinavian formation) and reorganized into an independent brigade. A reconstituted and enlarged Flemish formation was given the designation SS-Freiwilligen-Sturmbrigade "Langemarck." At the same time, the French Volunteer Regiment and the Wallonian Legion, both of which had been serving in the German Army, were transferred to the Waffen SS. Although none of these formations ever exceeded brigade strength, they ended the war as nominal divisions, under the designations 23rd SS-Freiwilligen-Panzergrenadierdivision "Nederland"; 27th SS-Freiwilligen-Grenadierdivision "Langemarck"; 28th SS-Freiwilligen-Grenadierdivision "Wallonien";

---

[55] Memorandum by Himmler, "Aufstellung des Germanischen Korps," March 3, 1943, Geheime Kommandosache, RFSS/T–175, 111/2635157ff.; and SSFHA, "14. (germ.) SS-Panzer-Grenadier-Division 'Nordland,' " March 22, 1943, Geheime Kommandosache, RFSS/T–175, 108/2631184 f.

33rd Waffen-Grenadierdivision der SS "Charlemagne" (franz. Nr. 1).[56]

Unlike the east European members of the Waffen SS, the west Europeans generally fought well; their combat performance even seems to have improved as German military fortunes declined. With no future in their homelands except a trial for treason, they often fought with greater determination than the Germans themselves. In the desperate struggle to prevent the Russians from reaching Berlin, the west European formations of the Waffen SS were the backbone of the defense. And it is surely one of the ironies of recent history that within the encircled German capital the last defenders of the entombed Führer included the Danes and Norwegians of SS Division "Nordland," a battle group of French SS men from the Division "Charlemagne," and a battalion of Latvian SS men belonging to the 15th SS Division.[57]

[56] SSFHA, "Bezeichnung der Feldtruppenteile der Waffen SS," October 22, 1943, Geheime Kommandosache, RFSS/T–175, 111/2635138ff.; *Hitlers Lagebesprechungen*, p. 536; Keilig, *Das Deutsche Heer*, II, Section 141, pp. 18ff. For a tendentious account of the combat achievements of "Langemarck" (previously Legion "Flandern"), see the three-part article in the February, March, and April 1965 issues of *Der Freiwillige*.

The Waffen SS also undertook the recruitment of an Italian SS formation after the capitulation of Italy in 1943. By June 1944, the Waffen-Grenadierbrigade der SS (ital. Nr. 1) had been established. Apparently this formation was not considered reliable enough to be used in combat against the advancing Allied forces, and it seems to have been employed exclusively against partisans behind the north Italian front. In 1945 the brigade was nominally redesignated a division and given the number 29, which was available after the dissolution of the Russian SS division that had previously borne it. There is also some evidence that a second SS division, the 24th SS-Gebirgskarstjägerdivision (roughly "rock-scaling mountain rifle division"), was created by enrolling ethnic German volunteers from northern Italy. Neither of these divisions is listed in the OKW list; this suggests that they were not under military control and therefore were at best part of Himmler's rear-area security forces. See Hausser, *op. cit.*, pp. 161, 192; Reitlinger, *op. cit.*, pp. 391 f.; *Hitlers Lagebesprechungen*, p. 536, n. 1; F. W. Deakin, *The Brutal Friendship: Mussolini, Hitler and the Fall of Italian Fascism* (New York, 1962), pp. 574, 593, 725 f.; "Die Aufstellung neuer italienischer Verbände und ihr Einstatz," KTB/OKW, IV, 585.

[57] Steiner, *Die Freiwilligen*, pp. 328ff.

CHAPTER SEVEN

The East European SS:

Mobilization of Foreign Nationals, II

THROUGHOUT the summer of 1941 the Wehrmacht surged ever deeper into the Soviet Union. One Russian army after another was routed, encircled, or annihilated. At the end of September the strategic objectives the German High Command had set at the beginning of the campaign were largely fulfilled: Leningrad had been placed under siege; Kiev had been taken and the Ukraine was in German hands as far as the Donetz; and Bock's Army Group Center was preparing to make its final push toward Moscow. To many Germans (including Hitler) it seemed as if Russia had been militarily defeated.

On November 21, German tanks entered Rostov, opening the way to the oil-rich Caucasus. In the center the last mass Russian army had been shattered, and German forces formed a semicircle only twenty to thirty miles from Moscow. But the Russian bear was not quite dead. To their amazement, the Germans found the resistance of the Red Army increasing in the face of what seemed imminent defeat. And by the end of November, the icy Russian winter had set in.

The Russian Winter Counteroffensive

At this moment of crisis, the Russian High Command decided to play its last card: the so-called Siberian troops of the Far Eastern Command, which contained some of the most formidable units in the entire Red Army. Assured by its agents in Tokyo (the Sorge group) that the Japanese intended to strike south into the Pacific rather than north against Mongolia and Siberia, the Soviet High Command early in November began transferring troops from the Far East to positions behind the Moscow front. Although the Russians held back the bulk of the Siberian troops, on November 18, the German 112th Infantry Division

was attacked by a Siberian division from the Russian 10th Army and an armoured brigade newly arrived from the Far East with a full complement of T 34's. . . . To these shivering and practically defenceless men the sight of the Siberians in their white quilted uniforms, lavishly equipped with tommy guns and grenades, riding along at thirty miles an hour on the dreaded T 34's, was too much, and the division broke up.[1]

This was only a taste of things to come. On November 27, the Russians counterattacked in the south, retaking Rostov and driving the Germans back nearly fifty miles in what was the first major setback suffered by the German Army in World War II.

Meanwhile, Hitler, convinced that the Red Army was incapable of a sustained counteroffensive, ordered a final, all-out attack on the Russian capital. On December 1, in subzero temperatures, the greatest armored force ever concentrated for one operation surged toward Moscow. On the second day of the drive a German reconnaissance unit penetrated into a Moscow suburb and reported that it was within sight of the Kremlin's towers. This was the nearest the Wehrmacht ever got to the city. On December 3, the reconnaissance unit was thrown out of the suburb, and within two more days the German drive ground to a halt against bitter Russian resistance; the Red Army's massive counteroffensive, which Stalin had approved on November 30, was only hours away.

After more than five months of steady advance, the German offensive had finally burned itself out; along a 200-mile semicircular front, Army Group Center lay exhausted in temperatures which plunged as low as minus 40 degrees Centigrade. While Hitler's generals counseled withdrawal to a winter

[1] Clark, *op. cit.*, p. 174.

defense line, the Russians struck. On December 6, 1941, seventeen armies, spearheaded by Siberian divisions trained and equipped for winter warfare, smashed into Army Group Center. This sudden and unexpected blow by a superior force shattered the German line before Moscow, driving it back a full forty miles. Only Hitler's order calling for each unit to stand fast and offer "fanatical resistance" regardless of the cost prevented a complete German rout. [2]

In the wake of the debacle in Russia, Hitler once again conducted a wholesale purge of the Army's leadership. Some thirty-five general officers were relieved of their commands and sent home in varying degrees of disgrace. Brauchitsch was dismissed, and Hitler himself assumed the position of Commander-in-Chief of the Army (Oberbefehlshaber des Heeres). "This little matter of operational command," he declared, "is something anyone can handle." After 1941, no major, and few minor, operational decisions affecting the Army were taken without Hitler's approval. In retrospect it is evident that the Führer's increasing disdain for the generals worked to the advantage of the SS. Certainly Himmler's position improved as that of the High Command declined. Nevertheless, despite the almost superhuman efforts of the SS divisions during the fall and winter of 1941, Hitler was not yet prepared to approve a major change in the status of the Waffen SS.

By February 1942 the Russian offensive had slackened, and during the following month the Germans managed to stabilize a line about 100 miles behind that of their farthest advance. Although Russian losses were much higher than those of the Germans, the Wehrmacht had suffered over a million casualties since the beginning of the war in the East, some 35 per cent of the force committed. Of this number, well over 200,000 were dead, nearly ten times as many as had been killed in the western campaign of 1940.[3]

Characteristically, Waffen SS losses were proportionally much higher than those of the Army. The SS Division "Das

---

[2] Philippi and Heim, *op. cit.*, pp. 94ff. There is an excellent evaluation of Hitler's role during the winter crisis in Clark, *op. cit.*, pp. 182 f.

[3] Philippi and Heim, *op. cit.*, p. 109; Werth, *op. cit.*, pp. 259 f.

Reich," for example, had lost 60 per cent of its combat strength by mid-November, including 40 per cent of its officers; yet it spearheaded a major attack on Moscow, achieving one of the deepest penetrations of the offensive. During the course of the Russian winter counteroffensive, "Das Reich" (like all the Waffen SS units on the eastern front) attempted to obey Hitler's "no withdrawal" order to the letter and hence suffered even greater losses; as of February 10, 1942, the division had lost a total of 10,690 men (not including officers). While "Das Reich" was the hardest hit of all the SS divisions, the others also bore heavy casualties.[4] Before long all of Himmler's reserves were required merely to keep the field units of the Waffen SS battleworthy.

By the time the Russian counteroffensive was halted, the Waffen SS had suffered losses totaling more than 43,000 men. It quickly became apparent that the quota of native German recruits which the OKW had allotted to the Waffen SS would barely cover losses in the existing field formations.[5] Any expansion of the Waffen SS would therefore depend on the success of the foreign recruitment drive. In view of the difficulties encountered with the west European or "Germanic" volunteers, the SS authorities directed their attention toward the East.

Volksdeutsche in the Waffen SS

It has already been noted that by the last year of the war foreign-born SS men outnumbered those of German birth. Many of these were ethnic Germans, or *Volksdeutsche*, from areas outside the Reich. According to a document issued by the German government in 1938, *Volksdeutsche* were those who were not citizens of the German Reich but who were German in language and culture. By mid-1944 more than 150,000 ethnic Germans were serving in the Waffen SS.[6]

[4] The casualty figures for "Das Reich" and the other SS formations are given in SSFHA, "Gesamtaufstellung des Mannschaftserzatzes für die SS-Divisionen und Regimenter seit Beginn des Ostfeldzuges," March 3, 1942, RFSS/T–175, 108/263178ff.

[5] Berger to Himmler, "Einberufungen im Jahr 1941," March 6, 1942, Geheime Kommandosache, RFSS/T–175, 109/2633780 f.

[6] Nuremberg Document NG–295, USMT IV, Case 11, PDB 72–D, p. 12. The number of *Volksdeutsche* in the Waffen SS was given in the "Rede des

The first large-scale recruitment of ethnic Germans for the SS took place in Romania shortly after the beginning of the war. During the spring of 1940, Berger, working through the political leader of the German community in Transylvania, his son-in-law, Andreas Schmidt, secured more than 1000 young volunteers. To avoid diplomatic complications, the men were sent to Germany in the guise of industrial and agricultural laborers.[7]

Flushed by his success in Romania, Berger began to think in terms of an SS recruitment effort that would embrace all the ethnic German communities in the world. In a memorandum he submitted to Himmler in August 1940, Berger suggested that the Balkans, especially Romania, Hungary, and Yugoslavia, with an estimated million and a half ethnic Germans, would be the most fertile area in which to launch his plan.[8] At the time, only clandestine recruitment was possible. But by mid-1941, Yugoslavia was under Axis control, and Romania and Hungary were allies of Germany.

Shortly after the fall of Yugoslavia a small-scale SS recruiting effort in Serbia yielded a modest number of ethnic German volunteers, who were incorporated directly into SS Division "Reich." On its way through Romania en route from Yugoslavia to Germany, the division picked up an additional 600 ethnic German volunteers and smuggled them out of the country in its vehicles.[9] But Berger had more ambitious plans. He believed that with the proper backing and organization it would be possible to create an entire SS division composed of ethnic Germans from Yugoslavia. Himmler liked the idea; it would

---

Reichsführers-SS auf der Ordensburg Sonthofen," May 5, 1944, RFSS/T–175, 92/2613482. An excellent study based on the Nuremberg material is Robert Herzog, *Die Volksdeutschen in der Waffen-SS* ("Studien des Instituts für Besatzungsfragen in Tübingen zu den deutschen Besetzungen in 2. Weltkrieg," No. 5; Tübingen, 1955), mimeographed.

[7] Nuremberg Documents NO–1605, NG–1112, NO–3362; USMT IV, Case 11, PDB 66–G, pp. 73ff., and PDB 43, p. 42.

[8] Berger to Himmler, "Population Movement," August 7, 1940, Top Secret, Nuremberg Document NO–1825, USMT IV, Case 11, PDB 65, pp. 1ff.

[9] Berger to Wolff, "Lage in Rumänien," April 15, 1941, Geheim, RFSS/T–175, 110/2634795ff.

give him a seventh division. He agreed to discuss the matter with the Führer.

By the end of 1941 partisan operations in Serbia and Croatia were on the increase, and German forces were being tied down in these areas at a time they were badly needed in Russia. Himmler's constant pleas, underscored by the sudden Russian counteroffensive before Moscow, led Hitler to agree to Berger's plan. On December 30, 1941, Keitel informed Himmler that the Führer had ordered the establishment of a new SS division composed of ethnic Germans from Yugoslavia; it was to have a strength of two brigades, each with ten or eleven self-supporting battalions trained and equipped for antipartisan warfare.[10]

An existing SS-led militia (*Selbstschutz*) composed of Serbian *Volksdeutsche* was quickly transformed into a nucleus for the new division, which, on March 1, 1942, was officially designated the SS-Freiwilligen-Division "Prinz Eugen." [11] It was the Waffen SS' seventh division, and the first of the many foreign divisions that were to alter its complexion so drastically in succeeding years.

Establishing a new division was of course only part of the task; it still had to be manned. Himmler, acting on information supplied by Berger, had assured Hitler that there would be no difficulty in finding the necessary ethnic German volunteers. But he was wrong. Despite an intensive recruiting effort in Serbia and Croatia during the spring and summer of 1942, few *Volksdeutsche* volunteered for service in the Waffen SS. Berger was understandably concerned. Failure to man "Prinz Eugen" might well mean the end of Hitler's support for the foreign-volunteer program. If the members of the German community in Serbia did not know their duty, the SS would quickly make it clear to them. Accordingly, Berger ordered his recruiting teams to employ stronger methods. Thus coercion was added to propaganda as a means of securing "volunteers," and before long outright conscription was introduced.

[10] Keitel to Himmler, "Aufstellung von volksdeutschen Verbänden in Serbien durch den Reichsführer-SS," December 30, 1941, Geheime Kommandosache, RFSS/T–175, 109/2633912 f.

[11] SSFHA, "Aufstellung der Freiwilligen-Gebirgs-Division," March 1, 1942, Geheim, RFSS/T–175, 109/2633790.

The spring of 1942 was another turning point in the development of the Waffen SS. At that time it was still an elite fighting force, overwhelmingly German and largely voluntary. During the second half of 1942, however, it began to take on a new profile; increasing numbers of foreigners, many of whom were not volunteers, entered the ranks. By 1943 even native Germans were being conscripted. In short, the Waffen SS lost both its ethnic uniformity and its voluntary elitism.

Unofficial conscription for the Waffen SS began in Serbia during the middle of 1942. Acting on complaints received from members of the German community there, the Hauptamt SS-Gericht (Main SS Legal Office) ordered the SS and Police Court in Belgrade to investigate the methods employed by Berger's recruiters in the area. The results of the investigation (conveyed to Himmler in a tactfully worded letter of complaint from SS Oberführer Dr. Guenther Reinecke, Chief of the Hauptamt SS-Gericht) indicated that SS-Freiwilligen-Division "Prinz Eugen" was "no longer an organization of volunteers, that on the contrary, the ethnic Germans from the Serbian Banat were [according to the findings of the SS and Police Court in Belgrade] 'drafted, to a large extent under threat of punishment by the local German leadership, and later by the [SS] Ergänzungsamt.' " [12]

To forestall criticism of this kind, Himmler approved the introduction of formal compulsory military service for *Volksdeutsche* in the German-occupied areas of Serbia. Berger, concerned about the legal and political implications, questioned the necessity of such a step: "Nobody cares what we do down there with our racial Germans. . . . to proclaim Compulsory Service for Croatia and Serbia is impossible under public law. And it is not at all necessary either, for when a racial group is under a moderately good leadership everybody volunteers all right, and those who do not volunteer get their houses broken to pieces." [13]

Nevertheless, Himmler preferred to ensure his supply of Serbian *Volksdeutsche* by legislation. Accordingly, the German-occupied portion of Serbia was declared *deutsches Hoheitsgebiet*

---

[12] Nuremberg Document NO–1649, USMT IV, Case 11, PDB 66–G, p. 57.
[13] Nuremberg Document NO–5901, *ibid.*, p. 54.

(territory under German sovereignty), and the Imperial *Tiroler Landsturmordnung* (Tyrolese General Levy Act) of 1872 was resurrected to provide a juridical basis for the introduction of obligatory military service (*Allgemeine Wehrpflicht*) for the German community in the area.[14]

With the recruiting situation in Yugoslavia well in hand, Berger turned his attention to Hungary. On the basis of an agreement with the Hungarian Army (Honved) Ministry, the SS was given permission to recruit among the ethnic Germans of that land. In a whirlwind campaign, SS recruiters managed to enlist and ship to Germany 16,527 men between March and May 1942. By 1944 some 42,000 *Volksdeutsche* from Hungary were serving in the Waffen SS.[15]

Berger might crow to Himmler about the phenomenal success of "Operation Hungary," but the SS Führungshauptamt did not share his enthusiasm. During August 1941 and again the following March, SS Gruppenführer Jüttner compained about the methods employed by Berger's recruiters. And it was not only in connection with the induction of ethnic Germans but also with the procedures used in the recruitment of native Germans and west European volunteers that Jüttner found fault. In September 1942, the chief of the SSFHA wrote a third and stronger letter to Berger in which he complained that, once again, he was being saddled with "entirely unsuitable replacements," this time from Hungary. Many of the recruits had "obviously not been seen by a doctor or SS officer, because their physical disabilities are so obvious that a soldier could never declare these men fit for military service." Among them, Jüttner pointed out, were many men "with epilepsy, severe tuberculosis, and other serious physical disabilities." These recruits had "to be discharged and sent back to Hungary." In addition, it was discovered that many of the recruits were

14 Herzog, *op. cit.*, p. 13. Cf. Absolon, *op. cit.*, pp. 122ff.

15 Berger to Himmler, "Operation Hungary," n.d. (probably May 1942), Secret, Nuremberg Document NO–5024, USMT IV, Case 11, PDB 66–G, p. 95; Himmler's Sonthofen Speech, May 5, 1944, RFSS/T–175, 92/2613482; and SSFHA "Aufstellung eines Rekruten-Depots der Waffen SS auf dem SS-Tr. Ub. Platz Debica," March 17, 1942, Geheim, RFSS/T–175, 109/2633756 f.

"not volunteers, but men who have been included in the transports under false pretences or by force." Still others were "not ethnic Germans, but Hungarian nationals who were persuaded to join the transports under the assurance that it was only a question of a short sports training." Jüttner also drew Berger's attention to the fact that "complaints and objections are constantly being received . . . from relatives of the recruits about the methods used in these recruitments by the *Volksbund* of Hungary." [16]

Berger's response to the SSFHA, if indeed there was one, has not been found. Jüttner's letters of complaint clearly indicated the pitfalls inherent in the indiscriminate recruitment of recalcitrant foreigners. Nevertheless, they seem to have had little effect on Berger's plans for the future.

During 1942 and 1943 the recruitment of ethnic Germans was intensified in order to meet the ever-increasing needs of an expanding Waffen SS. Agreements were concluded with the governments of Romania and Hungary, and with the puppet regimes of Croatia and Slovakia, permitting almost unrestricted conscription of *Volksdeutsche* in these areas. In the case of German-occupied areas such as Serbia, Poland, and portions of the Soviet Union, ethnic Germans were simply conscripted into the Waffen SS in the same fashion native Germans were drafted into the Wehrmacht. By the end of 1943, the number and origin of *Volksdeutsche* serving in the Waffen SS was: North Schleswig (Denmark) 1292; Slovakia 5390; Hungary 22,125; Romania 54,000; Serbia 21,516 (including Police); Croatia 17,538. As the war moved into its fourth year, more than a quarter of the men in the Waffen SS were ethnic Germans from areas outside the Reich.[17]

Having virtually exhausted the supply of civilian *Volksdeutsche* of military age in Eastern Europe, the SS early in 1944 forced the governments of Slovakia and Hungary to transfer

[16] Jüttner to Berger, "Recruiting of Racial Germans and Germanic Volunteers," September 5, 1942, Geheime Kommandosache, Nuremberg Document NO–2476, USMT IV, Case 11, PDB 66–G, pp. 70ff.

[17] "Auszug aus dem Informationsblatt der Reichsleiterdienst vom 28. 12. 1943," Nuremberg Document NO–2015, *ibid.*, pp. 80ff.

to the Waffen SS all ethnic Germans serving in their armed forces. Thus another 50,000 or so *Volksdeutsche* found their way into the SS.[18]

Baltic Legions of the SS, 1942–1945

In 1940 the Soviet Union annexed Estonia, Latvia, and Lithuania. A year later the Russians were ousted by the Wehrmacht, and the Baltic lands became the *Ostland*. Within a few weeks of the German occupation, the SS began recruiting Baltic volunteers for SS Police formations. On July 31, 1941, the first group of 396 Estonian volunteers was turned over to the Höhere SS- und Polizeiführer Russland-Nord for police work.[19] In the following months the SS established a number of security battalions (*Schutzmanns-Bataillone*) composed of Latvian and Estonian volunteers, while the Army recruited eight Estonian battalions, of which four were sent as combat formations to Army Group North. An early attempt by Himmler to gain control of these battalions was blocked by the Army.[20] During the Russian winter counteroffensive of 1941–1942, the Baltic battalions were thrown into the front line to plug gaps. Although they fought bravely enough, the poorly trained and inadequately armed *Schutzmannschaften*—like the national legions—were decimated.

When it appeared that the Russian counterthrust along the northern front might break through the German defense, the Army in desperation considered the emergency mobilization of Latvian, Lithuanian, and Estonian military formations to defend the *Ostland*. Informed of the Wehrmacht's intention, the SS representative in the area demanded that the SS be entrusted with the task, since only under its supervision would the Balts receive "the proper ideological orientation and

[18] SS Obersturmbannführer Letsch to Berger, "Slovakia: Introduction of Compulsory Labor and Military Service," January 19, 1944, Secret, Nuremberg Document NO–3067, *ibid.*, pp. 106ff. Concerning the agreement with Hungary see Herzog, *op. cit.*, p. 10.

[19] SSFHA, "Einberufungen zur Waffen-SS," July 31, 1941, Geheim, RFSS/T–175, 110/2634485ff.

[20] KTB/OKW, December 2, 1943, IV, 1328 f.

National Socialist leadership." [21] The danger of a Russian break-through passed before a decision was reached on the formation of a Baltic SS, but the idea had taken root in Berlin.

For the time being the Germans confined themselves to an increased recruitment of Estonians and Latvians for additional police battalions. Some of these formations were established by the Army, others by the SS. Intended primarily for anti-partisan operations, they were nevertheless frequently committed to battle in the front lines. [22]

In the meantime, however, local interest had gone beyond what Berlin had in mind. To nationalist collaborators intent on securing autonomy for their nations, the prospect of re-establishing indigenous armed forces was extremely attractive. Particularly in tiny Estonia, the agitation for the creation of a national military formation grew during 1942. Berger, quick to sense the possibilities in the situation, threw his support behind the Balts. When the proposal for the establishment of a Baltic SS was submitted to Himmler in May 1942, he was ambivalent: "The formation of SS units consisting of Estonians, Latvians, or even Lithuanians is surely enticing; however, it [is fraught with] very great dangers." [23] Within a few months, Himmler's doubts had yielded to a thirst for manpower. Estonia was chosen to provide the first unit of the eastern Waffen SS; pro-German sentiment there was stronger than elsewhere in the Baltic region, and Himmler had fewer reservations about the racial purity of the inhabitants. By the end of August 1942, he had given his approval to the creation of an Estonian Legion within the Waffen SS. [24]

In January 1943, Himmler inspected a group of fifty-four Estonian legionnaires undergoing training at a Waffen SS non-

[21] Copy of telegram from SS Brigadeführer Stahlecker to SS Obergruppenführer Heydrich, forwarded to Himmler on January 25, 1942, Geheim-Dringend, RFSS/T–175, 109/2633024 f.

[22] See Steiner, *Die Freiwilligen*, pp. 141, 185.

[23] Quoted in Dallin, *op. cit.*, p. 597.

[24] SSFHA, "Aufstellung der Estnischen SS-Legion," September 29, 1942, Geheim, RFSS/T–175, 111/2635437ff. Sometime after the establishment of the Estonian Legion, the Army was forced to turn its Estonian battalions over to the Waffen SS. See KTB/OKW, December 2, 1943, IV, 1329.

commissioned officers' academy; he came away very favorably impressed. "Racially," Himmler observed, "they could not be distinguished from Germans. . . . The Estonians really belong to the few races that can, after the segregation of only a few elements, be merged with us without any harm to our people." He was also of the opinion that the proper ideological and linguistic education would enable the legionnaires to "spread the idea that a nation of 900,000 Estonians cannot survive independently, and that as a racially related nation Estonia must join the Reich." [25]

Taking its cue from the Estonians, the Latvian puppet regime requested the Reichskommissar for the *Ostland* to permit the re-establishment of the Latvian Army at a strength of 100,000 men. When the petition came to Berger's attention, he had the matter investigated and reported to Himmler that it was nothing more than "an old trick to gain special political advantages." If the Latvians really wanted to fight the Bolsheviks, he suggested that they "create a unit of volunteers who are racially acceptable and put them at the disposal of the Reichsführer SS . . . as Police battalions for combating partisans or, if they are especially suitable, as a Latvian Legion." [26] Berger's suggestion was endorsed by the Minister for Eastern Territories, Reichsleiter Rosenberg. Prompted by the increasingly critical situation along the Stalingrad front, Himmler added his support to the proposal, and Hitler gave his approval to the establishment of a Latvian Legion for the Waffen SS.

As with the Germanic legions, the first response from the youth of the two Baltic countries seemed to augur a promising future for the new organizations. Within two months of its foundation the Estonian Legion had a strength of over 200 Germans and 700 Estonians. Four months later some 15,000 Latvians and 6500 Estonians had been signed up for the legions. But shortages in equipment, lack of barracks, and other short-

[25] Himmler to SSHA and SSFHA, January 13, 1943, Geheim, Nuremberg Document NO–3301, USMT IV, Case 11, PDB 66–G, pp. 146ff.

[26] Berger to Himmler, "Latvian Operation," December 11, 1942, Secret, Nuremberg Document NO–3300, *ibid.,* pp. 119 f.

comings in the administration of the program delayed their induction. By April 15, 1943, only 2478 Latvians and 2850 Estonians had been called up for service.[27]

It will be recalled that the early part of 1943 was a period of major reorganization for the Waffen SS. The Germanic legions, mainly because of their small size, had been found inadequate for the type of warfare being waged in the East; they were therefore regrouped into brigades and later into divisions. The same procedure was now also applied to the nascent Baltic legions.

Even before they had completed their basic training, the legions were reorganized and enlarged. The Estonian Legion, reinforced by a portion of the 1st SS Infantry Brigade, was redesignated the Estnische SS-Freiwilligen Brigade. The Latvian Legion, with the addition of the remaining men from the 2nd SS Infantry Bridgade, became the Lettische SS-Freiwilligen Brigade.[28] Since many of the men transferred from the two SS infantry brigades were either native or ethnic Germans, the Baltic SS was never an exclusively national formation.

Shortly after the legions had been converted into brigades, the SS leadership, influenced in part by further German military reverses, ordered that they be enlarged into divisions. In addition, the remaining Latvian security battalions were to become the nucleus of a third Baltic SS division.[29] Realizing that a reliance on voluntary enlistments would never provide sufficient

[27] Berger to Himmler, "Replacements situation of the Replacement Command Ostland, Riga," April 17, 1943, Secret, Nuremberg Document NO–3379; "The situation regarding replacements in the Ostland," June 4, 1943, Secret, Nuremberg Document NO–3303, *ibid.,* pp. 122, 124 f. See also telegram from SSFHA to Himmler, "Estnische Legion," December 20, 1942, Geheime Kommandosache, RFSS/T–175, 111/2635404 f.

[28] SSFHA, "Umgliederung der 1. SS-Inf. Brig. (Mot) in die Estnische SS-Freiw. Brigade," May 5, 1943, RFSS/T–175, 111/2635291ff.; SSFHA, "Umgliederung der 2. SS-Inf. Brig. (Mot) in die Lett. SS-Freiw. Brig.," May 18, 1943, 111/2635256.

[29] While the expansion to divisions was taking place, the existing Baltic formations—sometimes called legions and at other times referred to as brigades—were in action along the northern sector of the Russian front. For details see Steiner, *Die Freiwilligen,* pp. 201, 233ff.

manpower to fill three divisions, Himmler ordered the introduction of compulsory military service in the *Ostland*. As a
result, Latvians and Estonians (Himmler refused to accept
Lithuanians in the SS on the grounds that they were politically
unreliable and racially inferior) in age groups 1915–1924 were
made subject to conscription for the Waffen SS. In 1944, conscription was broadened to include those in age groups 1904–
1914 and 1925–1926. Moreover, all former Estonian Army officers and NCOs were made liable to military service through
the ages of sixty and fifty-five respectively.[30]

By 1944 the Waffen SS had at its disposal three new divisions: the 15th Waffen-Grenadierdivision der SS (lett. Nr. 1),
the 19th Waffen-Grenadierdivision der SS (lett. Nr. 2), and the
20th Waffen-Grenadierdivision der SS (estn. Nr. 1). When the
SS began setting up its own army corps, the two Latvian divisions were brought together to form the VIth (lett.) SS-Freiwilligen Armee-Korps.[31] All three Baltic divisions fought in the
futile defense of their homelands during the Soviet advance of
1944. The Latvian 19th SS Division was part of the force cut

[30] Nuremberg Documents NO–3474, NO–2817, NO–3044, NO–2812,
NO–2816, NO–2804, NO–2810, NO–4884, and NO–4885, USMT IV, Case
11, PDB 66–G, *passim*. The OKW war diary indicates that the Germans
had a great deal of difficulty with the conscription program in Latvia. The
operation was at first left in the hands of the indigenous collaborators
(Rudolf Bangerskis, a former Latvian War Minister, was appointed an SS
Gruppenführer and Inspector General of the Latvian SS), but they were so
inefficient that large numbers of *Wehrpflichtige* managed to avoid service.
Consequently, the German Army established fifty recruiting offices of its own
throughout the country. By the end of 1943 the whole operation had been
taken over by the SS. In the words of the OKW war diary: "The Führer
has transferred to the Reichsführer SS the task of mobilizing those Latvians
and Estonians who are fit for military service. For this purpose, SS
Ergänzungskommandos [recruiting offices] have been established in Reval
and Riga; they have the authority of a German Wehrbezirkskommando
[military district headquarters]." Entry for December 2, 1942, KTB/OKW,
IV, 1328 f.

[31] See *Hitlers Lagebesprechungen*, pp. 519, n. 4, 837, n. 2, 939, n. 1;
Steiner, *Die Freiwilligen*, pp. 201, 269, 280ff., 311ff.; and SSFHA, "Aufstellung
des Gen. Kdo. VI. SS-Freiw. Korps," October 8, 1943, RFSS/T–175,
111/2635214ff.

off in Courland (Latvia), which maintained a useless German enclave behind the Soviet lines until the end of the war. After the German withdrawal from the Baltic states, the Latvian 15th SS Division was decimated in the desperate defense of Pomerania. The Estonian 20th SS Division was routed in Silesia and then retreated into Bohemia, where its survivors surrendered at the end of the war.[32]

The Eastern Waffen SS

For Himmler, the fundament of the SS was its racial purity; its purpose "to create an order of good blood which is able to serve Germany." Although he was forced to relax the rigid pre-war standards, he struggled mightily to preserve some semblance of the Waffen SS' former racial exclusiveness. When Hitler ordered the establishment of the national legions in 1941, Himmler refused to have the French and Walloons in the Waffen SS on the grounds that they were not "Germanic" peoples. Yet even the Germanic legionnaires did not have to meet SS racial requirements, and this worried Himmler. In July 1942 he ordered the SSFHA to make certain that men serving in the legions were wearing national emblems on their collar tabs in place of the SS runes. His reason: "I want purely and simply, for all time, to prevent the admission, as a result of the exigencies of war, of all men who are not from the strictest point of view qualified to be SS men." [33]

Himmler was waging a losing battle. By 1943 the exigencies of war had reduced SS racial requirements to the point where former legionnaires—west European and Baltic—had become, for all intents and purposes, regular members of the Waffen SS. Step by step, regulations were modified, until the Waffen SS was accepting recruits from ethnic groups which could not by any stretch of the imagination be considered "Germanic."

The first major Waffen SS formation to be recruited with-

[32] See "Gliederung des deutschen Heeres in den Jahren 1944/45 (Schematische Übersicht)," March 1, 1945, KTB/OKW, IV, 189ff.

[33] Himmler to Jüttner, July 7, 1942, Geheime Kommandosache, RFSS/T–175, 111/2635402ff.

out regard for racial and ethnic factors was ordered into existence by Adolf Hitler in February 1943. It was to be composed
of Moslems from Bosnia and Herzegovina, and was to assist the
ethnic German 7th SS Division "Prinz Eugen" in combating
the partisans of Yugoslavia.[34]

Capitalizing upon the traditional Moslem hatred for the
Christian Serbs who made up the bulk of Tito's partisans, the
Waffen SS was able quickly to recruit thousands of young
Moslems. Yet once again, as in the case of the Germanic legions,
the flow of volunteers tapered off after an initial surge. This
time, however, the reason was not lack of interest but the
resistance of the puppet Croatian regime, which was nominally
in control of the areas in which a large part of Yugoslavia's
Moslem population lived.

Himmler discovered that the local authorities were arresting
or drafting into the Croatian Army men who had shown a
desire to volunteer for the Waffen SS. His informants reported
that the "Croatian concentration camps in Novogradieca and
Jasenovac are full of youths who had attempted to enlist in
the SS." In a strongly worded letter to his representative in
Croatia (Beauftragte des Reichsführers SS in Kroatien), Police
Major General Kammerhofer, Himmler demanded that "strong
steps" be taken to remind the Croatian authorities that they
were supposed to be puppets. "I expect to receive, by August 1,
1943, your report that the division, at a strength of about 26,000
men, is completely ready." Two days later Himmler ordered
Berger to send Kammerhofer two million *Reichsmarks* to help
finance the recruiting operation.[35]

Kammerhofer promptly set about his new task. Although
the Croatian authorities dragged their feet, they quickly gave
up their earlier tactics: recruitment of Moslems increased
almost immediately. When voluntary enlistments fell short of
the need, conscription was introduced to bring the Moslem divi-

---

[34] SSFHA, "Aufstellung der Kroatischen SS-Freiwilligen-Division,"
April 30, 1943, Geheime Kommandosache, RFSS/T–175, 111/2635334ff.

[35] Himmler to Kammerhofer, July 1, 1943, Geheime Kommandosache,
RFSS/T–175, 111/2635371ff.; Himmler to Berger, July 3, 1943, Geheime
Reichsache, *ibid.,* 111/2635386.

sion up to its authorized strength.[36] Training was conducted in France and later in Silesia. By the end of 1943 the division was back in Croatia to participate in the fight against the growing menace of Tito's partisan bands.

As the first SS formation of its type—and certainly the strangest ever to wear the SS uniform—the Moslem division warrants a closer examination. For many months after its creation the unit remained nameless. It was sometimes referred to as the Kroatischen SS-Freiwilligen-Division and at other times it was called the Muselmanen-Division. In October a SSFHA directive officially designated it the 13th SS-Freiwilligen b.h. Gebirgs-Division (Kroatien).[37] A short time later, as part of a plan to distinguish the elite units from those of inferior racial composition,[38] the division received a new and final designation: 13th Waffen-Gebirgsdivision der SS "Handschar" (kroat. Nr. 1).

In January 1944, Himmler described his Moslem division to Goebbels and other leaders of the Propaganda Ministry as

[36] SS-Freiw.-Geb.-Division "Prinz Eugen," Kommandeur Notiz, "Abgabe von Muselmanen aus der kroat. Wehrmacht," July 31, 1943, Geheime Kommandosache, *ibid.*, 108/2631276ff.; Berger to Himmler, "Muselmanen-Division," August 4, 1943, Geheim, *ibid.*, 108/2631142.

[37] SSFHA, "13. SS-Freiw. b.h. Gebirgs-Division (Kroatien)," October 9, 1943, Geheime Kommandosache, *ibid.*, 108/2631269.

[38] During the early years of the war, SS divisions were identified by name only (e.g., SS Division "Reich"). In 1942, however, all SS divisions were numbered consecutively in the order in which they had been established; the lower the number, the older the division. The distinguishing factor in determining the racial and physical profile of any given formation was the placement of the letters SS in the unit designation. Thus an elite formation composed largely of native Germans was designated "SS-Division" (e.g., 3rd SS-Panzerdivision "Totenkopf"); a formation composed largely of ethnic German or "Germanic" (west European) volunteers was designated "SS-Freiwilligen-Division" (e.g., 11th SS-Freiwilligen-Panzergrenadierdivision "Nordland"); a formation composed largely of "non-Germanic" personnel (volunteers or conscripts) was designated "Division der SS," with the nationality given in brackets following the name (e.g., 13th Waffen-Gebirgsdivision der SS "Handschar" [kroat. Nr. 1]). Cf. "Rede des SS-Obergruppenführers Jüttner auf der SS-Führer-Tagung in Prag am 13. April 1944," NSDAP/T-81, 154/157541ff.

"being very religious." Each battalion had its *imam*, each regiment its *mullah*, and with Hitler's consent the Moslems were given the same privileges they had had in the old Imperial Austro–Hungarian Army: special rations and permission to observe their religious rites en masse. And the aggressively anti-religious Himmler told Goebbels that he had "nothing against Islam because it educates the men in this division for me and promises them heaven if they fight and are killed in action; a very practical and attractive religion for soldiers!" Nevertheless, the SS did contribute something to the education of the Moslems; according to Himmler, eight weeks of SS training taught them not to steal from one another.[39]

Although the original directive establishing the division called for "special care to ensure the rapid training of young Moslems with leadership potential,[40] "Handschar," like the Bosnian units of the Imperial Army, was officered largely by Germans and *Volksdeutsche*. It may be imagined that the most difficult adjustment that had to be made by the German SS men assigned to the division was in connection with the strange headgear worn by all personnel. This was a field-gray fez (red with the dress uniform), complete with tassel, but bearing on the front the *Hoheitszeichen* (eagle and Swastika) and the SS *Totenkopf* (skull and crossbones). In place of the SS runes on their right collar tab, members of this division wore an insignia depicting a Swastika and a hand grasping a *Handschar,* a Turkish sword resembling a scimitar.[41] With the possible exception of the Russian cossacks who later served with the SS, this was certainly the most picturesque unit in the Waffen SS.

Despite their elaborate uniforms and the spiritual ministrations of the pro-Nazi Grand Mufti of Jerusalem, Haj Amin el Hussein, the Moslems never seem to have repaid the attention lavished on them. They mutinied while in training in France,

---

[39] "Rede des Reichsführers-SS auf der Tagung der RPA-Leiter am 28. Januar 1944," Geheim, RFSS/T–175, 94/2614801. Cf. Kersten, *op. cit.*, pp. 259 f.

[40] SSFHA, "Aufstellung der Kroatischen SS-Freiwilligen Division," April 30, 1943, Geheime Kommandosache, RFSS/T–175, 111/2635334ff.

[41] Kersten, *op. cit.*, p. 259; photographs in Kanis, *op. cit.*, pp. 125, 137.

and discipline was restored only after the personal intervention of the Grand Mufti. Late in 1943, "Handschar" was returned to the area from which it had been recruited. For a few months the division skirmished with Tito's partisans, and in the process distinguished itself largely by the number of atrocities it committed.[42] The two standard accounts of the Waffen SS state that the Moslems were later transferred to the Hungarian front, where they supposedly fought bravely against the Red Army; Hausser even has Moslems defending Vienna during the last days of the war.[43] Actually the Moslems fought nowhere but in Yugoslavia, and even there they were not very successful.

On October 2, 1944, the commander of the German southeastern front (OB Südost) requested Himmler's permission to transfer the Moslem division from Bosnia to the Yugoslav–Hungarian frontier, to help prevent a link-up between the partisans and the advancing Red Army, "although he was aware of the risk involved in moving the Moslems from their home area to the East." Himmler, apparently unwilling to take the risk, demurred. The Moslems were growing increasingly unreliable, and soon they became reluctant to take any action beyond the protection of their native region. Since the focal point of the fighting had shifted to the northeast, Himmler decided to order the dissolution of the division and make use of its equip-

[42] Himmler's liaison officer at Hitler's headquarters, SS Brigadeführer Hermann Fegelein, describing to his Führer the ferocity of the Moslems, said that "the enemy takes off [*abhauen*] with all its things when they [the Moslems] move in. They kill them only with their knives. There was one man who was wounded. He allowed his arm to be bandaged and then went on to finish off 17 more of the enemy with his left hand. Cases also occur where they [the Moslems] cut the heart out of their enemy." Hitler, apparently annoyed by Fegelein's gory intrusion into a high-level military conference, responded with an abrupt *"Das ist Wurst."* "Mittagslage vom 6. April 1944," *Hitlers Lagebesprechungen,* p. 560.

[43] Hausser, *op. cit.,* pp. 104 f.; Reitlinger, *op. cit.,* p. 200. It is interesting to note that nowhere in his paean to the foreign volunteers does Steiner make any mention of the Moslem "Handschar" Division, although he devotes many pages to the campaign in the Balkans and often refers to foreign units that were not even part of the SS. One can only conclude that Steiner cannot think of anything good to say about the "brave Mujos," and therefore prefers to say nothing.

ment and German personnel elsewhere. The Moslems were discharged and the German cadre formed into a regimental combat group. By November 1944 the 13th Waffen-Gebirgsdivision der SS "Handschar" (kroat. Nr. 1) had ceased to exist. In its place remained the truncated and predominantly German Rgt.-Gr. (Regimental Combat Group) 13th SS-Geb. "Handschar." It was this unit, not the "brave Mujos," that later fought along the Drau (Drava) River line.[44]

The mystery of the SS Division "Handschar" in Hungary, and later in Vienna, still remains to be cleared up. Hausser, who spent the last months of the war commanding army groups in the north and west, had no personal knowledge of events in the southeast and was therefore misled by an OKW security measure. Early in 1945 it was decided to transfer the crack 16th SS-Panzergrenadierdivision "Reichsführer-SS" from northern Italy to the hard-pressed Hungarian front. In order to mislead the enemy, "Reichsführer-SS" was camouflaged as the non-existent 13th Waffen-Gebirgsdivision der SS "Handschar."[45] The purpose was to prevent the Allies from discovering that the Italian front had been weakened by the transfer of "Reichsführer-SS" and at the same time to lull the Russians into the belief that they would be facing a motley collection of Moslems rather than a formidable mechanized division. It is not known whether the Allies were misled by the OKW's stratagem, but Hausser certainly was. It was the "Reichsführer-SS" wolf masquerading in "Handschar" sheep's clothing that fought along the Drau, then north of the Plattensee, and finally in Vienna.[46]

During 1944 the SS organized two other Moslem formations along the same lines as "Handschar." The first was recruited in Albania and designated the 21st Waffen-Gebirgsdivision der SS "Skanderbeg" (alban. Nr. 1); the second was composed largely of Croatians and given the title 23rd Waffen-Grenadier-

[44] See "Titos Verhältnis zu Sowjetrussland und das Vordringen der Russen im Südostraum," KTB/OKW, IV, 699; "Gliederung des deutschen Heeres in den Jahren 1944/45 (Schematische Übersicht)," November 26, 1944, *ibid.*, p. 1893.
[45] "Lagebuch 7. 3. 45, Heeresgr. Süd: Angriff in Ungarn," *ibid.*, p. 1151.
[46] "Lagebuch 28. 3. 45, Heeresgr. Süd," *ibid.*, p. 1204.

division der SS "Kama" (kroat. Nr. 2). "Skanderbeg" was no sooner established than it began to show signs of unreliability. By September so many of its men had deserted that it was decided to disband the unit.[47] As in the case of "Handschar," the German personnel were formed into a regimental combat group, Rgt.-Gr. 21st SS-Geb. "Skanderbeg," which fought in Yugoslavia (with the 7th SS Division "Prinz Eugen") until February 1945, when it was sent north to help defend the Oder line.[48] "Kama" apparently was never fully established. At least the fact that it is nowhere mentioned in the war diary of the OKW makes safe the assumption that it never saw action.

It will be recalled that as early as April 1941 Berger had recruited Ukrainian volunteers from Poland in the hope of establishing the nucleus of a Ukrainian SS formation, but had been overruled by Himmler for racial reasons. The German Army, less bound by Nazi ideology, toward the end of 1941 established a number of volunteer units composed of Russian racial minorities. Over the next two years, regular legions of Caucasians, Georgians, Turkomens, Cossacks, and similar groups were created. Later Ukrainian and Russian units were added, so that by the end of the war approximately one million *Osttruppen* (not counting military construction workers) were serving in the Wehrmacht.

Having openly compromised its racial exclusiveness by the formation of the Moslem "Handschar" Division, the Waffen SS no longer had any good reason for denying itself a share in the Slavic manpower pool. On April 28, 1943, a call went out for volunteers for a "Galician" SS division. The response was overwhelming: nearly 100,000 Ukrainians volunteered, fewer than 30,000 of whom were accepted.[49] Although a special effort was made to limit recruiting to that part of German-occupied Poland which had before 1919 been Austrian Galicia, the fact remained that the division was composed of Ukrainians;

[47] "Der Kampf gegen die Aufstandsbewegung im Südosten," *ibid.*, p. 685.

[48] "Gliederung des deutschen Heeres in den Jahren 1944/45 (Schematische Übersicht)," November 26, 1944, *ibid.*, p. 1893; "Lagebuch 22. 2. 45, Südosten," *ibid.*, p. 1117. Also cf. Reitlinger, *op. cit.*, p. 403.

[49] Dallin, *op. cit.*, p. 598.

the euphemistic designation 14th SS-Freiwilligen-Division "Galizien"[50] fooled no one, least of all the personnel of the division, who were mostly Ukrainian nationalists. But after years of Slav-baiting it was difficult for the SS leaders to admit that they had created an SS division of "subhumans."

By May 1944 the division had completed its training in Germany. Before leaving for the eastern front it was honored with a visit by the Reichsführer SS. Speaking to the predominantly German officer corps of the division, Himmler admitted that the Galicians were really Ukrainians, and he appealed for "comradeship" between the German and Ukrainian personnel. In answer to those who claimed that the SS was only interested in recruiting "cannon fodder" for the German war machine, Himmler, with dubious logic, pointed out that if this were so, the division would not have been given a whole year of expert training to prepare it for combat. He also stressed the fact that 250 Galicians belonging to the division had been chosen to attend the SS Junkerschule and had returned as officers. With Himmler denied the use of his customary material on this occasion, his speech was colorless and restrained. There were a few tentative remarks about the "Jewish–Bolshevik enemy," but not a word about "Asiatic hordes" and "Slavic subhumans."[51]

Shortly after Himmler's visit the division was redesignated the 14th Waffen-Grenadierdivision der SS (galiz. Nr. 1) and sent to the eastern front. There, in the area where it had been recruited, it was thrown into battle in a desperate effort to stem the Russian advance. As part of the German XIVth Army Corps, the division was cut off and surrounded in the so-called Brody–Tarnow pocket. After days of heavy fighting, in which the division was decimated, the surviving Ukrainians managed to break out of the encirclement; 14,000 had gone into the

---

[50] SSFHA, "Aufstellung der SS-Freiw. Division 'Galizien,'" July 30, 1943, Geheime Kommandosache, RFSS/T–175, 108/2631288ff.

[51] "Rede des Reichsführers-SS auf dem Appell des Führerkorps der Galizischen SS-Freiw.-Infantrie-Division in Neuhammer am 16. Mai 1944," RFSS/T–175, 94/2614657ff.

cauldron, 3000 came out. The Ukrainians had indeed been little more than cannon fodder, for their contribution to the battle was negligible. The remnants of the division were sent to Slovakia for refitting and never fought again.[52]

With both the Ukraine and Galicia in Soviet hands, the SS could afford to make a concession to Ukrainian national pride; early in 1945 the bracketed portion of the division's title was changed from "Galician No. 1" (galiz. Nr. 1) to "Ukrainian No. 1" (ukrain. Nr. 1). On March 23, 1945, only a few weeks before the collapse of the Third Reich, Hitler became incensed upon discovering that the division had recuperated to the point where it had a strength of 14,000 men (3000 more than its most recent authorization) and, as he put it, "nearly enough weapons to equip two divisions" and yet was still "refitting" far from any fighting.[53]

The somewhat less than outstanding performance of the Galician division proved to be the high point of the eastern SS program. By the summer of 1944 the continuing need for manpower had led Himmler to give up his remaining reservations about admitting *Ostvölker* into the Waffen SS. Shortly after the Galicians left France for the front, the SS began recruiting additional east European formations. None of these units were to match even the mediocre military performance of their predecessor.

Russians and Ukrainians serving in security units (*Schuma-Bataillonen*) were brought together to form the nuclei of two

[52] Steiner, *Die Freiwilligen*, p. 291; *Hitlers Lagebesprechungen*, p. 941, n. 1; Reitlinger, *op. cit.*, p. 203; Dallin, *op. cit.*, p. 599, n. 3. An entry in the OKW war diary for February 2, 1945, states that "the 14th SS-Div. ('Galizien') will be transferred to Vienna." (Lagebuch 2. 2. 45, Slowakei, KTB/OKW, IV, 1065.) There is, however, no reason to believe that the move was actually made; the official OKW list still has the division in Slovakia on March 1, and it was not in action three weeks later when Hitler discovered its existence. See "Gliederung des deutschen Heeres in den Jahren 1944/45," March 1, 1945, *ibid.*, p. 1904.

[53] *Hitlers Lagebesprechungen*, p. 940. Reitlinger, *op. cit.*, p. 205, n. 1, states that "the bulk of the Ukrainian SS, numbering 15,000, surrendered to the British in Austria and were interned at Rimini."

new divisions: the 29th Waffen-Grenadierdivision der SS (russ. Nr. 1) and the 30th Waffen-Grenadierdivision der SS (russ. Nr. 2). Neither of these units was ever enlarged beyond regimental size. The 29th was turned over to the so-called Russian Liberation Army of General Vlasov before it ever saw action.[54] The 30th was badly mauled during the German retreat from France late in 1944, and many of its survivors were then also turned over to the Vlasov Army. In March 1945 the "division" was reconstituted as a brigade, this time with the national designation changed from "russiche Nr. 2" to "weissruthenische." But it was no longer considered reliable, and was not committed to battle again.[55]

During the last six or eight months of the war the following additional eastern SS formations were established: 25th Waffen-Grenadierdivision der SS "Hunyadi" (ungar. Nr. 1), 26th Waffen-Grenadierdivision der SS (ungar. Nr. 2), 31st SS-Freiwilligen-Grenadierdivision "Böhmen-Mähren" (Hungarians and *Volksdeutsche*), Osttürkischer Waffenverband der SS, Kaukasischer Waffenverband der SS, Serbisches SS-Freiwilligenkorps, Waffen-Grenadierregiment der SS (rumän. Nr. 1), Waffen-Grenadierregiment der SS (rumän. Nr. 2), and Waffen-Grenadierregiment der SS (bulgar. Nr. 1).[56] Moreover the SS, late in 1944, also fell heir to a division of cossack cavalry that had been under German Army command. From among the thousands of Russian cossacks who fled into the Balkans before the advancing Red Army, the Waffen SS formed a second division, and the two Kosaken-Kavalleriedivisionen were brought together to form the XVth (SS) Kosaken-Kavalleriekorps. The cossacks, who remained under the command of their own leaders and a handful of German Army officers, were used to combat Tito's partisans in Yugoslavia, which apparently they did with only moderate success. During the great retreat of 1945, the surviving cossacks escaped into Austria, where they eventually surrendered to the British. They were later turned over to the

54 On the Vlasov movement in general see Dallin, *op. cit.*, pp. 553ff.; Reitlinger, *The House Built on Sand,* pp. 317ff.
55 *Hitlers Lagebesprechungen*, pp. 536, n. 1; 674, nn. 1, 2; 941, n. 1.
56 *Ibid.*, p. 536, n. 1.

Left: Reichsführer SS Heinrich Himmler in 1937. (Ullstein)
Right: SS Oberführer Felix Steiner, commander of SS Regiment "Deutschland," shortly after he was awarded the Knight's Cross for his regiment's role in the Western campaign, 1940. As an SS Gruppenführer (Lieutenant General), Steiner later commanded the 5th SS Division "Wiking" and the IIIrd SS Panzerkorps. (Ullstein)

Left: SS Obergruppenführer (General) Josef (Sepp) Dietrich, commander of the 1st SS Panzergrenadierdivision (later Panzerdivision) "Leibstandarte Adolf Hitler," shortly after receiving the Oak Leaves to the Knight's Cross from Adolf Hitler in 1941. In July 1943, Dietrich became commander of the Ist SS Panzerkorps; later, as an SS Oberstgruppenführer (Colonel General), he commanded the 5th Panzerarmee and the 6th Panzerarmee. (Ullstein–Copress)
Right: SS Obergruppenführer (General) Paul Hausser, molder of the prewar SS Verfügungstruppe, commander of the SS Verfügungsdivision (later "Das Reich"), and commander of the SS Panzerkorps during the battle for Kharkov in 1943. Later in the war, as an SS Oberstgruppenführer (Colonel General), Hausser commanded the 7th Armee, Heeresgruppe Oberrhein, and, finally, Heeresgruppe G. (Ullstein)

Left: SS Obergruppenführer (General) Theodor Eicke, prewar chief of Germany's concentration-camp system and wartime commander of the SS Totenkopf-division (later SS Panzerdivision "Totenkopf"), shortly before his death in Russia early in 1943. (Ullstein)

Right: SS Standartenführer (Colonel) Fritz Witt, commander of the 1st SS Panzergrenadierregiment of the 1st SS Panzerdivision "Leibstandarte Adolf Hitler," 1942. In 1943, at the age of 35, Witt became the first commander of the newly established 12th SS Panzergrenadierdivision (later Panzerdivision) "Hitler Jugend." He was killed in July 1944 during the battle for Normandy. (Ullstein)

Left: SS Sturmbannführer (Major) Kurt Meyer as he appeared after Hitler awarded him the Knight's Cross for his exploits during the Balkan campaign of 1941. In 1944, Meyer became the second commander of the 12th SS Panzerdivision "Hitler Jugend." (Ullstein)

Right: SS Obergruppenführer (General) Hans Jüttner, head of the SS Führungs-hauptamt and after July 22, 1944, also Himmler's deputy as Commander of the Reserve (Ersatz) Army and Chief of Army Ordnance. (Ullstein)

Soviets; the leaders were tried and executed and the others disappeared into Stalin's labor camps.[57]

Flights of Fancy: The British and Indian Legions

In the spring of 1941 the leader of the militant Indian liberation movement, Subhas Chandra Bose, arrived in Germany to seek support for his cause. A short time later the German Army took steps to create an Indian Legion, which was intended to serve as the nucleus of an Indian "army of liberation." Starting with eight of Bose's followers, "Legion Indien" grew during the following years (by the recruitment of Indian POWs captured by the Germans in North Africa and Italy) to a maximum strength of about 2000 men.[58]

The Indians were not considered battleworthy and were maintained primarily for their propaganda value. The Allied invasion of France in 1944 found the legion stationed in a quiet sector along the Bay of Biscay. It did no actual fighting, but was swept into the hectic German retreat and apparently lost some of its personnel and equipment in the process. On its arrival in Germany, the legion was turned over to the Waffen SS.[59]

The SS leaders decided to convert the Indian Legion into a genuine fighting force. But they made a poor start. The Indians were forced to give up their remaining heavy equipment to a newly formed elite SS division, the 18th SS-Freiwilligen-Panzergrenadierdivision "Horst Wessel." And their first SS commander, a former official of the Foreign Ministry by the name of Heinz Bertling, took so little interest in his command that he had to be replaced. Nevertheless, the legion was eventually reorganized and re-equipped.

In March 1945, when Hitler was scraping the bottom of his manpower barrel, he came across the Indian Legion and was angered to learn that it had more weapons than its size warranted and that, although it had never fought, it was undergoing

[57] *Ibid.*, pp. 660, n. 1, 674, 864, n. 2. See also Steiner, *Die Freiwilligen*, pp. 228, 293 f., 308ff.
[58] *Hitlers Lagebesprechungen*, p. 939, n. 2.
[59] *Ibid.*

"rest and rehabilitation" miles from the front at a time when the Red Army was nearing Berlin. Turning to SS Sturmbannführer (Major) Johannes Göhler, an SS liaison officer, Hitler remarked sarcastically: "As I see it, units in rest and rehabilitation are those who have been engaged in heavy fighting and therefore require refreshing. Your units are always refreshing and never fighting." [60] And the Indian Legion never did fight.

Prompted by its success in recruiting former enemy soldiers from the POW camps, the Waffen SS in 1943 decided to establish a British Legion to take part in the European crusade against Bolshevism. A number of British turncoats were available in Germany to assist in the endeavor. The most prominent of these, John Amery, a former Fascist and son of one of Churchill's ministers, was sent around to the prison camps to seek recruits among his captured countrymen. [61] By the spring of 1944, the first 50 or so Britons were established at the legion's camp in Hildesheim. [62]

On March 3, 1944, Gottlob Berger reported to Himmler's headquarters that the British volunteers had "uniformly expressed the desire to have Brigadier General (corresponding to our SS Oberführer) Parrington as the future leader of the 'British Free Corps.' " The English general had been captured in Greece in 1941 and according to Berger had "the reputation of being both enthusiastically and sincerely devoted to the Führer." In closing his report the chief of the SS Hauptamt expressed his belief that there would be some difficulty in getting the British to swear an oath to the Führer and he therefore requested Himmler's adjutant to "please ask the Reichsführer SS whether the . . . *soft* formula is appropriate." [63]

Himmler's answer to Berger's report has not been found, but apparently the Reichsführer was willing to make extra concessions to British national pride: he gave the Free Corps per-

[60] *Ibid.,* p. 942.

[61] *Ibid.,* p. 267, n. 2.

[62] "Rede des SS-Obergruppenführers Jüttner auf der SS-Führer-Tagung in Prag am 13. April 1944," NSDAP/T–81, 154/157544.

[63] Berger to Brandt, March 3, 1944, Geheime Kommandosache, Nuremberg Document NO–2757, USMT IV, Case 11, PDB 66–H, pp. 46 f.

mission to wear English uniforms with German insignia. Nevertheless, despite the special privileges, the Free Corps never seems to have attracted any significant number of Britons. By June 1944 the SS Hauptamt was complaining that "the method of recruiting hitherto used among the British prisoners of war is not leading to the success we hoped for." It was suggested that SS men with a knowledge of English be assigned to the POW camps to ascertain "the attitude of the individual Englishmen and . . . [to report] immediately if they discover any adherents of the British Legion idea so that they can be transferred. This transfer must be made immediately so that the other inmates of the camp will no longer be able to exert any influence over them." [64]

No additional information concerning the British Free Corps has been found in the records examined for this study. But by mid-1944 the Allies had invaded France and whatever appeal the Free Corps might have had surely must have evaporated. Although the "British Freecorps (SS)" was still listed as a formation of the Waffen SS in 1945, there is no evidence that it ever attained a status other than that of a propaganda device.

Conclusions

The foreign SS presents such a combination of contrasts that it is difficult to assess its value. Nevertheless, one fact emerges quite clearly: the enlargement of the Waffen SS resulting from the massive mobilization of foreign nationals did not lead to a corresponding increase in its military capability.

Only the west Europeans—numerically the smallest group—fought consistently well. The best of them—and this included most of the early volunteers from Norway, Denmark, and Holland—were practically indistinguishable in quality from the native Germans in the crack SS divisions. Having learned their craft in the hard but victorious battles of the early war years, they remained a formidable and reliable fighting force until the very end. When large numbers of west Europeans entered

[64] Klumm (Amt B, SSHA) to Brandt, "British Volunteer Unit," June 13, 1944, Secret, Nuremberg Document NO–909, USMT IV, Case 11, PDB 66–G, pp. 173 f.

the Waffen SS in the last year of the war, their veteran countrymen helped provide the leadership, experience, and élan which
made the new brigades and divisions useful additions to the SS
war machine.

The combat record of the *Volksdeutsche* is considerably
more difficult to evaluate. Most of them were, at first, assigned to
existing SS formations as replacements. As early as November
1941, Gruppenführer Eicke, commander of the SS Division
"Totenkopf," complained to the SSFHA that the *Volksdeutsche*
replacements being sent to him were "mostly undernourished
and less suited for physical strain." Many were not only physically deficient but "spiritually weak" as well. He reported that
they "tend to be disobedient and evasive," often using their
alleged inability to understand German as an excuse to avoid
carrying out unpleasant or dangerous assignments. This, Eicke
pointed out, had led to numerous cases of "cowardice" in combat. In concluding his list of complaints, Eicke reminded Berlin
that his was an elite division and that he had no use for
"undisciplined and dishonest scoundrels [*Lumpen*] and
criminals." [65]

In short, the integration of large numbers of *Volksdeutsche*
—many of whom had difficulty with the German language—
was a serious problem for the Waffen SS, and quite a few of
Himmler's speeches before SS officers included pleas for patience
and understanding in the handling of ethnic German personnel. Of course, the best of the SS divisions remained predominantly German and apparently managed to absorb those *Volksdeutsche* assigned to them without any drastic diminution in
fighting ability. Less elite SS units, however, were largely, and
in some cases almost entirely, composed of ethnic Germans.
In general it is possible to discern a correlation between the
number of *Volksdeutsche* in a given SS division and its combat
efficiency: the higher the percentage of ethnic Germans, the
lower the level of performance. Indeed, this fact was recognized
by Hitler and his military staff.

At one conference of which we have a record, the Führer

[65] Eicke to SSFHA, "Erfahrungen über den Nachersatz," November
15, 1941, RFSS/T–175, 108/2632012ff.

inquired about the personnel composition of two SS divisions with which he was unfamiliar. The answer was *"Volksdeutsche und Reichsdeutsche,"* and he seems to have been pleasantly surprised to discover that there were at least some native Germans in the units. At a time when most of the new SS divisions were composed of foreigners or *Volksdeutsche,* the proportion of Germans to non-Germans in a given unit had become the yardstick with which to measure its reliability.[66]

The eastern SS—numerically many times larger than the western SS—was, with the exception of the three Baltic divisions, nearly useless in regular warfare. To be sure, Himmler had originally intended to use the eastern formations only against irregular forces. But the exigencies of a losing war forced them out of the forests and into the front line. It was a challenge the eastern SS could not meet. Aside from their generally inferior morale, these formations were neither trained nor equipped to fight against the massive tank and artillery concentrations employed by the Red Army during the last stages of the war.

The Moslems, as we have seen, were not even reliable in antipartisan operations and had to be disbanded before the end of the war. The multitude of eastern SS regiments and brigades established during the last months of the war were no less unreliable. So many Romanians and Hungarians deserted to the Russians along the lower Oder front that the rest had to be disarmed.[67] The Vlasov Army, which included numerous SS men from the 29th and 30th SS divisions, never fought against the Red Army at all. "In fact," Reitlinger tells us, "the Waffen SS were the only enemy it ever fought and the story is one of the queerest of the whole war."[68]

[66] The SS divisions in question were the 8th SS-Kavalleriedivision "Florian Geyer" and the 22nd Freiwilligen-Kavalleriedivision der SS; the former was 40 per cent *Volksdeutsch,* the latter 70 per cent. Neither division was considered an elite SS formation. See "Besprechung des Führers mit Generaloberst Jodl am 31. Juli 1944 in der Wolfsschanze," *Hitlers Lagebesprechungen,* p. 607.

[67] "Lagebuch 5. 4. 45, Heeresgr. Weichsel," KTB/OKW, IV, 1224.

[68] The clash took place in Prague during the last week of the war. See Reitlinger, *op. cit.,* p. 391.

The Baltic SS divisions, which had fought well while defending their homelands, lost much of their zeal after the Soviet Army occupied Estonia and Latvia. The 15th Waffen-Grenadierdivision der SS (lett. Nr. 1) performed better than the others during the last months, and some of its units (including a battalion in Berlin) fought grimly to the end.[69] Its sister division, the 19th Waffen-Grenadierdivision der SS (lett. Nr. 2), which was cut off in Courland, erupted in a series of mutinies during December 1944, while the previously reliable 20th Waffen-Grenadierdivision der SS (estn. Nr. 1) fell apart when it was again committed to battle in Silesia early in 1945.[70]

During the night of March 23–24, 1945, with the Russians less than 100 miles from Berlin, Hitler held a conference in the living quarters of his underground bunker. The proceedings were taken down stenographically and the record provides us with Hitler's own final assessment of the eastern SS.[71]

HITLER: One never knows what's floating around. I've just heard, to my surprise, that a Ukrainian SS-Division has suddenly turned up. I knew absolutely nothing about this Ukrainian SS-Division.

GÖHLER: [SS Liaison Officer] It has been in existence for a long time.

HITLER: But it has never been mentioned at any of our conferences. Or do you recall otherwise?

GÖHLER: No, I don't remember.

. . . .

HITLER: [In reference to foreign units in general and the Ukrainian Division in particular] Either the unit is reliable or it isn't reliable. At the moment I can't even create new formations in Germany because I have no weapons. Therefore it is idiocy to give weapons to a Ukrainian division which is not completely reliable. I would

[69] See "Lagebuch 29. 1. 45, Heeresgr. Weichsel," KTB/OKW, IV, 1050; Steiner, *Die Freiwilligen,* pp. 311ff.

[70] *Hitlers Lagebesprechungen,* pp. 939, 537, n. 2. The collapse of the Estonian division was mentioned in the conference of March 23, 1945, excerpts from which are reproduced below. The location and the circumstances of the event are not known, but the division was part of Korps-Gruppe Schlesien in southern Silesia in March. See "Gliederung des deutschen Heeres in den Jahren 1944/45," March 1, 1945, KTB/OKW, IV, 1896, Cf. Steiner, *Die Freiwilligen,* p. 335.

[71] "Abendlage vom 23. Marz 1945 in Berlin (Führerwohnung)," *Hitlers Lagebesprechungen,* pp. 938ff.

much rather take their weapons away and set up a new German division. I assume that it is outstandingly equipped, probably much better armed than most of the German divisions we are creating at present.

BURGDORF: [General and Chief Wehrmacht Adjutant to the Führer] It is the same with the Latvian 20th [sic]. It also collapsed immediately down there [Silesia].

DE MAIZIERE: [Lieutenant Colonel on the General Staff] The Latvian is fighting in Courland at the moment, and quite well at that. It was the Estonian [20th Waffen-Grenadierdivision der SS (estn. Nr. 1)] down there.

BURGDORF: Yes, it was the Estonian that disintegrated immediately. One has to look at it also from a psychological viewpoint. A bit too much has been demanded of these people.

HITLER: After all, why should they still fight? They are far from their homeland.

. . . .

HITLER: The Indian Legion is a joke. There are Indians that can't kill a louse, and would prefer to allow themselves to be devoured. They certainly aren't going to kill any Englishmen. . . . I imagine that if one were to use the Indians to turn prayer wheels or something like that they would be the most indefatigable soldiers in the world. But it would be ridiculous to commit them to a real blood struggle. . . . The whole business is nonsense. If one has a surplus of weapons, one can permit oneself such amusements for propaganda purposes. But if one has no such surplus [it] is simply not justifiable.

. . . .

HITLER: [Again referring to the Ukrainian–Galician Division] If it is composed of [former] Austrian Ruthenians, one can do nothing other than immediately to take away their weapons. The Austrian Ruthenians were pacifists. They were lambs, not wolves. They were miserable even in the Austrian Army. The whole business is a delusion.

. . . .

HITLER: I don't want to maintain that nothing can be done with these foreigners. Something can indeed be made of them. But it requires time. If one had them for six or ten years and controlled their homelands as the old monarchy did, they would naturally become good soldiers. But if one gets them when their homelands lie somewhere over there [in enemy territory]—why should they be expected to fight?

. . . .

HITLER: [After listening to a list of the Ukrainian Division's equipment] . . . First thing tomorrow morning, I want to speak to the Reichsführer [Himmler]. He is in Berlin anyway. It must be established, in a professional manner, exactly what can be expected from such a formation. If one can't expect anything, then it has no sense. Such formations are a luxury that we cannot afford.

The outcome of Hitler's talk with Himmler remains unknown. But with final defeat only weeks away it could hardly have mattered. For over a year the Reichsführer had been setting up one eastern SS formation after another. As Chef der Heeresrüstung und Befehlshaber des Ersatzheeres [72] he was able to equip them with arms that would have been of far more use in the hands of German troops. In addition, the eastern SS drained veteran German officers and NCOs from existing SS divisions at a time when they were already in critically short supply. As Hitler clearly indicated, the eastern SS—which by 1945 consisted of some two dozen separate formations—was a luxury the German war machine could ill afford.

[72] Himmler was appointed to the position of Commander of the Replacement Army and Chief of Army Ordnance by Hitler a few hours after the bomb plot on July 20, 1944. Colonel General Fromm, the man Himmler replaced, was tried and later executed for his ambiguous role in the plot.

CHAPTER EIGHT

The Waffen SS Comes of Age: 1942-1943

IN his authoritative account of the SS organization, Gerald Reitlinger makes much of the fact that the first great expansion of the Waffen SS did not take place until 1943. He explains the long delay by saying that Hitler "did not trust Himmler sufficiently to allow him a complete army corps," and contends that it was not until the three classic SS divisions ("Adolf Hitler," "Das Reich," and "Totenkopf") temporarily snatched victory from defeat by recapturing Kharkov in March 1943 that "Hitler's own objections to the creation of more SS divisions, his fear of private armies, his anxiety not to provoke the General Staff too far, both [sic] disappeared." The result, according to Reitlinger, was the removal of the check on SS recruiting and the sanctioning of "a large and immediate increase" in the strength of the Waffen SS. He goes on to say that "four completely new armored divisions were recruited with a large component of western European volunteers. They were named Hohenstauffen, Frundsberg, Nordland and Hitlerjugend." [1]

In the absence of any other explanation, Reitlinger's exegesis has become the standard interpretation of the turning point in the development of the Waffen SS. Unfortunately, aside from the names of the four new SS divisions, little in the account quoted above is accurate. The turning point in the development of the Waffen SS was reached in 1942, not 1943. The first SS army corps was authorized by Hitler in May 1942, a full ten

[1] Reitlinger, *op. cit.*, pp. 87, 154, 191, 194.

months before the SS victory at Kharkov. And the establishment of all four of the SS divisions mentioned by Reitlinger was
approved by Hitler before the successful termination of the
battle; indeed, two of them were ordered into existence before
the end of 1942.

Moreover, Hitler's reasons for keeping a tight rein on the
growth of the Waffen SS had nothing to do with a lack of trust
in Himmler. If there was anyone among his top lieutenants
whom Hitler trusted in 1942, it was *"der getreue Heinrich."*
And since the Waffen SS was under military command, it is
difficult to see why Hitler should have feared that its expansion
would create a "private" army for Himmler; all the more so
since Hitler was by then personally directing the war as head
of both the OKH and OKW.[2]

To understand Hitler's long delay in creating new SS divisions, it is necessary to re-examine his basic conception of the
Waffen SS. It will be recalled that for Hitler the armed SS was
first and foremost an elite, militarized, and politically reliable
police force. He reiterated this view as late as January 1942. The
SS, he declared, had to go to the front in order to maintain its
prestige. But it must remain small and selective; quality, not
quantity, was what mattered. Hence only the elite should be
sought. Youths who merely wanted to show off must be made
aware that casualties in the Waffen SS were higher than in other
formations. When peace returned, he concluded, the Waffen SS
would be freed for its intended role as an elite police force.[3]

Reitlinger has interpreted Hitler's remarks as a polite rebuff
to "Himmler's hope of a private army." [4] But there is no
reason to believe that they were any more or less than they
seem. The fact is that Hitler was at this time still under
the impression that the war would soon be over. Despite the
reverses being suffered by the Wehrmacht as a result of the
unexpected Russian winter offensive, Hitler was confident that
he was witnessing the death throes of the Bolshevik bear. While

[2] In taking issue with Reitlinger's views on this subject, the author is
in no way attempting to depreciate the over-all value of his book.
[3] *Hitler's Secret Conversations*, pp. 177 f.
[4] Reitlinger, *op. cit.*, p. 191.

WORLD WAR II IN EUROPE
1942-1943

→ Allied troop movements
→ Axis troop movements
▨ Extent of Axis domination
at the end of 1943

Miles
0   500
Kilometres
0   500

NORTH SEA

IRELAND

GREAT BRITAIN

London

ATLANTIC OCEAN

English Channel

NETHERLANDS

BELG.

LUXEM-BOURG

Paris

FRANCE

GERMAN OCCUPATION NOV., 1942

Vichy

Bordeaux

SWITZ.

Munich

Milan

Marseille   Nice

Lisbon
PORTUGAL

Madrid

SPAIN

Strait of Gibraltar

SP. MOROCCO

Casablanca

FRENCH MOROCCO

ALLIED TASK FORCE NOV. 8, 1942

Oran   Algiers

Bône

Tunis

ALGERIA

TUNISIA

CAPTURED BY ALLIES MAY 7, 1943

GERMAN POSITION FEB., 1943

NORWAY

SWEDEN

DENMARK

BALTIC SEA

FINLAND

Lake Ladoga

Gulf of Finland

Leningrad

ESTONIA

LATVIA

LITHUANIA

Memel

Danzig

GERMANY

EAST PRUSSIA

Berlin

Warsaw   Brest-Litovsk

POLAND

CZECHOSLOVAKIA

AUSTRIA   HUNGARY

ITALY

CORSICA

OCT., 1943

SEPT., 1943

SARDINIA

Rome
Anzio

ALLIED POSITION JAN., 1944

Naples
JAN. 1944
SEPT. 8 1943
Salerno
SEPT. 3, 1943

Palermo   Messina

SICILY INVADED BY ALLIES JULY 10, 1943

MALTA

YUGOSLAVIA

ADRIATIC SEA

ALBANIA

Taranto

GREECE

AEGEAN SEA

RUMANIA

Bucharest

BULGARIA

Sofia

Odessa

SEA OF AZOV

Yalta

BLACK SEA

Moscow

Smolensk

EASTERN FRONT JAN., 1944

Kursk

Kiev   Kharkov

LIMIT OF GERMAN PENETRATION NOV., 1942

Stalingrad

U.   S.   S.   R.

CAUCASUS MTS.

CASPIAN SEA

Dardanelles

CRETE

CYPRUS

TURKEY

Teheran

IRAN

OCCUPIED BY ALLIES, 1941

SYRIA
OCCUPIED BY ALLIES 1941

IRAQ
OCCUPIED BY ALLIES, 1941

MEDITERRANEAN   SEA

Tripoli

PURSUIT OF ROMMEL NOV., 1942-FEB., 1943

LIBYA

Benghazi   Derna   Tobruk
Bardia
Sidi Barrani

El-Alamein

BATTLE OF EL-ALAMEIN OCT. 23-NOV. 1, 1942

EGYPT

Cairo

Suez Canal

Gulf of Suez

RED SEA

PALESTINE

TRANSJORDAN

Gulf of Aqaba

SAUDI ARABIA

a good many of the generals were exhibiting signs of panic and even defeatism, Hitler was planning a new offensive which he believed would bring final victory.[5]

Hitler did not have to wait until the battle of Kharkov in 1943 to appreciate the value of the SS divisions. Their fighting ability had been amply demonstrated in the campaigns of 1939, 1940, and 1941. At the very time that he was envisioning a speedy return of the Waffen SS to its postwar police functions, Hitler did not fail to recognize its outstanding combat performance. "I am proud," he told a group of dinner guests, "when an army commander can tell me that 'his force is based essentially on an armored division and the SS Reich Division.' " For Hitler the SS was "an extraordinary body of men, devoted to an idea, loyal unto death. . . . At the present time [the Soviet counteroffensive] we have it confirmed that every division of the SS is aware of its responsibility. The SS knows that its job is to set an example . . . and that all eyes are upon it." [6] While many Army units and their commanders panicked in the face of the unexpected Russian onslaught, the Waffen SS stood firm. And Goebbels noted in his diary that "if we had twenty men like [Sepp Dietrich] we wouldn't have to worry at all about the Eastern Front." [7]

It was during the winter of 1941–1942 that the Waffen SS displayed what was for Hitler to become its greatest virtue: the ability to retain its fighting spirit even in defeat.[8] It was this quality that led Hitler to order an expansion of the Waffen SS toward the end of 1942. For by then events had forced him to give up his earlier optimism and to face the fact that Germany was in for a long, hard war.

As the Führer had predicted, the Wehrmacht survived the

[5] For a description of Hitler's state of mind during the winter of 1942–1943, see *The Goebbels Diaries, 1942–1943,* Louis P. Lochner, ed. (New York, 1948), pp. 62, 79.

[6] *Hitler's Secret Conversations,* p. 178.

[7] *The Goebbels Diaries,* p. 51.

[8] For Hitler's opinion regarding the importance of "fanatical tenacity" as a soldierly quality see "Besprechung des Führers mit Generalmajor Thomale am 29. Dezember 1944 im Adlerhorst," *Hitlers Lagebesprechungen,* pp. 779 f.

Soviet winter offensive. By standing firm in hedgehog positions and permitting the Russians to sweep around their flanks, the Germans maintained a hold on the key towns along their front; Hitler's "no retreat" order had exposed his troops to terrible sufferings, but it had saved the eastern front. By March the Russian thrust had run its course and Hitler ordered preparations for the launching of a new German offensive.[9]

Although Himmler continued to plead for an expansion of the Waffen SS, Hitler demurred. He was certain the war would be over by the end of the year. The only completely new SS division established during the first half of 1942 was the *Volksdeutsche* 7th SS Freiwilligen-Gebirgsdivision "Prinz Eugen," which was confined to antipartisan operations in Yugoslavia. Hitler did, however, authorize the reorganization and reinforcement of the existing SS formations. By the middle of the year, the bulk of the three elite SS divisions—"Leibstandarte Adolf Hitler," "Das Reich," and "Totenkopf"—had been taken out of the line and sent west to be reorganized into panzergrenadier divisions.[10]

In the meantime, the German summer offensive was launched in the Kursk–Kharkov sector. In line with Hitler's plan to seize the Caucasian oil fields in a lightning thrust along the southern front, a panzer army under the command of Field Marshal Kleist broke through the Soviet line and surged into the Caucasus. The Soviet armies once again crumbled under the German onslaught, and in six weeks the entire Don River bend as well as the Maikop oilfields were in German hands; one of the deepest penetrations had been made by the SS Division "Wiking."[11]

For the Russians this was the most critical period of the war. Hitler's optimism ("The Russian is finished," he told his Chief of Staff on July 20) had seemingly been vindicated.

---

[9] The best account of these events is in Clark, *op. cit.*, pp. 187ff. See also "The Russo-German Campaign," *The Red Army*, B. H. Liddell Hart, ed. (New York, 1956), pp. 109ff.; Manstein, *op. cit.*, pp. 175ff.; Philippi and Heim, *op. cit.*, pp. 107ff.

[10] Panzergrenadier divisions were mechanized infantry formations whose riflemen were transported in armored halftrack personnel carriers.

[11] Steiner, *Die Freiwilligen*, p. 158.

By the middle of September German troops were in the heart of Stalingrad. Here the war would be decided, for if the Germans captured this strategically placed city, they would be in a position to wheel north (along the line of the Volga) and roll up the entire Russian front. What followed is well known. Stalingrad did not fall; and on November 19, 1942, the Red Army launched a counteroffensive which, despite local setbacks and long delays, brought it to Berlin some two and a half years later.

In the last months of 1942 the tide of war turned everywhere against the Third Reich. On November 4, Rommel's Afrika Korps, standing on the threshold of Alexandria, was forced into retreat at the battle of El Alamein; four days later an Anglo–American army under the command of General Eisenhower landed in North Africa; and on November 22, the Russians closed the ring around the German 6th Army at Stalingrad.[12] After three years of steady advance, the Wehrmacht lost the initiative and began its long retreat. That it took the Allies another two and a half years to encompass Germany's defeat was, in no small measure, due to the efforts of the elite panzer divisions of the Waffen SS which Hitler ordered into existence in 1942 and 1943.

Development of the Waffen SS in 1942

During the first months of 1942, the entire field strength of the Waffen SS was engaged in the bitter battles raging along the eastern front; six divisions, two infantry brigades, one cavalry brigade, four national legions, and a handful of smaller independent formations constituted the Waffen SS' contribution to the campaign.[13]

By the time the Russian offensive petered out in February, the SS formations were in some cases mere shadows of their

[12] See summary of Germany's military situation in *Hitlers Lagebesprechungen,* p. 49.

[13] See Himmler's Memorandum of April 27, 1942, RFSS/T–175, 105/2628463ff. A complete listing of the field units of the Waffen SS at the beginning of 1942 may be found in SSFHA, "Feldpostübersicht," January 10, 1942, Geheim, RFSS/T–175, 105/2628746ff.

former strength. In view of Hitler's intention to launch a summer offensive designed to knock Russia out of the war, it was
decided to reinforce and re-equip the elite SS divisions. As early
as August 1941, SS Gruppenführer (Lieutenant General)
Hausser had requested that the SS Divisions "Leibstandarte
Adolf Hitler" and "Das Reich" be supplied with a tank component.[14] The following January, Hitler approved the request,
issuing orders that a tank battalion be established for each of
the two divisions. By the end of May the two remaining elite
SS divisions ("Totenkopf" and "Wiking") had also been
allotted a tank battalion each.[15] Thus, by mid-1942, the four
classic SS divisions had taken the first step toward becoming
the armored "fire brigade" of the Third Reich. During this
same period Hitler finally made good his 1938 promise to
establish an SS army corps; to lead the reorganized SS divisions,
he authorized the establishment of an SS Generalkommando (SS
army corps headquarters) under the command of Paul Hausser.[16]

While three of the four elite SS divisions were refitting in
the West, the German summer offensive, which had opened so
brilliantly, ground to a halt at Stalingrad. As the German position in Africa and Russia continued to deteriorate, Hitler made
the decision to expand the Waffen SS. His first step was to
authorize the enlargement of the SS Cavalry (Kavallerie) Brigade into the 8th SS Kavalleriedivision "Florian Geyer." [17] This
was followed in November by new orders calling for the
further strengthening of the elite SS Divisions "Leibstandarte

[14] Hausser's Memorandum of August 31, 1941, RFSS/T–175, 107/
2630666.

[15] SSFHA, "Aufstellung einer Panzer-Abteilung für die LSSAH,"
January 30, 1942, Geheime Kommandosache, RFSS/T–175, 108/2631615ff.;
SSFHA, "Aufstellung einer Panzer-Abteilung für die SS-Div. 'Reich,' "
February 11, 1942, Geheim, 106/2629425ff.; SSFHA, "Aufstellung einer 3.
SS-Panzer-Abteilung," April 18, 1942, Geheim, 106/2629382ff.; SSFHA,
"Aufstellung einer SS-Panzer-Abteilung für die SS-T-Div.," May 20, 1942,
Geheim, 108/2631827ff.

[16] SSFHA, "Aufstellung eines SS-Generalkommandos," May 28, 1942,
Geheim, RFSS/T–175, 109/2633566ff. Before the end of the year, Hausser's
command had been redesignated SS Panzer-Generalkommando.

[17] SSFHA, "Gliederung der SS-Kavallerie-Division," September 9, 1942,
Geheime Kommandosache, RFSS/T–175, 109/2632762ff.

Adolf Hitler," "Das Reich," and "Totenkopf." Equipped with additional tanks, assault guns, and armored personnel carriers, they now were redesignated SS panzergrenadier divisions.[18] And in December Hitler ordered the creation of two new German SS divisions, the first since 1940; both of them were to be elite panzergrenadier divisions and were to constitute a second SS army corps.[19]

Increasing battle losses and the requirements of expansion combined to create a new manpower crisis for the Waffen SS. Now, however, Hitler stood solidly behind the SS in its dealings with the OKW, the RAD, and the Army. As early as August, Keitel reluctantly authorized the Waffen SS to recruit three times its normal quota from the 1924 class,[20] and the lid was never again successfully clamped down. On September 1, 1942, the Waffen SS had a field strength of 141,975 men, with an additional 45,663 in training and reserve; exactly a year later the figures had almost doubled—280,000 in the field units and 70,000 in training and reserve.[21]

[18] SSFHA, "Umgliederung der SS-Div. 'Das Reich' in SS-Panzer-Grenadier-Div. 'Das Reich,' " November 14, 1942, Geheime Kommandosache, RFSS/T–175, 106/2629210ff.; SSFHA, "Umbenennung und Umgliederung der SS-Div. 'LSSAH,' " November 24, 1942, Geheime Kommandosache, 108/2631443; SSFHA, "Umgliederung der SS-T-Div. in SS-Panzer-Grenadier-Division 'Totenkopf,' " November 16, 1942, Geheime Kommandosache, 108/2631857. The 5th SS Division "Wiking" was not redesignated until the following March; see SSFHA, "Umgliederung der SS-Division 'Wiking' in SS-Panzer-Grenadier-Division 'Wiking,' " March 29, 1943, Geheime Kommandosache, 111/2635184ff.

[19] The SSFHA directives establishing these two divisions have not been found in the SS records examined for this study, but other evidence indicates that Hitler authorized both divisions (eventually designated 9th SS Panzergrenadierdivision "Hohenstauffen" and 10th SS Panzergrenadier-division "Frundsberg") before the end of 1942. See KTB/OKW, January 5, 1943, III, 20; *Hitlers Lagebesprechungen*, p. 207, n. 2; "Rede des SS-Obergruppenführers Jüttner auf der SS-Führer-Tagung in Prag am 13. April 1944," NSDAP/T–81, 154/157539.

[20] Keitel to SS Ergänzungsamt, "Ersatzverteilung Jahrgang 24," August 7, 1942, Geheim, RFSS/T–175, 110/2634193.

[21] "Iststärke der Waffen-SS Stand vom 1. 9. 1942," Geheime Kommandosache, RFSS/T–175, 105/2627497 f.; KTB/OKW, III, 1576. For the strength of the Waffen SS by units see "Gesamstärke der Waffen-SS," December 31, 1942, Geheime Kommandosache, RFSS/T–175, 111/2635898ff.

Organization and Development
of the Waffen SS in 1943

The beginning of 1943 found the combat formations of the Waffen SS distributed as follows: 1st SS Panzergrenadierdivision "Leibstandarte Adolf Hitler," 2nd SS Panzergrenadierdivision "Das Reich," 3rd SS Panzergrenadierdivision "Totenkopf," and SS Panzer-Generalkommando (SS Panzer Corps Headquarters Staff) in the West (mostly in France); 4th SS Polizeidivision and 2nd SS Brigade (including Dutch, Flemish, and Norwegian legions) fighting in Russia with Army Group North; 5th SS Division "Wiking" in southern Russia with Army Group Don; 6th SS Gebirgsdivision "Nord" in action along the northern Finnish front with the German 20th Gebirgsarmee; 7th SS Freiwilligen-Gebirgsdivision "Prinz Eugen" in Serbia with Army Group Southeast; 8th SS Kavalleriedivision "Florian Geyer" and 1st SS Brigade (including Freikorps "Danmark") fighting in Russia with Army Group Center.[22]

To these formations were now added the 9th SS Panzergrenadierdivision "Hohenstauffen" and the 10th SS Panzergrenadierdivision "Frundsberg," which Hitler had authorized in December. In spite of Himmler's boast that 25 per cent of each yearly class volunteered for the Waffen SS, his recruiters were unable to obtain the number of volunteers that had been authorized for the two new divisions.[23] As a result, the Waffen SS for the first time had to resort to the large-scale conscription of native Germans. Thousands of youths who met SS standards, some 70 to 80 per cent of the necessary personnel, were drafted from the work camps of the Reichsarbeitsdienst (Reich Labor Service). SS Obergruppenführer (General) Jüttner, chief of the SS Führungshauptamt, later described to his colleagues the great agitation that resulted from this procedure. Complaints and letters from "parents, ministers, bishops, and cardinals" poured into Berlin (some directly to the Führer) demanding

[22] See particularly "Schematische Kriegs-Gliederung," January 1, 1943, KTB/OKW, III, 3ff.

[23] Himmler's boast was made on November 23, 1942, in a speech at the SS Junkerschule Tölz, RFSS/T–175, 90/2612788.

the release of the conscripted youths. According to Jüttner, the SS authorities agreed to a compromise: the youths were to be kept in training for a month or so and then offered the choice of volunteering or being released from SS service. "I believe," Jüttner reported, "that there were three [who asked to be released] out of the entire two divisions. All the rest said: 'No, we stay!' They had not known what the Waffen SS really was, only what their ministers and parents had told them." Both divisions, concluded Jüttner, turned into crack formations.[24]

In January, while recruiting for "Hohenstauffen" and "Frundsberg" was still in progress, Reichsjugendführer (Reich Youth Leader) Arthur Axmann came to Himmler with an offer to establish a volunteer division for the Waffen SS. It would be composed of members of the Hitler Youth born in 1926, and would, according to Axmann, have "a value equal to that of the Leibstandarte." On February 13, Himmler informed Axmann that he had received Hitler's approval, and he requested the youth leader to work out the details for the new division with Berger.[25] So dazzled was the chief of the SS Hauptamt at the prospect of a new elite division composed of handpicked young Nazis that he begged Himmler to appoint him its commander. Berger's dream of becoming another Sepp Dietrich was shattered by Himmler's polite but firm refusal; Berger, it seems, was much more valuable behind his desk, and Himmler admonished him not to "become impatient." [26] Instead the post was awarded to a regimental commander in the 1st SS Panzergrenadierdivision "Leibstandarte Adolf Hitler," the much-decorated thirty-five-year-old SS Standartenführer (Colonel) Fritz Witt. With him as cadre for the new division came a

---

[24] "Rede des SS-Obergruppenführers Jüttner auf der SS-Führer-Tagung in Prag am 13. April 1944," NSDAP/T–81, 154/157539ff.; KTB/OKW, January 5, 1943, III, 20.

[25] Himmler to Axmann, February 13, 1943, Geheim, RFSS/T–175, 108/2631254.

[26] Berger to Himmler, February 9, 1943, Geheim, RFSS/T–175, 108/2631262ff. and Himmler to Berger, February 16, 1943, Geheim, 108/2631245. For details concerning Berger's negotiations with Axmann see Berger to Himmler, "Aufstellung der Division Hitler Jugend," February 18, 1943, 108/2631249ff.

sizable number of officers, NCOs, and specialists from the Waffen SS' senior formation. By midsummer of 1943 the first 10,000 youths for the 12th SS Division "Hitler Jugend" were in training at an SS camp near Beverloo, Belgium.[27]

In the meantime, Hitler's relationship with the Army generals and his attitude toward the Waffen SS changed drastically as a result of the defensive battles following the debacle at Stalingrad and culminating in the great SS victory at Kharkov in March 1943. As the Russians surged into the Donetz basin, the generals counseled withdrawal, arguing that an attempt to hold on to the area would result in another Stalingrad. On February 6, Field Marshal von Manstein, commander of Army Group South, flew to Hitler's headquarters at Rastenburg in the hope of convincing him to "shorten the front" in order to make additional forces available for a defense farther to the west. But Hitler refused, insisting that "if one fought bitterly for every foot of ground and made the enemy pay dearly for every step he advanced, even the Soviet armies' offensive power must some day be exhausted." Manstein's professional views seemed to make no impression on the Führer: "All Hitler actually had to say about the operational position was to express the belief that the SS Panzer Corps would be able to remove the acute threat to the middle Donetz front. . . . His faith in the penetrating power of this newly established SS Panzer Corps was apparently unbounded."[28]

Unable because of Hitler's intransigence to conduct the campaign in terms of long-range objectives, Manstein did the best he could. As the Russians approached the Dnieper after capturing Kharkov, he launched a counterstroke which slashed through the hinge of the advance and threw the Russians back in disorder. Although the success of the operation owed much to Manstein's masterful strategy, it was the three divisions

[27] Meyer, *op. cit.*, p. 205. Apparently a good many of the youths for the "Hitler Jugend" Division were drafted. See Berger to SSFHA, "Aufstellung der SS-Division 'Hitler-Jugend,'" March 21, 1943, Geheime Kommandosache, RFSS/T–175, 108/2631228ff.

[28] Manstein, *op. cit.*, pp. 410 f.

("Leibstandarte Adolf Hitler," "Das Reich," and "Totenkopf") of the SS Panzerkorps that spearheaded the operation and recaptured Kharkov.[29] The effect of the SS victory on Hitler was exhilarating. That part of the mineral-rich Donetz basin which was so essential to the German war effort had been held. The great Soviet Stalingrad offensive seemed to have been stemmed; and Hitler's no-retreat policy, as well as his faith in the elite divisions of the Waffen SS, had been vindicated.

The transcript of Hitler's military conferences in the months following the Kharkov battle reflects his increased appreciation of the Waffen SS. "The SS Panzerkorps is worth twenty Italian divisions," he said on one occasion.[30] He worried a good deal about the SS, and told General Zeitzler, his Army Chief of Staff, that "we must see to it that the SS gets the necessary personnel."[31] He was impatient to pull the three SS armored divisions out of the line, to spare them for a new emergency. On Hitler's orders they received the latest heavy tanks. Moreover, even the two new SS divisions, despite Army objections, were given priority in the distribution of the latest model Panther medium tanks.[32]

When Himmler made one of his rare appearances at a military conference, Hitler took the opportunity to question him about the new SS divisions, "Hohenstauffen" and "Frundsberg." Himmler's comment that the average age of the two divisions, including officers, was only eighteen, drew from Hitler the remark that this was fine, since Germany's youth fights "magnificently and with incredible bravery." He indicated that battle reports show that "the youngsters who come from the Hitler Youth are fanatical fighters. . . . These young German lads, some only sixteen years old, . . . fight more fanatically

[29] *Ibid.*, pp. 420ff.; KTB/OKW, March 15, 1943, III, 214 f. According to Hausser, *op. cit.*, p. 95, his SS Panzerkorps lost 365 officers and 11,154 men in the battle.

[30] "Besprechung des Führers mit Feldmarschall v. Kluge am 26. Juli 1943," *Hitlers Lagebesprechungen*, p. 383.

[31] "Fragment einer Abendlage vermutlich zwischen 12. und 15. März 1943 in der Wolfsschanze," *ibid.*, p. 197.

[32] Various conferences, *ibid.*, pp. 212 f., 303 f., 364 f., 380.

than their older comrades." He was certain that the new SS divisions—"Hohenstauffen," "Frundsberg," and especially "Hitler Jugend"—would fight equally well.[33]

The temporary stabilization of the Russian front and the invasion of Sicily on July 10, 1943, followed two weeks later by the capitulation of Italy, led Hitler to order the transfer of part of the SS Panzerkorps to the West.[34] It was the type of sudden shift which was to characterize the employment of the elite SS divisions during the remainder of the war; wherever in Hitler's opinion the threat was greatest, there the panzer divisions of the Waffen SS were sent.

In the second half of 1943 the expansion of the Waffen SS moved rapidly ahead. The 9th SS Panzergrenadierdivision "Hohenstauffen" and the 10th SS Panzergrenadierdivision "Frundsberg" were now entering the last phase of their training. On March 22 the 11th SS Freiwilligen-Panzergrenadierdivision "Nordland" was created by merging the four Germanic legions, a cadre from the 5th SS Division "Wiking," and a large group of new west European recruits.[35] On June 24, the 12th SS Panzergrenadierdivision "Hitler Jugend," which had been recruiting since early spring, was officially activated. During the same period, it will be recalled, three eastern SS divisions—the 13th "Handschar" (Bosnian), the 14th (Galician), and the 15th (Latvian) were established.[36] More important, however, two additional German SS divisions were authorized by Hitler the following October: the 16th SS Panzergrenadierdivision "Reichsführer SS" and the 17th SS Panzergrenadierdivision "Götz von Berlichingen." [37] Finally, the survivors of

[33] "Mittagslage vom 26. July 1943," *ibid.,* pp. 334 f. Hitler repeated his comments almost verbatim to von Kluge at another conference the same evening. See *ibid.,* pp. 381 f.

[34] See p. 214.

[35] See pp. 162 f.

[36] See Chapter Seven, *passim.*

[37] The 16th SS Division was based on the Sturmbrigade "Reichsführer SS," which in turn had been created out of Himmler's personal SS escort battalion. See SSFHA, "Umgliederung des Begleit-Btls. RFSS zur Sturmbrigade RFSS," February 23, 1943, Geheime Kommandosache, RFSS/T–175, 108/2631347ff.; SSFHA, "Aufstellung der 16. SS-Pz. Gren. Div. 'RFSS,' "

the long-suffering 4th SS Polizeidivision were pulled out of the Russian front and shipped off to Greece, where in the comparative quiet of guerrilla warfare they were reorganized as a panzergrenadier division.

Normally, German panzergrenadier divisions possessed no tank component, the designation simply standing for a partially armored, motorized infantry division. But the elite SS panzergrenadier divisions had long been equipped with tanks—indeed, "Leibstandarte Adolf Hitler" and "Das Reich" had more and better tanks than most Army panzer divisions.[38] In October 1943, therefore, the seven crack SS panzergrenadier divisions—"Leibstandarte Adolf Hitler," "Das Reich," "Totenkopf," "Wiking," "Hohenstauffen," "Frundsberg," and "Hitler Jugend"—were redesignated SS panzer divisions.[39] Despite the continued expansion of the Waffen SS in succeeding years, no additional SS panzer divisions were ever created. These seven divisions became Hitler's emergency "fire brigade"; with occasional assistance from the half-dozen or so somewhat less elite SS panzergrenadier divisions, they maintained and enhanced the military reputation of the Waffen SS until the final collapse of the Third Reich.

In the last years of the war, the deciding factors in ground warfare were tanks, self-propelled artillery, and mechanized infantry. It was a measure of the increased importance of the Waffen SS that by the end of 1943, seven of the thirty panzer

---

October 19, 1943, Geheime Kommandosache, 108/2631300ff.; *Hitlers Lagebesprechungen*, pp. 283 f. On the 17th SS Division see SSFHA, "Aufstellung der 17. SS-Pz. Gren. Div. 'Götz von Berlichingen,' " October 30, 1943, Geheime Kommandosache, 108/2631385ff.; *Hitler's Lagebesprechungen*, p. 758, n. 6.

[38] In December 1942, when Germany's inventory of the new Tiger and Panther tanks totaled only 74, two companies of the latest Tiger tanks went to the "Leibstandarte Adolf Hitler," which was then not technically a panzer division. See SSFHA, "Aufstellung einer schweren SS-Panzer-Abteilung," December 24, 1942, Geheim, RFSS/T–175, 110/2633944 f.

[39] See RFSS Adjutantur, "Aufstellung der Verbände der Waffen SS," November 15, 1943, Geheime Kommandosache, RFSS/T–175, 111/2635237ff. The "Umgliederung" directives for the individual SS divisions are scattered throughout roll 111.

divisions and six of the seventeen panzergrenadier divisions in the Wehrmacht were SS formations.[40] Given the larger size, better equipment, and generally superior morale of the SS divisions, it is clear that their combat potential was considerably greater than their number alone might indicate.

To provide the necessary tactical leadership for the many new SS divisions, Hitler authorized the formation of additional SS Generalkommandos, or army corps. Altogether, six new SS corps were created during 1943, of which four were armored. Hausser's pioneer SS corps was redesignated IInd SS Panzerkorps, and a new corps, the Ist SS Panzerkorps, was created with Sepp Dietrich as its commander. For the Germanic volunteer divisions "Wiking" and "Nordland" (plus the SS Brigade "Nederland"), Hitler approved the formation of the IIIrd (Germanisches) SS Panzerkorps, under the leadership of Felix Steiner. The last of the four new corps, the IVth SS Panzerkorps, was established in June, with Herbert Gille as its commander.[41] Although the original intention was permanently to group two SS panzer or panzergrenadier divisions under each corps, the constant shifting of the elite SS divisions from one trouble spot to another made it impossible to maintain the intended assignments. Consequently, the mobile SS divisions were moved from corps to corps as the situation demanded.

In addition to the four SS Panzerkorps, two non-elite SS corps were organized in 1943: the Vth SS Gebirgskorps in Yugoslavia and the VIth SS Freiwilligenkorps (Lettisches) in the *Ostland*. Early in 1944, another SS mountain corps, the IXth

[40] Determined by the author on the basis of figures given in "Zahlenmässige Übersicht der Divisionen" and "Neuaufstellungen," October 4, 1943, and December 26, 1943, KTB/OKW, III, 1161, 1403, 1404; and "Gliederung des Feldheeres 1943," Keilig, *Das Deutsche Heer*, I, Section 15, pp. 51, 55.

[41] SSFHA, "Aufstellung des Germ. SS-Panzerkorps," April 19, 1943, Geheime Kommandosache, RFSS/T–175, 111/2635181 f.; SSFHA, "Aufstellung des Gen. Kdo. I. SS-Pz. Korps 'Leibstandarte,' " July 27, 1943, 111/2635170 f.; SSFHA, "Aufstellung des Gen. Kdo. IV. SS-Pz. Korps," August 5, 1943, 111/2635196ff.; SSFHA, "Aufstellung des Gen. Kdo. V. SS-Geb. Korps," July 8, 1943, 111/2635204ff.; and copies of five "Führer-Befehle" issued on October 3, 1943, 111/2635149ff.

Waffen-Gebirgskorps der SS (Kroatisches), was established in the Balkans; and by the end of the year, six more SS army corps (XIth, XIIth, XIIIth, XIVth, XVth, and XVIIIth) had been thrown together by Himmler in his new capacity as Commander of the Reserve Army. Since the Waffen SS had neither the divisions to man them nor the qualified officers to command them, they were SS corps in name only; most of the commanders were Police generals and many of the troops were drawn from the ranks of the Reserve Army. In short, the whole business reflected Himmler's ambition to establish as many "SS formations" as possible, to enhance his own prestige in Hitler's eyes.

Similarly, between 1943 and the end of the war, the personnel strength of the Waffen SS more than doubled and the number of nominal SS divisions rose from eighteen to thirty-eight. Yet only one of these, the 18th SS Panzergrenadierdivision "Horst Wessel," could even remotely be considered an elite German formation. As for the numerous regiment-sized SS "divisions" scraped together in the last months of the war, only two or three, composed of training personnel from various SS combat schools, were more than chaff in the wind. Inasmuch as the considerable military value of the Waffen SS lay primarily in the elite, largely German, SS panzer divisions, which were the spiritual successors of the prewar Leibstandarte and Verfügungstruppe, it may be concluded that all the SS divisions that were to be of any real worth in the final year and a half of the war were already in existence in 1943.

CHAPTER NINE

To the Bitter End:

The Waffen SS and the Defense

of the Third Reich, 1943-1945

BY their consistently outstanding performance during the early years of the war and by their unshakable tenacity in the defensive battles of 1942 and 1943, the classic divisions of the Waffen SS won the confidence as well as the gratitude of their Führer. After the SS Panzerkorps' victory at Kharkov, Hitler decided to establish a strong central reserve composed of SS armored divisions. By mid-1943 the Germans were everywhere on the defensive and Hitler, against the will of his field commanders, replaced the previously successful mobile tactics with an uninspired strategy of rigid defense of established lines. But it was also his intention to conduct an active defense by counterattacks, with the object of wresting the initiative from the enemy. It was for this purpose that he required an aggressive and loyal SS striking force that could be counted upon to snatch victory from defeat.

Despite Hitler's best efforts, the constantly deteriorating military situation made it impossible to withdraw all of the elite SS divisions from the front at the same time. Consequently, they were shuttled from one danger spot to another, with only an occasional brief rest for refitting. For example, the "Leibstandarte Adolf Hitler," the most peripatetic of the SS divisions, made the trip between the eastern and western fronts seven times in the last two years of the war. After each transfer the division mounted an offensive operation. Thus the panzer and panzergrenadier divisions of the Waffen SS became the "fire brigade" of the Third Reich. Wherever they were committed they attacked; sometimes with great success, at other times with little or none. But whatever the outcome of the individual action, the end result was to delay the enemy advance. That, in the final analysis, was the value of the Waffen SS in the last two years of the war.

Defensive Battles in the East, 1943–1944

After stemming the Soviet offensive at Kharkov in March 1943, the three divisions of the SS Panzerkorps ("Leibstandarte Adolf Hitler," "Das Reich," "Totenkopf") spearheaded the German summer offensive on the central sector of the eastern front, in the area of Orel and Kursk. It was the last major offensive operation undertaken by the Germans in the East. Despite its initial success, the attack had to be given up in the face of stiffening Soviet resistance and Hitler's desire to transfer the SS Panzerkorps to Italy in order to bolster Mussolini's tottering regime.[1]

The impact of the Tunisian defeat and the imminence of an Allied invasion had brought the Fascist regime in Italy near collapse. Defeatism was rife in the armed forces and among the people, and Hitler had for some time envisaged the possibility of an Italian defection. During a military conference held on May 19, he stated that under such circumstances, he would have to employ his three elite SS divisions in Italy "because they understand Fascism the best." Other units, he continued, "do not have the experience and, from a political standpoint, lack the skill of my old SS divisions, who are propagandists. I am positive that if the three best SS divisions go down there they will very quickly establish complete fraternization with Fascism." [2]

---

[1] The offensive was code-named *Zitadelle;* its purpose, like that of Hitler's subsequent offensives, was to regain the initiative and restore confidence in the German cause. For details see " 'Zitadelle' und die Abwehrschlachten im Osten," KTB/OKW, III, 1619ff., and Kriegstagebuch entries beginning with July 5, 1943, pp. 748ff. See also Manstein, *op. cit.,* pp. 443ff.; *Hitlers Lagebesprechungen,* pp. 269, 274, 297, n. 1; Clark, *op. cit.,* pp. 322ff.

[2] "Besprechung des Führers mit Feldmarschall Keitel am 19. Mai 1943," *Hitlers Lagebesprechungen,* p. 207.

On July 10, 1943, Anglo-American forces landed on Sicily. During the night of July 24–25, the Fascist Grand Council, meeting for the first time since December 1939, voted to depose Mussolini. The next day, Il Duce was summoned to a meeting with the King, summarily dismissed from office, and placed under arrest.[3] On the same day, Hitler ordered the transfer of the SS Panzerkorps to Italy. Field Marshal von Kluge, commander of Army Group Center, immediately flew to the Führer's headquarters to protest. But Hitler remained adamant:

The point is I can't just take units from anywhere. I have to take politically reliable units. . . . It is a very difficult decision, but I have no choice. Down there, I can only accomplish something with elite formations that are politically close to Fascism. If it weren't for that I could take a couple of Army panzer divisions. But as it is, I need a magnet to gather the people together. . . . [To accomplish this] I must have units down there which come under a political banner.[4]

Nevertheless, in the end, a renewed Russian counteroffensive succeeded where von Kluge's arguments had failed; SS Divisions "Das Reich" and "Totenkopf" remained in the East, and only the "Leibstandarte Adolf Hitler" was shifted to Italy.[5]

Shortly after its departure, the two remaining SS divisions took part in a counterattack which threw the Soviet spearheads back across the Muis and resulted in a temporary restoration of the front in that area.[6] There followed a period of Soviet offensives which alternated from area to area along the central and southern front, continuing with only short pauses until the onset of the muddy season in the spring of 1944. The Germans were forced to give up hundreds of miles of ground, and

[3] The best discussion of events in Italy at this time may be found in F. W. Deakin, *op. cit.*, pp. 439ff.

[4] "Besprechung des Führers mit Feldmarschall v. Kluge am 26. Juli 1943," *Hitlers Lagebesprechungen*, p. 373. A portion of this conference, in English translation, may be found in Felix Gilbert, *Hitler Directs His War* (New York, 1950), pp. 55ff.

[5] KTB/OKW, III, 836, 879; *Hitlers Lagebesprechungen*, pp. 309, 339, 371, n. 2.

[6] *Ibid.*, p. 310, n. 1; Manstein, *op. cit.*, pp. 452 f.; Clark, *op. cit.*, pp. 346 f.

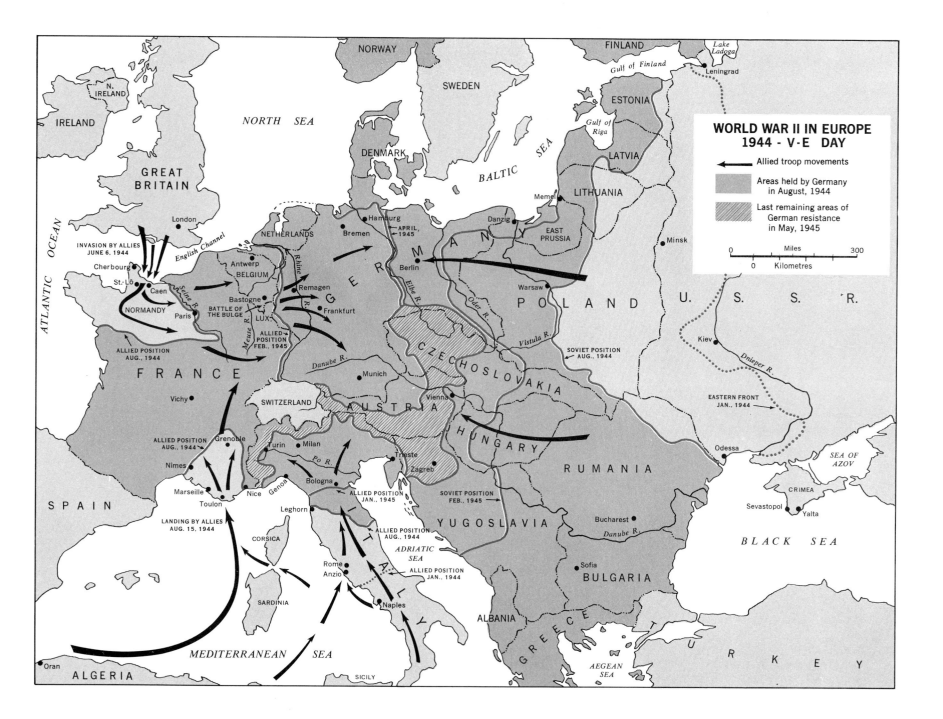

**WORLD WAR II IN EUROPE
1944 - V-E DAY**

→ Allied troop movements

Areas held by Germany
in August, 1944

Last remaining areas of
German resistance
in May, 1945

0 ——— Miles ——— 300
0 ——— Kilometres

ATLANTIC OCEAN

IRELAND

N. IRELAND

GREAT BRITAIN

London

NORTH SEA

NORWAY

SWEDEN

DENMARK

Hamburg
APRIL, 1945
Bremen

FINLAND

Lake Ladoga
Leningrad

Gulf of Finland

ESTONIA

Gulf of Riga

LATVIA

BALTIC SEA

Memel

LITHUANIA

Danzig

EAST PRUSSIA

Minsk

English Channel

Cherbourg
St.-Lô   Caen
NORMANDY
Paris

INVASION BY ALLIES
JUNE 6, 1944

Seine R.

NETHERLANDS

Antwerp
BELGIUM
Bastogne
BATTLE OF
THE BULGE
LUX.
Meuse R.
ALLIED
POSITION
FEB., 1945

Rhine

Remagen
R.
Frankfurt

G E R M A N Y

Berlin

Elbe R.

Oder R.

Warsaw

P O L A N D

Vistula R.

SOVIET POSITION
AUG., 1944

U. S. S. R.

Kiev

Dnieper R.

EASTERN FRONT
JAN., 1944

ALLIED POSITION
AUG., 1944

F R A N C E

Vichy

Danube R.

Munich

SWITZERLAND

CZECHOSLOVAKIA

AUSTRIA

Vienna

H U N G A R Y

R U M A N I A

Odessa

SEA OF AZOV

ALLIED POSITION
AUG., 1944

Grenoble

Turin   Milan

Po R.

Trieste

Zagreb

SOVIET POSITION
FEB., 1945

Bucharest

Danube R.

CRIMEA

Sevastopol   Yalta

Nimes

Marseille
Toulon

Nice   Genoa

Bologna

ALLIED POSITION
JAN., 1945

I T A L Y

Y U G O S L A V I A

BLACK SEA

SPAIN

LANDING BY ALLIES
AUG. 15, 1944

CORSICA

Leghorn

ADRIATIC SEA

ALLIED POSITION
AUG., 1944

BULGARIA

Sofia

SARDINIA

Rome
Anzio

ALLIED POSITION
JAN., 1944

Naples

ALBANIA

GREECE

Oran

MEDITERRANEAN SEA

SICILY

ALGERIA

AEGEAN SEA

TURKEY

by the end of the year had withdrawn behind the Dnieper. But despite repeated breakthroughs, the Russians were unable to gain a decisive victory. Penetrations were counterattacked, while the German forces on either side withdrew to new positions.

Many of the defensive battles fought in Russia during this period owed their success to the efforts of the SS divisions. It is therefore an understandable cause of bitterness among Waffen SS veterans that little or no mention of this fact is made in the many memoirs published by former Army leaders since the end of the war. Whole histories of the eastern campaign have been written with barely a reference to the exploits of the Waffen SS.[7]

The wartime records tell a different story. On August 17, 1943, for example, the SS Division "Das Reich" received the following commendation from the commander of Army Group South, Field Marshal von Manstein:

In a daring and energetically led attack along the west flank of the army, the division has destroyed a considerable enemy force, and thus created the necessary condition for further operations. I convey to the division and its officers my special recognition. Mention of the division in the Wehrmacht communiqué has been proposed.[8]

On August 26, the Wehrmacht war diary describes the action in these terms:

The 6th Army was forced to pull back its front in some places in the face of strong enemy attacks. The 1st Panzer and 8th Armies warded off enemy attacks. In this connection the SS Panzergrenadier-division "Das Reich" achieved an especially successful defensive victory.[9]

Nevertheless, there is no mention of the Waffen SS in connection with this action in von Manstein's published memoirs. The Army leaders were quick to complain about the failures of the Waffen SS, but they were equally quick to credit to the

[7] Two notable exceptions are the very recent (previously cited) works by Alan Clark and Paul Carrel.

[8] Kanis, *op. cit.*, p. 237.

[9] KTB/OKW, III, 1010.

Army the accomplishments of the Waffen SS formations under their command. This trend, already noticeable during the war, became increasingly evident in the postwar literature.

The contribution of the Waffen SS to the successful defensive battles of 1943–1944 may be summarized by again quoting the wartime words of an Army leader. General Wöhler, commander of the 8th Army, commended an SS panzer division for having "stood like a rock in the Army [*Wie ein Fels im Heer*], while the enemy broke through in neighboring sectors." In another *Tagesbefehl*, the same officer describes the SS Panzerdivision "Totenkopf" as "a lightning sword of retribution," which fulfilled its tasks "with unshakable fortitude [*unerschütterlicher Kampfkraft*]." [10] Moreover, as a corrective to the postwar accounts, one has only to scan the pages of the Wehrmacht war diary or the record of Hitler's military conferences to appreciate the extent to which the divisions of the Waffen SS figured in the calculations of the German war leaders.

As the situation worsened along the eastern front during the autumn of 1943, Hitler was forced to order the return of the "Leibstandarte Adolf Hitler" from Italy. By November, barely three months after leaving, the division—now rested and completely re-equipped with the latest-model tanks—was back in Russia.[11] And on November 15, along with two fresh Army panzer divisions, the Leibstandarte launched a counterattack against a Soviet armored corps that had pierced the German Dnieper line near Kiev. The assault crushed the Russian force, and on November 19 the Germans recaptured Zhitomir. Once again an operation spearheaded by an SS division had temporarily re-established a front. [12]

But the fierce efforts of the SS and Army panzer units, as well as the sharp counterattacks by fresh infantry formations,

---

[10] These commendations, as well as others, are reprinted in Kanis, *op. cit.*, pp. 233ff.

[11] *Hitlers Lagebesprechungen*, pp. 371, n. 2, 399; KTB/OKW, III, 1209, 1215.

[12] Manstein, *op. cit.*, p. 489; *Hitlers Lagebesprechungen*, pp. 408, 494, n. 1; Kriegstagebuch entries November 15–November 19, 1943, KTB/OKW, III, 1281ff.

were only momentarily successful in holding back the Soviet flood. The decisive blow came with the great winter offensive. On December 13, the Russians broke out of the Nevel salient toward the southwest, overwhelming Army Group Center. On Christmas Eve, they rolled forward from the Kiev area, and within a week had regained Zhitomir and Korosten. Then, swinging in a southwesterly direction, the Soviet forces reached the prewar Polish frontier, thus threatening to outflank the entire southern sector of the German line. Moreover, on January 14, the Red Army struck at Army Group North, forcing it to give up the encirclement of Leningrad.[13]

In the course of the Soviet offensive, and for the first time since Stalingrad, large German formations were twice encircled —two corps at Cherkassy in February and the whole 1st Panzer Army in the area of Kamenets–Podolsk in March. Two elite SS panzer divisions were caught in these traps: "Wiking" in the Cherkassy pocket and the "Leibstandarte Adolf Hitler," along with a 2500-man battle group from "Das Reich," in the south.[14]

After having defended the constantly shrinking perimeter of their position for over two weeks, the encircled German units in the Cherkassy "cauldron" were ordered to break out. As the only panzer division in the trap, "Wiking" was assigned to spearhead the attempt. The breakout was partially successful, but the SS division lost its remaining tanks, all of its equipment, and half of its personnel in the process.[15]

The effort to re-establish a link with the encircled 1st Panzer Army was a far more difficult task, for it required the stemming of the Soviet offensive in the region of Tarnopol. The German troops available for the task had tried and failed. But after a good deal of agonizing and the repeated pleas of the front commanders, Hitler released the last of his SS reserve for a renewed

---

[13] See situation summaries in *Hitlers Lagebesprechungen*, pp. 408, 434 f., 469, 526.

[14] The greater part of the SS Division "Das Reich" had been sent to France to be refitted. See KTB/OKW, IV, 285.

[15] For details see Steiner, *Die Freiwilligen*, pp. 238ff. For two dramatic eyewitness accounts of the breakout (one Russian, the other German), see Werth, *op. cit.*, pp. 780 f., and Clark, *op. cit.*, pp. 376 f.

attempt. In April 1944, the IInd SS Panzerkorps, with the 9th
SS Panzerdivision "Hohenstauffen" and the 10th SS Panzerdivision "Frundsberg," arrived from France under the command
of the able Paul Hausser. The SS divisions quickly launched a
flank attack which neatly amputated the tip of the Soviet spearhead and made possible the extrication of the trapped 1st Panzer
Army.[16] Thus, barely a year after the original disaster, units of
the Waffen SS had on two separate occasions prevented another
Stalingrad.

Immediately after their rescue, the Leibstandarte and the
Kampfgruppe "Das Reich" were sent to the West; the former
to Belgium for refitting and the latter to rejoin the rest of its
division in southern France. Hitler, with good reason, was
expecting an Allied invasion of the continent, and was feverishly
at work attempting to rebuild his SS reserve. The IInd SS
Panzerkorps ("Hohenstauffen" and "Frundsberg") had to be
kept in Poland to prevent a renewal of the Soviet advance, but
Hitler warned his commanders that he would recall it in the
event of an Allied landing.

In the meantime, some of the survivors of the SS Division
"Wiking" had been formed into a 4000-man Kampfgruppe and
sent back into action, while the remainder were moved back to
Poland to serve as a nucleus around which to rebuild the division. As for the other elite SS divisions, "Totenkopf" continued
its uninterrupted year-long defense on the south-central front,
while Felix Steiner's IIIrd SS Panzerkorps (11th SS Panzergrenadierdivision "Nordland" and SS Brigade "Nederland")
played a major role in the defense of the Baltic region.[17]

The Russian advance in the south had brought the Red
Army dangerously close to Hungary. Hitler reacted to this
threat by ordering the execution of Operation Margarethe—
the German occupation of Hungary. The plan, conceived in
September 1943, was carried out between March 19 and 31,
1944. The operation, largely an SS affair, made use of the
second-string units of Hitler's SS "fire brigade." By April, the

---

[16] KTB/OKW, IV, 112, 274; Liddell Hart, *The Red Army*, p. 119;
Hitlers Lagebesprechungen, pp. 549, n. 3, 550, 552, 615, n. 4.

[17] Steiner, *Die Freiwilligen,* pp. 187ff.

16th SS Panzergrenadierdivision "Reichsführer SS," the 18th SS Panzergrenadierdivision "Horst Wessel," and the 8th SS Kavalleriedivision "Florian Geyer" had taken up positions in Hungary.[18]

Allied Invasion and the Battle for France, 1944

On the eve of the Allied invasion, four of the ten German armored divisions in France and Belgium were Waffen SS. They were: 1st SS Panzerdivision "Leibstandarte Adolf Hitler," 2nd SS Panzerdivision "Das Reich," 12th SS Panzerdivision "Hitler Jugend," and 17th SS Panzergrenadierdivision "Götz von Berlichingen." [19] As early as June 7, 1944 (D-Day + 1), "Hitler Jugend" was in action against Allied forces in the area of Caen. On June 11, Hitler ordered the cancellation of a planned offensive near Kowel on the eastern front and the immediate transfer of the IInd SS Panzerkorps to France. Before the end of the month, the SS Panzer Divisions "Hohenstauffen" and "Frundsberg" had added their considerable weight to the German effort to push the Allies back into the sea.[20] They were unsuccessful. Nevertheless, the six crack SS armored divisions were by far the most formidable adversaries the Anglo–American forces had to face.

On June 22, barely two and a half weeks after the invasion, the Russians launched their main summer offensive. The overwhelming power of the Soviet assault shattered Army Group Center and tore a 200-mile gap in the German front. On July 13, the Red Army mounted an attack against Army Group North, and the following day moved forward against Army Group North–Ukraine. By the middle of July, the German front in the East had been pierced from top to bottom. At the

[18] See "Deutsche Gegenmassnahmen: Die Vorbereitung und Durchführung des Unternehmens 'Margarethe' (Besetzung Ungarns) . . . ," KTB/OKW, IV, 189ff.

[19] *Hitlers Lagebesprechungen*, p. 575, n. 2.

[20] See "Die Kämpfe in der Normandie von der Landung bis zum Durchbruch bei Avranches (6. Juni–31. Juli)," KTB/OKW, IV, 311ff. For details of the battle through the eyes of the commander of the 12th SS Panzerdivision "Hitler Jugend" see Meyer, *op. cit.*, pp. 208ff.

end of the month, the Soviet Army stood at the Gulf of Riga in the north, in the suburbs of Warsaw in the center, and on the line of the San River in the Ukraine.[21]

For Hitler and his Third Reich this was a moment of general crisis. In the West, the loss of France and Belgium was imminent; on the home front, morale had been shaken by the attempt on the Führer's life;[22] in the East, the Red Army continued to advance and—while Russian troops were fighting in the suburbs of Warsaw—the Polish resistance movement in the capital rose in open revolt. But once again, the Waffen SS came to the rescue.

During the first week in August, the newly established IVth SS Panzerkorps, composed of the elite SS Panzer Divisions "Wiking" and "Totenkopf" (reinforced by the Army's 19th Panzerdivision), launched a counterattack which threw the Russians out of Warsaw and back across the Vistula. For the next two months the three divisions held off two entire Soviet armies. And in October the Russians finally gave up the attack.[23] They had advanced up to 450 miles in the first five weeks, but overextended communications and the setback at Warsaw finally brought their offensive to a halt. Consequently, the Germans were able to crush the Warsaw uprising, and until January 1945 the situation along the Vistula remained comparatively quiet.[24]

Despite this temporary stabilization of the main front, a new Soviet offensive in the far south began on August 20. Romania capitulated within three days, and the Russians were able without difficulty to occupy the vital oilfields at Ploesti. By the end

[21] See situation summaries in *Hitlers Lagebesprechungen,* pp. 583, 609; also "Der Kriegsverlauf an der Ostfront im Jahre 1944," KTB/OKW, IV, 856ff.

[22] The best account may be found in Wheeler-Bennett, *op. cit.,* pp. 635ff.

[23] Steiner, *Die Freiwilligen,* pp. 288ff.; cf. Liddell Hart, *The Red Army,* p. 121.

[24] On the Warsaw uprising see *Hitlers Lagebesprechungen,* pp. 625ff., and (a Russian view) Werth, *op. cit.,* pp. 867ff. With the exception of some Hungarian *Volksdeutsche* from the 22nd SS Kavalleriedivision, no regular Waffen SS units seem to have been involved in the brutal suppression of the uprising. For the role played by the Kaminski and Dirlewanger SS Brigades see below, pp. 265ff.

of the month the whole country was in Soviet hands, and on September 8 the Russians began the occupation of Bulgaria. It was also during September that the Finns withdrew from the war and turned on the German 20th Gebirgsarmee when it refused to evacuate their territory. In the following months Hitler lost Greece and most of Yugoslavia; and by the beginning of December the Russians were laying siege to Budapest.[25]

Once again the Waffen SS stood out in the defense. Although there were no elite SS panzer divisions in the Balkan sideshow, the ethnic Germans of the 7th SS Gebirgsdivision "Prinz Eugen" did their best in Yugoslavia, while the 8th SS Kavalleriedivision "Florian Geyer" and the 22nd SS Kavalleriedivision fought to the end in the encircled Hungarian capital.[26] A commentary on the low level to which the Army formations had sunk by 1945 is the emergence of these second-rate SS divisions as the backbone of the German defense in their respective areas of operation.

Although Hitler diverted a few low-grade formations to the defense of the eastern and southeastern fronts, his primary interest had shifted to the West. There, on July 25, the Americans launched a major offensive to break out of the Normandy bridgehead. While the British and Canadian forces kept seven of the remaining nine German panzer divisions occupied in the Caen sector, six divisions of the United States First and Third Armies moved south on the western side of the Cherbourg Peninsula. The only German armored divisions in their path were the 2nd SS Panzerdivision "Das Reich" and the 17th SS Panzergrenadierdivision "Götz von Berlichingen"; both SS formations fought a stubborn rear-guard action, but were unable to check the American advance.[27]

[25] Liddell Hart, *The Red Army*, p. 121; KTB/OKW, IV, 859ff.; *Hitlers Lagebesprechungen*, pp. 650 f.

[26] For details see "Der Südöstliche Kriegsschauplatz," KTB/OKW, IV, 599ff., and "Die Ereignisse in Ungarn von Anfang April bis zum Ende der Schlacht um Budapest . . . ," *ibid.*, pp. 827ff.

[27] *Report by the Supreme Commander to the Combined Chiefs of Staff on the Operations in Europe of the Allied Expeditionary Force, 6 June 1944 to 8 May 1945* (Washington, 1946), pp. 36ff. Hereafter cited as SHAEF Report. For the German side of the picture see KTB/OKW, IV, 327ff.

The decisive breakthrough took place on July 31, when the United States 4th Armored Division "forced the lock of the door" at Avranches. Racing through the gap, the tanks of General Patton's Third Army quickly overran most of Brittany. As General Eisenhower described the situation in his report to the Combined Chiefs of Staff: "The enemy infantry was in no condition to resist us, and only the weary, badly battered armor put up any considerable fight." While the Germans streamed back "in a state of complete disorganization," the SS divisions were still dangerous antagonists: "Following heavy fighting, Vire was entered on August 2, only to be recaptured by two SS panzer divisions on the next day. There was a bitter struggle for some days before the enemy was finally forced back from this sector." [28]

The German left flank had collapsed completely, so that there was no longer any possibility of stopping the rapid sweep of Patton's flying armored columns. The one danger to this onrushing flood was that the Germans might manage to mount a counterattack to cut the narrow Avranches bottleneck through which its supplies had to be maintained. On Hitler's orders the Germans began preparations for just such an attack. Regardless of the risk, all available German armored formations were to mount an all-out assault from the area of Mortain westward through Avranches to the coast. Then, "ignoring the American forces which have broken into Brittany," the attackers were to "turn north and northeast, and from the western wing, attack and destroy the American divisions . . . thus bringing about the collapse of the front in Normandy." [29]

The German assault was launched on the night of August 7 with the 1st SS, 2nd SS, 2nd and 116th Panzer Divisions, supported by infantry and elements of the 17th SS Panzergrenadier-division. This formidable force was under the command of SS Oberstgruppenführer (Colonel General) Paul Hausser.[30] But the Americans were prepared, and in a bitter battle stemmed

28 SHAEF Report, p. 40.
29 KTB/OKW, IV, 336 f.
30 *Ibid.*, p. 338. Among Waffen SS field commanders, only Hausser and Dietrich held this highest of SS ranks.

the attack. Once checked, the German spearhead became the target of a furious Allied air attack. Rocket-firing fighter-bombers destroyed and damaged many tanks in addition to large quantities of unarmored vehicles. In his official report the Allied Supreme Commander concluded that "the result of the vigorous action by ground and air forces was that the enemy attack was effectively brought to a halt, and a threat was turned into a great victory." [31]

For the elite divisions of the Waffen SS the two months since the Allied invasion had been bitter and frustrating. They were not accustomed to failure. Even during the great retreats in the East, an all-out assault by two elite SS panzer divisions invariably resulted in at least a local victory. But in the West, the SS troops had to face what they bitterly called the *Materialschlacht.* Against heavy naval fire, unending streams of tanks, fully motorized infantry, superior artillery, and above all crippling attacks from the air, even the determination of the SS troops came to nothing.

But back at his remote headquarters in East Prussia, Hitler continued to view events in the light of his past experience. He ordered a renewal of the attack with additional forces drawn from other sectors of the front. Events were moving too fast, however, to permit the implementation of the Führer's plan. Although the units previously committed to the assault persisted in an attempt to break through to Avranches, it was clear to the Germans at the front that their efforts were to be in vain. Allied advances elsewhere made it impossible to gather the necessary forces; only the 10th SS Panzerdivision "Frundsberg" and an Army Rocket-Artillery (*Werfer*) Brigade reinforced the continuing assault. On August 11, Hitler was informed that even "SS Oberstgruppenführer Hausser no longer believes that the attack against Avranches is possible." On the following day it was decided to abandon the attack and to withdraw the forces involved.[32]

In the supercharged atmosphere of the *Führerhauptquartier* following the attempt on Hitler's life, the failure of the counter-

[31] SHAEF Report, p. 43.
[32] KTB/OKW, IV, 339 f.; SHAEF Report, p. 43.

offensive was interpreted as another case of treason. It was Hitler's opinion that "success only failed to come because Kluge [the German commander in the West] did not want to be successful." [33] And on August 14, when Kluge was cut off from his headquarters for twelve hours by an enemy artillery barrage, Hitler leaped to the conclusion that the Field Marshal was attempting to establish contact with the Allies in order to surrender his forces. He immediately relieved Kluge and ordered SS Oberstgruppenführer Hausser to take over command of Army Group B pending the appointment of a new Oberbefehlshaber West.[34] Nevertheless, the Waffen SS—for the first time—also seemed to have failed its Führer, and both Hausser and Sepp Dietrich had officially protested the order to renew the attack against Avranches. Hitler did not fail to notice this, and it gave rise to his first doubts concerning the reliability of the Waffen SS.

In reality, the SS divisions had made almost superhuman efforts to carry out the directives from Berlin. "As on former occasions," reported General Eisenhower, "the fanatical tenacity of the Nazi leaders and the ingrained toughness of their men had led the Germans to cling too long to a position from which military wisdom would have dictated an earlier retreat." [35] The result was fatal for the German defenders: in mounting the attack, they had drawn some of their strongest forces to the west; by stubbornly refusing to withdraw they allowed themselves to be encircled by the American armored forces that were

[33] Quoted in Alan Bullock, *Hitler: A Study in Tyranny* (rev. ed.; New York, 1962), p. 745.

[34] Hitler's opinion on the von Kluge affair may be found in "Besprechung des Führers mit Generalleutnant Westphal und Generalleutnant Krebs am 31. August 1944 in der Wolfsschanze," *Hitlers Lagebesprechungen,* pp. 610ff. A partial translation of this conference record may be found in Gilbert, *op. cit.,* pp. 101ff. See also Kluge's farewell letter to Hitler (written just before his suicide), "Abschiedsschreiben des Gen.-Feldm.s von Kluge . . . an Hitler v. 18. August," KTB/OKW, IV, 1573ff. Kluge had been both OB West and commander of Army Group B. Hausser replaced him in the latter capacity only. See *ibid.,* p. 345.

[35] SHAEF Report, p. 43. In addition to the OKW war diary entries already cited see KTB/OKW, IV, 462ff.

sweeping eastward behind their rear. Thus the stage was set for
the battle of the Falaise–Argentan pocket.

By mid-August, five SS panzer divisions, six Army panzer
divisions, and eight infantry divisions were caught in a pocket
between the United States Third Army and the Canadian First
Army; only a small gap remained open between Falaise and
Argentan. But the bitter resistance of the German armored
formations—especially the 12th SS Panzerdivision "Hitler
Jugend"—kept the jaws of the pincers open long enough to
enable some of the trapped forces to escape. By August 17, the
gap had so narrowed that panic broke out among the retreating
troops. The IInd SS Panzerkorps (2nd and 9th SS Panzer
Divisions), which had managed to escape earlier, now mounted
a counterattack that aided the escape of some of its trapped
comrades.[36] While the remnants of the German Army in the
West were streaming across the Seine in headlong retreat, the
Falaise pocket continued to shrink under the sledgehammer
blows of the Allied attackers. In his report to the Combined
Chiefs of Staff, General Eisenhower observed that "while the SS
elements as usual fought to annihilation, the ordinary German
infantry gave themselves up in ever-increasing numbers." By
August 20, the Allied pincers had met near Chambois, and two
days later the pocket was eliminated. Some "50,000 prisoners
were taken and 10,000 corpses found on the battlefield."[37]

While part of the 10th SS Panzerdivision "Frundsberg" had
been trapped in the pocket and annihilated, the remaining SS
divisions had made good their escape, but with heavy casualties
and the loss of the better part of their equipment. The 12th SS
Panzerdivision "Hitler Jugend," for example, lost 80 per cent
of the combat troops with which it had gone into action. Its
support personnel also suffered unusually high losses as a result
of air attacks. The division lost over 80 per cent of its tanks, 70

[36] While leading this relief attack, SS Oberstgruppenführer Hausser was
seriously wounded. *Ibid.*, p. 357. A vivid description of the battle of the
Falaise pocket by the commander of the 12th SS Panzerdivision "Hitler
Jugend" may be found in Meyer, *op. cit.*, pp. 297ff.

[37] SHAEF Report, pp. 44 f. The German casualty figures are given in
B. H. Liddell Hart, *Strategy* (rev. ed.; New York, 1961), p. 317.

per cent of its armored vehicles, 60 per cent of its artillery, and 50 per cent of its motor vehicles. At the beginning of September the fighting strength of "Hitler Jugend" amounted to only 600 men and no tanks.[38] The other five elite SS divisions were probably in no better shape. Indeed, they were carried on the official OKW roster for September 16, 1944, as Kampfgruppen (Battle Groups) rather than divisions.[39]

Field Marshal von Rundstedt, who took over command as Oberbefehlshaber West in September, told Allied interrogators after the war that "as far as I was concerned the war was ended in September." But Hitler apparently was not of the same opinion. He seems to have realized that Germany could no longer win, but he hoped to prolong the war until he secured a favorable peace. In his military conference on August 31 Hitler made it very clear to his generals that he intended to continue the struggle.[40]

The time hasn't come for a political decision. . . . It is childish and naive to expect that the time for favorable political dealings is during a period of grave military defeats. Such moments come when you are having successes. . . .

But the time will come when the tension between the Allies will become so great that a break will occur anyway. All the coalitions in history disintegrated sooner or later. No matter how difficult it is, the only solution is to wait until the right moment. . . .

If necessary we will fight on the Rhine. It makes absolutely no difference. Regardless of the circumstances we will continue this long struggle until, as Frederick the Great said, one of our damned enemies becomes too tired to fight any more and until we secure a peace that will ensure the existence of the German nation for the next 50 or 100 years and which, above all, does not damage our honor a second time, as happened in 1918.

Shortly after this meeting Hitler ordered that plans be prepared for what was to become the famous German Ardennes offensive against the western Allies.

[38] Meyer, *op. cit.,* pp. 312 f.

[39] See "Gliederung des deutschen Heeres . . . ," September 16, 1944, KTB/OKW, IV, 1879.

[40] *Hitlers Lagebesprechungen,* pp. 614, 615, 617. Cf. Gilbert, *op. cit.,* pp. 105 f.

Last German Offensive in the West:
The Ardennes, 1944–1945

Just as the main Soviet offensive drew to a halt in August, so the Allied offensive in the West petered out in the following month. General Hans Speidel described it after the war as "a German variation of the 'miracle of the Marne' for the French in 1918. The furious advance of the Allies suddenly subsided." Actually there was nothing very miraculous about it. The Anglo–American forces were simply suffering from what Liddell Hart has called "the strategic law of overstretch": Allied lines of communication were lengthening while those of the Germans were being shortened. In addition, the flying weather was unusually bad and there were differences of opinion among the Allies as to how the campaign should be run. And perhaps as important as all the other factors combined was the extraordinary power of recovery shown by the Germans now that they were faced with the defense of their homeland.[41] In any event, by the end of September they had succeeded in forming a continuous front west of the Rhine, along the line of the German frontier.[42]

Meanwhile, behind the front, Germany was being organized for total war. In the wake of the plot on Hitler's life, Himmler had been made Commander of the Reserve Army and Chief of Army Ordnance (Oberbefehlshaber des Ersatzheeres und Chef der Heeresrüstung) and Goebbels had been appointed Plenipotentiary for Total War. The Himmler–Goebbels team, with the support of Martin Bormann (who controlled the Nazi Party organization), quickly turned Germany into an armed camp.[43]

Despite the heavy Allied bombings, Germany's armaments production was maintained and in some cases even increased in the last half of 1944. But motor fuel and raw materials were in very short supply. "Germany made a remarkable recovery in the

[41] Liddell Hart, *Strategy*, p. 319; SHAEF Report, p. 121.

[42] For details see "Der Wiederaufbau des Westheeres. Die Instandsetzung des Westwalls und die Sicherung der Deutschen Bucht," KTB/OKW, IV, 376ff.

[43] See Reitlinger, *op. cit.*, pp. 381ff.

last three months of 1944, but it was the last reserves of men, materials, and morale on which Hitler was now drawing; if he squandered these there was nothing left." [44] In December, Hitler gambled everything in one last offensive in the West—and lost.

Ever since the Allies had broken out of the Normandy beachhead Hitler had been searching for an opportunity to regain the initiative in the West. The comparative quiet which settled over the front in September gave him his chance. On September 16, Hitler announced to a handful of his military lieutenants his intention of launching an offensive. The area eventually chosen for the assault was the Ardennes sector, where the Wehrmacht had made its decisive breakthrough during the victorious days of 1940. [45]

Hitler gave his reasons for attacking in a rambling harangue before an audience of generals who were to participate in the operation. In summary, he hoped "to deprive the enemy of his belief that victory is certain" and thus hasten the split between the Allies upon which he counted to win the peace, if not the war. In choosing the West over the East as the place to strike his blow, Hitler was motivated by his belief that the British and the Americans were less dangerous adversaries than the fanatical Russians. [46]

The preparations for Operation *Wacht am Rhein* (Hitler's cover name for the offensive) were, from a technical standpoint, brilliantly conceived and faultlessly executed. Tanks, assault guns, artillery, armored vehicles, motor transport, gasoline, and even aircraft were gathered in quantities that had not been seen on the German side since the early years of the war. [47] In

[44] Bullock, *op. cit.*, p. 759.

[45] See "Die Vorbereitung einer eigenen Offensive zwischen Monschau und Echternach (bis 16. Dezember)," KTB/OKW, IV, 430ff., and John Toland, *Battle: The Story of the Bulge* (Signet edition; New York, 1960), pp. 22ff.

[46] "Ansprache des Führers vor Divisionskommandeuren am 12. Dezember 1944 im Adlerhorst," *Hitlers Lagebesprechungen*, pp. 713ff.

[47] See report by a German quartermaster officer, "Mitteilungen des Oberst d. G. Poleck (Qu) am 3. 1. 1945," KTB/OKW, IV, 981ff.; Toland, *op. cit.*, pp. 22, 31.

the summer of 1943, three SS divisions had spearheaded the last major German offensive in the East. Now, a year and a half later, Hitler chose four SS divisions to lead what was to be the last major German offensive in the West.

The newly refitted SS Panzer Divisions "Leibstandarte Adolf Hitler," "Das Reich," "Hohenstauffen," and "Hitler Jugend" were organized into the 6th Panzer Army (later 6th SS Panzer Army), under the command of SS Oberstgruppenführer Sepp Dietrich. The aim of the German assault was to drive through the Ardennes, cross the Meuse on the first day, and move on to capture the main Allied supply port of Antwerp by the end of the week. If all went according to plan, the British forces would be separated from their American allies as well as from their source of supply; they could then be crushed between the Germans in their rear and those along their front. Of the three German armies taking part in the operation Dietrich's was the most powerful, and it was assigned the leading role: an advance along the northern flank of the attack, the shortest route to Antwerp.[48]

On the morning of December 16, some twenty German divisions moved forward along a seventy-mile front between Monschau and Echternach and smashed into the four American divisions defending the sector. Aided by surprise and by weather that grounded the Allied air forces, the Germans made considerable gains in the early stages of the assault. By the morning of December 18, more than fifty German columns were moving through the Ardennes. The greatest penetration had been made by a combat group from the 1st SS Panzerdivision "Leibstandarte Adolf Hitler." Led by hard-driving SS Obersturmbannführer (Lieutenant Colonel) Jochen Peiper, this strong force of tanks and armored cars had advanced nearly thirty miles and was only twenty-five miles short of the Meuse. But the other columns of Dietrich's panzer army had become tangled in a gigantic traffic jam, which limited their advance to only a mile or two.

[48] KTB/OKW, IV, 435ff.; Toland, *op. cit.*, pp. 29 f.; B. H. Liddell Hart, *The German Generals Talk* (Berkley edition; New York, 1958), pp. 229 f.

To the south, Manteuffel's 5th Panzer Army, which was composed of three Army panzer divisions and a number of Volksgrenadier (infantry) divisions, was doing better. Much to Dietrich's chagrin, even the infantry of the second-rate 7th Army had penetrated farther on foot than had most of the vaunted SS panzers.[49] In response to Hitler's growing concern, Dietrich promised a major breakthrough for the following day. It never materialized. As if this were not enough, Hitler delivered another blow to Dietrich's pride when he transferred the 2nd SS Panzerdivision "Das Reich" to Manteuffel's army in order to exploit the far more successful penetration in that area.

The details of the "Battle of the Bulge" are well known and have been often described. The German offensive failed for a variety of reasons, perhaps the most important of which was that the bulk of the elite SS panzer forces never really got into the fight. As General Ridgway wrote after the war: "The whole Ardennes fight was a battle of road junctions, because in the wooded country, in the deep snows, armies could not move off the roads." And even though their units had been shattered and overrun, small groups of bypassed American soldiers persisted in defending the road junctions. They were invariably wiped out, but they managed to delay the advance of the German road-bound armored units long enough to cause monumental traffic jams that often stretched back for miles. As Hitler later pointed out to his generals, only the spearheads of the panzer columns ever clashed with the enemy; the rest of these formidable formations were often impotently backed up along the roads, waiting for the lead units to clear obstructions.[50]

Having failed to exploit the initial surprise and thus reach

[49] SHAEF Report, pp. 76 f.; Toland, *op. cit.,* pp. 32ff.; "Das Unternehmen 'Wacht am Rhein': die Ardennen-Offensive bis zum Beginn des Zurückweichens (16. Dezember 1944 bis 13. Januar 1945)," KTB/OKW, IV, 1342ff.

[50] See "Ansprache des Führers vor Divisionskommandeuren am 28. Dezember 1944 im Adlerhorst," *Hitlers Lagebesprechungen,* p. 750. This long speech is of special interest because it contains Hitler's personal evaluation of the Ardennes offensive. An unusually good English translation of the speech may be found appended to Gilbert, *op. cit.,* pp. 157ff.

the Meuse during the first stage of the attack, the German offensive was doomed. The Allies responded energetically, the Bulge was sealed, and fresh troops rushed to the scene soon forced the Germans back on the defensive. The deepest penetration—some sixty miles—had been made by the Army's 2nd Panzer Division, but it too fell short of the Meuse. SS Kampfgruppe Peiper, which at first led the advance, had been left far behind. Its thirty-mile dash was as far as Dietrich's SS army ever got. Less than a week after the start of the offensive Peiper's men were fighting for their lives in the area of La Gleize and Stoumont. Out of fuel, low on ammunition, and facing the newly arrived paratroopers of the veteran United States 82nd Airborne Division. Peiper's position was hopeless. On December 24, the SS commander ordered the destruction of his remaining vehicles, then led 800 surviving SS troopers (and a captured American major) on a long retreat to the German lines. The men of the SS Kampfgruppe had gained nothing by their efforts except the Swords to the *Ritterkreuz* for their commander and opprobrium for having massacred a large group of American prisoners near Malmédy.[51]

In an attempt to assist the failing offensive in the Ardennes, Hitler threw in additional forces and ordered the launching of a new offensive in Alsace, where the American line had been thinned in order to send reinforcements north to the Bulge. The operation, code-named *Nordwind,* was launched on New Year's Day with eight divisions spearheaded by an SS corps consisting of the 17th SS Panzergrenadierdivision "Götz von Berlichingen" and the 36th Volksgrenadierdivision. Despite some gains, the assault did not achieve a breakthrough. The subsequent commitment of the 10th SS Panzerdivision "Frundsberg" and the 6th SS Gebirgsdivision "Nord" failed to alter the situation.[52]

[51] The saga of Kampfgruppe Peiper is related in Toland, *op. cit., passim.* On the controversial Malmédy massacre, see below, pp. 278ff.

[52] Hitler's hopes for *Nordwind* were expressed in his speech to the division commanders on December 28, *Hitlers Lagebesprechungen,* pp. 738ff. An account of the operation from the German side is given in "Das Unternehmen 'Nordwind': das Freikämpfen des nördlichen Elsasses (21. Dezember 1944 bis 13. Januar 1945)," KTB/OKW, IV, 1347ff.

From a tactical viewpoint the Ardennes and Saar counter-offensives were not without success. Even though they fell short of their objectives, they seriously delayed the Allied invasion of Germany and in the process inflicted heavy damage at a not unreasonable cost.[53] But Germany could no longer afford even reasonable losses, especially among its elite armored units. In light of Germany's over-all situation, Hitler's gamble proved fatal.[54]

To Colonel General Guderian, Chief of the Army General Staff and commander of the eastern front, the dangers inherent in Hitler's all-out attempt in the West were already clear by December 22: "A sensible commander would on this day have remembered the looming dangers on the Eastern Front which could only be countered by a timely breaking-off of the operation in the West that was already, from the long view, a failure." He thereupon decided "to drive to supreme Headquarters and to request that the battle, which was causing us heavy casualties, be broken off and that all forces that could be spared be immediately transferred to the Eastern Front." [55]

On December 24, at a conference with Hitler, Guderian presented the view of his staff that the Russians would renew their attack on January 12 with a total superiority of 15 to 1 on the basis of the present German strength on the eastern front. Consequently, he pleaded for the release of troops from the Ardennes

[53] The official SHAEF Report, p. 79, estimated German casualties for the month ending January 16, 1945, at 120,000. The losses in matériel were estimated at 600 tanks and assault guns, 1620 planes, and 13,000 motor vehicles and 1150 locomotives destroyed or damaged. By the end of January, the Allies claimed, "the enemy had lost 220,000 men, including 110,000 prisoners." But the OKW recorded a maximum loss of only 98,024 German troops between December 12, 1944, and January 25, 1945, estimating the casualties inflicted on the Allies during the same period at about 120,000. KTB/OKW, IV, 1362. Cf. table of comparative casualties in *Hitlers Lagebesprechungen*, p. 742, n. 2.

[54] General Eisenhower (SHAEF Report, p. 79) stated that "more serious in the final analysis [than the material losses] was the widespread disillusionment within the German Army and in Germany itself which must have accompanied the realization that the breakthrough had failed to seize any really important objective and had achieved nothing decisive."

[55] Heinz Guderian, *Panzer Leader* (London, 1952), p. 381.

and the Upper Rhine. "But all of this was of no avail,"
Guderian wrote after the war; "I was rebuffed . . . [and] dismissed with instructions that the Eastern Front must take care
of itself." [56]

Last German Offensive in the Southeast: Hungary, 1945

While Guderian was trying in vain to draw Hitler's attention
to the East, a report arrived that the last contact with the German
defenders in Budapest had been lost. Trapped in the city were
50,000 men of the IXth SS Korps, including the 8th SS Kavalleriedivision "Florian Geyer" and the 22nd SS Freiwilligen-
Kavalleriedivision, under the command of the veteran Police
general SS Obergruppenführer Pfeffer-Wildenbruch.[57]

Hitler reacted to this news by ordering an attack to relieve
the Hungarian capital; but, to Guderian's chagrin, he drew
the necessary forces not from the West but from the East. While
Guderian was returning to his headquarters (and without
informing him), the OKW ordered the two elite SS divisions
(SS Panzer Divisions "Totenkopf" and "Wiking") of Gille's
IVth SS Panzerkorps from the defense of Warsaw to "raise the
siege of Budapest."

The attack was scheduled to begin on New Year's Day.
Guderian, present at the *Führerhauptquartier* on the day of
the assault, reported that although "Hitler expected great results
from this attack, I was skeptical since very little time had been
allowed for its preparation and neither the troops nor the commanders possessed the same drive as in the old days." [58]
Guderian's skepticism was well founded; the attack continued
for nearly two weeks, but despite the destruction of some of
the encircling Russian forces, it did not succeed in breaking
through to the city.[59] Thus, for the third time in less than six

[56] *Ibid.*, p. 382.
[57] *Hitlers Lagebesprechungen,* p. 803, n. 1.
[58] Guderian, *op. cit.*, p. 384.
[59] For details of the relief attempt see Steiner, *Die Freiwilligen,* pp. 294ff.,
and Lagebuch entries beginning with February 2, 1945, in KTB/OKW, IV,
977ff.

months, the elite divisions of the Waffen SS had failed their Führer.

In the meantime, Hitler had at last accepted the hopelessness of the situation in the Ardennes. On January 8, he issued instructions to pull the 6th SS Panzer Army out of action. A few days later he ordered the rapid refitting of the four SS panzer divisions and their corps organizations (Ist and IInd SS Panzerkorps).[60]

On January 12, 1945, the Russians launched their last and greatest offensive. By the end of the month they had reached the lower Oder, only forty miles from Berlin. The German front, stretching from the Baltic to the Bohemian foothills and running along the Oder–Neisse line, was now only 190 miles wide. This shortened line, requiring fewer troops for its defense, largely compensated for the losses suffered by the Germans in the preceding weeks and, with other factors, helped to bring the Soviet advance to a temporary halt in mid-February.[61]

Four days after the start of the Soviet offensive, Hitler returned to Berlin from *Adlerhorst,* the western headquarters at Bad Nauheim, from which he had directed the Ardennes operation. He was met by Guderian's entreaties to transfer forces from the West to face the Russians along the Oder. The Führer had other plans. He informed the Chief of Staff that he had indeed decided to go over to the defensive in the West to free troops for transfer to the East; but these troops, Sepp Dietrich's 6th SS Panzer Army, were to go to Hungary. Despite Guderian's vehement opposition, Hitler "reaffirmed his intention to attack in Hungary, to throw the Russians back across the Danube and to relieve Budapest." [62]

Hitler had been thwarted in the West, but he had not given up his dream of a great last-minute offensive; the recapture of the Hungarian capital was to be his badly needed prestige victory. On January 20, the OB West was notified to prepare for the immediate shipment of "the entire 6th Panzer

---

[60] See "Der Übergang der Initiative in den Angriffsräumen an den Gegner (14. bis 28. Januar 1945)," *ibid.,* p. 1353, and "Mittagslage vom 10. Januar 1945 im Adlerhorst," *Hitlers Lagebesprechungen,* pp. 794 f.

[61] Liddell Hart, *The Red Army,* pp. 124 f.

[62] Guderian, *op. cit.,* p. 393.

Army, with four SS panzer divisions" to the East. The next day, a directive was received which outlined Hitler's intentions in regard to the changing military situation.[63]

The British attack south of Roermond, the American attack in the Ardennes Bulge, the tenacious resistance in lower Alsace, as well as the French attack in the upper Vosges indicate that the enemy is trying to prevent the German Command from making use of its reserves. This is being done in the hope of aiding the Soviets in their effort to bring about the collapse of the national defense. In light of this, the Führer has decided to make provisions for halting the Russians and going over to the offensive. Therefore the transfer of the 6th SS Panzer Army and . . . [other units] has been ordered.

Once again Hitler was staking everything on the efforts of his SS divisions.

Why did Hitler choose to mount an offensive in Hungary rather than along the Oder front? He had a very practical reason, aside from his desire for a prestige victory. By the end of January 1945 the Allied bombings had destroyed the greater part of Germany's synthetic oil plants; hence the already fuel-starved Wehrmacht became dependent on oil from the wells at Zistersdorf in Austria and around Lake Balaton in Hungary.[64] And even Guderian, who long and violently opposed the attack, conceded that Hitler "wanted to keep control of the remaining wells and refineries which were of vital importance both to the armored forces and to the air force." [65]

Meanwhile, the SS Panzer Divisions "Wiking" and "Totenkopf" persisted in their futile efforts to relieve Budapest; their third and last attempt failed on January 29. Nevertheless, the beleaguered defenders refused to surrender, conducting a bitter house-to-house fight for another two weeks. Finally, with no

[63] KTB/OKW, IV, 1353 f.

[64] In January 1945 German supplies of motor fuel were only 28 per cent of what they had been the previous August, and aviation fuel was down a full 94 per cent since May. The shortage of fuel was one of the reasons for the long delay in the transfer of the 6th SS Panzer Army to Hungary. See "Mitteilungen des Oberst d. G. Poleck (Qu) am 26. 1. 45, 10 Uhr," KTB/OKW, IV, 1042 f. See also Poleck's report of 3. 1. 45, *ibid.*, p. 986.

[65] Guderian, *op. cit.*, p. 417.

hope of rescue (they were not informed of the pending offensive by the 6th SS Panzer Army), the survivors attempted to break out, but only 785 of the original 50,000-man garrison managed to reach the German lines.[66]

By the beginning of February the Russians had returned to the offensive, and the pressure of their attacks increased after the fall of the Hungarian capital. The battered divisions of Army Group South, including "Wiking" and "Totenkopf," were hard put to maintain the front. Finally, after long delays occasioned by poor railway connections and a shortage of gasoline, the first units of the 6th SS Panzer Army began to arrive. Other reinforcements, including the 16th SS Panzergrenadierdivision "Reichsführer SS," were added, and on March 6 the German offensive rolled forward on both sides of the Plattensee (Lake Balaton).[67]

On the southern side of the lake the attack soon ground to a halt. But to the north Dietrich's SS panzer divisions made good progress at first. By the time they approached the Danube, however, they were at the end of their strength; the spring mud made movement difficult and the fierce resistance of the Soviet troops took a heavy toll. Moreover, the SS Panzer Army had never completely recovered from the Ardennes offensive and many of its replacements were sailors and airmen inexperienced in land warfare. By mid-March, the German offensive was over and the SS divisions were in retreat.[68] Hitler's orders to renew the attack were in vain, and even his usual "stand fast"

[66] *Hitlers Lagebesprechungen,* p. 803, n. 1. The details of the final battle for Budapest may be found in the daily Lagebuch entries under Heeresgruppe Süd, KTB/OKW, IV, 1072ff.

[67] "Lagebuch 6. 3. 45," *ibid.,* p. 1146. Cf. *Hitlers Lagebesprechungen,* p. 907, n. 2. Even before the start of the main offensive, the 12th SS Panzerdivision "Hitler Jugend" and elements of the 1st SS Panzerdivision "Leibstandarte Adolf Hitler" took part in a successful operation which destroyed a long-established Soviet bridgehead over the Gran River. See Lagebuch entries beginning with February 18, 1945, KTB/OKW, IV, 1104ff., and "Der Einsatz der 12. SS-Panzerdivision vom Invasionsende bis zum Kriegsschluss," Meyer, *op. cit.,* pp. 338ff.

[68] See Lagebuch entries under Heeresgruppe Süd beginning with March 6, 1945, KTB/OKW, IV, 1146ff.; Meyer, *op. cit.,* 339ff.; *Hitlers Lagebesprechungen,* pp. 907, n. 2, 925, n. 3.

directives were ignored. Guderian, who was with Hitler at the time, states that when he learned of this "he almost went out of his mind. He flew into a towering rage and ordered that the divisions—which included his own bodyguard, the Leibstandarte—have their armbands taken away from them." When the order reached Sepp Dietrich, he refused to pass it on. In any case, the SS troops had long since removed their telltale sleeve stripes for security reasons.[69] By early April the 6th SS Panzer Army, minus much of its heavy equipment, had withdrawn across the Austrian border.

In 1944 Himmler had concluded a speech before Goebbels and his staff with these words: "So far the Waffen SS has never under any circumstances caused disappointment, and it will not —even under the most severe hardships yet to come—disappoint in the future." This statement had been met with "strong, sustained applause." [70] But in April 1945 there was no longer any applause in Germany, not even for the Waffen SS. Four times in less than a year Hitler had pinned his hopes on his elite SS divisions, and four times he had been disappointed. His final disillusionment was only a few weeks away.

Battle of Berlin and the Fall
of the Third Reich

While the survivors of the once-elite SS panzer divisions fought to hold the *Ostmark* and its capital, the front in the West collapsed; on April 1, Army Group B was encircled in the Ruhr and ten days later the Americans reached the Elbe. Then it was the turn of the East. On April 9, Königsberg, the capital of East Prussia, fell. Four days later Dietrich's SS troops were finally forced out of Vienna. And on the sixteenth the Russians burst through the Oder line. Berlin was threatened and Germany was in danger of being cut in two.[71]

[69]The elite SS troops wore a thin stripe on their lower left sleeve on which was emblazoned the name of their division or, in some cases, their regiment. Guderian, *op. cit.,* p. 419; Meyer, *op. cit.,* pp. 342 f.; cf. Reitlinger, *op. cit.,* p. 370.

[70] "Rede des Reichsführers-SS auf der Tagung der RPA-Leiter am 28. Januar 1944," Geheim, RFSS/T–175, 94/2614818.

[71] KTB/OKW, IV, 1216, 1232, 1238, 1241, 1244.

At this crucial moment the majority of the best SS formations were in the South and West. Of the many units in the
East bearing the designation SS, only a handful were of top
quality. These had been gathered together in the newly established 11th Panzer Army (under the command of SS Obergruppenführer [General] Felix Steiner), which was ordered to
launch an offensive designed to dislocate the threatened Soviet
advance on Berlin. On February 16, the 10th SS Panzerdivision
"Frundsberg," the 4th SS Polizei-Panzergrenadierdivision, the
11th SS Panzergrenadierdivision "Nordland," the SS Brigade
"Nederland," the SS Kampfgruppe "Wallonie," and a number
of miscellaneous formations thrust in a southwesterly direction
into the northern flank of Marshal Zhukov's 1st White Russian
Front (Army Group). Within the first few hours the SS troops
retook Arnswalde and freed its trapped garrison. But the Russians redeployed their forces to meet the assault, and by the
eighteenth Steiner's offensive had been brought to a halt.[72]

In the next weeks, Russian advances on other sectors of the
front drew Steiner's best divisions away one by one. When the
final Soviet push on Berlin began on April 16, the 11th Panzer
Army retained only three reliable divisions. One of these, the
18th Panzergrenadierdivision, was transferred to the front east
of Berlin the same day. Two days later the 11th SS Panzergrenadierdivision "Nordland" was ordered into the beleaguered
capital and the SS Brigade "Nederland" was sent south of the
city to help parry a Soviet breakthrough. Finally, the Wallonians
were decimated while attempting to defend the bridgehead at
Altdamm, and the survivors retreated into Mecklenburg. As
Steiner himself described it: "I was a general without any
troops." [73]

Meanwhile, inside the ruined capital, Hitler had lost all
control over events and no longer was adequately informed
of what was going on outside. His original intention had been
to leave Berlin on his birthday, April 20, for Obersalzberg and
there, with the still-formidable divisions of the 6th SS Panzer
Army, to conduct the defense of the "Alpine Redoubt." But

[72] Steiner, *Die Freiwilligen,* pp. 317ff.
[73] *Ibid.,* p. 324.

during the military conference held on that day he hesitated. Present for the occasion were all of the remaining leaders of the Third Reich—Himmler, Göring, Goebbels, Bormann, Ribbentrop, Speer, and the military chiefs Keitel, Jodl, Krebs, Burgdorf, and Dönitz. They entreated Hitler to leave the doomed city; he still hoped that Berlin could be saved. He agreed, however, to the establishment of two separate commands in case Germany was split by a junction of the United States and Soviet forces. Admiral Dönitz was given command of all German forces in the north and Hitler left open the possibility that he might shortly move south and take over the command there himself. [74]

But first he would organize one more attempt to relieve Berlin. While Hitler planned, most of his visitors fled the city: Dönitz, Himmler, and Speer to the north; Göring and Ribbentrop to the south. Only Goebbels, Bormann, and the generals remained with their Führer. The next day, April 21, Hitler unfolded his plan: Busse's 9th Army, holding the Oder line southeast of the city, would turn around and advance on Berlin; Wenck's 12th Army, holding the Elbe against the Americans to the southwest, would also turn about and fight through to relieve the city; and, finally, SS Obergruppenführer Steiner would lead his 11th Panzer Army south from Eberswalde in an all-out attack from the north. Since the 9th and 12th Armies were still heavily engaged, Steiner was to begin the operation immediately; the other forces would participate as soon as possible. Accordingly, all the available personnel in the area north of Berlin were to be sent to reinforce Steiner's attack. Feverishly Hitler began issuing the necessary orders.[75]

But Hitler was living in what Trevor-Roper has described

[74] H. R. Trevor-Roper, *The Last Days of Hitler* (3rd ed.; New York, 1962), pp. 173ff., and "Übersicht über den Zusammenbruch des 'Dritten Reiches' (20. April bis 23. Mai 1945)," KTB/OKW, IV, 1436. Cf. Hitler's orders, pp. 1587, 1590.

[75] Steiner, *Die Freiwilligen*, pp. 324ff., and Jürgen Thorwald, *Die grosse Flucht* (Stuttgart, n.d.), pp. 350ff. The latter work is a new one-volume edition of Thorwald's two classic studies on the last days of the Third Reich: *Es begann an der Weichsel* and *Das Ende an der Elbe*, both published in 1950.

as a "cloud-cuckoo-land; . . . his orders bore no relation now
to any reality. He was moving imaginary battalions, making
academic plans, disposing non-existent formations." [76] There
had once been an 11th Panzer Army under Steiner's command,
but it had been blown to the winds in the heavy fighting of the
previous weeks. In fact, at the time Hitler issued his orders, the
11th Panzer Army consisted of little more than a small headquarters staff, which had been assigned the task of creating a
battle group out of sailors, airmen, and whatever stragglers they
could lay their hands on.

Either Hitler was unaware of this situation or else he did
not care, for he continued to issue orders: the Hitler Youth was
to be mobilized and sent to Steiner; a battalion of Luftwaffe
ground troops guarding Göring's estate (Karinhall) was "to be
unconditionally put under the command of SS Obergruppenführer Steiner"; and the Luftwaffe Chief of Staff, Karl Koller,
received a verbal order direct from Hitler demanding that
"all Luftwaffe personnel available for action on the ground
must immediately be sent to Steiner. Any commander who
holds back his troops will forfeit his life in five hours. You
yourself will guarantee with your head that the last man is
thrown in." [77]

When Koller called the *Führerbunker* to report that he had
issued the necessary instructions, an elated Hitler reassured him
that everything would turn out all right: "You'll see, the Russians will yet suffer the greatest and bloodiest defeat in their
history at the gates of Berlin." Nonetheless, it was obvious to all
those around the Führer that he was building the most exaggerated hopes on the success of Steiner's attack. [78]

While Hitler anxiously awaited news of Steiner's advance,
the Russians broke through the outer defense ring and entered
northern Berlin. Throughout the morning of the twenty-second
a series of increasingly agitated phone calls from the bunker

[76] Trevor-Roper, *op. cit.*, p. 179.
[77] "Die Vorgänge im FHQu. (Bunker unter der Reichskanzlei in Berlin)
am 21. bis 23. April 1945 (Tagebuchaufzeichnungen von General d. Fl. Karl
Koller Chef des Gen.-Stabs der Luftwaffe)," KTB/OKW, IV, 1687 f.
[78] *Ibid.*, p. 1689.

failed to elicit any reliable information about the progress of Steiner's attack; from Hohenlychen, Himmler called to say it had begun, but the Luftwaffe reported that it had not. Finally, late in the afternoon, a reliable report was received: Steiner had not launched the attack because the assigned Army and SS units had not appeared. But, the report stated, he hoped to attack the following day—if the troops were available.[79]

The news was broken to Hitler during the afternoon *Lage-besprechung*. He had been on edge all day and those who knew him were aware that he was on the verge of hysteria. It now erupted, and for the next five hours Hitler raged. The end had come. He could no longer continue. He would die in Berlin; those who wanted to leave the city were free to do so. [80]

This dramatic scene has been described many times. All the accounts rely heavily on the investigations of Trevor-Roper, whose study in turn rests on the evidence of a number of those who were present at the conference.[81] All the published works on the subject agree that Hitler's decision to die in Berlin resulted from the failure of the Steiner attack. But no effort has been made to analyze in greater depth the reason for Hitler's hysterical outburst and sudden spiritual collapse. Perhaps it is thought that the failure of the attack speaks for itself. But there had been many failures before. Moreover, Hitler did not permanently give up his interest in the military situation. Indeed, the very next day, and every day until he took his own life on the thirtieth, Hitler continued to direct relief attacks on Berlin.

What then caused Hitler temporarily, but completely, to

[79] *Ibid.*, p. 1691.

[80] *Ibid.*, p. 1692, and "Die Vorgänge im Bunker der Reichskanzlei am 22. April (nach Auskünften des Stenographen Dr. Gerhard Herrgesell)," *ibid.*, p. 1696. Hitler's decision to remain in Berlin was relayed to the Wehrmacht's northern headquarters and there entered into the Kriegstagebuch des Führungsstabs Nord (A) on April 22, *ibid.*, p. 1453. A public announcement of the decision was made on the following day, see "Wehrmachtbericht 23. April," *ibid.*, p. 1262.

[81] See Bullock, *op. cit.*, pp. 783 f.; William L. Shirer, *The Rise and Fall of the Third Reich: A History of Nazi Germany* (New York, 1960), pp. 1112ff.; Trevor-Roper, *op. cit.*, pp. 180ff.; Reitlinger, *op. cit.*, pp. 428 f.

lose his usual fanatical determination? The answer was clearly given three weeks after the event by one of the few persons who was in the conference room for the entire five hours and therefore in a position to hear every word that was said—the stenographer, Gerhard Herrgesell. Herrgesell (along with the transcript of the conference) was flown to Berchtesgaden in the last passenger flight out of Berlin. There, a few days after the end of the war, he told a *Time* correspondent that Hitler had lost all hope because he had been *betrayed by the Waffen SS*. Not simply *betrayed*, as Trevor-Roper describes it. After all, Hitler had been complaining about treason for quite some time before the Steiner affair. Beyond question, the decisive factor was his belief that he had been deserted by his praetorian guard.[82]

In recalling Hitler's words, Herrgesell said: "He had lost confidence in the Wehrmacht quite a while ago. . . . This afternoon [22 April] he said that he was losing confidence in the Waffen SS, for the first time. He had always counted on the Waffen SS as elite troops which would never fail him." Moreover, he had always been determined to fight as long as any part of Germany remained unoccupied; but "the failure of the SS troops to hold the Russians north of Berlin had apparently convinced Hitler that his elite troops had lost heart." Herrgesell recalled that "the Führer always maintained that no force, however well trained and equipped, could fight if it lost heart, and now his last reserve [the Waffen SS] was gone."[83] But the Waffen SS was far from gone. In reality, the great majority of the rank-and-file SS men were still true to their motto—*Meine Ehre heisst Treue.*[84] The fact is that the troops of the Waffen

[82] Herrgesell's interview with *Time* correspondent Percival Knauth was published in the May 21, 1945, issue of the news magazine. It has been recently reviewed for accuracy by Herrgesell and reprinted in English in KTB/OKW, IV, 1696ff. It should be noted that Trevor-Roper interviewed Herrgesell but makes no mention of Hitler's statements about the SS. Cf. Thorwald, *op. cit.,* p. 383, who comes close to pinpointing Hitler's loss of faith in the Waffen SS as the cause of his temporary breakdown.

[83] KTB/OKW, IV, 1696 f.

[84] Perhaps best rendered as "My Honor is my Loyalty"; this motto was engraved on the belt buckle worn by all SS men.

SS, on the whole, fought bitterly until the end of the war; it was only some of their senior officers, and eventually their Reichsführer, who lost heart.

One of these senior officers was Felix Steiner. From Hitler's point of view he had forsworn his oath. Despite a direct order, he had not launched his attack. The reason has already been mentioned: Steiner felt that he lacked sufficient strength. In his book Steiner writes that the forces at his disposal amounted to less than a "weak corps." [85] Moreover, he knew that his attack would receive little or no support: Busse's 9th Army was already surrounded and Wenck's 12th Army consisted of only a few battered divisions. "Considering the situation," Steiner concluded, "the operation seemed ridiculous." As for Hitler's "reinforcements," they consisted of fewer than 5000 Luftwaffe personnel and a band of Hitler Youth, armed only with hand weapons. Steiner sent them back to their bases; "their commitment," he decided, "would have been irresponsible." [86]

The day after his outburst, Hitler regained his interest in the military situation. One of the first things he did was order Steiner relieved of his command and replaced by Lieutenant General Holste, a corps commander in Wenck's army. Holste and Steiner, however, agreed to ignore the order and to continue in command of their own units. Hitler now also ordered Keitel and Jodl to the front, with instructions to establish contact with the relief forces and to spur their advance on Berlin. Accordingly, Jodl left for Steiner's headquarters, Keitel for Wenck's. [87]

On April 25, Steiner's "army," now somewhat reinforced, was once more ordered to attack toward Berlin. According to the OKW war diary, Steiner obeyed his orders on this occasion, and his troops (largely Army, not SS) managed to establish a bridgehead across the Ruppiner Canal, on the route to Berlin. Nevertheless, the relatively weak German force was no match for the Soviet armored divisions that were quickly deployed

[85] Steiner, *Die Freiwilligen*, p. 326.

[86] *Ibid.* Cf. Reitlinger, *op. cit.*, pp. 432 f.

[87] "Kriegstagebuch des Führungsstabs Nord (A)," April 22, 1945, KTB/OKW, IV, 1454. See also Thorwald, *op. cit.*, pp. 403 f.

against it; before long, the advance ground to a halt. On the twenty-seventh, the Russians broke into Steiner's rear, and his two best divisions were drawn away to counter the threat. At 3 P.M., the war diary recorded that "as difficult as it is, there remains no choice other than to give up the Steiner attack." [88] Understandably, neither Keitel nor Jodl had the nerve to report this decision to Hitler, who in any case had no idea that Steiner was still in command of the northern relief force.

But the truth emerged the following day (April 28), when the Russians broke through Berlin's inner defenses and the fighting shifted into the heart of the city. With the sounds of the approaching battle ringing in his ears, General Krebs, Hitler's remaining military adviser, telephoned Keitel and anxiously demanded news about the progress of the relief operation. An illuminating extract from the conversation was entered in the OKW war diary.[89]

KREBS: The Führer is mainly interested in the attack west of Oranienburg [Steiner's attack]. What's the situation there? Is the attack moving forward? The Führer removes Steiner from command there!!! Has Holste taken over the command there yet? If we are not helped in the next 36 to 48 hours, it will be too late!!!

There follows a description of the military situation by Keitel, the sense of which is that the bridgehead won by Steiner across the canal west of Oranienburg is not large enough for German tanks to operate in and the enemy is attacking from three sides. In addition, Russian tanks have broken through near Templin, threatening Steiner's rear so strongly that "a further continuation of the attack will in any case *lead to defeat!!!*"

KREBS: Why is Holste not in command there? The Führer has no trust in Steiner!

88 KTB/OKW, IV, 1460. Cf. Thorwald, *op. cit.*, p. 418. Although Thorwald's book is not documented, it is obvious that he had early access to some of the material contained in the "Kriegstagebuch des Führungsstabs Nord (A)." His bibliography indicates that he was provided with a set of "Tagebuchnotizen" by Joachim Schultz, who as a major had been responsible for the maintenance of the official war diary of Führungsstab Nord during the last month of the war. Schultz later published a book entitled *Die letzten 30 Tage: aus dem Kriegstagebuch des OKW* (Stuttgart, 1951).

89 KTB/OKW, IV, 1461 f. Emphasis in the original.

KEITEL: Holste is on the western wing of his very broad front and I have not been able to bring him over. At the moment, the way things stand, there is nothing that can be done about it.

KREBS: The Führer awaits immediate help; there remains at most only 48 more hours. If help doesn't come by then it will be too late! The Führer asks me to remind you again of that!!!

KEITEL: We will drive Wenck and Busse with utmost energy; there still lies the possibility of rescue by a northerly advance.

This was the last telephone conversation with Berlin; at 5 A.M. the connection to the capital was broken.[90]

In the meantime, reports of Hitler's outburst during the conference of April 22, and particularly his comments about having been betrayed by the SS, led Himmler to succumb to the persistent appeals of SS Gruppenführer Schellenberg that he open negotiations for an armistice.[91] On the night of April 23, Himmler met with Count Bernadotte at the Swedish Consulate in Lübeck to discuss the matter. News of the contact leaked to the press, was reported in a BBC broadcast from London, and was picked up by a Propaganda Ministry monitor amid the ruins of Berlin.[92]

The scene that followed was a shorter, but sharper, repetition of Hitler's earlier outburst. When the news was delivered to the Führer, "his color rose to a heated red and his face was unrecognizable. . . . After the lengthy outburst, Hitler sank into a stupor, and for a time the bunker was silent." [93] But he soon recovered. It all seemed clear now. The failure of Sepp Dietrich in Hungary and the disobedience of Steiner had been part of a larger plot; Himmler—*der getreue Heinrich*—and the SS had been conspiring to betray him all along. Hitler's first thought was of revenge. Himmler's deputy, SS Obergruppenführer (General) Fegelein, who had already been put under

[90] *Ibid.,* p. 1462.

[91] Himmler was in contact with SS Obergruppenführer Fegelein, his deputy at the Führer's headquarters. (See Trevor-Roper, *op. cit.,* p. 186.) Walter Schellenberg was head of military intelligence during the last year of the war.

[92] *Ibid.,* p. 224.

[93] Hanna Reitsch's interrogation, Nuremberg Document 3734–PS, quoted in Bullock, *op. cit.,* p. 791.

arrest after he left the bunker without authorization, was now closely interrogated. Apparently he admitted some knowledge of Himmler's intention to open negotiations; in any case, he was taken out into the Chancellery courtyard and shot. Interestingly enough, the execution was conducted by members of Hitler's SS escort, which was composed of members of the "Leibstandarte Adolf Hitler." Apparently Hitler's distrust of the SS did not extend to the members of his personal staff, for he retained his SS adjutants and guards until the end. After the execution, Hitler's thoughts turned toward Fegelein's master. Himmler was more difficult to reach, but Hitler ordered the new Luftwaffe chief, Ritter von Greim, to fly out of Berlin and see to the Reichsführer's arrest. "A traitor must never succeed me as Führer," he declared. "You must go out to make sure that he does not." Greim and the female test pilot Hanna Reitsch did manage to escape in a small airplane. They were even able to confront Himmler at Dönitz's headquarters at Ploen, but were unable to take any action against the still-powerful SS leader.[94]

During all of his outbursts, Hitler need only have gone a little way from his bunker to see that he had not really been betrayed by the Waffen SS. Aside from the two understrength Army divisions of General Mummert's LVIIth Army Corps, the only regular troops in Berlin were the men of the 11th SS Panzergrenadierdivision "Nordland," reinforced by 300 French SS men from the 33rd Waffen-Grenadierdivision der SS "Charlemagne" and a battalion of Latvian SS men from the 15th Waffen-Grenadierdivision der SS (lett. Nr. 1). An additional 600 SS men were added to the defense when Himmler sent his *Begleitbataillon* (Escort Battalion) to Berlin at the last moment.[95]

From the evidence available it seems that the SS and the members of the *Hitlerjugend* were, as usual, the most determined fighters. In addition to fighting the enemy, young officers of Himmler's SS Escort were formed into *fliegende Feld- und Standgerichte*, which hunted for shirkers and deserters and

---

[94] Trevor-Roper, *op. cit.*, pp. 230ff., 309.

[95] Steiner, *Die Freiwilligen*, pp. 330ff.; Thorwald, *op. cit.*, pp. 424ff.; Reitlinger, *op. cit.*, p. 428.

when they found them hanged them from the nearest lamppost. The diary of a German Army officer in Berlin described these flying tribunals as "mostly very young SS officers. Hardly a single decoration. Blind and fanatical." But they served their purpose. "The hope of relief and at the same time the fear of the tribunals always serves to rally the men," concluded the officer.[96] The SS men of "Nordland" were still in action on May 1, when they heard that Hitler was dead and the city was about to capitulate. According to one of the few survivors, less than 100 men—all that remained of the division—attempted to break out during the night; but they were cut down or driven back by enemy fire.[97]

Meanwhile, on the evening of the twenty-ninth, Keitel, at his headquarters outside Berlin, received a radio message from General Krebs and Reichsleiter Bormann in the bunker. "The foreign press," read the message, "spreads word of new betrayal. The Führer expects that, with the speed of lightning and the hardness of steel, regardless of the circumstances, you will break through. Concerning Wenck, Schörner and others, the Führer awaits proof of their loyalty to him by their coming to his immediate rescue."[98]

At 11 P.M. Colonel General Jodl, who was coordinating the rescue attempt from the south and west, received the following radio message from Hitler:[99]

You are to report to me immediately:
1. Where is Wenck's spearhead?
2. When will they move forward?
3. Where is the 9th Army?
4. Where will the 9th Army break through?
5. Where is Holste's spearhead?

On receipt of the query, Keitel and Jodl met to discuss the answer that should be given. It was decided that for the first time in months Hitler must be told the unvarnished truth; it

[96] Quoted in Thorwald, *op. cit.,* p. 427.

[97] See report by Rolf Holzboog, SS-Panzer-Flak-Abteilung 11, in Steiner, *Die Freiwilligen,* p. 332.

[98] KTB/OKW, IV, 1466.

[99] *Ibid.*

would no longer serve any useful purpose to maintain the fiction of a possible rescue. At 1 A.M. on April 30, Keitel reported to Berlin:

1. Wenck's spearhead is stuck fast south of the Schwielow-See.
2. Therefore 12th Army cannot renew its advance toward Berlin.
3. The mass of the 9th Army is encircled.
4. Holste's corps has been forced over to the defensive.[100]

With the last hope of rescue shattered and the Russians only two blocks from the bunker, Hitler prepared to end his life; by the afternoon he was dead. Less than a month later, with the war already over, Reichsführer SS Heinrich Himmler followed in the footsteps of his former master.[101]

On May 7, 1945, in the French city of Reims, the capitulation of the German Wehrmacht was signed; it went into effect two days later.[102] With matters back in the hands of the professional soldiers, the Waffen SS once more became "invisible." The capitulation and the various directives issued in its wake by the OKW were addressed to the Army, Navy, and Air Force only. But the generals did not forget the still formidable Waffen SS forces concentrated in Austria. The OKW war diary entry for May 9 states that "Field Marshal Kesselring informed SS Oberstgruppenführer [Colonel General] Dietrich that the terms of the cease fire are also binding on the formations of the Waffen SS. [He] expects that, like the entire Wehrmacht, the Waffen SS will also conduct itself in an irreproachably correct manner." [103]

And so it did. As a recent apologetic put it: "All the divisions of the Waffen SS went directly from battle into captivity." [104] But unlike the many cowed and dispirited Army troops who shuffled dejectedly off to the prisoner-of-war cages,

[100] *Ibid.*, p. 1467; also "Kriegstagebuch des Führungsstabs Süd (B)," May 1, 1945, p. 1450.
[101] For the events leading to Himmler's suicide see Reitlinger, *op. cit.*, pp. 438ff.
[102] For text see "Urkunde über die militärische Kapitulation," KTB/OKW, IV, 1676 f.
[103] *Ibid.*, p. 1488.
[104] Kanis, *op. cit.*, p. 232.

the SS men retained a measure of their arrogance and defiance even in defeat. On May 9, the SS Panzergrenadier-Regiment "Deutschland," the oldest in the Waffen SS, sent the following message to the headquarters of the 2nd SS Panzerdivision "Das Reich":

The Regiment "Deutschland"—now completely cut off, without supplies, with losses of 70 per cent in personnel and equipment, at the end of its strength—must capitulate. Tomorrow the regiment will march into captivity with all heads held high. The regiment which had the honor of bearing the name "Deutschland" is now signing off.

As a former SS officer described the regiment's final ride, the vehicles maintained "a more exact formation than usual. The grenadiers sat stiffly at attention. With exemplary bearing we drove westward. There were the Americans." [105]

A similar description by a former officer of the 12th SS Panzerdivision "Hitler Jugend" tells of how his division ignored the "demeaning" orders of the Americans to drape its vehicles with white flags and, less than a mile from the demarcation line, passed in review before its commander: "Disciplined and with proud bearing," the division drove into captivity.[106]

---

[105] "Aus einem Bericht des holländischen Freiwilligen, Leutnant der Waffen-SS van Tienen," quoted in Steiner, *Die Freiwilligen,* pp. 339ff.

[106] "Der Einsatz der 12. SS-Panzerdivision vom Invasionsende bis zum Kriegsschluss," Meyer, *op. cit.,* p. 341. For obvious reasons the Waffen SS formations chose (where they had a choice) to surrender to the western Allies.

CHAPTER TEN

The Tarnished Shield:

Waffen SS Criminality

NO study of the Waffen SS would be complete without a close look at the question of its criminal activities. Ever since the SS was indicted as a criminal organization before the International Military Tribunal at Nuremberg, defenders of the Waffen SS have insisted that the only similarity between it and the SS was that of title. The Waffen SS, they argue, was a purely military organization no different from any other component of the Wehrmacht and had no connection with the crimes committed by other branches of the SS.[1] The prosecution at Nuremberg rejected this claim and concluded that the Waffen SS "was in theory and practice as much an integral part of the SS organization as any other branch of the SS."[2]

This view was accepted by the Tribunal, and the Waffen SS was included in the judgment that "the SS was utilized for purposes which were criminal under the Charter [of the International Military Tribunal], involving the persecution and extermination of the Jews, brutalities and killings in concentration camps, excesses in the administration of occupied territories, the administration of the slave-labor program and the mistreatment and murder of prisoners of war."[3] Specifically,

[1] See, for example, testimony of Paul Hausser before the International Military Tribunal, August 6, 1946, TGMWC, XX, 300, and summary by SS defense counsel Dr. Horst Pelckmann, TGMWC, XXII, 102ff.

[2] Summary by deputy chief prosecutor Sir David Maxwell-Fyfe, *ibid.*, p. 282.

[3] Judgment of the International Military Tribunal, *ibid.*, p. 480. The

the Waffen SS was singled out for having participated "in steps leading up to aggressive war" such as "the occupation of the Sudetenland, of Bohemia and Moravia, and of Memel." In connection with the charges of War Crimes and Crimes Against Humanity, the Tribunal concluded that "units of the Waffen SS were directly involved in the killing of prisoners of war and the atrocities in occupied countries. It supplied personnel for the Einsatzgruppen, and had command over the concentration-camp guards after its absorption of the Totenkopf SS, which originally controlled the system." [4]

With regard to the organizations indicted before the Tribunal, the proceedings were designed only "to identify and condemn," and the declaration of criminality did not empower the Tribunal to impose sentence upon them or to convict any individual merely because of membership.[5] In separate trials before Allied military courts, however, a few hundred Waffen SS personnel, including some members of fighting formations, were convicted, and in a few cases executed, for specific criminal acts. In addition, all officers and noncommissioned officers of the Waffen SS were kept in prison camps for as long as four years after the war. After their release, these men were haled before German de-Nazification courts; 99 per cent were found to be free of personal guilt. But, in keeping with the haphazard administration of this program, a portion of the group was convicted of membership in a "criminal organization" and deprived

---

Charter of the International Military Tribunal is reproduced in *ibid.*, pp. 550ff.

[4] *Ibid.*, pp. 479 f.

[5] This statement on the law and policy advocated by the prosecution in regard to the Nazi groups and organizations indicted at Nuremberg was delivered by Justice Jackson before the Tribunal on February 28, 1946: "It was the intent of the Charter to utilize the hearing processes of this Tribunal to identify and condemn those Nazi and militaristic forces that were so organized as to constitute a continuing menace to the long-term objectives for which our respective countries have spent the lives of their young men. . . . The only issue in this trial concerns the collective criminality of the organization or group. It is to be adjudicated by what amounts to declaratory judgment. It does not decree any punishment, either against the organization or against individual members." (NCA, II, 5 f.)

for a time of certain civil rights.[6] Generally speaking, this type of harassment decreased as the years passed, and only an occasional ex-member of the Waffen SS was singled out for trial on a specific charge.

These were the years of silence, when members of the Waffen SS were too ashamed or intimidated to call attention to themselves. It was a period when former officers of the Wehrmacht were attempting to divest themselves of any responsibility for the horrors of Nazism and for the loss of the war. In a flood of memoirs, articles, and historical studies, German military circles drew a sharp dividing line between themselves and the Waffen SS; and they ascribed to the activities or influence of the SS much of what had been charged against the Wehrmacht. Perhaps the wildest and least-deserved charge made by military spokesmen against the Waffen SS was that it had been a complete failure in battle and was responsible for the defeat of the Wehrmacht.[7]

As the war-crimes trials passed into memory and people in Europe and the United States stopped talking and thinking about Nazi atrocities, leading Waffen SS veterans decided that the time was ripe to remove the stigma on their "honor." They were, of course, also motivated by other considerations. For despite their successful reintegration into civilian life, the aura of criminality surrounding veterans of the Waffen SS kept the German authorities from granting them the same treatment in regard to pensions and allotments that was accorded to other ex-members of the Wehrmacht.

In order to press their claims for personal, political, and financial rehabilitation, former Waffen SS men began to organize on a local basis. Out of these local efforts grew the Mutual Aid Society of the Waffen SS, or HIAG der Waffen SS (Hilfs-organisation auf Gegenseitigkeit der Waffen SS), which publishes a magazine called *Der Freiwillige,* finances the publication of apologetics by former members of the Waffen SS, runs a library devoted to circulating neo-Nazi tracts, holds annual

---

[6] See Kanis, *op. cit.,* p. 243; Dornberg, *op. cit.,* pp. 9ff.

[7] See, for example, Siegfried Westphal, *Heer in Fesseln* (Bonn, 1950).

"help-find-lost comrades conventions" drawing thousands of ex-SS men, and lobbies incessantly for legitimacy for its members.[8]

The first attempt at rehabilitating the Waffen SS seems to have been the campaign to revise the verdict of the famous Malmédy massacre trial, in which SS Standartenführer (Colonel) Joachim Peiper and seventy-two members of his Kampfgruppe, which belonged to the 1st SS Panzerdivision "Leibstandarte Adolf Hitler," had been found guilty of murdering seventy-one American soldiers during the Ardennes counteroffensive in 1944.[9] With the support of right-wing publications and conservative clergymen, sharp accusations were leveled at the trial investigators and the prosecution staff. Further backing for the revisionist campaign came from the late Senator Joseph McCarthy and other interested circles in the United States. Although a special congressional investigating committee upheld the fairness of the trial, none of the forty-three defendants sentenced to death was executed. The campaign continued with the publication of Dietrich Ziemssen's *Der Malmedy Prozess* in 1952. Four years later Peiper was paroled from the U.S. War Crimes Prison at Landsberg; in June 1964 West German officials disclosed that he was once more under investigation, this time on a charge that he was responsible for atrocities in northern Italy in 1943.[10]

Meanwhile, the Waffen SS received assistance in its rehabilitation efforts from an unexpected source. Colonel General Guderian, second-to-last Chief of the General Staff (OKH),

[8] See Dornberg, *op. cit.*, pp. 42, 111ff.; Kurt Hirsch, *SS: Gestern, heute und* . . . (Darmstadt, 1960), *passim*. The HIAG journal was first published in 1953 under the title *Wiking Ruf;* in 1958 it merged with a similar publication to become *Der Freiwillige/Wiking Ruf;* its present title is *Der Freiwillige: Kamaradschaftsblatt der HIAG* and it is published monthly in Osnabrück by Verlag "Der Freiwillige."

[9] See pp. 278ff. Peiper preferred the name Jochen to Joachim, and the two names are used interchangeably in the SS files.

[10] See pp. 275 f. For the congressional investigation see United States Senate Committee on Armed Forces, *Malmedy Massacre Investigation Hearings 1949* (Washington, 1949).

in his memoirs praised the conduct and fighting ability of the SS divisions.[11] And when former SS Oberstgruppenführer (Colonel General) Paul Hausser published the first history of the Waffen SS, Guderian contributed this introduction:

"Our Honor is our Loyalty [*Unsere Ehre heisst Treue*]." This was the motto according to which the Waffen SS was trained, and it was the motto according to which it fought. Whoever saw them in battle is bound to confirm that. After the collapse this formation faced exceptionally heavy and unjust charges. . . . Since so many untrue and unjust things have been said and written about them, I welcome most cordially the initiative of their prewar teacher and one of the most outstanding wartime commanders, who has taken up his pen to give evidence of the truth. His book will help to disperse the clouds of lies and calumnies piled up around the Waffen SS and will help those gallant men to resume the place they deserve alongside the other branches of the Wehrmacht.[12]

The efforts of HIAG and the revisionists soon produced some major successes. As early as August 1953, Chancellor Adenauer stated in a public speech in Hannover that members of the combat formations of the Waffen SS had been soldiers like any others.[13] In the following months a number of ex-Waffen SS men imprisoned for war crimes were released from Allied captivity. Among them was the still-youthful former commander of the 12th SS Panzerdivision "Hitler Jugend," Kurt (Panzermeyer) Meyer, who quickly became the chief spokesman for HIAG. Many of the released war criminals applied for, and received, returnee payments or prisoner-of-war compensation from local governments. In 1955, Hasso von Manteuffel, a former Wehrmacht general and then FDP member of the Bundestag, took up the fight for rehabilitation of the Waffen SS. And finally, in 1956, the German Ministry of Defense announced that former members of the Waffen SS, through the grade of SS Obersturmbannführer (lieutenant colonel), would be accepted in the Bundeswehr at their old rank.[14]

[11] Guderian, *op. cit.*, p. 447.
[12] Quoted in Hirsch, *op. cit.*, p. 84.
[13] *Deutsche Soldaten-Zeitung*, August 1956, cited in *ibid.*, pp. 90, 98.
[14] See *ibid.*, pp. 88, 91 f.; "Allgemeine Ausnahmegenehmigung für das Überspringen von Dienstgraden durch Soldaten," *Ministerialblatt des*

The trend toward rehabilitation of the Waffen SS did not go unchallenged, and so far the Federal Government has refused to extend to ex-members of the Waffen SS the provisions of the so-called 131 Law, which provides retirement benefits and pensions for former career soldiers of the Wehrmacht. But the efforts of the HIAG circle continue, and the controversy surrounding the criminality of the Waffen SS has increased in recent years. Despite the passage of time, however, little new evidence has been introduced by either those who condemn or those who defend the Waffen SS. The arguments put forward by both sides are, in effect, simply repetitions or variations of those heard before the International Military Tribunal in 1945 and 1946.

Speaking before some 8000 former SS men at a HIAG convention held in Karlberg, Bavaria, during 1957, Kurt Meyer stated the position of the apologists in simple terms. "SS troops," he claimed, "committed no crimes except the massacre at Oradour, and that was the action of a single man. He was scheduled to go before a court-martial, but he died a hero's death before he could be tried." The Nuremberg Tribunal's charge that the Waffen SS had been involved in the destruction and massacre of Lidice was denied, and Meyer insisted that "the Waffen SS was as much a regular army outfit as any other in the Wehrmacht." He went on to condemn the theory of "collective guilt" and demanded an end to governmental policies which "treat former SS troopers as second-class citizens [when] they did nothing more than fight for their country." [15]

In his book, which was published the same year, Meyer gave

Bundesministers für Verteidigung, Bonn, No. 1, September 1, 1956, reproduced in Reimund Schnabel, *Macht ohne Moral: Eine Dokumentation über die SS* (Frankfurt am Main, 1957), pp. 548 f. By the end of September 1956, the following figures of former Waffen SS personnel serving in the Bundeswehr had been released: 33 officers, 5 officer candidates, 5 musicians, 270 noncommissioned officers, and 1917 enlisted men. In addition, 4 former members of the Allegemeine SS were serving in the Bundeswehr. See Hirsch, *op. cit.*, pp. 91 f.

[15] Quoted in Dornberg, *op. cit.*, p. 113. Meyer was right about Lidice; the Waffen SS had nothing to do with the massacre there. See action report in Schnabel, *op. cit.*, p. 468.

a somewhat more detailed version of his views. His choice of
words is important. "The charge that units belonging to the
divisions of the Waffen SS [*Einheiten der Divisionen der Waffen
SS*] were assigned to carry out extermination operations is a
deception designed to defame the formation." But Meyer did
not, like some neo-Nazis, deny that such crimes were committed:

> In the interests of historical truth nothing must be glossed over.
> Things happened during the war that are unworthy of the German
> nation. The former soldiers of the Waffen SS are men enough to
> recognize and deplore actual cases of inhuman behavior. It would
> be foolish to label all the charges laid at our doorstep as the
> propaganda of our former enemies. Of course they made propaganda
> out of it. . . . But crimes were committed. It is useless to argue
> about the toll of victims—the facts are burdensome enough.[16]

This relatively candid admission is not, however, followed by
a thorough discussion of the specific crimes charged to the
Waffen SS. Meyer offers only a vague rejoinder to one of the
most frequently made accusations:

> The Waffen SS is at present being reproached for what took place
> in the concentration camps because leading personalities of the
> state placed special formations on the budget of the combat
> troops . . . [which] knew no more and no less about these activities
> in the homeland than the mass of the German people.

The soldiers of the Waffen SS, concludes Meyer, "have been
subjected to inhuman suffering for crimes which they neither
committed, nor were able to prevent." [17]

The opposing view is set forth succinctly in the preface to
a recent German documentary publication specifically intended
to combat the trend toward the rehabilitation of the Waffen
SS: Hitler was evil, the SS was the embodiment of the most
brutal aspects of his reign, and the claims of the Waffen SS
apologists "do not alter the fact that the Waffen SS was a part
of the SS party formation [*Parteigliederung SS*] and that the
majority of the Waffen SS at least knew about the atrocities." [18]

[16] Meyer, *op. cit.,* p. 412.
[17] *Ibid.,* p. 413.
[18] Schnabel, *op. cit.,* pp. 12 f.

Much depends on one's definition of the term *Waffen SS*. The accusers stress the unity of the SS organization and base their condemnation in large part on the theory of collective guilt originally formulated at Nuremberg. When referring to the Waffen SS they include all units, departments, organizations, and individuals bearing this designation. They consequently reject all arguments or explanations which attempt to distinguish between "combat formations" and "noncombatant formations," or "regular Waffen SS" and "nominal Waffen SS." Indeed, this group generally refuses to recognize any differences between the Waffen SS and its parent organization. Hence their publications, ostensibly directed against a rehabilitation of the Waffen SS, contain much shocking evidence attesting to the crimes committed by Himmler's SS organization but little relating to the criminal activities of the Waffen SS.[19]

The apologists, on the other hand, define the Waffen SS in only the narrowest terms. For example, Kurt Meyer, in the passage quoted above, offers a sweeping defense of the Waffen SS; yet he refers specifically only to "units belonging to the divisions of the Waffen SS." The fact that the guardians of the concentration and extermination camps were members of the Waffen SS is passed off as a betrayal of the combat troops by "leading personalities of the state." In connection with the charge that Waffen SS units and personnel other than those at the front were involved in criminal activities, the apologists are silent.

A close reading of the material offered by the two principal factions in the controversy makes inescapable the conclusion that neither the apologists nor the accusers are primarily interested in the truth. Both sides are in fact playing for higher stakes. Kurt Hirsch, author of one of the more convincing tracts in the recent crop of journalistic indictments of the Waffen SS, is of the opinion that "the [apologist] propaganda of the past few years is really not concerned with the welfare of 'widows

[19] In addition to the works previously cited see the formidable volume prepared by the Komitee der Antifaschistischen Widerstandskämpfer in der Deutschen Demokratischen Republik (East Germany) entitled *SS im Einsatz: Eine Dokumentation über die Verbrechen der SS* (Berlin, 1964).

and orphans' or 'disabled veterans'; rather, it is directed toward a rehabilitation of the wartime Waffen SS, and with it the whole evil National Socialist system." [20] The controversy surrounding the criminality of the Waffen SS, then, may be viewed as part of a larger political and ideological struggle between liberal and conservative elements in present-day Germany.

Despite their tendentiousness, the works published in the course of the controversy are useful. Those that condemn the SS present some interesting insights and at the same time provide a convenient compilation of otherwise scattered material. As for the books published by the HIAG circle, Karl O. Paetel has pointed out that they are "trying to prove only what no tolerably informed person has ever attempted to deny, viz., that the soldiers of the Waffen SS were brave fighters, suffered big losses and, as far as they served in the front line, did not run extermination camps." [21] Unfortunately there is no work available at present which offers a meaningful and objective discussion of the criminal activities of the Waffen SS.[22] A full analysis of this type would transcend the limits of the present study, but an attempt will be made here to examine, or re-examine, some of the more important questions and to offer an opinion on the criminality of the Waffen SS.

Waffen SS, Totenkopfverbände, and Concentration Camps

In October 1939, some 6500 members of the SS Totenkopfverbände were transferred to the newly established SS

[20] Hirsch, *op. cit.,* p. 118.

[21] Karl O. Paetel, "The Black Order: A Survey of the Literature on the SS," *The Wiener Library Bulletin,* XII, Nos. 3–4 (London, 1959), p. 35. This is a translation of an article originally published in the *Neue Politische Literatur,* No. 4 (Stuttgart and Düsseldorf, 1958).

[22] The best existing treatment of the subject is in Reitlinger, *op. cit.,* but references to the criminal activities of the Waffen SS are scattered throughout the book and do not constitute a coherent and meaningful discussion of the subject. See also Robert M. W. Kempner, *SS im Kreuzverhör* (Munich, 1964), which, although little concerned with the Waffen SS, presents an interesting and valuable compilation of extracts from various war-crimes trials, including some of those held in Germany in recent years.

Totenkopfdivision. The former guardians of Germany's concentration-camp system thus constituted the nucleus of one of the elite fighting formations of the Waffen SS. The commander of this division, until his death in 1943, was Theodor Eicke, the notorious boss of the entire concentration-camp system from 1934 until 1939. Although the prewar German concentration camps were not yet the extermination camps of the later war years, the former members of the Totenkopfverbände hardly fit the apologists' description of decent young soldiers who "knew no more and no less about these activities than the mass of the German people." [23]

During the first two years of the war, 30,000 to 40,000 members of the fourteen reinforced SS Totenkopfstandarten were engaged in "special police tasks" in various parts of German-occupied Europe. In the East, Totenkopf personnel conducted the deportations and executions which characterized the first stages of Hitler's racial policy. These tasks were eventually turned over to other SS or Police formations; and by the time the Germans invaded the Soviet Union the remaining Totenkopfstandarten had been converted into SS Totenkopf infantry regiments. Some were integrated directly into SS front-line formations, but others remained for a time under Himmler's control for use in operations against partisans behind the front lines. Because the fight against partisans often served as a cloak for the mass extermination of civilians, the criminal activities of some of these troops did not end with their transfer to combat elements of the Waffen SS.[24]

By the end of 1941, then, there were tens of thousands of men serving in the front-line formations of the Waffen SS who had participated in, supported, or witnessed criminal acts. This fact is particularly damaging to the claim that the fighting men of the Waffen SS had no connection with the atrocities committed behind the front.

When spokesmen for HIAG deny responsibility for what happened in the concentration camps, they are on firmer ground. Until the latter part of 1940, the Inspectorate of Con-

[23] Meyer, *op. cit.*, p. 413.
[24] See pp. 274ff.

centration Camps was formally under the authority of the SS Hauptamt. In practice, its chief was responsible only to Himmler.[25] Some months after the beginning of the war, the Wehrmacht High Command (OKW) issued a directive listing those components of the SS that were officially recognized as formations of the Waffen SS; neither the SS Hauptamt nor the concentration-camp system was included.[26]

In August 1940, Himmler established a new main office, the SS Führungshauptamt, under whose authority all formations of the Waffen SS were placed.[27] The Inspectorate of Concentration Camps, now headed by SS Brigadeführer (Major General) Richard Glücks, became Amt VI of the SS Führungshauptamt. The transfer did not affect the special position enjoyed by Glücks, and the Inspectorate remained an autonomous organization.[28] But by virtue of its position within the SS Führungshauptamt, the concentration-camp system became a nominal part of the Waffen SS.

By April 1941, Himmler felt strong enough to ignore the OKW in the matter of designating SS components as Waffen SS. During that month, he issued a directive listing 163 separate units, departments, and installations which were henceforth to be considered part of the Waffen SS establishment. On the list were all the existing concentration camps.[29] It is now known that this step was taken for economic and administrative reasons; Himmler, despite the inconsistency of his actions, intended to keep the concentration-camp system carefully separated from his beloved Waffen SS.[30] Nevertheless, the concentration-camp personnel wore Waffen SS uniforms and carried Waffen SS paybooks.

Early in 1942, Himmler decided to transform the camps into large-scale economic enterprises. On March 3, 1942, he

[25] Enno Georg, *Die wirtschaftlichen Unternehmungen der SS* ("Schriftenreihe der Vierteljahrshefte für Zeitgeschichte," No. 7; Stuttgart, 1963), pp. 39 f.

[26] See p. 49.

[27] See pp. 105 f.

[28] Georg, *op. cit.,* pp. 39 f.

[29] See p. 110.

[30] Kersten, *op. cit.,* pp. 250 f.; Reitlinger, *op. cit.,* p. 265.

transferred the entire concentration-camp system from the SS Führungshauptamt to the SS Wirtschafts- und Verwaltungshauptamt (Main SS Economic and Administrative Office), or WVHA. As Amtsgruppe D of this organization, the Inspectorate of Concentration Camps was formally under the command of SS Obergruppenführer (General) Oswald Pohl, chief of the WVHA; but once again Glücks retained his autonomy, and until the end of the war he received his orders directly from the Reichsführer SS. Although Pohl, Glücks, and most of their staff held nominal Waffen SS ranks, their organization had no direct connection with the SS combat formations.[31]

Nevertheless, there was a continual exchange of personnel between the field units of the Waffen SS and the concentration-camp service throughout the war. Until the personnel records of the SS are thoroughly analyzed, the extent of this practice can only be estimated. Rudolf Höss, the commandant of Auschwitz from May 1940 until December 1943, recalled after the war that during his tenure approximately 2500 members of his staff were posted to field units of the Waffen SS and replaced by others.[32] The commandant of the smaller Sachsenhausen camp estimated that about 1500 of his guards were similarly transferred between August 1942 and May 1945.[33] In the last months of the war large numbers of concentration-camp guards, many of whom had previously been rejected as unfit for combat, were redrafted into the field divisions of the Waffen SS. They were replaced to a considerable extent by older men from other branches of the Wehrmacht or its auxiliaries who had never been members of the SS. All guard personnel, regardless of their origin, were incorporated into the Waffen SS. Where a camp was near a Waffen SS installation, recruits or personnel in training were also employed as guards in the latter part of the war. Reitlinger tells of the British general who, in April

[31] Hans Buchheim, "Die SS in der Verfassung des Dritten Reiches," *Vierteljahrshefte für Zeitgeschichte*, III, No. 2 (April 1955), pp. 142, 149; Reitlinger, *op. cit.*, pp. 262ff.; TGMWC, XXII, 122ff.; Nuremberg Documents NO–498 and NO–1210.

[32] Nuremberg Document D–749–B, NCA, VII, 212 f.

[33] Nuremberg Document D–745–A, NCA, VII, 208 f.

1945, saw German guards at Belsen "shooting indiscriminately among the mob of gibbering skeletons." The guards turned out to be *Volksdeutsche* recruits from Hungary who had been in training at a nearby Waffen SS panzergrenadier school.[34]

The transfer of personnel between the field units and the concentration camps was not confined merely to enlisted men but also included officers. Again, the extent of such exchanges is not known, and the final word on the subject must await a study of the records of the SS Personalhauptamt. It seems that competent combat officers were rarely transferred to the concentration camps unless wounded or otherwise rendered unfit for front-line duty. But officers who proved unqualified to hold a field command might be shipped off to a camp assignment. A case in point is that of SS Obersturmbannführer (Lieutenant Colonel) Friedrich Hartjenstein, a defendant in the postwar Natzweiler Trial. Hartjenstein voluntarily transferred from the Wehrmacht to the SS Totenkopfverbände in 1938; and he was for a time employed as the commander of a guard company at the Sachsenhausen concentration camp. In 1940 he became an officer in Eicke's Totenkopfdivision and served at the front until 1942, when he was relieved of his duties because of incompetence and shipped off to Auschwitz to become commander of its guard detachment. In 1944 Hartjenstein became commandant of the Birkenau extermination camp, and from May 1944 until January 1945 he commanded the notorious Natzweiler camp.[35]

In summary, the concentration-camp system shared a common establishment with the Waffen SS for administrative reasons and carried the name *Waffen SS;* but it was a separate organization within Himmler's SS empire and fulfilled a function which had little in common with that of the field formations. Nevertheless, the transfer of personnel between the two was extensive enough to destroy the claim that the combat troops

[34] Reitlinger, *op. cit.,* p. 266.

[35] Höss, *op. cit.,* p. 118, n. 1. On the attitude of guards, and on the concentration-camp system in general, see Kogon, *op. cit., passim.* The service records of a number of the defendants in the so-called Auschwitz-Prozess (which began in Germany in 1963) indicate that they served for some time in regular combat units of the Waffen SS either before or after a tour of duty in the concentration-camp system. See Kempner, *op. cit.,* pp. 165ff.

had absolutely no connection with the concentration camps and had no knowledge of what transpired there.

Waffen SS and Einsatzgruppen

Another charge that must be examined is that of Waffen SS participation in the activities of the notorious Einsatzgruppen, the special extermination squads created by Himmler to follow the German armies into the Soviet Union for the purpose of combating resistance groups and executing "political and racial undesirables." In this case the apologists have had nothing to say; even the late Kurt Meyer, the most outspoken defender of the Waffen SS, maintained a discreet silence on the subject.

The four Einsatzgruppen created just prior to the invasion of Russia numbered only some 3000 men, yet they managed to murder nearly half a million people in a period of six months.[36] The operations were under the direction of the Reichssicherheitshauptamt (RSHA) in Berlin, and the extermination units were officered by personnel of the Gestapo, SD, and Kripo. The rank and file, however, were drawn largely from the Waffen SS and the Ordnungspolizei. The posting of SS combat troops to the Einsatzgruppen "was a recognized part of Waffen SS discipline." The commander of the 2nd SS Panzerdivision "Das Reich," Georg Keppler, described the procedure in this fashion:

They are late or fall asleep on duty. They are court-martialled but are told they can escape punishment by volunteering for Special Commandos. For fear of punishment and in the belief that their career is ruined anyway, these young men ask to be transferred to the Special Commandos. Well, these commandos, where they are first put through special training, are murder commandos. When the young men realize what they are being asked to do and refuse to take part in mass murder, they are told the orders are given them as a form of punishment. Either they can obey and take that punishment or they can disobey and be shot. In any case their career is over and done with. By such methods decent young men are frequently turned into criminals.[37]

[36] Reitlinger, *op. cit.*, p. 185; NCA, II, 265ff.
[37] Quoted in Reitlinger, *op. cit.*, p. 171.

In examining the composition of the Einsatzgruppen, one finds that Einsatzgruppe A, while operating behind the northern sector of the Russian front during the fall of 1941, included 340 members of the Waffen SS in its complement of 990 men.[38]

On the basis of the evidence at hand it may be concluded that perhaps as many as 1500 members of the Waffen SS served with the Einsatzgruppen, that at least some of the senior SS combat officers were aware of the manner in which they were employed, and that for these reasons the Waffen SS must bear its share of responsibility for the cold-blooded murder of hundreds of thousands of civilians.

The SS Sonderkommandos Dirlewanger and Kaminski

Before examining the charges made against the front-line troops of the Waffen SS, something must be said about the infamous Dirlewanger and Kaminski formations. Both units committed numerous atrocities, most notably during the abortive Warsaw uprising of August 1944; and these were added to the charges laid against the Waffen SS at Nuremberg. High-ranking SS leaders like Paul Hausser, Gottlob Berger, and Erich von dem Bach-Zelewski testified that neither unit was considered part of the Waffen SS. They did not, however, deny the crimes. These were a matter of record; even German authorities had protested about them to Berlin on a number of occasions.[39]

In looking at the evidence one discovers that Kaminski was a Russian engineer who had collaborated with the German military occupation authorities and was therefore permitted to govern a semiautonomous province behind Army Group Center. To defend his appanage against Soviet partisan bands, Kaminski was allowed to establish an armed militia. For the next two years, Kaminski's militia cooperated with German troops in

[38] Nuremberg Document L–180, NCA, II, 227. The best brief summary of the activities of the Einsatzgruppen and Einsatzkommandos may be found in Kempner, *op. cit.,* pp. 18ff.

[39] See Hellmuth Auerbach, "Der Einheit Dirlewanger," *Vierteljahrshefte für Zeitgeschichte,* X, No. 3 (July 1962), pp. 252 f.

antipartisan operations. With the approach of the Red Army in the fall of 1943, Kaminski and his band—now grown to the size of a brigade and armed with artillery and captured Soviet tanks—were forced to retreat along with the German forces. Until this time neither Kaminski nor his troops had had any official connection with the SS. But now the Russian collaborators, reinforced by turncoats from the prisoner-of-war camps, were assigned to full-time duty with the antipartisan forces under the command of the SS Obergruppenführer (General) von dem Bach-Zelewski, and Kaminski was given the rank of SS Oberführer.[40]

During the Warsaw rebellion, the Kaminski Brigade was officially incorporated into the Waffen SS at Himmler's personal order. The 6500 Russians under Kaminski's command composed the largest individual unit used by the Germans in suppressing the rebellion. The atrocious behavior of the Russians, many of them Ukrainians with a traditional antipathy toward Poles, was rivaled only by that of the 4000 men of the Dirlewanger Brigade. So shocking were the crimes they committed that Colonel General Guderian, Chief of the Army General Staff, and SS Gruppenführer Fegelein, the SS Liaison Officer at Hitler's headquarters, prevailed upon the Führer to order the withdrawal of both units. This was done; but neither formation was disbanded. Kaminski disappeared under mysterious circumstances; the most probable explanation is that offered by von dem Bach, who had been in charge of the action at Warsaw and who claimed that he had Kaminski tried and executed.[41] Kaminski's men were incorporated into Andrei Vlasov's German-sponsored "Russian Army of Liberation." [42]

The other SS Sonderkommando (Special Command) under investigation here is the SS Dirlewanger Brigade, perhaps the most irregular of the many irregular military formations estab-

[40] *Hitlers Lagebesprechungen*, p. 378, n. 1. An SS Oberführer ranked higher than a German Army colonel, but lower than a major general.

[41] Reitlinger, *op. cit.*, p. 377; Guderian, *op. cit.*, pp. 322ff. On this point and the Kaminski Brigade in general see also the undocumented but remarkably candid "Die Brigade Kaminski," *Der Freiwillige*, X, No. 8 (August 1964), pp. 13ff.

[42] See Dallin, *op. cit.*, pp. 553ff.

lished by the Nazis during World War II. It was created during
the summer of 1940 as a result of Gottlob Berger's imaginative
search for manpower for the SS. The SS recruiting chief suggested to Himmler the establishment of a special formation util-
izing the many convicted poachers serving sentences in the
SS-controlled prisons and concentration camps.[43]

The proposal seems to have appealed to the romantic streak
in the Reichsführer's personality, and he gave Berger his
approval. But he was somewhat more reluctant to accept Berger's friend Oskar Dirlewanger as the unit's commander. Even
by SS standards, Dirlewanger was an unsavory character. His
ideological commitment to National Socialism was beyond
reproach: he was a Freikorps veteran, a violent anti-Semite, and
had been a member of the NSDAP since 1923. But in 1934,
while serving as a Nazi official, Dirlewanger was arrested for
contributing to the delinquency of a minor with whom he was
sexually involved, and he was sentenced to two years' imprisonment. No sooner was he released than he was once more arrested
on the same charge; this time he was sent to a concentration camp.
Fortunately for Dirlewanger, his powerful friend Berger was
in a position to effect his release. He quickly left the country
and in the next few years served the Fascist cause in Spain—
first in the Spanish Foreign Legion and later, at Berger's recommendation, in the German Condor Legion. Upon Dirlewanger's
return to Germany in the middle of 1939, Berger secured him
a commission in the General SS. With the outbreak of war, the
faithful Berger attempted to get his friend a berth in the Waffen
SS, but the strangely puritanical Himmler refused, fearing that
Dirlewanger might revert to his former habits. By mid-1940,
however, the Reichsführer had changed his mind. Giving in to
Berger's urgings, he appointed Dirlewanger an Obersturmführer
(1st lieutenant) in the Waffen SS and entrusted to him the task
of training a unit composed of convicted poachers.[44]

There has been a good deal of debate about the official
status of the Dirlewanger unit. Because its commander was an

[43] Nuremberg Document NO–2920, USMT IV, Case 11, PDB 66–C,
pp. 1ff.; Auerbach, *op. cit.,* p. 250.

[44] Auerbach, *op. cit.,* p. 251.

officer in the Waffen SS and because it ended the war as the 36th Waffen-Grenadierdivision der SS, the Nuremberg prosecutors concluded that it was indeed a formation of the Waffen SS. Defense witnesses, however, claimed that the unit was under the direct command of Berger's SS Hauptamt and was therefore not a part of the Waffen SS.[45]

Actually, Dirlewanger's unit was an organizational orphan for its first year and a half. Under the designation "Wilddieb-Kommando-Oranienburg" it was carried on the records of the 5th SS Totenkopfstandarte, and thus was at best only nominally a formation of the Waffen SS. Until the beginning of 1942 it was employed in Poland, first as a labor battalion and then to guard a camp for Jewish laborers. On January 29, 1942, just before its transfer to Russia to participate in antipartisan operations, Himmler issued a directive which established the position of the "SS Sonderkommando Dirlewanger" as that of a volunteer formation of the Waffen SS similar to the units composed of volunteers from the Germanic lands of Western and Northern Europe.[46]

Himmler's directive placed the Dirlewanger Kommando under the jurisdiction of the SS Führungshauptamt, thus making it technically a part of the Waffen SS. Berger, however, continued to serve as its protector, and from his vantage point in Berlin was able to intercede in Dirlewanger's behalf. This has led to the erroneous conclusion that the Dirlewanger unit was under the command of the SS Hauptamt and hence was no part of the Waffen SS.[47]

The transfer of the Dirlewanger unit to the Waffen SS did not put an end to its irregularity. Indeed, in terms of its recruitment, discipline, and employment, it differed sharply from the other fighting formations of the Waffen SS. The development and the activities of the Dirlewanger unit can only be outlined here. Rarely serving in the front lines, it was most often under the command of Himmler's Höheren SS- und Polizeiführer (Higher SS and Police Leaders) in operations against partisans

---

[45] Reitlinger, *op. cit.*, p. 172; Hausser's testimony, TGMWC, XX, 331.
[46] Auerbach, *op. cit.*, p. 253.
[47] *Ibid.*, p. 252.

or civilians. In the process, the formation committed so many atrocities that even SS officials were led to complain about its activities. Attempts by the Hauptamt SS-Gericht (Main SS Legal Office) to indict Dirlewanger and to bring his men under its jurisdiction were foiled by Berger's intercession.[48]

By the beginning of 1942 the supply of convicted poachers had been exhausted, and ordinary criminals were recruited or impressed into Dirlewanger's band. Moreover, native Russians and ethnic Germans from the Soviet Union were added in such numbers that by February 1943 about half of the 700 men in unit (now designated a battalion) were non-Germans. In time, members of the SD, court-martialed Waffen SS men, and convicts from the military prisons of the Wehrmacht were also dragooned. In this fashion the Dirlewanger unit grew into a regiment and then into a brigade. Toward the end of the war even political prisoners from the concentration camps were sent to serve with Dirlewanger.[49]

Discipline within the formation was nearly as brutal as the behavior of the formation toward civilians. Beatings with clubs and shootings out of hand were common practice. Dirlewanger did not hesitate to shoot, with his own pistol, men who displeased him. It is therefore little wonder that his men—especially the conscripted political prisoners, many of whom were former Communists—deserted to the enemy at the first opportunity.[50]

It has been estimated that only 10 to 15 per cent of Dirlewanger's men were Waffen SS members on probation. Another 30 per cent were former concentration-camp inmates, and more than 50 per cent were former members of the three branches of the Wehrmacht—Army, Navy, and Air Force. Most of the noncommissioned officers were veteran poachers, whereas most of the "officers" were degraded former officers who served without rank insignia.[51]

48 Nuremberg Document NO–3028, USMT IV, Case 11, PDB 66–C, pp. 28ff.; Auerbach, *op. cit.*, pp. 258ff.

49 Nuremberg Documents NO–2713, NO–2061, NO–2061–B, NO–070, 1309–PS, USMT IV, Case 11, PDB 66–C, pp. 49ff.; Auerbach, *op. cit.*, pp. 253ff.

50 *Ibid.*, p. 259.

51 *Ibid.*, p. 258. The remaining 5 to 10 per cent of the personnel were foreign.

The most notorious crimes of the Dirlewanger Brigade were committed during the suppression of the 1944 Warsaw uprising. While Kaminski paid for his activities with his life, Dirlewanger was awarded the *Ritterkreuz,* Nazi Germany's most coveted military decoration. He received this honor despite complaints by Army and SS authorities that he had encouraged his troops to act in the most brutal fashion, had given them permission to plunder, and had even shot some of his own men in order to seize their loot for himself.[52]

None of the charges made against Dirlewanger had any effect. His protector, Berger, had been appointed Supreme Commander of the German Forces in Slovakia, and he had the brigade transferred there to help suppress a national revolt that had broken out as the Soviet Army neared. In the last weeks of 1944 the Dirlewanger Brigade was sent to the front in northern Hungary, but so many of its men deserted to the Russians that it had to be withdrawn. After being reinforced and redesignated the 36th Waffen-Grenadierdivision der SS, the unit was committed to battle along the Oder front. In mid-February 1945, after only a few days in action, Dirlewanger was wounded. He thus avoided the fate of his division, which was encircled and forced to surrender southeast of Berlin on April 29.[53]

There is no lack of source material relating to the Dirlewanger Brigade. Its development, structure, composition, activities, and crimes are largely a matter of record. The evidence makes untenable the claim that the unit was not a part of the SS. It is true that few of its members were SS men, but like the SS Police regiments the Dirlewanger Brigade was an integral part of Himmler's SS organization. One question remains,

[52] *Ibid.,* p. 263.

[53] One recent account adds the following information about the fate of Dirlewanger's unit after its surrender: "In one of the most gruesome massacres of the Eastern campaign the whole unit and a large number of German civilians were put to the sword by the Russians" (Clark, *op. cit.,* p. 460). Dirlewanger was arrested shortly after the war and died of unspecified causes on June 7, 1945. Rumors that he was still alive and had escaped justice (for example, see *ibid.,* which has Dirlewanger living in Egypt in 1955) led German officials to exhume his body in 1960; a coroner's report definitely established that the corpse buried at Althausen (Oberschwaben) was Dirlewanger. See Auerbach, *op. cit.,* p. 252.

however: Can this highly irregular formation truly be considered a part of the Waffen SS?

Gerald Reitlinger offers no direct answer but concludes that the award of the *Ritterkreuz* to Dirlewanger after the Warsaw affair and his inclusion in Ernst Krätschmer's *Die Ritterkreuzträger der Waffen SS* "proved very destructive of the alibi that the Dirlewanger regiment formed no part of the Waffen SS." [54] Hellmuth Auerbach, on the other hand, concludes that the composition and activities of the unit caused so much opposition within the ranks of the SS that it was "never made into a full-fledged [*vollgültigen*] formation of the Waffen SS." [55]

Nevertheless, it is important to note that Auerbach's definition of the Waffen SS is a very narrow one. Hence he is able to state that:

while it is true that Dirlewanger and the SS men sent to his unit on probation were members of the Waffen SS and the unit was carried as a field formation on a Waffen SS list of 30 June 1944 prepared by the Statistical Science Institute of the Reichsführer SS, it nevertheless was not considered a full-fledged formation of the Waffen SS because its members (with the exception of those who came from the Wehrmacht) were, so to speak, only second-class SS members [*SS-Angehörige mindern Rechts*] just like the Latvian, Croatian, and similar non-German "Waffen-Grenadier-Divisionen der SS." [56]

It has been shown in earlier chapters that the foreign formations were in terms of size, if not performance, an important part of the Waffen SS. And on this ground alone, Auerbach's equation could well be disputed. But it is doubtful that anything of value to the historian would result from this type of argument. In the end, as in the beginning, the degree to which one assigns criminal guilt to the Waffen SS depends to a large extent on one's definition of the term *Waffen SS*.

Military Atrocities of the Waffen SS

Because of the organizational and administrative complexity of the SS there will undoubtedly always be some confusion or

[54] Reitlinger, *op. cit.*, p. 174, n. 4.
[55] Auerbach, *op. cit.*, p. 258.
[56] *Ibid.*, pp. 252 f.

difference of opinion in regard to the Waffen SS' connection with the concentration camps, the Einsatzgruppen, and "special commands" like the Dirlewanger Brigade. But no terminological difficulties exist to cloud the criminal guilt of the *Feldtruppenteile*, or field formations, of the Waffen SS. According to the apologists' own definition, the field formations of the Waffen SS were those that fought at the front under the operational control of the Army. And even within this narrow limitation Kurt Meyer's statement still applies: "The facts are burdensome enough." [57]

The first recorded atrocity committed by a member of a field unit of the Waffen SS occurred on September 19, 1939, during the Polish campaign. An SS private named Ernst (a member of the SS Artillery Regiment attached to Panzerdivision Kempf) and an Army military policeman herded fifty Jews of a work detail into a synagogue and shot them. The men were arrested, court-martialed, and found guilty of manslaughter. The SS man was sentenced to three years' imprisonment *(Gefängnis)* and the military policeman received nine years' penal servitude *(Zuchthaus)*. But the prosecuting officer insisted on the death penalty for murder and appealed the sentences to Berlin. There a senior military judge upheld the lesser sentence for the SS man on the grounds that

he was in a state of irritation as a result of the many atrocities committed by Poles against ethnic Germans. As an SS man he was also particularly sensitive to the sight of Jews and the hostile attitude of Jewry to Germans; and thus acted quite unpremeditatedly in a spirit of youthful enthusiasm [*jugendlichem Draufgängertum*].

The judge's report closed with the observation that Ernst was an "excellent soldier" who had never been punished before. In the case of the military policeman the higher court reduced the sentence to three years. Shortly thereafter both sentences were dropped under amnesty; neither man served a day in prison for his crime.[58]

[57] Quoted, p. 256.

[58] Nuremberg Document D–421, reproduced in Poliakov and Wulf, *op. cit.*, p. 485. See also transcript of proceedings at Nuremberg, TGMWC, XX, 355.

The prosecution at Nuremberg made much of this case, pointing out the incongruity of a three-year prison sentence for the murder of fifty people. But in the light of subsequent events, the greater incongruity lies in the fact that the men were brought to trial at all. And it was to avoid similar situations that the SS established its own court system in October 1939.[59]

If there were any other crimes committed by members of the combat units of the SS during and after the Polish campaign, they have become entangled beyond any hope of separation with the many atrocities perpetrated by the SS Totenkopfstandarten during the same period.[60]

The next Waffen SS atrocity of which there is a record was the massacre of about one hundred British prisoners at Le Paradis by members of the SS Totenkopfdivision during the battle of Flanders in the summer of 1940. Once again the Army sought to bring the perpetrators to justice, but on this occasion SS authorities were able to quash the proceedings before they got under way. Not until after the war was the responsible officer punished; in 1948 he was brought before a British military court, found guilty of murder, and hanged.[61]

The Le Paradis massacre was only the first incident of its kind to take place in the West. The greatest number of Waffen SS atrocities, however, seem to have occurred in the East. Taught that they were engaged in an ideological and racial war against a "subhuman" enemy, the SS troops often applied a standard to warfare which differed sharply from accepted practices. The shooting of prisoners, the massacre of civilians, and the wanton destruction of villages, while not universal, seem to have occurred frequently enough to become a hallmark of Waffen SS operations along the eastern front.

Thus we find that barely two weeks after the German invasion of the Soviet Union, the SS Division "Wiking" murdered six hundred Galician Jews "as a reprisal for Soviet cruelties."[62] In another reprisal, this one for the brutal murder of six cap-

---

[59] See p. 30.
[60] See Broszat, *op. cit.,* p. 60.
[61] See pp. 76ff.
[62] Reitlinger, *op. cit.,* p. 157.

tured SS soldiers by the GPU early in 1942, the SS Division "Leibstandarte Adolf Hitler" shot every Russian taken prisoner over a three-day period; according to a former officer of the division, "it was a question of the lives of 4000 men, for that was the number that fell into our hands during those three days that were so fatal to them." [63] It hardly need be added that none of the Russians who were executed had anything to do with the murder of the six SS men.

In contrast to the activities of the SS Einsatzgruppen and the SS antipartisan formations, atrocities committed by SS combat troops were rarely recorded, and the captured SS documents offer little to the investigator in this regard. The extent of this type of criminal activity, then, can often only be inferred on the basis of circumstantial evidence.

The Russian representatives at the Nuremberg Trial offered surprisingly little evidence in support of the case against the Waffen SS; what they did present was largely hearsay. For instance, the Russians charged that "the units of the SS—particularly the SS Division of Adolf Hitler [1st SS Panzerdivision 'Leibstandarte Adolf Hitler'] under the leadership of Obergruppenführer Dietrich, and the SS Division 'Totenkopf' (Death's Head) under the leadership of Obergruppenführer Simon, are responsible for the extermination of more than 20,000 peaceful citizens of Kharkov, for the shooting and burning alive of prisoners of war." [64] No convincing evidence was submitted to support this charge, but judging by proven Waffen SS atrocities elsewhere it may have some basis in fact. If the allegation is true, then Kharkov was not only the scene of the Waffen SS' greatest military victory, but also the scene of its greatest military atrocity.

Perhaps the most shocking evidence against the Waffen SS

[63] Quoted in *ibid.*, p. 171; also see above p. 133. A few months later, in a rare display of indignation, Colonel General Georg Lindemann, commander of the German 18th Army, filed with SS headquarters a complaint listing specific instances in which members of the 2nd SS Infantry Brigade had shot prisoners of war. Himmler defended his SS men and refused to take disciplinary action against them. See Himmler's letter to Lindemann, August 23, 1942, Geheim, RFSS/T–175, 109/2633404 f.

[64] TGMWC, XXII, 352.

was presented on behalf of the Yugoslav delegation. It dealt with the criminal activities of the 7th SS Gebirgsdivision "Prinz Eugen" and offered graphic descriptions of the burning of villages, the massacre of their inhabitants, and the torture and murder of captured partisans. One irrefutable piece of evidence was a photograph taken from a Waffen SS prisoner showing a Yugoslav being decapitated with a woodsman's axe while grinning SS men looked on.[65] Even evasive witnesses before the International Military Tribunal, like SS Obergruppenführer Paul Hausser, did not seek to deny these crimes but fell back on the excuse that "Prinz Eugen" was composed largely of ethnic Germans from Yugoslavia and that warfare in the Balkans was traditionally brutal. That both statements are true does not absolve the Waffen SS of its responsibility for the behavior of its troops; all the more so since the "Prinz Eugen" division was led, for the most part, by German officers and noncommissioned officers.

Shortly before the invasion of the Soviet Union, the OKW and OKH agreed to permit Himmler's SS Police Leaders to exercise control over security operations behind the combat zone. In theory the SS could call on the rear-area commands of the Army to provide the additional forces necessary to deal with partisan activity. But inasmuch as these operations seem to have been directed against the Jewish population as often as against the partisans, the SS Police Leaders preferred to use units of the Waffen SS to reinforce their security forces. Since the combat elements of the SS divisions were usually engaged at the front, rear-area support or replacement units were most frequently utilized. For example, in September 1941, while the SS Division "Das Reich" was on the move from one sector of the front to another, one of its rear-area companies assisted an SS extermination squad in the shooting of 920 Jews near Minsk.[66] Similarly, the final reduction of the Warsaw Ghetto in the spring of 1943 was largely the work of fledgling Waffen

[65] The photograph is reproduced in Schnabel, *op. cit.,* p. 489, and *SS im Einsatz,* p. 454. For other evidence see TGMWC, XXII, 305 f.
[66] Reitlinger, *op. cit.,* p. 169.

SS men drawn from two training and replacement units quartered in the area.[67]

In some cases combat units of the Waffen SS were withheld or withdrawn from the front at Himmler's request, and assigned instead to the SS Police Leaders for large-scale antipartisan operations. During the late summer of 1941, for example, the SS Kavallerie Brigade (later 8th SS Kavalleriedivision "Florian Geyer") participated in a "pacification operation" in the area of the Pripet Marshes in the course of which one of its regiments reported the shooting of 259 Russian soldiers and the execution of 6504 civilians.[68]

The following year found both the 1st SS Infantry Brigade and the SS Freikorps "Danemark" operating behind Army Group Center under the command of SS Obergruppenführer von dem Bach-Zelewski, Himmler's special representative in charge of combating guerrilla bands (Sonderbevollmächtigten des Reichsführers SS für Bandenbekämpfung).[69] And there were many other occasions when field units of the Waffen SS were employed against partisans, suspected partisans, or ordinary civilians who had the misfortune of being proscribed under Nazi racial policies.

Shortly after the fall of Mussolini in 1943, the elite 1st SS Panzerdivision "Leibstandarte Adolf Hitler" arrived in Italy to bolster what was left of the Fascist regime. It has generally been accepted that the SS division, during its short stay in Italy before returning to the Russian front, did little more than act as a palace guard for Il Duce, after his dramatic rescue by a group of SS parachutists.[70] But in June 1964, West German officials disclosed that Joachim Peiper, the former Leibstandarte officer once condemned to death for the massacre of American prisoners at Malmédy, Belgium, was under investigation on a new charge

[67] See p. 47.

[68] TGMWC, XXII, 352.

[69] See Document No. 50, *The Case against General Heusinger* (Chicago: Translation World Publishers, 1961), p. 170. This publication is tendentious, but the documents in it are photostatically reproduced and are reliable.

[70] See F. W. Deakin, *op. cit.*, pp. 543ff.

—that he played a leading role in the destruction of the town of Boves in northern Italy and the mass execution of its inhabitants in September 1943.[71] This atrocity was part of an SS operation against anti-Fascist partisans in the area. Nor was it the only incident of its kind that took place in Italy.

In the late summer of 1944, the 16th SS Panzergrenadier-division "Reichsführer SS," resting after a bitter battle against British forces along the Arno front, participated in a reprisal operation that resulted in the massacre of 2700 Italian civilians. The division's commander, SS Gruppenführer Max Simon, "was condemned to death by a British court in Padua; but the sentence was commuted, and he was freed in 1954." [72]

The early months of 1944 found the elite 2nd SS Panzer-division "Das Reich" in southern France recuperating after a hard winter of fighting on the Russian front. While there, the division assisted the local security forces in a drive against partisan bands operating in the mountains of Auvergne. In the small village of Tulle alone, ninety-nine people—men and women—were hanged, and the SS operation soon became known as the "Blood and Ashes Action." Immediately after the Allied invasion of France, the SS Division "Das Reich" was ordered north to help defend Normandy. As elements of the division passed near the village of Oradour-sur-Glane, a French resistance sniper shot and killed an SS officer. In reprisal, the First Battalion of the division's SS Panzergrenadier Regiment 4 "Der Führer" burned the village and massacred its entire population; 642 inhabitants, including 207 children, were shot or burned to death. The SS regiment's action report for the day refers to a "cleansing action" in which the village was burned after "munitions were discovered in almost every house." The mass murder of unarmed men, women, and children was treated as if it had been a military operation, and the SS report listed the casualties as "548 enemy dead" at a cost of "2 men wounded." [73] Apparently two SS men got too close to a fire or

71 *The New York Post,* June 29, 1964.

72 Reitlinger, *op. cit.,* p. 245.

73 The action report is reproduced in Schnabel, *op. cit.,* p. 493. For accounts of the massacre see Reitlinger, *op. cit.,* p. 400, and Lord Russell

were accidentally shot by their comrades. An almost identical case involving an SS division occurred in Greece during the same year. When a convoy belonging to the 4th SS Polizei-Panzergrenadierdivision, refitting in northern Greece after a disastrous year on the Russian front, was ambushed by Greek guerrillas near Klissura, members of the SS unit conducted savage reprisals against the local inhabitants.[74]

With the Allied invasion of France in June 1944, western soldiers clashed with the Waffen SS for the first time since 1940. For the Americans and Canadians it was an entirely new experience, while the British found the SS troops as skillful and tough as they remembered them. Moreover, Allied soldiers soon discovered that the Waffen SS thoroughly lived up to the reputation for brutality it had gained along the eastern front.

In the ten days after the establishment of the Allied bridgehead in Normandy, sixty-four unarmed Canadian and British prisoners, many of whom had previously been wounded, were shot by members of the 12th SS Panzerdivision "Hitler Jugend." Although many of its officers and noncommissioned officers had been transferred from the Leibstandarte, the division had never been in combat before. A SHAEF court of inquiry established that some units of the division had been given secret orders to shoot their prisoners after they were interrogated and the "conclusion was irresistible that it was understood throughout the division that a policy of denying quarter or executing prisoners after interrogation was openly approved."[75]

As a result of the inquiry, the division's commander, SS Brigadeführer (Major General) Kurt Meyer, was brought to trial before a Canadian military court and sentenced to death. The verdict, delivered on December 28, 1945, made Meyer, who was the youngest divisional commander in the Wehrmacht at the time of his appointment, the first German war criminal to

of Liverpool, *The Scourge of the Swastika* (New York, c. 1954), pp. 99ff. A recent account of the Oradour affair appearing in the Waffen SS veterans' journal also provides some interesting details in the course of its attempt to justify the massacre. See "Die Wahrheit über Oradour," *Der Freiwillige*, X, No. 7 (July 1964), pp. 5ff.

[74] Görlitz, *op. cit.*, p. 27.
[75] NCA, II, 229.

be condemned to die by the western Allies. But like many of the other capital sentences passed on men of the Waffen SS, this one was commuted, and Meyer was released on September 7, 1954.[76]

The most publicized, although by no means the most flagrant, atrocity committed by SS combat troops was the murder of seventy-one American prisoners of war at Malmédy on December 17, 1944, during the German counteroffensive in the Ardennes. The deed was the work of an armored battle group detached from the 1st SS Panzerdivision "Leibstandarte Adolf Hitler" and led by SS Obersturmbannführer Joachim (Jochen) Peiper.

The exact circumstances surrounding the massacre remain a matter of dispute; some SS apologists have claimed that the prisoners, who had been herded into a field beside the road, were shot down when they were mistaken for an attacking enemy force in a fog. Others claimed that the men were shot when they attempted a mass escape. But the only American officer to survive the massacre testified:

It was decided that it would be best to surrender to this overwhelming force, the First Adolph Hitler SS Panzer Division, as we learned later. This we did. . . . We were all placed in this field approximately 150 to 160, maybe 175 men. . . . The Germans then, at the particular time, were continuing to advance in a southerly direction toward Bastogne, and one of their self-propelled 88-millimeter guns was ordered to stop, and it was backed around facing the group of personnel as they were standing in the field. After what happened, I have no doubt today that if they had been able to depress the muzzle of this gun into our group, they would have fired at point-blank range with their artillery into that group of men. They were not able to do that, however, because we were more or less in a depression below the gun and they couldn't lower it. So this particular self-propelled weapon was blocking their advance and it was ordered off. At that time they drove up two halftracks and parked them facing the group, at a 15- or 20-foot

[76] For an account of the trial through the eyes of the defendant see Meyer, *op. cit.*, pp. 358ff. A digest of the trial may be found in United Nations War Crimes Commission, *Law Reports of Trials of War Criminals*, Vol. IV, Case No. 22, pp. 97ff.

interval between the two. A man stood up in this vehicle, who I later identified at Dachau, and fired a pistol . . . into the group. At the time we ordered our men to stand fast because we knew if they made a break that they would have a right then to cut loose on us with their machine guns. His first shot killed my driver. The second shot that he fired into the group then set off a group of machine guns firing into this helpless group of unarmed American prisoners of war. Those of us who were not killed immediately in the initial burst fell to the ground. . . . We continued to lay on the ground and the fire continued to come into us. . . . When they ceased firing after approximately 5 minutes, maybe 3 minutes, they came into the group to those men who were still alive, and of course writhing in agony, and they shot them in the head. . . . During the initial firing I was only hit one time.[77]

He then went on to describe how he and perhaps twenty others who were overlooked and left alive lay for hours in the field whispering plans for escape. As vehicles full of Germans roared by he "could hear them laughing and every once in a while they would fire into the group of men as they lay on the ground, more or less as target practice."

Finally, at dusk, the surviving Americans leaped up and ran toward the woods. Some were immediately shot down by SS guards stationed at the nearby crossroads, and others were shot after they were flushed from a house in which they sought cover. After hiding in a nearby shed until well into the night, the surviving officer reached some American troops in Malmédy.[78] A few weeks later, when the Americans recaptured the lost ground, they found the victims lying frozen in the snow just as they had fallen.

Himmler is said to have addressed his SS commanders before the counteroffensive with the words: "I rely on you to prove yourselves worthy of your SS runes and to guarantee victory *so oder so*."[79] The Waffen SS was not ultimately victorious in the Ardennes, but it proved once and for all that its peculiar

[77] Testimony of former 1st Lieutenant Virgil T. Lary, Jr., *Malmedy Massacre Investigation Hearings,* pp. 1032ff.
[78] *Ibid.,* p. 1033. For other accounts see *ibid.,* pp. 105 f.; Toland, *op. cit.,* pp. 67ff.
[79] Quoted in Reitlinger, *op. cit.,* p. 394.

standards of warfare were not reserved exclusively for the fight against "Bolshevik subhumans."

For the murder of the American soldiers as well as of an undetermined number of Belgian civilians, Peiper, commander of the Kampfgruppe; Hermann Priess, commander of the Leibstandarte; Fritz Krämer, commander of the 1st SS Panzerkorps; and Sepp Dietrich, commander of the 6th SS Panzerarmee, together with sixty-nine of their subordinates, were tried before an American military court sitting at Dachau. On July 16, forty-three of the accused, including Peiper, were condemned to death, twenty-three to life imprisonment, and the rest to shorter sentences. Among the latter, Dietrich received twenty-five years, Priess eighteen, and Krämer ten. All of the death sentences were later commuted; by 1956 the last of the group had been freed from prison.[80]

The crimes of the Waffen SS were not confined to the enemy; German soldiers and civilians were also among its victims. During the last months of the war, hundreds, perhaps thousands, of Germans were shot or hanged for lack of determination or what was called "cowardice in the face of the enemy." It has been said that "there is hardly a German community where some Nazi atrocity was not committed toward the end of the war."[81] By no means all of these were committed by the Waffen SS, but SS *Standgerichte,* or emergency courts, which any SS commander was empowered to convene on his own initiative, were particularly zealous in handing down death sentences for "treachery or negligence." Thus SS Gruppenführer Max Simon (whose 16th SS Panzergrenadierdivision "Reichsführer SS" had been responsible for the mass murder of Italian civilians in 1944) tried and executed a number of Germans in the Swabian town of Brettheim on April 7, 1945. Among those condemned to die was an elderly farmer who had disarmed a group of Hitler Youths to keep them from being killed by the advancing American forces. Late in 1955, a year after his release from a

---

[80] *Ibid.,* p. 395, n. 1. For the names of all the defendants see Military Government Court Charge Sheet, *Malmedy Massacre Investigation Hearings,* pp. 1191 f.

[81] Dornberg, *op. cit.,* p. 31.

British military prison, Simon was brought before a German court at Ansbach for the Brettheim affair. He was acquitted because the court ruled that he had simply obeyed a legal order which Himmler had issued in his dual capacity as Minister of the Interior and Chief of the SS and Police.[82]

In Berlin during the last days of the battle, fanatical young Waffen SS officers belonging to Hitler's and Himmler's bodyguard battalions conducted drumhead courts-martial that ended in the hanging or shooting of uncounted numbers of German soldiers and conscripted civilians who had been found guilty of cowardice, desertion, or "resisting the war effort." For days after the fall of the capital, and long after Hitler's suicide, groups of fanatical SS men continued to resist, as often shooting at those who surrendered as at the Russian conquerors.[83]

The lengthy but by no means definitive compilation of atrocities presented above makes it clear that, whatever else may be said in its behalf, the Waffen SS was not free of guilt, and its conduct both in and out of battle belies the claim that it was no different from the Army with which it fought. But to go to the other extreme and to view the Waffen SS primarily as an organization of terrorists and murderers would be no less at variance with the facts.

Actually, only a minority of the nearly one million men who passed through the ranks of the Waffen SS during World War II were involved in any of the known atrocities. To recognize this is not to agree with the apologists who picture the overwhelming majority of the men in the Waffen SS as idealistic, clean-living, decent, and honorable soldiers. As a group they were hard, tough, ruthless, and capable of the most savage behavior. Nevertheless the extent of Waffen SS atrocities should not be exaggerated. Neither should those that actually occurred be permitted to obscure the historical significance of the Waffen SS, which is to be found not so much in its role in the massacre of Le Paradis or Malmédy as in its part in the great battles for the defense of Hitler's Europe.

[82] Reitlinger, *op. cit.,* p. 450.

[83] See Historical Division, Headquarters United States Army, Europe, *Foreign Military Studies: The German Defense of Berlin,* MS #P–136.

CHAPTER ELEVEN

Reprise and Assessment

ONE characteristic that the three great totalitarian systems of the twentieth century—Communism, Fascism, and National Socialism—had in common was the development of a paramilitary party militia alongside the regular state security organs: the armed forces and police. Originally the instrument of terror and repression, whose function was to ensure the primacy of the dictator, the party militia characteristically grew a new appendage in the face of war. Thus the elite GPU and NKVD divisions of the Soviet Union during Stalin's rule, the Italian divisions composed of members of Mussolini's Fascist Militia (MSVN), and the armed SS formations of Hitler's Third Reich were all similar manifestations of the modern totalitarian party-state.[1] The Waffen SS emerged during World War II as the largest, most highly developed, and most efficient of the militarized party armies.

It would be more accurate to describe the Waffen SS as the dictator's private army, or praetorian guard, rather than as a party army. The NSDAP was a mass party, a nondescript agglomeration, which was far from being the elite group necessary to assure the success of the Nazi revolution. Indeed, it was the SS, not the National Socialist Party, that proved to be the dynamic core of the Nazi system. And the SS, from the earliest days of the Nazi movement, was bound to Hitler, the future dictator, rather than to the Party.

When the Leibstandarte SS "Adolf Hitler" was created by

[1] This point is made in Görlitz, *op. cit.*, pp. 5 f.

Hitler, during his first year as Chancellor of the German Reich, its members took this oath: "I swear to you, Adolf Hitler, as Führer and Reichschancellor, loyalty and bravery. I vow to you, and those you have named to command me, obedience unto death, so help me God." [2] This oath, taken by all members of the armed SS, set the tone for the Waffen SS of the war years. And of vital significance to the later development of the armed SS, it raised the Leibstandarte from the position of a party formation to that of a true praetorian guard, standing above both party and state. But a fact of far more immediate importance was that Hitler, without legal authority, had created a standing armed force responsible to himself and not to Hindenburg, who was still President and Commander-in-Chief of the Armed Forces.[3] Hitler thus established a new area of sovereignty for himself as party chief and head of government and took an important step toward becoming a totalitarian dictator.[4]

Among the many specialized SS organizations that developed during the early years of the Third Reich were a number of armed formations patterned after the Leibstandarte. By 1936 these had crystallized into two branches: the SS Verfügungstruppe and the SS Totenkopfverbände. Legitimized as "organizations in the service of the state," both formations were placed on the police budget of the Ministry of the Interior. In this way the two standing SS military formations became firmly entrenched alongside the Wehrmacht and Police.

The oft-quoted Führer Decree of August 17, 1938, issued in the midst of German military preparations against Czechoslovakia, clarified and underscored the position which the armed SS had in fact achieved during the preceding four years. Its importance for the future, however, lay in its equivocal and often contradictory formulation, which separated the armed

[2] For German text, see *Dich ruft die SS*, New York Public Library Microcopy Z–941.

[3] For the complexities of the constitutional and legal position (verfassungsrechtliche Stellung) of the various components of the SS see Buchheim, "Die SS," *passim*.

[4] For a definition of the term *totalitarian dictator* see Carl J. Friedrich and Zbigniew K. Brzezinski, *Totalitarian Dictatorship and Autocracy* (New York, 1961), pp. 3ff.

SS from the Wehrmacht but at the same time forged links between them.

The more important provisions separating the armed SS from the Wehrmacht stated that the SS Verfügungstruppe was a special formation unconditionally at Hitler's personal disposal; that it was part neither of the Wehrmacht nor of the Police; that during peacetime its command was vested in the Reichs-führer SS and Chief of the German Police; that regardless of its employment it remained "politically" (but not juridically) a formation of the NSDAP; and that its financial support was to continue to come from the police budget of the Ministry of the Interior.

Included among the provisions linking the armed SS to the Wehrmacht were those which decreed that duty in the SS Verfügungstruppe counted as military service (*Wehrdienst*); that its weapons and equipment were to be provided by the Army; that its officers were to attend Army training courses; that its personnel were to receive their pay and allotments according to Wehrmacht regulations; and that in the event of mobilization it might (with Hitler's approval) serve within the framework of the Wehrmacht and under the tactical command of the Army.

Hitler's decree also clarified some of the differences between the SS Totenkopfverbände and the SS Verfügungstruppe. In brief, the Death's Head troops were tied far more closely to the Police than to the Wehrmacht. Although the decree stipulated that their "political police duties" were to be assigned by the Führer, they were not at his "unconditional disposal." Their primary function was to guard the concentration camps. Unlike the Verfügungstruppen, they were not Hitler's household troops. Duty in the Totenkopfverbände did not count as military service, and the Death's Head troops had to fulfill their military obligation in either the Verfügungstruppe or the Wehrmacht.

By 1939 the armed SS consisted of the Leibstandarte, three regiments of Verfügungstruppen (plus support formations), and five undersized Totenkopf regiments. Although Himmler and the men of the Verfügungstruppe hoped that it might become the nucleus of an entirely new type of political army, there is no evidence that Hitler shared their aspiration. On the contrary, his purge of the High Command in 1938 had clearly established his authority over the Army, which was now a reasonably pliant instrument for the execution of his aggressive plans. In any event, on the eve of a war he had been planning for some time, Hitler was in no position to tamper with the existing structure of Germany's military machine.

So for Hitler, the armed SS remained an elite guard: the Leibstandarte to protect him and his regime, the other regiments of the Verfügungstruppe to act as a militarized police force, and the Totenkopfverbände to run the concentration camps and "clean up" the areas he intended to annex to the Reich.

By the beginning of the war the armed SS had grown into a small professional army of some 28,000 men. Rigid selection of personnel and intensive physical, military, and ideological training had created a tough, dedicated, and efficient cadre for the much expanded Waffen SS of later years.

Hitler's decision to allow the armed SS to take an active part in the war was based on his conviction that it would not be able to retain the respect of Germans unless it did its share at the front. Hitler regarded the Waffen SS [5] in its military role as a Guard formation, in the eighteenth- and nineteenth-century meaning of the term. As the military apotheosis of National Socialism, its task was to set an example for the Army. But Hitler assured the generals in 1940 that after the war the Waffen SS would become the "militarized state police" of the Third Reich and would not exceed 5 to 10 per cent of the Army's peacetime strength.

Therefore, despite its excellent showing in the victorious campaigns of 1939–1940, Hitler rejected Himmler's pleas for a greatly enlarged Waffen SS. For the first half of the war, then,

[5] The term *Waffen SS* to describe the armed formations of the SS came into use late in 1939 and was made official early in 1940.

the SS leaders had to content themselves with a slow but steady growth, which the best efforts of the Army proved unable to halt.

The claims of apologists notwithstanding, it is evident from Hitler's attitude toward the Waffen SS during the early years of the war that he had no intention of creating a fourth branch of the Wehrmacht. Theodor Eschenburg, editor of postwar Germany's leading journal of modern history, believes that the Nazis thought of the Waffen SS as "the antipode of the Army" and that "its comradeship with the Army in battle and its role as the 'fourth branch of the Wehrmacht' grew out of the exigencies of the war, but were not in line with the National Socialist plan." [6]

If the Waffen SS of the last years of the war can be described as a branch of the Wehrmacht, it was at best a *de facto* branch. To be sure, with a peak strength of thirty-eight divisions and some 600,000 men, it was a most formidable organization. Nonetheless, the Waffen SS never became a serious rival of the Army. Despite its many special privileges, it never achieved complete independence of command; nor did its officers manage to invade the upper echelons of the German High Command. Attempts by the Waffen SS to establish its own procurement system were only partially successful, and it remained dependent on the Army for its heavy weapons and much else. Perhaps the final verdict on the position of the Waffen SS was delivered on May 9, 1945, when the German surrender was signed in Berlin by representatives of the Army, the Navy, and the Air Force; the Waffen SS was neither invited nor mentioned.[7]

And yet, if the Waffen SS was not officially a branch of the Wehrmacht, its formations were among the most effective in the German war machine. By the end of 1941, the Waffen SS had six divisions in the field and the equivalent of two more in the form of independent brigades, regiments, and battalions. From a military standpoint, the best of these SS formations had

[6] Preface to "Die Rede Himmlers vor den Gauleitern am 3. August 1944," *Vierteljahrshefte für Zeitgeschichte*, I, No. 4 (October 1953), p. 360.

[7] A copy of this surrender agreement is reproduced in KTB/OKW, IV, 1679 f.

earned the title of Guards. The Leibstandarte, for example, had participated in every one of Hitler's military adventures: the remilitarization of the Rhineland; the occupation of Austria, the Sudetenland, and Czechoslovakia; the invasion of Poland; the campaign in the West; the campaign in the Balkans; and the invasion of the Soviet Union.

In the fighting before Moscow during the winter of 1941–1942, the Waffen SS displayed what was to become in Hitler's eyes its greatest virtue: the ability to retain its fighting spirit in defeat. But the fanaticism, or spirited recklessness, that characterized the combat performance of the elite SS formations resulted in an enormous number of casualties. In fact, most of the old guard—the professionals of the prewar SS—died on the eastern front.

As military setbacks increased and personnel losses became more critical, the demands for manpower forced the Waffen SS to give up a good deal of its racial and physical selectiveness; by the end of 1942, it was accepting men who could pass the ordinary Wehrmacht physical examination. The manpower needs of the Waffen SS also led to the large-scale recruitment of foreigners. Before long, foreigners outnumbered native Germans in the ranks of the Waffen SS. Of the thirty-eight SS divisions in existence in 1945, none was exclusively German and at least nineteen consisted largely of foreign personnel. Serving in the Waffen SS were Netherlanders, Norwegians, Danes, Finns, Swiss, Swedes, Flemings, Walloons, Frenchmen, and a handful of Britons; Latvians, Estonians, Ukrainians, Croats, Bosnians, Italians, Albanians, Caucasians, Russians, Turko-Tatars, Azerbaijanis, Romanians, Bulgarians, Hungarians, and some Indians; and large numbers of ethnic Germans from Alsace, Denmark, Czechoslovakia, Italy, Hungary, Romania, Poland, and Yugoslavia. It is quite possible that the Waffen SS was the largest multinational army ever to fight under one flag.

The enlargement of the Waffen SS as a result of the massive mobilization of foreign nationals, however, did not lead to a corresponding increase in military effectiveness. Only the west Europeans, numerically the smallest group, fought consistently well. The *Volksdeutsche* varied from excellent to poor in their combat performance. And the eastern Europeans, with very few exceptions, seem to have been more of a liability than an asset.

By the end of 1942 the tide of war had turned against the Third Reich. After three years of almost steady advance, the Wehrmacht had lost the initiative and begun its long retreat. Under these circumstances there was no immediate future for the Waffen SS of Hitler's earlier conception; if Germany could not hold on to its empire, there would be no need for an elite formation to police it. But there was an increasingly urgent need for a reliable striking force that could be counted upon to fight tenaciously, without equivocation, regardless of the general military situation. It was Hitler's recognition of this need that led him to sanction an immediate and substantial enlargement of the Waffen SS. From the fall of 1942 onward, the size of the Waffen SS more than doubled each year until the end of the war.

Although at the beginning of 1944 the Waffen SS constituted numerically less than 5 per cent of the Wehrmacht, nearly one-fourth of the panzer (armored) divisions and one-third of the panzergrenadier (mechanized) divisions in the German military establishment were SS formations. Furthermore, in view of their large size, superior equipment, and high morale, the combat potential of these elite SS divisions was even greater than their number would indicate. The military value of the Waffen SS lay not in the hordes of the eastern SS but in the largely German armored divisions that in terms of selection, training, and leadership were the spiritual successors of the prewar Verfügungstruppe.

The Waffen SS has often been described as the spearhead of Nazi aggression. And, as we have seen, SS units were invariably in the van of Hitler's armies as they marched into neighboring lands. Nonetheless, the military significance of the Waffen SS is to be found not so much in its accomplishments during the years of German victory as in its victories during the years of German defeat. The German offensives of the early war years could have succeeded without the participation of the Waffen SS, but the defense of the Third Reich would have collapsed much earlier had it not been for the elite SS divisions.

During the last two years of the war the divisions of the Waffen SS fought on all fronts. Wherever the Allied threat was greatest, the SS panzer and panzergrenadier divisions of Hitler's "fire brigade" appeared; at Kharkov, Warsaw, Normandy, the Ardennes, Budapest, and Berlin, SS divisions spearheaded counterattacks that temporarily rolled back or halted the Allied advance.

From a military standpoint, and aside from moral considerations, the combat achievements of the elite SS divisions were remarkable. Certainly their adversaries recognized their fighting qualities; General Dwight D. Eisenhower, for example, reported to the Combined Chiefs of Staff that even in defeat SS "morale, backed by a blind confidence in ultimate Nazi victory, was extremely good, and whether in attack or defense they fought to a man with fanatical courage."[8]

A recent study has confirmed that the much-criticized decision to divert U.S. troops from the drive toward Berlin was based largely on the presumed existence of an Alpine redoubt, from which the Nazis were planning to make a last-ditch stand built around the still powerful SS divisions of Sepp Dietrich's 6th SS Panzer Army.[9] The Alpine redoubt proved to be a myth, but the author concludes that "there was nothing about the wartime performance of [the] Waffen SS that might lead Allied observers to believe that [Hitler's] orders would not be carried out with efficiency and fanaticism."[10]

But the price of fanaticism is high: perhaps as many as one-third of the million men who passed through the ranks of the Waffen SS were killed or seriously wounded in battle. Moreover, thirty-six general officers of the Waffen SS lost their lives, a ratio of nearly one for each SS division.[11]

Many serious students of the SS agree with the German political scientist Ermenhild Neusüss-Hunkel that "most of the

[8] SHAEF Report, p. 30.

[9] The 6th SS Panzer Army was withdrawing westward after its unsuccessful attempt to drive the Russians back from the Hungarian oilfields.

[10] Rodney G. Minott, *The Fortress That Never Was: The Myth of Hitler's Bavarian Stronghold* (New York, 1964), p. 17.

[11] See figures given in Neusüss-Hunkel, *op. cit.*, pp. 104ff.; also Kanis, *op. cit.*, p. 241.

SS combat units were of great military value, were not spared and thus suffered unusually heavy losses, and in general did not differ from Wehrmacht formations in their fighting habits [*Kampfesweise*]." [12] Like most generalizations, however, this one requires qualification. The Waffen SS had many faces, and even its front-line formations were not completely indistinguishable from those of the Army.

The difference was not, as many have supposed, that the Waffen SS was composed largely of active Nazis. On the contrary, the available evidence indicates that the great majority of the most active Nazis—members of the NSDAP, the SA, the Allgemeine SS, and the Hitler Youth—performed their military service in the Wehrmacht. Although a good deal of research remains to be done on the subject, there appears to have been no single Waffen SS type. Diversity was the hallmark of the wartime SS. Rubbing shoulders in the ranks of the Waffen SS were young idealists, hard-bitten soldiers of fortune, dull-witted yokels, dehumanized concentration-camp guards, flaming-eyed Hitler Youths, bewildered conscripts, hard-core Nazis, and thousands of foreigners who understood little or no German, let alone Nazi ideology. [13]

And yet there can be little doubt that the Waffen SS possessed a distinct character, one that served to set it apart from the Army. Eugen Kogon, in his pioneering study *Der SS-Staat*, offers a valuable insight into this character: "There was much naive and boyish idealism in the ranks of the Waffen SS, coupled with a savage soldier of fortune spirit." Most Waffen SS men, Kogon believes, "knew little or nothing concrete about the SS superstate or about SS aims." They limited themselves to "the realization of a single SS ideal—a tough recklessness. To them this was the epitome of the SS." [14]

With the proviso that this "tough recklessness" and "savage soldier of fortune spirit" had a marked National Socialist hue, Kogon's interpretation rings true. Few of the men in the Waffen SS were old enough to have had any personal contact with the

[12] Neusüss-Hunkel, *op. cit.*, p. 110.
[13] Cf. Paetel, *op. cit.*, pp. 22ff.
[14] Kogon, *op. cit.*, pp. 32, 338.

post-World War I Freikorps movement;[15] yet it was the spirit of this movement, its nihilism and elitism, which perhaps comes closest to that of the Waffen SS.

The most important popularizer of this spirit was the German poet and novelist Ernst Jünger, who in 1919 wrote of a "new man, the storm soldier, the elite of central Europe. A completely new race, cunning, strong and packed with purpose . . . battle proven, merciless both to himself and others."[16] Jünger's warrior was only a figment of his imagination; but he might well have been describing the model SS officer, the ideal of the Junkerschulen (Cadet Schools) of the Waffen SS.

It was the new National Socialist *Volksoffiziere*—men qualifying on the basis of physical fitness, racial purity, and presumed ideological conviction rather than by virtue of education, social background, and emotional stability—who characterized the officer corps of the wartime Waffen SS. Although their influence cannot be entirely discounted, the *alte Kämpfer* or Police generals turned into field commanders by a stroke of Himmler's pen—butchers like Theodor Eicke, Friedrich Jeckeln, Friedrich Krüger, Heinz Reinefarth, Erich von dem Bach-Zelewski, and Oskar Dirlewanger—did not represent the essence of the Waffen SS. Of far greater significance was the influence of the former regular Army officers who had commanded the SS Verfügungstruppen—men like Paul Hausser, Felix Steiner, Herbert Gille, Wilhelm Bittrich, and Georg Keppler. If the divisions of the Waffen SS seemed at times indistinguishable from those of the Army, it was in no small measure due to the efforts of these men.

But the real spirit of the Waffen SS was exemplified by the great mass of younger SS officers who were graduates of the SS Junkerschulen or who had come up through the ranks of the prewar SS. By and large these were men who had consecrated themselves to the blind obedience of all orders emanating from the Führer or his representatives, and whose highest aims were

[15] On the Freikorps see Robert G. L. Waite, *Vanguard of Nazism: The Free Corps Movement in Postwar Germany, 1918–1923* (Cambridge, Mass., 1952).

[16] Quoted in George L. Mosse, *The Culture of Western Europe* (Chicago, 1961), p. 297.

loyalty and toughness. They recognized no universal standards of conduct and were guided by a perverted moral code that put a low value on human life—including their own.

Harsh, ruthless, and often arrogant, these officers nevertheless established a close personal relationship with their men, one that went far beyond the traditional Army distinction between officers and men. Espousing a particularly demanding brand of "follow me" leadership, the young SS officers—even those of high rank—were often in the van of the attack. Just as they readily risked their own lives and those of their men, they killed without compunction and rarely discouraged their men from committing excesses. Sometimes loved by their men, other times hated, often respected but always obeyed, this elite within an elite left their mark on the Waffen SS.

By the last year of the war there were hundreds of these younger SS officers in command of regiments and battalions. And in the last months before the collapse a number of them, still in their thirties, commanded divisions. It was such men who often tried to organize last-ditch stands, shot shirkers, hanged deserters, and threatened local officials who showed signs of surrendering. It is instructive to recall that the first German to be tried as a war criminal by the western Allies was SS Brigadeführer Kurt Meyer, commander of the 12th SS Panzerdivision "Hitler Jugend" and youngest divisional commander in the Wehrmacht, who was sentenced to death for permitting his men to shoot Canadian prisoners during the battle for Normandy.

While neither SS ideological training materials nor Himmler's inspirational speeches need be accepted at face value as Waffen SS beliefs in practice, it is true that the nihilism of the Waffen SS was reinforced and given direction by National Socialist ideology. Nazi ideology per se, however, was not the primary causative factor in the committing of most Waffen SS atrocities. The most publicized of these atrocities—the massacre of British soldiers at Le Paradis in 1940, the massacre of French civilians at Oradour in 1944, and the massacre of American soldiers at Malmédy later the same year—were all unpremeditated and instigated by junior officers on the scene. Those murdered were not proscribed by Nazi racial policies. Rather they were victims of a freebooter spirit that the men of the Freikorps would have readily understood.

There was, as we have seen, a tenuous connection between the Waffen SS and those SS formations engaged in carrying out Hitler's racial policies. When called upon, as individuals or units, to assist in such operations—whether it was the reduction of the Warsaw Ghetto or the extermination of Jews at Minsk—the men of the Waffen SS displayed their cardinal virtue: blind obedience. Nevertheless, relatively few SS combat troops took part in such activities, although a good many must have known about them.

Nazi occupation policies brought some Waffen SS troops into contact with a type of combat that is harsh and savage even under the best circumstances. Those SS men who accepted the *Herrenmensch–Untermensch* [17] dichotomy found in partisan warfare a perfect opportunity to put Nazi racial theory into practice. Others displayed the usual Waffen SS contempt for life, and the remainder simply obeyed orders. The result was often large-scale atrocities. Indeed, most of the crimes attributed to the Waffen SS were committed during the course of operations styled as "antipartisan drives" or "pacification campaigns." Significantly, no SS apologist has yet tried to explain how the innocent civilians—men, women, and children—murdered by soldiers of the Waffen SS in such places as Minsk, Kharkov, Boves (Italy), Klissura (Greece), and Oradour (France) could have been mistaken for partisans. [18]

Even after the false charges against the Waffen SS are set aside, there remain more than enough legitimate ones to support the conclusion that the men of the Waffen SS deviated from the accepted rules of warfare too often to claim that they were merely "soldiers like any others."

[17] Roughly, superman–subhuman, or master race–inferior race.

[18] An unconvincing attempt to explain and justify the massacre at Oradour appeared in a recent issue of the HIAG journal; it may be considered an exception to this statement. See "Die Wahrheit über Oradour," *Die Freiwillige*, X, No. 7 (July 1964), pp. 5ff.

It is important to remember that in many respects the Waffen SS was an organization molded by the demands of a long and desperate war. The fact is that the Waffen SS played a role in World War II for which it was not originally intended. Conceived as the Führer's elite guard and militarized police force of the Nazi revolution, it became instead the elite combat arm of Hitler's Wehrmacht.

It was a long road from the handful of black-uniformed security guards Sepp Dietrich commanded during the Röhm purge of 1934 to the formidable SS panzer army he led during the Ardennes offensive a decade later. Along the way the Leibstandarte, the Verfügungstruppe, and the Totenkopfverbände merged in the Waffen SS; and the divisions of the Waffen SS, swelled by hundreds of thousands of new recruits—volunteers and conscripts, German and foreign—became to all intents and purposes a part of the Army. "And the longer the war went on," concluded Colonel General Heinz Guderian, "the less distinguishable they became from the Army." [19]

But the Waffen SS never did become indistinguishable from the Army. Although it lost some of its original character during the course of the war, it retained an ethos that was distinctly National Socialist. Nor did it ever wholly emerge from the sinister shadow cast by its parent organization—Himmler's SS.

[19] Guderian, *op. cit.*, p. 447.

Comparative Table of Waffen SS, German Army, and U.S. Army Ranks

Waffen SS	German Army	U.S. Army [1]
Commissioned		
Reichsführer-SS	Generalfeldmarschall	General of the Army
SS-Oberstgruppenführer	Generaloberst	General
SS-Obergruppenführer	General	Lieutenant General
SS-Gruppenführer	Generalleutnant	Major General
SS-Brigadeführer	Generalmajor	Brigadier General
SS-Oberführer	—	—
SS-Standartenführer	Oberst	Colonel
SS-Obersturmbannführer	Oberstleutnant	Lieutenant Colonel
SS-Sturmbannführer	Major	Major
SS-Hauptsturmführer	Hauptmann	Captain
SS-Obersturmführer	Oberleutnant	1st Lieutenant
SS-Untersturmführer	Leutnant	2nd Lieutenant
Noncommissioned [2]		
SS-Sturmscharführer	Stabsfeldwebel	Sergeant Major
SS-Standarten-Oberjunker	Oberfähnrich	—
SS-Hauptscharführer	Oberfeldwebel	Master Sergeant
SS-Oberscharführer	Feldwebel	Technical Sergeant
SS-Standartenjunker	Fähnrich	—
SS-Scharführer	Unterfeldwebel	Staff Sergeant
SS-Unterscharführer	Unteroffizier	Sergeant
Enlisted		
SS-Rottenführer	⌠Stabsgefreiter	—
	⌡Obergefreiter ⌉	
SS-Sturmmann	Gefreiter ⌋	Corporal
SS-Oberschütze	Oberschütze	Private 1st Class
SS-Schütze	Schütze	Private

[1] U.S. Army Warrant Officer grades have been omitted.

[2] The ranks used during World War II are given for U.S. Army noncommissioned and enlisted grades. German noncommissioned grades include those of officer candidates, for which there are no U.S. Army equivalents. Of course, all comparisons of German and U.S. ranks below the commissioned officer grades are only approximations.

List of Waffen SS Field Units,

1944 – 1945[1]

Key to Symbols:

*	Units that were divisions in name only, often no larger than regiments
F+	Units composed largely of foreign personnel
F–	Units including a sizable number of foreign personnel
V+	Units composed largely of *Volksdeutsche*
V–	Units including a sizable number of *Volksdeutsche*

I Divisions

1st   SS-Panzerdivision "Leibstandarte Adolf Hitler"
2nd   SS-Panzerdivision "Das Reich"
3rd   SS-Panzerdivision "Totenkopf"
4th   SS-Polizei-Panzergrenadierdivision
5th   SS-Panzerdivision "Wiking"   F–
6th   SS-Gebirgsdivision "Nord"
7th   SS-Freiwilligen-Gebirgsdivision "Prinz Eugen"   V+
8th   SS-Kavalleriedivision "Florian Geyer"   V–
9th   SS-Panzerdivision "Hohenstauffen"
10th SS-Panzerdivision "Frundsberg"
11th SS-Freiwilligen-Panzergrenadierdivision "Nordland"   F–
12th SS-Panzerdivision "Hitler Jugend"

[1] For a listing of components of the Waffen SS other than field units (such as reserve and training battalions, schools, training bases, supply and support formations, etc.), see Keilig, *Das Deutsche Heer*, II, Section 141, pp. 25ff.

13th Waffen-Gebirgsdivision der SS "Handschar"   F+
      (kroat. Nr. 1)
14th Waffen-Grenadierdivision der SS (galiz. Nr. 1)   F+
15th Waffen-Grenadierdivision der SS (lett. Nr. 1)   F+
16th SS-Panzergrenadierdivision "Reichsführer SS"   V—
17th SS-Panzergrenadierdivision "Götz von Berlichingen" V—
18th SS-Freiwilligen-Panzergrenadierdivision "Horst Wessel" V+
19th Waffen-Grenadierdivision der SS (lett. Nr. 2)   F+
20th Waffen-Grenadierdivision der SS (estn. Nr. 1)   F+
* 21st Waffen-Gebirgsdivision der SS "Skanderbeg" (alban. F+
      Nr. 1)
22nd Freiwilligen-Kavalleriedivision der SS "Maria   F+/V—
      Theresia"
* 23rd Waffen-Gebirgsdivision der SS "Kama" (kroat. Nr. 2); F+
      dissolved late in 1944, and numerical designation given to
      SS-Freiwilligen-Panzergrenadierdivision "Nederland"
* 24th Waffen-Gebirgskarstjägerdivision der SS
* 25th Waffen-Grenadierdivision der SS "Hunyadi"   F+
      (ungar. Nr. 1)
* 26th Waffen-Grenadierdivision der SS (ungar. Nr. 2)   F+
* 27th SS-Freiwilligen-Grenadierdivision "Langemarck"   F+
* 28th SS-Freiwilligen-Grenadierdivision "Wallonien"   F+
* 29th Waffen-Grenadierdivision der SS (russ. Nr. 1);   F+
      transferred to the Vlasov Army, and numerical desig-
      nation given to Waffen-Grenadierdivision der SS (ital.
      Nr. 1) as of April 1945.
30th Waffen-Grenadierdivision der SS (russ. Nr. 2)   F+
* 31st SS-Freiwilligen-Panzergrenadierdivision "Böhmen–   F—/V—
      Mähren" (established in 1945, around a nucleus of
      personnel from the various Waffen SS schools and
      training establishments in Bohemia–Moravia)
* 32nd SS-Panzergrenadierdivision "30. Januar" (created
      by mobilizing the students and instructors at the
      various panzer and panzergrenadier schools)
* 33rd Waffen-Kavalleriedivision der SS (ungar. Nr. 3); anni- F+
      hilated early in 1945 during the battle for Budapest,
      and numerical designation given to Waffen-Grenadier-
      division der SS "Charlemagne" (franz. Nr. 1)   F+
* 34th SS-Freiwilligen-Grenadierdivision "Landstorm Neder- F+
      land"

* 35th   SS-Polizei-Grenadierdivision (created in 1945 by mo-
         bilizing members of the Ordnungspolizei)
* 36th   Waffen-Grenadierdivision der SS (a titular upgrading
         of the notorious Dirlewanger penal brigade)
* 37th   SS-Freiwilligen-Kavalleriedivision "Lützow"   F+
* 38th   SS-Panzergrenadierdivision "Nibelungen" (composed
         in part of the staff and students of the SS-Junkerschule
         "Bad Tölz")

II   Other Field Units [2]

1st Kosaken-Kavalleriedivision der SS   F+
2nd Kosaken-Kavalleriedivision der SS   F+
Osttürkischer Waffenverband der SS   F+
Kaukasischer Waffenverband der SS   F+
Serbisches SS-Freiwilligenkorps   F+
Indische Freiwilligenlegion der SS   F+
British Freecorps (SS)   F+
Waffen-Grenadierregiment der SS (rumän. Nr. 1)   F+
Waffen-Grenadierregiment der SS (rumän. Nr. 2)   F+
Waffen-Grenadierregiment der SS (bulgar. Nr. 1)   F+
Norwegisches SS-Ski-Jäger Bataillon   F+
Begleitbataillon (mot) "Reichsführer SS"
Wachbataillon (mot) "Leibstandarte Adolf Hitler"

III   Army and Corps Commands [3]

Armee-Oberkommando 6th SS-Panzerarmee
Generalkommando Ist SS-Panzerkorps "Leibstandarte Adolf
    Hitler"
Generalkommando IInd SS-Panzerkorps
Generalkommando IIIrd (Germanisches) SS-Panzerkorps

[2] This is only a partial listing. In addition to the units mentioned, the Waffen SS maintained a number of corps troops, self-supporting units, and special-purpose formations such as heavy-artillery battalions, heavy-tank battalions, communications units, independent panzergrenadier brigades, rocket-launching battalions, and paratroop battalions. Other small units composed of foreigners, such as the Finnish Volunteer Battalion, also existed from time to time. See *ibid.*, pp. 23ff.

[3] Cf. *ibid.*, pp. 14 f.

Generalkommando IVth SS-Panzerkorps
Generalkommando Vth SS-Gebirgskorps
Generalkommando VIth SS-Freiwilligenkorps (Lettisches)
Generalkommando IXth Waffen-Gebirgskorps der SS (Kroatisches)
Generalkommandos XIth-XVth SS-Armeekorps (mixed Army-SS staffs)
Generalkommando XVIIIth SS-Armeekorps (Rhine front)

Glossary of Most Frequently Used German Terms

Abwehr, intelligence service of the German armed forces; taken over by the SS in 1944

Allgemeine SS, General SS; main body of the prewar SS, composed of part-time volunteers

Armee, an army (field formation usually composed of at least two corps)

Armeekorps (AK), an army corps (component of an army usually composed of at least two divisions)

Armeeoberkommando (AOK), army headquarters or headquarters staff

Barbarossa, code name for the invasion of the USSR

Befehlshaber, commander

Chef, chief, head, commander, superior

Deutsche Arbeitsfront (DAF), German Labor Front

Einsatzgruppe, action group; special SS/SD execution team responsible for liquidation of Jews and others proscribed by Nazi racial and political policies

Einsatzkommando, smaller component of an Einsatzgruppe

Eisernes Kreuz (E.K.), Iron Cross (military decoration)

Ergänzungstelle, recruiting center

Ersatz (heer, etc.), replacement or reserve (army, etc.)

Fall Gelb, code name for attack on France and Low Countries, May 1940

Fall Rot, code name for the second phase of the Battle of France, June 1940

Feldkommandantur, regional military government office

Freikorps, Free Corps; illegal military formations composed largely of World War I veterans, active in postwar Germany

Freiwillige, volunteers

Führer, in general, leader or officer; specifically, Hitler

Führerbefehl, order issued by Hitler

Führererlass, decree or edict issued by Hitler

Gebirgs (division, etc.), mountain (division, etc.)

Geheime Staatspolizei (Gestapo), Secret State Police; a branch of the SS organization

Generalgouvernment, Government-General; largest portion of German-occupied Poland

Generalkommando, headquarters of an army corps

Germanen, Germanics; non-Germans of "Nordic blood"

Gleichschaltung, the process of compulsory coordination by which Germany was brought under Nazi control

Heer, the Army

Heeresgruppe, army group (field formation usually composed of at least two armies)

Hitlerjugend, Hitler Youth

Höhere SS- und Polizeiführer (HSSPf.), Higher SS and Police Leader; commanding officer of SS and Police security forces, usually behind the front lines

Inspektion, inspectorate

Kampfgruppe, battle group

Kampfzeit, time of struggle; period during which the Nazis struggled to become masters of Germany (1919–1933)

Kommando (also *Kommandoamt*) *der Waffen SS,* operational command headquarters of the Waffen SS within the SS Führungshaupamt (see below)

Kommandostab RFSS, headquarters of the Reichsführer SS while in the field

Konzentrationslager (KZ), concentration camp

Kriegsmarine, German Navy

Kriminalpolizei (Kripo), Criminal Police; part of the SS organization

Landesgruppe, Nazi Party organization in a country outside Germany

Landwehr, military reserve of men between ages 35 and 45

Lebensraum, living space

Legion, legion; military formation composed of foreigners serving in the German Armed Forces

Luftwaffe, German Air Force

Marita, code name for the German invasion of Greece

Nationalsozialistische Deutsche Arbeiterpartei (NSDAP), National
Socialist German Workers Party (Nazi Party)

(SS) *Oberabschnitt,* SS district equivalent to a Wehrkreis (see below)

Oberbefehlshaber (Ob.), Commander-in-Chief (of a large military
formation)

Oberbefehlshaber des Heeres (ObdH), Commander-in-Chief of the
Army

Oberkommando des Heeres (OKH), Army High Command (headquarters)

Oberkommando der Wehrmacht (OKW), Armed Forces High Command (headquarters)

Ordnungspolizei (Orpo), Order Police; regular uniformed police,
incorporated into the SS organization

Organisation Todt (OT), military construction agency founded by
Fritz Todt (until his death in 1942, Reich Minister for Armaments and Munitions)

Ostland, Baltic countries and White Russia

Ostmark, Austria after its incorporation into the Reich

Panzer (*division, korps*), armor (armored division, armored corps)

Panzergrenadier (*division*), Mechanized infantry (division)

Rasse- und Siedlungs-Hauptamt (RuSHA), SS Main Office for Race
and Settlements

Reichsarbeitsdienst (RAD), Reich Labor Service (compulsory for
youths)

Reichsdeutsche, German citizens residing in Germany

Reichsführer SS (RFSS), Reich Leader of the SS (Himmler's title)

Reichsgesetzblatt (RGBl.), Reich Legal Gazette

Reichskommissariat für die Festigung deutschen Volkstums
(RKFDV), SS agency (headed by Himmler) for the "strengthening of Germanism"; primarily concerned with ethnic Germans

Reichssicherheitshauptamt (RSHA), Main Office of Reich Security;
SS agency headed by Reinhard Heydrich, later Ernst Kaltenbrunner

Reichswehr, the German Armed Forces from 1920 to 1935

Ritterkreuz, Knight's Cross of the Iron Cross

Schutzstaffel (SS), Protection Squad; originally elite corps of the
NSDAP; later, all-inclusive designation for components of the
complex organization headed by Heinrich Himmler

Sicherheitsdienst (SD), security and intelligence service of the SS

Sicherheitspolizei (Sipo), Security Police; component of the SS
organization

Sonderkommando, special command; extermination squad equivalent to an Einsatzkommando, but operating in a civil government area

SS Führungshauptamt (SSFHA), Main Leadership Office of the SS; operational headquarters of the SS established shortly after the beginning of World War II

SS Hauptamt (SSHA), Main Office of the SS; principally concerned with administrative matters, recruiting, and ideological training

Standarte, SS or SA formation equivalent to a regiment

Sturm, SS or SA formation equivalent to a company

Sturmabteilung (SA), Storm Troops; brown-shirted militia of the Nazi Party

Sturmbann, SS or SA formation equivalent to a battalion

(SS) *Totenkopfstandarten,* Death's Head regiments; armed SS formations created at the beginning of the war to handle "special tasks of a police nature"; disbanded in 1941, and personnel absorbed by field units of the Waffen SS

(SS) *Totenkopfverbände* (SSTV), Death's Head formations; armed, full-time component of the SS during the prewar period, employed primarily in the guarding of political prisons and concentration camps

(SS) *Totenkopfwachsturmbanne,* designation for Death's Head guard battalions of the Waffen SS, which guarded concentration and extermination camps during the war

(SS) *Verfügungstruppe* (SSVT), full-time, militarized component of the SS in the prewar period; direct predecessor of the Waffen SS

Verlag, publishing house

Volksdeutsche, ethnic or racial Germans; persons of German blood but of non-German citizenship residing outside the Reich, who were considered by the Nazis as members of the German "race" or *Volk*

Wehrbezirk, military recruiting subdistrict

Wehrbezirkskommando (WBK), military recruiting subdistrict headquarters

Wehrkreis, military district; in peacetime, equivalent to an Army corps area

Wehrkreiskommando, military district headquarters

Wehrmacht, the German armed forces (Army, Navy, and Air Force)

(SS) *Wirtschafts- und Verwaltungshauptamt* (WVHA), SS Main Economic and Administration Office; after March 1942 responsible for operation of concentration camps

APPENDIX IV: Chart of the SS Organization, 1943

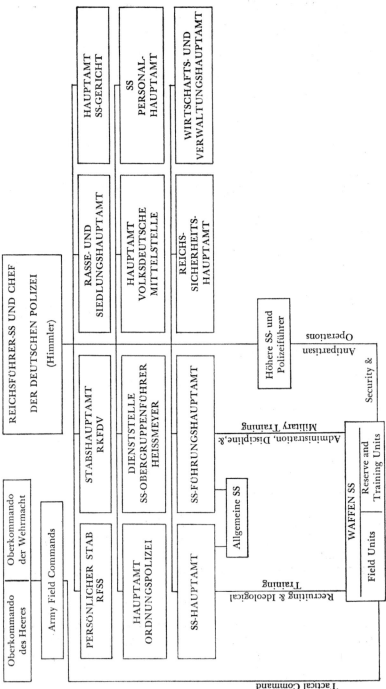

Selected Bibliography

1. Unpublished Documentary Material

Documents: Series PS, F, L, R, C, D, EC. Nuremberg: International Military Tribunal, n.d. (Mimeographed.)

Documents: United States Military Tribunal IV, Case 11. Nuremberg: U.S. Military Tribunals, 1948. (Mimeographed.)

Documents and Staff Evidence Analysis: Series NG, NI, NO, NOKW. Nuremberg: U.S. Military Tribunals, 1947–1948. (Mimeographed.)

Miscellaneous SS Records: Einwandererzentralstelle, Waffen-SS, and SS-Oberabschnitte. Washington: National Archives, Microcopy T–354. (Cited as SS/T–354.)

Official Transcript of Testimony for the Defense of Organizations. Nuremberg: International Military Tribunal, 1946. (Mimeographed.)

Records of Headquarters, German Armed Forces High Command (Oberkommando der Wehrmacht/OKW). Washington: National Archives, Microcopy T–77. (Cited as OKW/T–77.)

Records of Headquarters, German Army High Command (Oberkommando des Heeres/OKH). Washington: National Archives, Microcopy T–78. (Cited as OKH/T–78.)

Records of the National Socialist German Labor Party (Nationalsozialistiche Deutsche Abeiterpartei). Washington: National Archives, Microcopy T–81. (Cited as NSDAP/T–81.)

Records of the Reich Leader of the SS and Chief of the German Police (Reichsführer SS und Chef der Deutschen Polizei). Washington: National Archives, Microcopy T–175. (Cited as RFSS/T–175.)

2. Published Documentary Material, Handbooks, and Reports

Hitler Directs His War: The Secret Record of His Daily Military Conferences. Edited by Felix Gilbert. New York: Oxford University Press, 1950. (Selected fragments.)

Hitlers Lagebesprechungen: Die Protokollfragmente seiner militärischen Konferenzen, 1942–1945. Edited by Helmut Heiber. (Quellen und Darstellungen zur Zeitgeschichte, Vol. 10.) Stuttgart: Deutsche Verlags-Anstalt, 1962. (All extant fragments.)

Hitler's Secret Conversations, 1941–1944. Translated by Norman Cameron and R. H. Stevens. New York: Signet Books, 1961.

Hitlers Weisungen für die Kriegführung, 1939–1945. Edited by Walther Hubatsch. Frankfurt am Main: Bernard & Graefe Verlag für Wehrwesen, 1962. (English translation: *Blitzkrieg to Defeat: Hitler's War Directives, 1939–1945.* Edited by H. R. Trevor-Roper. New York: Holt, Rinehart and Winston, 1965.)

Hofer, Walther (ed.). *Der Nationalsozialismus: Dokumente, 1933–1945.* Frankfurt am Main: Fischer Bücherei, 1957.

Jacobsen, Hans-Adolf (ed.). *Dokumente zum Westfeldzug, 1940.* Göttingen: Musterschmidt Verlag, 1960.

———, and Hans Dollinger (eds.). *Der Zweite Weltkrieg: In Bildern und Dokumenten.* 3 vols. Munich: Verlag Kurt Desch, 1962–1964.

———, and Werner Jochmann (eds.). *Ausgewählte Dokumente zur Geschichte des Nationalsozialismus, 1933–1945.* Bielefeld: Verlag Neue Gesellschaft, 1961ff. (Looseleaf collection.)

Kriegstagebuch des Oberkommandos der Wehrmacht (Wehrmachtführungsstab), 1940–1945. Vols. IV–V. In four volumes. Vol. IV edited by Walther Hubatsch, Vol. V by Percy Ernst Schramm. Frankfurt am Main: Bernard & Graefe Verlag für Wehrwesen, 1961–1963. (Cited as KTB/OKW.)

Nationalsozialistische Deutsche Arbeiterpartei. *Organisationsbuch der NSDAP.* Munich: Zentralverlag der NSDAP, 1943.

———. *Verfügungen/Anordnungen/Bekantgaben.* Vol. III. Munich: Zentralverlag der NSDAP, 1943.

Nazi Conspiracy and Aggression. 10 vols. Washington: U.S. Government Printing Office, 1946. (Cited as NCA.)

Poliakov, Leon, and Josef Wulf (eds.). *Das Dritte Reich und Seine Diener: Dokumente.* Berlin: Arani Verlag, 1956.

Schnabel, Reimund (ed.). *Macht ohne Moral: Eine Dokumentation über die SS.* Frankfurt am Main: Röderberg Verlag, 1957.

SS im Einsatz: Eine Dokumentation über die Verbrechen der SS. Edited by the Komitee der Antifaschistischen Widerstandskämpfer in der Deutschen Demokratischen Republik. (East) Berlin: Deutscher Militärverlag, 1964.

Supreme Headquarters Allied Expeditionary Force. *Report by the Supreme Commander to the Combined Chiefs of Staff on the Operations in Europe of the Allied Expeditionary Force, 6 June 1944 to 8 May 1945.* Washington: U.S. Government Printing Office, 1946. (Cited as SHAEF Report.)

The Trial of German Major War Criminals: Proceedings of the International Military Tribunal Sitting at Nuremberg, Germany. 23 vols. London: H.M. Stationery Office, 1949–1951. (Cited as TGMWC.)

Trial of the Major War Criminals before the International Military Tribunal. 42 vols. Nuremberg: International Military Tribunal, 1947–1949. (Cited as IMT.)

Trials of War Criminals before the Nuremberg Military Tribunals. 15 vols. Washington: U.S. Government Printing Office, 1951–1952. (Cited as NMT.)

United Nations War Crimes Commission. *Law Reports of Trials of War Criminals.* 15 vols. London: London: H.M. Stationery Office, 1947–1949.

United States Senate Committee on Armed Forces. *Malmedy Massacre Investigation Hearings, 1949.* Washington: U.S. Government Printing Office, 1949.

3. *Memoirs, Diaries, and Letters*

Blücher, Wipert von. *Gesandter zwischen Diktatur und Demokratie.* Wiesbaden: Limes Verlag, 1951.

Bormann, Martin. *The Bormann Letters.* Edited by H. R. Trevor-Roper. London: Weidenfeld & Nicolson, 1954.

Bryant, Arthur. *The Turn of the Tide, 1939–1943: A History of the War Years Based on the Diaries of Field-Marshal Lord Alanbrooke, Chief of the Imperial General Staff.* Garden City: Doubleday, 1957.

Gisevius, Hans B. *To the Bitter End.* Boston: Houghton Mifflin, 1947.

Goebbels, Joseph. *The Goebbels Diaries, 1942–1943.* Edited and translated by Louis P. Lochner. Garden City: Doubleday, 1948.

Guderian, Heinz. *Panzer Leader*. London: Michael Joseph, 1952.

Halder, Franz. *Kriegstagebuch*. Vol. I. Edited by Hans-Adolf Jacobsen. Stuttgart: W. Kohlhammer Verlag, 1962.

Hanfstaengl, Ernst. *Hitler: The Missing Years*. London: Eyre & Spottiswoode, 1957.

Höss, Rudolf. *Kommandant in Auschwitz: Autographische Aufzeichnungen von Rudolf Höss*. Edited by Martin Broszat. (Quellen und Darstellungen zur Zeitgeschichte, Vol. 5.) Stuttgart: Deutsche Verlags-Anstalt, 1958.

Kersten, Felix. *The Kersten Memoirs, 1940–1945*. New York: Macmillan, 1957.

Mannerheim, Carl G. *Erinnerungen*. Zurich: Atlantis Verlag, 1952.

Manstein, Erich von. *Lost Victories*. Chicago: Henry Regnery, 1958.

Rommel, Erwin. *The Rommel Papers*. Edited by B. H. Liddell Hart. New York: Harcourt, Brace, 1953.

Schlabrendorff, Fabian. *Offiziere gegen Hitler*. Zurich: Europa Verlag, 1946.

Warlimont, Walter. *Im Hauptquartier der deutschen Wehrmacht 1939–1945*. Frankfurt am Main: Bernard & Graefe Verlag für Wehrwesen, 1962.

———. *Inside Hitler's Headquarters 1939–1945*. New York: Frederick A. Praeger, 1964. (English translation)

Westphal, Siegfried. *Heer in Fesseln: Aus den Papieren des Stabschefs von Rommel, Kesselring und Rundstedt*. Bonn: Athenäum-Verlag, 1950.

4. Books by Former Members of the Waffen SS

Degrelle, Leon. *Die verlorene Legion*. Stuttgart: Veritas Verlag, 1952.

Hausser, Paul. *Waffen-SS im Einsatz*. Göttingen: Plesse Verlag, 1953.

Kanis, K., *et al. Waffen-SS im Bild*. Göttingen: Plesse Verlag, 1957.

Krätschmer, Ernst-Günther. *Die Ritterkreuzträger der Waffen-SS* Göttingen: Plesse Verlag, 1955.

Meyer, Kurt ("Panzermeyer"). *Grenadiere*. Munich: Schild Verlag, 1957.

Steiner, Felix. *Die Freiwilligen: Idee und Opfergang*. Göttingen: Plesse Verlag, 1958.

———. *Die Armee der Geächteten*. Göttingen: Plesse Verlag, 1963.

5. Wartime German Publications Relating to the Waffen SS

Aufbruch: Briefe von germanischen Freiwilligen der SS-Division Wiking. Berlin: Nibelungen Verlag, 1943.

Best, Walter. *Mit der Leibstandarte im Westen: Berichte eines SS-Kriegsberichters.* Munich: F. Eher, 1944. (New York Public Library Microcopy Z–921.)

Dich ruft die SS. Berlin: H. Hilger, 194? (New York Public Library Microcopy Z–941.)

Heiss, Friedrich. *Der Sieg im Westen: Ein Bericht vom Kampf des deutschen Volksheeres in Holland, Belgien und Frankreich,* Prague: Volk und Reich Verlag, 1943.

Zachakel, Friedrich. *Waffen-SS im Westen: ein Bericht im Bildern.* Munich: F. Eher, 1941.

6. Books and Pamphlets

Absolon, Rudolf. *Wehrgesetz und Wehrdienst, 1935–1945: Das Personalwesen in der Wehrmacht.* (Schriften des Bundesarchivs, Vol. 5.) Boppard am Rhein: Harold Boldt Verlag, 1960.

Benoist-Méchin, Jacques. *Soixante jours qui ébranlèrent L'Occident.* 3 vols. Paris: Editions Albin Michel, 1956.

Broszat, Martin. *Nationalsozialistische Polenpolitik, 1939–1945.* (Schrieftenreihe der Vierteljahrshefte für Zeitgeschichte, No. 2.) Stuttgart: Deutsche Verlags-Anstalt, 1961.

Buchheim, Hans. *SS und Polizei im NS-Staat.* (Staatspolitische Schriftenreihe.) Bonn: Selbstverlag der Studiengesellschaft für Zeitprobleme, 1964.

Bullock, Alan. *Hitler: A Study in Tyranny.* Completely revised edition. New York: Harper & Row, 1962.

Carell, Paul. *Unternehmen Barbarossa.* Frankfurt am Main: Verlag Ullstein, 1963.

———. *Hitler Moves East, 1941–1943.* Boston: Little, Brown, 1965. (English translation.)

Clark, Alan. *Barbarossa: The Russian–German Conflict, 1941–45.* New York: William Morrow, 1965.

Craig, Gordon. *The Politics of the Russian Army, 1640–1945.* New York: Oxford University Press, 1956.

Dallin, Alexander. *German Rule in Russia, 1941–1945: A Study of Occupation Policies.* New York: St. Martin's, 1957.

Deakin, F. W. *The Brutal Friendship: Mussolini, Hitler and the Fall of Italian Fascism.* New York: Harper & Row, 1962.

Dornberg, John. *Schizophrenic Germany.* New York: Macmillan, 1961.

Ellis, L. F. *The War in France and Flanders, 1939–1940.* London: H.M. Stationery Office, 1953. (U.K. Official History.)

Friedrich, C. J., and Z. K. Brzezinski. *Totalitarian Dictatorship and Autocracy.* New York: Frederick A. Praeger, 1961.

Georg, Enno. *Die wirtschaftlichen Unternehmungen der SS.* (Schriftenreihe der Vierteljahrshefte für Zeitgeschichte, No. 7.) Stuttgart: Deutsche Verlags-Anstalt, 1963.

Görlitz, Walter. *Die Waffen-SS.* (Das Dritte Reich, No. 5.) Berlin: Arani Verlag, 1960.

Gray, J. Glenn. *The Warriors: Reflections on Men in Battle.* New York: Harcourt, Brace, 1959.

Gutachten des Instituts für Zeitgeschichte. Munich: Institut für Zeitgeschichte, 1958.

Hegner, H. S. *Die Reichskanzlei, 1933–1945.* Frankfurt am Main: Verlag Frankfurter Bücher, 1960.

Herzog, Robert. *Die Volksdeutschen in der Waffen-SS.* (Studien des Instituts für Besatzungsfragen in Tübingen zu den deutschen Besetzungen im 2. Weltkrieg, No. 5.) Tübingen: Institut für Besatzungsfragen, 1955. (Mimeographed.)

Hirsch, Kurt. *SS: Gestern, heute und . . . .* Darmstadt: Progress Verlag, 1960.

Hory, Ladislaus, and Martin Broszat. *Der kroatische Ustascha-Staat, 1941–1945.* (Schriftenreihe der Vierteljahrshefte für Zeitgeschichte, No. 8.) Stuttgart: Deutsche Verlags-Anstalt, 1954.

Jacobsen, Hans-Adolf. *Fall Gelb: Der Kampf um den deutschen Operationsplan zur Westoffensive, 1940.* (Veröffentlichungen des Instituts für europäische Geschichte Mainz, Vol. 16.) Wiesbaden: Franz Steiner Verlag, 1957.

Keilig, Wolf. *Das Deutsche Heer, 1939–1945.* 2 vols. Bad Nauheim: Podzun Verlag, 1956. (Looseleaf collection.)

Kempner, Robert M. W. *SS im Kreuzverhör.* Munich: Rütten & Loening Verlag, 1964.

Koehl, Robert. *RKFDV: German Resettlement and Population Policy, 1939–1945.* Cambridge: Harvard University Press, 1957.

Kogon, Eugen. *Der SS-Staat: Das System der deutschen Konzentrationslager.* Frankfurt am Main: Verlag der Frankfurter Hefte, 1946.

Liddell Hart, B. H. *The German Generals Talk*. New York: Berkley Books, 1958.

———. *Strategy*. Revised edition. New York: Frederick A. Praeger, 1961.

———. (ed.). *The Red Army*. New York: Harcourt, Brace, 1956.

Lundin, Leonard C. *Finland in the Second World War*. Bloomington: Indiana University Press, 1957.

Meissner, Hans Otto, and Harry Wilde. *Die Machtergreifung: Ein Bericht über die Technik des Nationalsozialistischen Staatsstreiches*. Stuttgart: J. G. Gotta'sche Buchhandlung, 1958.

Minott, Rodney G. *The Fortress That Never Was: The Myth of Hitler's Bavarian Stronghold*. New York: Holt, Rinehart and Winston, 1964.

Neufeldt, Hans-Joachim, Jürgen Huck, and Georg Tessin. *Zur Geschichte der Ordnungspolizei, 1936–1945*. (Schriften des Bundesarchivs, Vol. 3.) Coblenz: Bundesarchiv, 1957.

Neusüss-Hunkel, Ermenhild. *Die SS*. (Schriftenreihe des Instituts für wissenschaftliche Politik in Marburg Lahn, No. 2.) Hannover: Norddeutsche Verlagsanstalt, 1956.

Philippi, Alfred, and Ferdinand Heim. *Der Feldzug gegen Sowjetrussland, 1941–1945*. Stuttgart: W. Kohlhammer Verlag, 1962.

Prittie, Terence. *Germans against Hitler*. Boston: Little, Brown, 1964.

Reitlinger, Gerald. *The SS: Alibi of a Nation, 1922–1945*. New York: Viking Press, 1957.

———. *The House Built on Sand: The Conflicts of German Policy in Russia, 1939–45*. London: Weidenfeld & Nicolson, 1960.

Ritter, Gerhard. *Karl Goerdler und die deutsche Widerstandsbewegung*. Stuttgart: Deutsche Verlags-Anstalt, 1954.

Rooney, Andrew A. *The Fortunes of War*. Boston: Little, Brown, 1962.

Saller, Karl. *Die Rassenlehre des Nationalsozialismus in Wissenschaft und Propaganda*. Darmstadt: Progress Verlag, 1961.

Shirer, William. *The Rise and Fall of the Third Reich*. New York: Simon and Schuster, 1960.

Shulman, Milton. *Defeat in the West*. New York: E. P. Dutton, 1948.

Taylor, Telford. *The March of Conquest: The German Victories in Western Europe, 1940*. New York: Simon and Schuster, 1958.

Thorwald, Jürgen. *Die grosse Flucht*. Stuttgart: Steingrüben Verlag, n.d. (Originally published in two volumes, 1950.)

Toland, John. *Battle: The Story of the Bulge.* New York: Signet Books, 1960.

Trevor-Roper, H. R. *The Last Days of Hitler.* 3rd edition. New York: Collier Books, 1962.

Waite, Robert G. L. *Vanguard of Nazism: The Free Corps Movement in Postwar Germany, 1918–1923.* Cambridge: Harvard University Press, 1952.

Werth, Alexander. *Russia at War, 1941–1945.* New York: E. P. Dutton, 1964.

Wheeler-Bennett, John W. *The Nemesis of Power: The German Army in Politics, 1918–1945.* 2nd edition. London: Macmillan, 1964.

Zipfel, Friedrich. *Gestapo und Sicherheitsdienst.* (Das Dritte Reich, No. 3.) Berlin: Arani Verlag, 1960.

7. *Articles and Periodicals*

Auerbach, Hellmuth. "Die Einheit Dirlewanger," *Vierteljahrshefte für Zeitgeschichte,* X, No. 3 (July 1962), pp. 250–263.

Berger, Gottlob. "Zum Ausbau der Waffen-SS," *Nation Europa: Monatsschrift im Dienst der europäischen Erneuerung,* III, No. 4 (April 1953), pp. 55–56.

Buchheim, Hans. "Die Höheren SS- und Polizeiführer," *Vierteljahrshefte für Zeitgeschichte,* XI, No. 4 (October 1963), pp. 362–391.

———. "Die SS in der Verfassung des Dritten Reiches," *Vierteljahrshefte für Zeitgeschichte,* III, No. 2 (April 1955), pp. 127–157.

Dmytryshyn, Basil. "The Nazis and the SS Volunteer Division 'Galicia,'" *American Slavic and East European Review,* XV, No. 1 (February 1956), pp. 1–10.

Himmler, Heinrich. "Die Rede Himmlers vor den Gauleitern am 3. August 1944," *Vierteljahrshefte für Zeitgeschichte,* I, No. 4, (October 1953), pp. 357–394.

Koehl, Robert. "The Character of the Nazi SS," *The Journal of Modern History,* XXXIV, No. 3 (September 1962), pp. 275–283.

Loock, Hans Dietrich. "Zur 'Grossgermanischen Politik' des Dritte Reiches," *Vierteljahrshefte für Zeitgeschichte,* VIII, No. 1 (January 1960), pp. 37–63.

Paetel, Karl O. "Die SS: Ein Beitrag zur Soziologie des Nationalsozialismus," *Vierteljahrshefte für Zeitgeschichte,* II, No. 1 (January 1954), pp. 1–33.

———. "The Black Order: A Survey of the Literature on the SS," *The Wiener Library Bulletin,* XII, Nos. 3-4 (1959), pp. 34–35.

Stein, George H. "The Myth of a European Army," *The Wiener Library Bulletin*, XIX, No. 2 (April 1965), pp. 21–22.

Wiking-Ruf: Zeitschrift der Soldaten der ehemaligen Waffen-SS. 1955–1958. Absorbed by *Der Freiwillige/Wiking-Ruf: Kameradschaftsblatt der HIAG (Hilfsgemeinschaft aus Gegenseitigkeit)* Stemmen über Hannover: Wiking Verlag, in 1958 and thereafter published monthly under the title *Der Freiwillige: Kameradschaftsblatt der HIAG.* Osnabrück: Verlag "Der Freiwillige."

Index

Aaltonen, Chief of the Finnish State Police, 159–160

Abbeville, 68

Abwehr, xxviii

Adenauer, Konrad: on Waffen SS, 254

Adlerhorst (Hitler's headquarters at Bad Nauheim), 234

Aisne River, 81, 82, 84, 87

Allgemeine SS, 93; brief history, xxv–xxvii; no longer the praetorian guard Hitler desired, 5; members called up for service in the Waffen SS, 152; *see also* SS, Waffen SS, *and* other specific components of the SS

Allier River, 85–86

"Alpine Redoubt," 238, 289

Amery, John, 190

Amsterdam, 67

Antwerp, 64, 229

Ardennes, 289; Canal, 87; offensive, 227–232

Argonne: Forest, 88; Pass, 88

Armed Forces High Command (German), *see* OKW

Army, German: attitude toward SA and SS, 6–8; and SS atrocities in Poland, 30–31; and *Fall Gelb*, 55–56; motorized divisions, 58; expansion for war against the USSR, 98–99; losses in Balkan campaign, 118; suffers first major setback of WW II, 166; and mobilization of Baltic manpower, 174; summer offensive (1942), 200–201; retreat in France (1944), 225

National legions: Wallonian, 163; composed of Russian national minorities, 185; composed of Ukrainians and Russians, 185; Indian, 189

Units:

  Army Groups (Heeresgruppen):

    A—60–61, 80–81

    B—60–61, 80–81, 224, 237

    C—60–61, 80–81

    North (Nord), 119–120, 174, 204 217, 219

    Center (Mitte), 119–120, 134, 165, 166–167, 204, 217, 219, 264

    South (Süd), 119–120, 236

    Southeast (Südost), 204

    Don, 204

    North-Ukraine (Nord-Ukraine), 219

  Armies (Armeen):

    1st Panzer, 215, 217–218

    2nd—58

    5th Panzer, 230

    6th—201, 215

    7th—230

    8th—215–216

    9th—239, 243, 247–248

    10th—28

    11th Panzer, 238

    12th—116, 239, 243, 247–248

    20th Gebirgs, 204, 221

  Groups:

    Panzer Group (Panzergruppe) Kleist, 81–88 *passim*

Army, German (*cont.*):
  Corps (Armeekorps):
    Afrika Korps, 201
    IIIrd Panzer, 134
    XIVth—84, 88, 186
    XVth—67
    XVIth—19, 77, 84
    XLIst Panzer, 115
    XLIVth—82
    LVIIth—246
  Divisions:
    2nd Panzer, 222, 230
    3rd Panzer, 72, 74
    5th Panzer, 67
    7th Panzer, 67, 69
    9th Panzer, 64–66, 88, 116
    10th Panzer, 88
    18th Panzergrenadier, 238
    36th Volksgrenadier, 231
    112th Infantry, 166
    116th Panzer, 222
  Brigades:
    4th Panzer, 28
  Regiments:
    "Gross Deutschland," 116
    French Volunteer, 163–164
Army High Command (German), *see*
  OKH
Arnswalde, 238
Arras, 68
Athens, 117–118
Auerbach, Hellmuth: on Dirlewanger
  detachment, 270
Auschwitz, 261–262
Austria (Ostmark), 19, 237
Avranches, 222
Avre River, 81
Axmann, Arthur, 205

Bach-Zelewski, Erich von dem, 291; on
  consequences of National Socialist
  ideology, 129; Dirlewanger and
  Kaminski detachments, 264–270
  passim
Bailleul, 80
Bakke, Jörgen (captain, Norwegian
  Army), 154
Baltic legions, *see under* Waffen SS:
  National legions *and* Foreign per-
  sonnel
Bangerskis, Rudolf, 178 n. 30
Bar le Duc, 88
Barbarossa, Operation or Case, 134;
  plans, 112–113; preparations and
  deployment, 119–120

Belgian Army, 61; in danger of collapse, 71
Belgium: and recruitment for Waffen
  SS, 94
Belgrade, 115
Belsen, 261
Berger, Gottlob, 32, 51, 93; establishes
  centralized SS recruiting system,
  36–38; negotiates with OKW on
  wartime status of Waffen SS, 38–
  49 *passim;* and OKW, 95–98; suggests increased recruitment of
  foreigners for Waffen SS, 99–100;
  and recruitment of west Europeans, 137–164 *passim;* on criminal
  element among Dutch volunteers,
  141; and European union, 145–146;
  and Greater Germanic Reich, 150
  n. 29; and SS recruiting, 151–152;
  and difficulties with Danish authorities over recruiting of Danes
  for Waffen SS, 153 n. 37; advocates
  changes in the foreign volunteer
  program, 160–161; and recruitment
  of *Volksdeutsche* for service in the
  Waffen SS, 168–174 *passim;* on
  conscription of *Volksdeutsche*, 171;
  and recruitment of Hungarian
  Volksdeutsche for the Waffen SS,
  172–173; supports Estonian desires
  for a national military formation
  (1942), 175; on re-establishment of
  Latvian Army, 176; suggests crea-
  tion of a Latvian legion of the
  Waffen SS, 176; and British Legion,
  190–191; and SS division composed
  of Hitler Youths, 205; and Dirle-
  wanger and Kaminski detachments,
  264–270 *passim*
Berlin, 289; Waffen SS executions in,
  281
Bethune, 72, 76
Birkenau, 262
Bittrich, Wilhelm, 291
Blaskowitz, Johannes, 31
Blomberg, Werner von, 18–19
Blomberg–Fritsch affair, 18–19
"Blood Purge," *see* SA
Bock, Fedor von, 119
Bordeaux, 88
Bormann, Martin, 227, 239, 247
Bose, Subhas Chandra, 189
Boulogne, 80
Boves, massacre of Italian civilians at,
  276, 293

Brauchitsch, Walther von, 19, 29, 31; friendship with Lutze, 43 n. 41; complains to Himmler about incidents in which Waffen SS and Army personnel involved, 114–115; dismissed by Hitler, 167

Breda, 64

Brettheim: execution by Waffen SS of German civilians at, 280–281

British Army: 2nd Division, 73, 74, 76; 4th Brigade, 76; 1st Royal Scots Regiment, 76; 1st/8th Lancashire Fusiliers Regiment, 76; 2nd Royal Norfolk Regiment, and massacre at Le Paradis, 76–78; 2nd Warwickshire Regiment, 79

British Expeditionary Force (BEF), 69–70, 72; decision to evacuate, 71; withdraws inside Dunkirk perimeter, 80; in Greece, 116; evacuates Greece, 117

Brittany, 222

Buchenwald, xxxiii

Budapest, 289; siege of, 221, 233, 234; fall of, 235–236

Bulgaria: signs Tripartite Pact, 114; entered by Soviet Army, 221

Bulge, battle of the, *see* Ardennes offensive (1944)

Bundestag, 254

Burgdorf, Wilhelm, 195, 239

Busse, Theodor, 239, 243, 245

Caen, 219, 221

Cambrai, 68, 80

Canadian Army: 1st Army, 225

Chambois, 225

Château-Thierry, 82–83

Chatillon, 85

Cherbourg peninsula, 221

Cherkassy, 217

Choltitz, Dietrich von, 66

Clermont-Ferrand, 86

Clerq, Staf de, 150; complains to Himmler about abuse of Flemish volunteers in Waffen SS, 154

Compulsory Labor Service, *see* RAD (Reichsarbeitsdienst)

Concentration camps, xxxii–xxxiv, 102; and arms for Waffen SS, 55; listed by Himmler as part of Waffen SS, 110–111; staffs, 111; and Waffen SS, 258–263 *passim;* Inspectorate of, 259–260; *see also* SS Totenkopfverbände

Cossacks, 188–189; *see also* Waffen SS: Foreign personnel

Courland, 179, 194–195

Croatia, 170; recruiting of *Volksdeutsche* in, 173; recruiting of Moslems in, 180–185

Czechoslovakia: occupation of, 24–25; and arms for Waffen SS, 51–52, 55

Dachau, xxxiii

DAF (Deutsche Arbeitsfront), 43

Daluege, Kurt, xxviii

Danube River, 236

Debica (SS military reservation), 109 n. 47

Degrelle, Leon, 140

Demelhuber, Karl, 10

Denmark: and SS recruiting, 94, 153 (*see also* Waffen SS: Foreign personnel); and Greater Germanic Reich, 148

Der Freiwillige (periodical), 252

Der Malmedy Prozess (book), 253

Die Ritterkreuzträger der Waffen SS (book), 270

Dietrich, Joseph (Sepp), 4–5, 57, 79, 245, 273, 289, 294; and murder of Röhm, 7; and Hitler, 10 n. 21; ignores "stop order," 71; awarded *Ritterkreuz*, 90; orders shooting of Russian prisoners, 133; praised by Goebbels, 199; appointed commander Ist SS Panzerkorps, 210; appointed commander 6th SS Panzerarmee, 229; and Hitler's "armband order," 237; and cease-fire, 248; sentence for Malmédy massacre, 280

Dijon, 84

Dirlewanger, Oskar, 264–270 *passim,* 291

Dirlewanger detachment (SS), 264–270 *passim;* and Warsaw uprising, 265, 269; composition of, 268; discipline in, 268

Dnieper River, 120, 215

Dönitz, Karl, 239, 246

Don River, 200

Donetz River, 165

Dunkirk, 71, 79, 80, 117

Dutch Army, 61, 62, 66

East Prussia, 237

Eberswalde, 239

Echternach, 229

Eicke, Theodor, 6, 57–58, 77, 87, 91–92, 259, 291; appointed Inspekteur der Konzentrationslager und Führer der SS Totenkopfverbände, xxxiii; appointed commander of SS Totenkopfdivision, xxxiv; role in murder of Röhm, 7; on *Volksdeutsche* in the Waffen SS, 192

Einsatzgruppen (SS), xxix, 126, 263; composition of, 263; and Waffen SS, 263–264

Eisenhower, Dwight D., 201, 222; on German defense of Normandy, 224; on combat performance of Waffen SS, 225, 289; on consequences for Germany of the Ardennes offensive, 232 n. 54

El Alamein, 201

Epernay, 82

Ergänzungsamt der Waffen SS, 36–37; *see also* Waffen SS: recruitment

Ernst, SS Sturmmann, 271

Eschenburg, Theodor: on Waffen SS as branch of Wehrmacht, 286

Esquebeck, 79

Estaires, 74

Estonia, 194; and agitation for a national military formation, 175

Ethnic Germans, *see Volksdeutsche*

Extermination camps, *see* Concentration camps

Falaise–Argentan pocket, 225–226

Falkenhorst, Nikolaus von, 131

Fascist Grand Council: votes to depose Mussolini, 214

Fegelein, Hermann, 245, 245 n. 91, 246; on Moslems in the Waffen SS, 183 n. 42

Finland, 120; and recruitment for the Waffen SS, 149; withdraws from war, 221

"Fortress Holland," 62

Frederick William I, King of Prussia, 143

Freikorps, 266, 291, 293

French Army, 62; 1st Army, 75; 7th Army, 64; 3rd Light Mechanized Division, 69

French Government: abandons Paris, 83

Fritsch, Werner Freiherr von, 18–19

Fromm, Friedrich (Fritz), 54, 196 n. 72

Führer Decree of August 17, 1938, xxi, 20–24, 283–284

Führer Decree of May 18, 1939, 33, 41, 49, 50

Gärtner, SS Oberführer: and arms for the Waffen SS, 50–54

Galicia, 119

Gannat, 86

Gelb, Fall (Case Yellow), 55; German deployment for, 60–61, plan of attack, 60–62

General SS, *see* Allgemeine SS

Gennep, 63–64

German Army, *see* Army, German

German Labor Front, *see* RAD

Germanic SS, *see* Waffen SS: Foreign personnel *and* National legions

Gestapo (Geheime Staatspolizei), xxviii–xxix, 102; and Einsatzgruppen, 263

Gille, Herbert, 233, 291; appointed commander of IVth SS Panzerkorps, 210

Giraud, Henri, 64

Glücks, Richard, 260

Goebbels, 102, 181, 237, 239; on Sepp Dietrich, 199; appointed Plenipotentiary for Total War, 227

Göhler, Johannes, 194

Gönner, Reichsarbeitsführer von, 44

Göring, Hermann, 7, 102, 239; and military manpower, 97

Gravelines, 69

Greece: invaded by Italy, 113; lost by Germans, 221

Greek Army: capitulates, 117

Greim, Robert Ritter von, 246

Guderian, Heinz, 19; and eastern front (1944–1945), 232–236; on Hitler and SS attempt to relieve Budapest, 233; on Hitler's decision to take offensive in Hungary, 235; praises Waffen SS, 253–254; complains to Hitler about atrocities, 265; on Waffen SS and Army, 294

Hague, The, 65–66

Halder, Franz: on SS recruiting, 45 n. 46; on SS Totenkopfdivision, 57–58; and invasion of USSR, 98

Hartjenstein, Friedrich, 262

Hauptamt Ordnungspolizei, xxix

Hauptamt SS-Gericht: investigates SS recruiting in Serbia, 171; and Dirlewanger detachment, 268

Hausser, Paul, 13, 57, 85, 91, 184, 218, 254, 291; appointed Inspector of

Hausser, Paul (*cont.*)
Verfügungstruppe, 9; on ideological training of Waffen SS, 145; appointed commander of first SS corps, 202; requests tanks for Waffen SS (1941), 202; and battle of Normandy, 222–224; appointed commander of Army Group (Heeresgruppe) B, 224; wounded (1944), 225 n. 36; and Dirlewanger and Kaminski detachments, 264; on Waffen SS atrocities in Yugoslavia, 274
Heimwehr Danzig, 28
Heissmeyer, August, 37 n. 26
Herrgesell, Gerhard: on Hitler's belief that the Waffen SS had betrayed him, 242
Heydrich, Reinhard, xxviii–xxix
HIAG der Waffen SS, *see* Waffen SS: Mutual Aid Society (HIAG)
Higher SS and Police Leaders, *see* Höheren SS- und Polizeiführer
Himmler, Heinrich, 31–33, 167; appointed Reichsführer SS, xxvi; appointed Chef der Deutschen Polizei, xxviii; and coordination of German Police, xxviii; authority over SS combat formations, xxxii; on role of SS in purge of SA, 7; on purpose of the SS Verfügungstruppe, 16; feud with Army, 18–19; on expansion of Waffen SS after outbreak of WW II, 27; and atrocities in Poland, 29–30; on admission of policemen into SS, 34 n. 19; and SS Polizeidivision, 57; thanked by Hitler, 90; on recruitment of foreigners for SS, 94; and plans for invasion of USSR, 97–98; seeks larger military role for SS, 102; and SSFHA, 105–106; retains private SS "army," 109–110; prohibits use of designations "SS Verfügungstruppe" and "SS Totenkopfverbände," 110; issues directive listing SS organizations considered part of Waffen SS (1941), 110–111; on aim as Reichsführer SS, 123; on ideology, 124; speech attempting to justify conquest of USSR, 126–127; on death rather than surrender, 131 n. 26; on effects of ideological conviction, 134; Kharkov speech, 135–136; on

foreign volunteers in Waffen SS, 140, 148, 196; and recruitment for Waffen SS of "Germanic" foreigners, 143; on Greater Germanic Reich, 146–148; and *Untermensch* philosophy, 151; refuses to recruit Ukrainians for Waffen SS (1941), 151; orders Berger to recruit 20,000 men for Waffen SS during May 1941, 151; and national legions, 152–153; and recruiting of Danes for Waffen SS, 153; issues directive governing status of national legions, 155–156; issues directive to correct abuses in treatment of foreign SS men, 161; and recruiting of *Volksdeutsche*, 170–172; approves compulsory military service for *Volksdeutsche* in Serbia, 171–172; on the formation of a Baltic SS, 175–176; on Estonians, 176; supports formation of a Latvian legion for the Waffen SS, 176; orders introduction of compulsory military service in the *Ostland*, 178; refuses to accept Lithuanians in the SS, 178; on Moslems in the Waffen SS, 181–182; speaks to officer corps of Ukrainian SS division, 186; agrees to accept *Ostvölker* in Waffen SS, 187; and *Volksdeutsche* in Waffen SS, 192; and expansion of Waffen SS, 200, 211; boasts of volunteers for Waffen SS, 204; and SS division composed of Hitler Youths, 205; on average age of recruits, 207–208; appointed Commander of the Reserve Army and Chief of Army Ordnance, 227; on Waffen SS, 237; and battle of Berlin, 239–248 *passim;* meets with Count Bernadotte, 245; commits suicide, 248; and concentration camps, 260; and Dirlewanger detachment, 266; and shooting of prisoners by Waffen SS, 273 n. 63
Hindenburg, Paul von, 1–3, 283
Hirsch, Kurt: on postwar propaganda by Waffen SS veterans, 257
Hitler, Adolf: released from prison (1924), xxvi; becomes Chancellor, 1–3; and need for bodyguard, 4–5; reintroduces conscription, 8; orders formation of SS Verfügungstruppe, 8; conception of Waffen SS, 16, 17,

Hitler, Adolf (*cont.*)
100, 102, 198, 199, 285; and decree of August 17, 1938, 20–23, 283–284; announces war with Poland to Reichstag, 26; decides to attack in West (1939), 29; on atrocities in Poland, 29–30; attitude toward armed SS, 31–32; orders heavy artillery for Waffen SS, 51; orders launching of *Fall Gelb*, 60; and "stop order" near Dunkirk, 71; praises combat performance of Waffen SS, 74, 91, 199; and *Fall Rot*, 83; Reichstag speech (July 19, 1940), 89–90; awards medals and promotions (1940), 90; uses term *Waffen SS* in Reichstag speech, 90; and demobilization, 96; declares intention to invade USSR, 98; sets peacetime strength of Army, 101; issues directive for Barbarossa, 112–113; requests plan for attack on Greece, 113; orders destruction of Yugoslavia, 114; his motives for invading USSR, 121; opposes exclusive national formations in Waffen SS, 149; and establishment of SS Freiwilligenstandarte "Nordwest," 150; sets date for Barbarossa, 151; approves creation of national legions, 152 (*see also* specific legions, *under* Waffen SS); on foreigners in the German armed forces, 161 n. 52; orders all-out attack on Moscow, 166; assumes position of Commander-in-Chief of the Army, 167; purges Army's leadership, 167; "no retreat" order (1941), 167, 200; and recruiting of *Volksdeutsche* for Waffen SS, 170; approves SS division composed of *Volksdeutsche* from Yugoslavia, 170; approves Latvian legion for Waffen SS, 176; approves SS division composed of Moslems from Yugoslavia, 180; and Moslem SS troops, 182 n. 42; and Ukrainian SS division, 187, 194; on the Indian Legion (SS), 189–190, 195; and *Volksdeutsche* in the Waffen SS, 192–193; assessment of foreign SS units, 194–196; and Himmler, 198; believes Russia defeated, 200; supports Waffen SS recruiting, 203; approves SS division composed of

Hitler Youths, 205; and conduct of war in the East, 206; relations with Army generals, 206; expresses confidence in the SS Panzerkorps, 206; attitude toward Waffen SS, 206–208; on the fanaticism of youths in German armed forces, 207–208; authorizes six new SS corps (1943), 210; and SS armored divisions, 212; and transfer of the SS Panzerkorps to Italy, 213–214; on political orientation of Waffen SS, 214; and preparations for Allied invasion of Continent, 218; shifts interest from eastern to western front, 221; and battle of Normandy, 222–226; and Ardennes offensive, 226–232 *passim;* orders offensive in Alsace, 231; gives up offensive in West for new offensive in Hungary, 234; orders withdrawal of 6th SS Panzerarmee from Ardennes, 234; orders Dietrich's SS divisions to remove sleeve stripes, 237; and battle of Berlin, 238–248 *passim;* appoints Dönitz commander of German forces in the North, 239; believes that Waffen SS has betrayed him, 242; orders Steiner relieved of his command, 243; and Steiner, 243–245; believes that he has been betrayed by Himmler, 245–246; commits suicide, 248; racial policy, 259; and Waffen SS (reprise), 283–288 *passim*

Hitler Youth, 205–206, 246, 290; *see also* 12th SS Panzer "Hitler Jugend," *under* Waffen SS: Units

Höheren SS- und Polizeiführer, xxx; in Russia, 111, 174; and Dirlewanger detachment, 267; and Waffen SS atrocities, 274

Hoepner, Erich, 77

Hoesel, A. F. G. van, 140

Höss, Rudolf, 261

Hohenlychen, 241

Holste, Rudolf, 243–245, 247–248

Hungary, 172–174, 218–219, 221, 233–236

Hussein, Haj Amin el, 182

International Military Tribunal, 250, 251, 255

Italy: **capitulation of,** 208

Jackson, Robert H., 251 n. 5
Jeckeln, Friedrich, 291
Jodl, Alfred, 25–26, 239; on SS recruiting, 95; and battle of Berlin, 243–248 *passim*
Jörgensen, SS Sturmbannführer, 156
Jünger, Ernst, 291
Jüttner, Hans: appointed chief of staff of the SSFHA, 105–106; issues directive for new SS division (1940), 106–107; complains to Berger about indiscriminate recruiting of *Volksdeutsche*, 172–173; on conscription of native Germans for Waffen SS, 204

Kaltenbrunner, Ernst: appointed chief of RSHA, xxix
Kaminski, Bronislav, 264, 265, 269
Kaminski detachment (SS), 264–265; and Warsaw uprising, 265
Kammerhofer, Konstantin, 180
Kastoria, 117
Kaul, SS Gruppenführer, 37
Keitel, Wilhelm, 19, 30, 40–41, 52, 170, 239, 243–248; and new SS division (1940), 106; orders OKH to provide weapons for Waffen SS, 106; and SS recruiting, 203; and battle of Berlin, 243–248 *passim*
Kempf, Werner, 28
Keppler, Georg, 291; receives *Ritterkreuz*, 91; on Waffen SS and Einsatzgruppen, 263
Kersten, Felix, 145
Kesselring, Albert: and Waffen SS, 248
Kharkov, 289; Waffen SS victory at, 197–198, 207
Kiev, 120, 165, 217
Kirkenes: garrisoned by SS Totenkopf battalion, 104
Kleist, Ewald von, 85–86, 200
Klidi Pass, 116
Klingenberg, SS Hauptsturmführer: awarded *Ritterkreuz*, 116
Klissura Pass, 116
Kluge, Günther von: protests Hitler's order to transfer the SS Panzerkorps from the Russian front to Italy, 214; accused by Hitler of treason, 223–224
Knauth, Percival, 242 n. 82
Knochlein, Fritz, 77–78
Königsberg, 237

Kogon, Eugen: on character of Waffen SS, 290
Koller, Karl, 240
Kommando der Waffen SS (also Kommandoamt der Waffen SS): redesignated Kommandoamt der Waffen SS and transferred from SS Hauptamt to SS Führungshauptamt, 105
Kommando Stab RFSS, 103, 111, 120
Kommissarbefehl, 133
Korosten, 217
Kowel, 219
Krämer, Fritz: sentence for role in Malmédy massacre, 280
Krätschmer, Ernst-Günther, 270
Krass, SS Obersturmführer, 63
Krebs, Hans, 239, 247
Krhyssing, Colonel (Danish Army), 154, 156–157
Kripo (Kriminalpolizei), xxviii, xxxix, 263
Kroll Opera House, 26, 90
Krüger, Friedrich-Wilhelm, 156–157, 291

Landwehr, 52
Latvia: requests permission to re-establish Latvian Army (1942), 176
Le Cateau, 68
Le Paradis: massacre of British at: 76–78, 92, 272, 292
Leeb, Wilhelm Ritter von, 119
Leibstandarte SS "Adolf Hitler," 21, 24, 51–52, 56, 61–63, 65–67, 120, 130, 147, 204, 213, 219, 222, 229, 231, 283, 285, 287, 294; creation of, 5; oath to Hitler, 5; role in purge of SA, 6–7; and remilitarization of the Rhineland, 8; and annexation of Austria, 19; reinforced for western campaign, 32; receives new artillery battalion, 52; in the Netherlands, 62–67; in Flanders and Artois, 69–80; battles near Dunkirk, 79–80; and *Fall Rot*, 80–89 *passim*; Hitler authorizes enlargement to brigade, 100; enlarged to brigade, 106; casualties in Balkans, 116, 118 n. 65; in Yugoslavia and Greece, 116–118; and atrocities on Russian front, 133–136 *passim*; reorganized as panzergrenadier division, 200; provides commander and cadre for SS Di-

Leibstandarte SS (*cont.*)
vision "Hitler Jugend," 205–206; in battle for Kharkov, 207; transferred from Russian front to Italy, 214; returns from Italy to Russian front, 216; encircled in area of Kamenets–Podolsk, 217; and destruction of Russian bridgehead over the Gran River, 236 n. 67; and Malmédy massacre trial, 253, 280; and shooting of Russian prisoners of war, 273; and massacre of Italian civilians at Boves, 275–276; and Malmédy massacre, 278–280, 292

Leningrad, 119, 156, 165, 217
Les Islettes, 88
Lestrem, 74
Ley, Robert, 43
Liddell Hart, Basil H., 227
Lidice massacre, 255
Lindemann, Georg: complains to Himmler about the shooting of Russian prisoners of war by Waffen SS, 273 n. 63
Lippert, Michael, 7 n. 12
Loire River, 85
Luftwaffe, 64–67 *passim;* recruiting, 96–97
Lutze, Viktor, 43 n. 41
Lyon, 86
Lys Canal, 73
Lys River, 75

McCarthy, Joseph: and Malmédy massacre trial, 253
Mackensen, Eberhard von: letter to Himmler praising Leibstandarte, 134–135
Maikop oilfields, 200
Maizière, Ulrich de, 195
Malmédy massacre, 78, 278–280, 292
Manstein, Fritz Erich von Lewinski *gen.*, 29; on SS Totenkopfdivision, 59; on Russian atrocities, 133; and differences with Hitler, 206; and German counteroffensive in the East (1943), 206–207; commends SS Division "Das Reich," 215
Manteuffel, Hasso von: and Waffen SS, 256
Margarethe, Operation, 218
Marita, Undertaking, 113–114
Marne River, 82–84
Mauthausen, xxxiii

Merville, 70, 72–74
Metzovon Pass, 117
Meuse River, 231
Meyer, Kurt, 116, 263, 271; awarded *Ritterkreuz*, 117; and HIAG, 254; on Waffen SS war crimes, 255–256; on Waffen SS criminality, 257; first German war criminal condemned to death by western Allies, 277–278; and shooting of British and Canadian prisoners in Normandy, 292
Military manpower, German: apportionment among armed forces, 99, 101
Moerdijk bridges, 64
Monastir, 116
Monschau, 229
Moscow, 120, 166–167, 287
Moulins, 85, 86
Muis River, 214
Mummert, Werner, 246
Munich putsch (1923), xxvi
Mussert, Anton, 140, 150
Mussolini: dismissed from office, 214

National legions, *see under* Waffen SS
National Socialism: ideology, 121
National Socialist Party, *see* NSDAP
Natzweiler, 262
Nazi party, *see* NSDAP
Netherlands, the: and recruitment for Waffen SS, 94
Neusüss-Hunkel, Ermenhild: on Waffen SS, 289–290
Norbecque, 80
Nordwind, Operation, 231
Normandy, 222, 289
Norway: and recruitment for Waffen SS, 94
Novgorod, 156
NSB (Nationaal Socialistische Beweging), 150
NSDAP (Nationalsozialistische Deutsche Arbeiterpartei), 18, 21, 282; and SS recruiting, 43, 45

Oder front, 235
Oder line, 237, 239
Oise River, 84
OKH (Oberkommando des Heeres), 22, 69, 198, 274; on performance of SS in Polish campaign, 28–29; and SS recruiting, 34–50 *passim;* and arms for the SS, 50–55; issues plans

OKH (*cont.*)
for *Fall Rot,* 80–81; issues memorandum on Hitler's conception of Waffen SS, 100; and deployment for Barbarossa, 113
OKL (Oberkommando der Luftwaffe): friction with OKW, 96–97
OKW (Oberkommando der Wehrmacht), 184, 198, 203, 260, 274; created by Hitler, 19; and SS recruiting, 34–50 *passim*, 96–97, 151–152; opposition to Waffen SS, 35–55 *passim*; negotiations with Berger on wartime status of Waffen SS, 38–49 *passim*; investigates SS recruiting operations, 95–96; fear of SS, 96; and apportionment of military manpower, 99; and Hitler's memorandum clarifying relationship between Wehrmacht and Waffen SS, 100 n. 43; lifts restrictions on recruitment for Waffen SS during May 1941, 151
Oradour-sur-Glane, massacre at, 255, 276, 292, 293
Oranienburg, xxxiii, 244
Ordnungspolizei (Orpo), xxviii–xxx, 103, 111; and SS, 33, 34 n. 19
Orpo, *see* Ordnungspolizei
Ostland (Baltic lands), 174; Himmler orders introduction of compulsory military service, 178; *see also* Estonia *and* Latvia

Paetel, Karl O.: on Waffen SS, 258
Paradis, *see* Le Paradis
Paris: abandoned by French Government, 83
Parrington, Brigadier (British), 190
Patton, George S., 222
Peiper, Joachim (Jochen), 229; and Malmédy massacre, 231, 278, 280; and Malmédy massacre trial, 253, 275, 280; and atrocities in Italy, 253, 275, 276; sentence for role in Malmédy massacre, 280
Pfeffer-Wildenbruch, Karl von, 57, 88, 92, 233
Plattensee (Lake Balaton), 236
Ploen, 246
Ploesti oilfields, 220
Pohl, Oswald, 261
Police, German (Polizei): brief history, xxviii (*see also:* Gestapo; Höheren SS- und Polizeiführer; Kripo; Ordnungspolizei; Sicherheitspolizei; SS Police regiments; SS Polizeidivision)
Police regiments, *see* SS Police regiments
Polizeidivision, *see* SS Polizeidivision
Prague, 118
Priess, Hermann: sentence for role in Malmédy massacre, 280

Quisling, Vidkun, 140

RAD (Reichsarbeitsdienst), 43–44, 203, 204
Rauter, Hanns Albin, 141
Red Army, *see* Russian Army
Reichenau, Walter von, 28
Reichsarbeitsdienst, *see* RAD
Reichssicherheitshauptamt (RSHA), 102; created by Himmler, xxviii
Reichstag, 26
Reims: German capitulation at, 248
Reinecke, Guenther: complains to Himmler about SS recruiting procedures in Serbia, 171
Reinecke, Hermann, 41
Reinhardt, Georg-Hans, 115
Reitlinger, Gerald, 12, 77, 193, 261; on the expansion of the Waffen SS, 197–198; on Dirlewanger detachment, 270
Reitsch, Hanna, 246
Rhine River, 227
Ribbentrop, Joachim von, 239
Ridgway, Matthew B., 230
Röhm, Ernst, xxvi, 6–7
Röhm purge, 294; *see also* SA
Romania: and recruitment for the Waffen SS, 94; capitulates to Russians, 220
Rommel, Erwin, 68, 201
Rosenberg, Alfred, 176
Rostov, 165
Rot, Fall (Case Red), 61; plans, 80–81
Rotterdam: bombed by Luftwaffe, 65
RSHA, *see* Reichssicherheitshauptamt
Ruhr, 237
Rundstedt, Gerd von, 120, 226
Ruppiner Canal, 243
Russian Army, 183, 193; resists stubbornly, 132–133; and atrocities, 133; winter counteroffensive (1941–1942), 165; recaptures Rostov, 166; and German summer offensive (1942), 200–201; launches counter-

Russian Army (*cont.*)
offensive (1942), 201; winter offensive (1943–1944), 217–218; approaches Hungary, 218; launches summer offensive (1944), 219–220; offensive in the Balkans (1944), 220–221; launches drive for Berlin, 234; and battle of Berlin, 237–248; 1st White Russian Front (Army Group), 238
Russian High Command, 166
Russian Liberation Army, 72; *see also* Vlasov Army

SA (Sturmabteilung), xxv–xxvi, 1–7 *passim*, 59; threat to Hitler, 6–7; purged, 6–8; and SS recruiting, 43
Sachsenhausen, xxxiii, 262
St. Étienne, 86
St. Pourcain, 86
St. Venant, 71–73
Salla: Waffen SS defeat at, 130–132
Salonica, 117
San River, 220
Scarpe River, 68
Schalburg, Christian von, 157
Schellenberg, Walter, 245
Schmidt, Andreas, 169
Schörner, Ferdinand, 247
Schultz, Joachim, 244 n. 88
Schutzmanns-Bataillone, 174
SD (Sicherheitsdienst), 102; brief history, xxvii–xxx; and Einsatzgruppen, 263; and Dirlewanger detachment, 268
Sea Lion, Operation, 112
Security Service (SS), *see* SD
Seine River, 84, 225
Sennheim, 144
Serbia, 204; SS recruiting in, 169–172
Sicherheitsdienst, *see* SD
Sicherheitspolizei (Sipo), xxviii–xxx
Sicily, 214
Simon, Max, 273; and massacre of Italian civilians, 276; and Brettheim affair, 280–281
Skoplje, 116
Slovakia, 173–174, 269
Somme River, 68, 81, 82
Sorge group, 165
South Beveland, 67
Soviet Army, *see* Russian Army
Speer, Albert, 55, 239
Speidel, Hans, 227
SS (Schutzstaffel), xxvi; purpose, xxvi;

role in purge of SA, xxvi; becomes separate formation of NSDAP, xxvi–xxvii, 7; Himmler purges unqualified members, 4; need for armed component, 4–5; armed units freed from legal jurisdiction of Wehrmacht, 30; ideology, 122–124; as dynamic core of Nazi system, 282; chart, 304; *see also* specific components
SS Beschaffungsamt, 50; *see also* Waffen und Geräteamt, *under* Waffen SS
SS Death's Head detachments, *see* SS Totenkopfverbände
SS Ergänzungsstellen, 36–38
SS Führungshauptamt (SSFHA), 107; establishment of, 105; purpose and authority of, 105–106; issues directive regarding status of components of Waffen SS, 108–109; friction with SSHA, 160; complains about indiscriminate SS recruiting practices, 172–173; and concentration camps, 260–261; and Dirlewanger detachment, 267
SS Hauptamt (SSHA), 144; and SS Verfügungstruppe, 9; friction with SSFHA, 160; and recruiting of British POWs for the Waffen SS, 190–191; and concentration camps, 260; and Dirlewanger detachment, 267
SS Junkerschulen, 291; "Braunschweig," 9, 12, 34; "Bad Tölz," 12, 34, 161
SS Oberabschnitte, 36–37
SS Personalhauptamt, 262
SS Police regiments, xxix–xxx, 269; recruitment, 93; deployment in Russia, 111 n. 53; duties and organization, 111–112; foreign personnel, 112
SS "Political Purpose Squads," 6
SS Polizeidivision, 52, 61, 98, 120; establishment of, 33–34; Army artillery regiment attached to, 52 n. 71; and *Fall Gelb*, 57; and *Fall Rot*, 87–89; casualties (1940), 88; reorganized as panzergrenadier division, 209; *see also* 4th SS Polizei-Panzergrenadier, *under* Waffen SS: Units: Divisions
SS Schulungsamt, 14
SS Totenkopfdivision, 56, 57, 98, 106, 120; establishment of, 33; in Flan-

SS Totenkopfdivision (*cont.*)
ders and Artois, 67–80 *passim;* and battle of Arras, 68–69; and massacre at Le Paradis, 76–78, 272; and *Fall Rot*, 80–89 *passim;* recruitment for, 96; *see also* 3rd SS Panzer "Totenkopf," *under* Waffen SS: Units: Divisions

SS Totenkopfstandarten, *see* SS Totenkopfverbände

SS Totenkopfverbände (SSTV), 6, 19–20, 38–50 *passim,* 56, 58–59, 272, 283–285, 294; brief history, xxxii–xxxiv; call-up of SS reservists as "police reinforcements," xxxiii, 23, 33; integrated into Waffen SS, xxxiv, 50, 102–110 *passim;* role in purge of SA, 6; legal status, 8, 283–284; and Führer Decree of August 17, 1938, 23–24, 283–284; and occupation of Sudetenland, 24–25; and Führer Decree of May 18, 1939, 33, 41, 49, 50; OKW refuses to recognize duty as military service, 39–40; and wearing of Army field-gray uniform, 42; and secrecy in recruiting, 42 n. 38; disposition (1940), 42 n. 40; requirements for wartime enlistment, 44–45; arms for, 50–53; recruitment, 93; definition, 102 n. 27; transformed into SS infantry regiments, 103; Inspectorate of SS Totenkopfstandarten dissolved, 104; under Army command, 104, 108; deactivation of units, 105; release of reservists, 105; Himmler prohibits further use of designation, 110; and antipartisan operations, 259

Units:

Regiments (Standarten):
SS Totenkopf "Brandenburg," xxxiii
SS Totenkopf "Oberbayern," xxxiii, 25
SS Totenkopf "Thüringen," xxxiii
1st SS Totenkopf, 35 n. 17
2nd SS Totenkopf, 35 n. 17, 77
3rd SS Totenkopf, 35 n. 17
6th SS Totenkopf, 107
7th SS Totenkopf, 107
8th SS Totenkopf, 108

Battalions (Sturmbanne):
Ist SS Totenkopf "Oberbayern," xxxiii
IInd SS Totenkopf "Elbe," xxxiii
IIIrd SS Totenkopf "Sachsen," xxxiii
IVth Totenkopf "Ostfriesland," xxxiii
Vth SS Totenkopf "Brandenburg," xxxiii
SS Totenkopf "Götze," *see* Heimwehr Danzig

SS Totenkopfwachsturmbanne, xxxiv, 103 n. 28

SS Verfügungsdivision, 32, 52, 56, 61, 63, 64, 67, 106–107; in the Netherlands, 63–67; in Flanders and Artois, 70–80 *passim;* and *Fall Rot*, 80–89 *passim;* casualties in *Fall Rot*, 81, 85; redesignated SS division "Reich" (later "Das Reich"), 107; *see also* 2nd SS Panzer "Das Reich," *under* Waffen SS: Units: Divisions

SS Verfügungstruppe (SSVT), xxx, 9–26 *passim,* 283–285, 288, 294; legitimized and placed on Police budget, 9, 283–285; selection of personnel, 10–13; and wearing of Army field-gray uniform, 11; training, 13–15; purpose, 15–17, 284–285; and Führer Decree of August 17, 1938, 20–22, 283–285; and occupation of Czechoslovakia, 24–25; stages maneuvers for Hitler, 25–26; integrated into Army for Polish campaign, 26; receives artillery regiment, 26; in the Polish campaign, 27–28; Himmler prohibits further use of designation, 110; and Wehrmacht, 283–284

Units:

Regiments (*see also under* Waffen SS: Units: Regiments):
Leibstandarte SS "Adolf Hitler," *see* Leibstandarte SS "Adolf Hitler"
1st SS "Deutschland," 10–11, 21, 25, 27
2nd SS "Germania," 10–11, 21, 24, 28
3rd SS "Der Führer," 19, 28 n. 3
SS Artillerie Standarte (Artillery Regiment), 26

SS Verfügungstruppe (cont.)
Units: Regiments: (cont.)
Battalions (Sturmbanne):
SS Aufklärungs (Reconnaissance),
27
SS Pionier (Engineer), 28
SS Wirtschafts- und Verwaltungshaupt-
amt (WVHA), xxxii, xxxiv, 261
Stabswache (SS), 4–5
Stahlhelm, 2–3, 9
Stalin, 166
Stalingrad, 201–202
Steiner, Felix, 10, 57, 74–75, 91, 218,
245, 291; awarded Ritterkreuz, 90–
91; appointed commander of SS
Division "Wiking," 106–107; on
foreign volunteers, 137–140 passim;
on Greater Germanic Reich, 146–
147; and Moslems in the Waffen
SS, 183 n. 43; appointed com-
mander of IIIrd (Germanisches)
SS Panzerkorps, 210; and battle of
Berlin, 238–248 passim
Stosstrupp "Adolf Hitler," xxv–xxvi
Stoumont, 231
Stroink, Colonel (Dutch Army), 154
Student, Kurt, 66
Sturmabteilung, see SA
Sudetenland, 24–25

Tarare, 86
Tarawa, 128
Tarnopol, 217
Taylor, Telford, 84
Terneuzen, 69
Tiroler Landsturmordnung (1872), 172
Todt, Fritz, 53–55
Totenkopf regiments, see SS Toten-
kopfverbände
Totenkopfstandarten, see SS Toten-
kopfverbände
Totenkopfverbände: transfer of mem-
bers to SS Totenkopfdivision, 258–
259; and executions and deporta-
tions, 259; integration into field
formations of Waffen SS, 259
Trevor-Roper, Hugh R., 239, 241, 242
Tulle: executions by SS of French
civilians at, 276

Ukraine, 165
United States Army: launches offensive
to break out of the Normandy
beachhead, 222; reaches Elbe
River, 237; units: 1st Army, 221;
3rd Army, 222, 225; 4th Armored

Division, 222; 82nd Airborne Division, 231
United States Marines, 128

Valenciennes, 69
Verfügungsdivision, see under SS Ver-
fügungsdivision
Vichy, 86
Villers-Cotterets, 82
Vistula River, 220
Vlasov, Andrei, 188
Vlasov Army, 188, 193–194
Vlissingen, 67
Völkischer Beobachter (newspaper), 7
Volga River, 201
Volksdeutsche, xxxi, 143, 192–193; from
Slovakia, 46; recruitment for Waf-
fen SS, 94; definition, 168; in the
Waffen SS, 168–174 (see also under
Waffen SS: Foreign personnel); and
concentration camps, 262
Volksoffiziere, 291–292
Voncq, 87
VNV (Vlaamsch Nationaal Verbond),
150

Wacht am Rhein, Operation, 228
Waffen SS; brief overview, xxx–xxxii;
nominal members, xxxiv; strength:
(September 1939) 27, (May 1940)
56, (May 1941) 101, (June 1941)
120 n. 3, (September 1942) 203,
(September 1943) 203, 211, 288,
289; casualties, 28, 134, 167, 289
(see also individual units); freed
from legal jurisdiction of Wehrmacht, 30; recruitment, 35–50
passim, 93–102 passim, 152, 203;
Ersatz formations, 46–48; title becomes official, 49; administrative
organizations (1940), 49 n. 62; fight
for arms, 50–55; Waffen und
Geräteamt, 53; independent procurement of arms, 53–54; use of
captured Czech arms, 55, 57; in
plans for Fall Gelb, 55–56; and
military regulations, 56; attitude
of Army field commanders toward,
56–59; deployment for Fall Gelb,
61; in the invasion of the Netherlands, 61–67; in Flanders and
Artois, 67–80; combat performance
(1940), 75; evaluation of role in
western campaign (1940), 89–92;
praised by Hitler in Reichstag, 90;

Waffen SS (*cont.*)
ideology, 92, 121–136 *passim;* relations with Army and OKW, 93–109 *passim* (*see also* Army, German, OKH, *and* OKW); demobilization of reservists (1940), 96–97; expansion and reorganization (1940–1941), 106–112; list of units serving with Army (April 1941), 108; status of units (1941), 108–109; units not serving under Army command (April 1941), 109; SS organizations considered part of, 110–111; in Yugoslavia and Greece (April 1941), 113–118; friction with Army, 114–115; deployment for Barbarossa, 120; Mutual Aid Society (HIAG), 124, 252–255, 258–259; ideological indoctrination, 125–130 *passim;* and suicide rather than surrender, 134; combat achievements praised by Army generals, 135; and myth of European army, 137–148; conscription for, 170–172, 204, 206 n. 27; system of designating divisions, 181 n. 38; expansion (1942–1943), 197–211; given priority in distribution of tanks, 201, 207, 209; as "fire brigade" of Third Reich, 202, 212–213; contribution to eastern campaign, 202; elite formations transformed into panzer-grenadier divisions, 202, 203, 209; field strength (1942–1943), 203; location of units (1943), 204; importance to German war machine, 209–210, 288–289; creates six new corps (1943), 210; elite divisions of, 211; value in last two years of war, 288–289; and defensive battles in the East (1943–1944), 214–221; and occupation of Hungary (1944), 218–219; and Allied invasion of France, 219–226; and battle for Warsaw (1944), 220; in defense of Balkans (1944–1945), 221, 233, 235, 236, 237; and battle of Falaise–Argentan pocket, 225; casualties in battle of Normandy, 225–226; and battle of Budapest, 233, 235, 236; use of sailors and airmen as replacements, 236; and German counteroffensive in Hungary (1945), 236–237; and Hitler's armband order, 237; forced out of Vienna, 237; and battle of Berlin, 238–248; not mentioned in capitulation, 248; and cease-fire, 248; arrogant in defeat, 248–249; and Nuremberg trials, 250–251; criminality, 250–281 (*see also* Atrocities); and concentration camps, 251, 256–263; and Einsatzgruppen, 251, 263–264; and German de-Nazification courts, 251; postwar imprisonment of members, 251; and Malmédy massacre trial, 253, 280; veterans in Bundeswehr, 254–255 n. 14; and postwar pensions, 255; and criminal guilt, 257; criminality and postwar German politics, 258; and Dirlewanger and Kaminski detachments, 264–270; as Hitler's praetorian guard, 282–285; oath, 283; as military apotheosis of National Socialism, 285; assessment of military role, 286–290; fanaticism, 289; composition of, 290; and Nazi ideology, 290–292; character of, 290–292; and Freikorps spirit, 291; influence of officers, 291–292; ranks (table), 295

Atrocities: destruction of Warsaw Ghetto (1943), 47; shooting of British prisoners at Le Paradis (1940), 77, 92, 272, 292; on Russian front, 133–136, 272–275; at Kharkov, 136, 293; during Warsaw uprising (1944), 220 n. 24, 265, 269; massacre at Oradour-sur-Glane, 255, 276, 292–293; and massacre at Lidice, 255 n. 15; shooting of Jews in Poland, 271; committed by field formations, 271–281; shooting of Jews in Galicia, 272; shooting of prisoners, 272–280; in Yugoslavia, 273–274; during antipartisan operations, 274–276, 293; shooting of Jews in Russia, 274, 293; massacre of Italian civilians, 275–276, 293; in southern France, 276; shooting of British and Canadian prisoners in Normandy, 277; in Greece, 277, 293; shooting of American prisoners at Malmédy, 278–280, 292; against Germans, 280–281; and Nazi ideology, 292

Waffen SS (*cont.*)

Foreign personnel: xxi, 138–139, 152, 287–288; *Volksdeutsche* from Slovakia, 46; recruitment of, 93–95, 143–144; motives for volunteering, 139–142; criminals among, 141; recruitment justified on ideological grounds, 144; ideological training of, 144–145; Finns, 149–150, 159–160; status of, 150; *Volksdeutsche* from Yugoslavia, 150; Danes, 153–155; Flemings, 154–155; Netherlanders, 154–155; problems with, 154–162; desertions, 158–159; disillusioned with SS service, 158–160; evaluation of combat performance, 161, 191–196, 287–288; recruitment of west European collaborators, 163; *Volksdeutsche* from Romania, 169; coercion in recruiting, 170–172; conscription of, 170–172; *Volksdeutsche* from Hungary, 172–174; *Volksdeutsche* in Hungarian and Slovakian armed forces transferred to Waffen SS, 173–174; number and origin of *Volksdeutsche* in Waffen SS (1943), 173; conscription of Latvians and Estonians, 178; Yugoslavian Moslems, 180–185, 193; Ukrainians (Galicians), 185–188, 194–196; Russians, 187–189, 193; Cossacks (Russian), 188–189; Indians, 189–190, 195; Britons, 190–191; problems with *Volksdeutsche*, 192–193; Hungarians, 193; Romanians, 193; Hitler's assessment of, 194–196; *see also Volksdeutsche and* Waffen SS: National legions

National legions: 152; Freiwilligen Legion "Niederlande" (also "Nederland"), 153–154; Freiwilligen Legion "Flandern," 153–154; strength of (July 1941), 154 n. 39; problems with, 154–162; Freiwilligen Legion "Norwegen," 154, 157; Freikorps "Danemark" (also "Danmark"), 155, 157, 204, 275; status of, 155; integrated into larger units of Waffen SS, 162–163; Estonian Legion, 175–177; Latvian Legion, 176–177; racial requirements for enlistment in, 179; Indian Legion, 189–190, 195; British Legion, 190–191; *see also* Waffen SS: Foreign personnel

Units (*see* complete list, 296–299):
Armies (Armeen):
6th SS Panzer, 229, 234–238, 289
Corps (Armeekorps):
SS Generalkommando (Corps Command), 202
SS Panzer-Generalkommando (previously SS Generalkommando), 204
SS Panzer (later IInd SS Panzer), 213
Ist SS Panzer, 210, 234
IInd SS Panzer, 210, 218, 225, 234
IIIrd (Germanisches) SS Panzer, 210, 218
IVth SS Panzer, 210, 220, 233
Vth SS Gebirgs, 210
VIth (Lettisches) SS Freiwilligen, 178, 210
IXth Waffen-Gebirgs (SS), 210–211, 233
XIth SS, 211
XIIth SS, 211
XIIIth SS, 211
XIVth SS, 211
XVth SS, 211
XVIIIth SS, 211
XVth (SS) Kosaken-Kavallerie, 188
Divisions:
1st SS Panzer "Leibstandarte Adolf Hitler," *see* Leibstandarte SS "Adolf Hitler"
2nd SS Panzer "Das Reich" (also "Reich"), 115, 116, 123, 133, 147, 150, 169, 200, 204, 207, 214, 215, 217, 219, 221, 222, 225, 229, 249, 263, 274; *see also* SS Verfügungsdivision
3rd SS Panzer "Totenkopf," 123, 147, 157, 200, 204, 207, 214–216, 218, 220, 233, 235, 236; *see also* SS Totenkopfdivision
4th SS Polizei-Panzergrenadier, 204, 277, 292; *see also* SS Polizeidivision
5th SS Panzer "Wiking," 107, 120, 123, 149, 150, 152, 159,

Waffen SS (*cont.*)
Units: Divisions (*cont.*)
200, 204, 208, 210, 217, 220,
233, 235, 236, 272
6th SS Gebirgs "Nord," 103, 204,
231
7th SS Freiwilligen-Gebirgs "Prinz
Eugen," 170, 179, 200, 204,
221, 273, 274
8th SS Kavallerie "Florian
Geyer," 193 n. 66, 202, 204,
219, 221, 233
9th SS Panzer "Hohenstauffen,"
204, 205, 208, 209, 218, 219,
225, 229
10th SS Panzer "Frundsberg,"
204, 205, 208, 209, 218, 219,
225, 231
11th SS Freiwilligen-Panzergren-
adier "Nordland," 162, 164,
208, 210, 218, 238, 246, 247
12th SS Panzer "Hitler Jugend,"
206, 208, 209, 219, 225, 229,
236 n. 67, 249, 277
13th Waffen-Gebirgs (SS) "Handschar" (kroat. Nr. 1), 181,
182, 183, 184, 208
14th Waffen-Grenadier (SS) (galiz. Nr. 1), 185–187, 208
15th Waffen-Grenadier (SS) (lett.
Nr. 1), 164, 178, 179, 194,
208, 246
16th SS Panzergrenadier "Reichsführer SS," 184, 208, 219,
236, 276
17th SS Panzergrenadier "Götz
von Berlichingen," 208, 219,
221, 222, 231
18th SS Freiwilligen-Panzergren-
adier "Horst Wessel," 211,
219
19th Waffen-Grenadier (SS) (lett.
Nr. 2), 178, 179, 194
20th Waffen-Grenadier (SS) (estn.
Nr. 1), 178, 179, 194, 195
21st Waffen-Gebirgs (SS) "Skanderbeg" (alban. Nr. 1), 184–
185
22nd Freiwilligen-Kavallerie (SS)
"Maria Theresia," 193 n. 66,
221, 233
23rd Waffen-Gebirgs (SS) "Kama"
(kroat. Nr. 2), 163, 184, 185
24th Waffen-Gebirgskarstjäger
(SS), 164 n. 56

25th Waffen-Grenadier (SS)
"Hunyadi" (ungar. Nr. 1),
188
26th Waffen-Grenadier (SS)
(ungar. Nr. 2), 188
27th SS Freiwilligen-Grenadier
"Langemarck," 163
28th SS Freiwilligen-Grenadier
"Wallonien," 163
29th Waffen-Grenadier (SS)
(russ. Nr. 1), 188, 193
30th Waffen-Grenadier (SS)
(russ. Nr. 2), 188, 193
31st SS Freiwilligen-Panzergren-
adier "Böhmen Mähren,"
188
33rd Waffen-Grenadier (SS)
"Charlemagne" (franz. Nr.
1), 164, 246
36th Waffen-Grenadier (SS)
267, 269
Brigades:
1st SS Infantry, 109, 121, 157,
204, 275
2nd SS Infantry, 109, 155, 204,
273 n. 63
SS Kavallerie, 121, 275
SS Freiwilligen-Sturm "Langemarck," 163
SS Freiwilligen-Sturm "Nederland," 238
Waffen-Grenadier (SS) (ital. Nr.
1), 164 n. 56
Regiments (*see also under* SS Verfügungstruppe):
SS "Deutschland," 57, 67, 73–76,
107, 249
SS "Germania," 57, 107
SS "Der Führer," 57, 61, 63, 81,
82, 107
SS "Nordland," 94, 106, 159
SS "Westland," 94, 106–107
SS Freiwilligenstandarte "Nord-
west," 150, 153
SS Panzergrenadier "Danmark,"
162
SS Panzergrenadier "Nederland,"
162
SS Panzergrenadier "Norge,"
162–163
Waffen-Grenadier (SS) (rumän.
Nr. 1), 188
Waffen-Grenadier (SS) (rumän.
Nr. 2), 188

Waffen SS (*cont.*)
Units: Regiments (*cont.*)
Waffen-Grenadier (SS) (bulgar. Nr. 1), 188
2nd SS Totenkopf Infantry, 77
4th SS Infantry, 109
5th SS Infantry, 109
8th SS Infantry, 109
9th SS Infantry, 120
10th SS Infantry, 109
11th SS Infantry, 107, 115
14th SS Infantry, 109
1st SS Kavallerie (Cavalry), 110
2nd SS Kavallerie (Cavalry), 110
SS Artillerie Standarte (Artillery Regiment), 26, 27, 30, 271
5th SS Artillerie (Artillery) Regiment, 107
Battalions:
Begleitbataillon "Reichsführer SS," 246
Finnish Volunteer Battalion (Finnische Freiwilligen-Bataillon der Waffen SS), 149, 162
Battle Groups (Kampfgruppen):
SS Kampfgruppe "Nord," 103, 107, 108, 120, 130–132
SS Kampfgruppe Peiper, 229, 231
SS Kampfgruppe "Wallonie," 238
Rgt.-Gr. 13th SS-Geb. "Handschar," 184
Rgt.-Gr. 21st SS-Geb. "Skanderbeg," 185
Miscellaneous formations:
Kaukasischer Waffenverband (SS), 188
Osttürkischer Waffenverband (SS), 188
Serbisches SS Freiwilligenkorps, 188

Walcheren, 67
Warsaw, 29, 220, 233, 289; Ghetto, 47; uprising, 220, 265, 269
Watten, 71
Wawrzinek, Emil, 117
Wehrbezirkskommandos (WBK), 35, 46, 95
Wehrkreise, xxx
Wehrkreiskommandos, 108, 109 n. 46
Wehrmacht: losses in Russian campaign, 167–168; capitulates to Allies, 248; and Waffen SS, 283–294 *passim; see also* Army, German, *and* OKW
Weichs, Maximilian Freiherr von: and SS Totenkopfdivision, 58–59
Wenck, Walter, 239, 243, 245, 247, 248
Weserübung, Fall, 60 n. 1
Wheeler-Bennett, Sir John W., 7–8
Wiele, Jef van de, 150 n. 29
Witt, Fritz, 205
Wöhler, Otto: commends SS panzer divisions, 216
Wolff, Karl, 41, 77
Wormhoudt, 79
WVHA, *see* SS Wirtschafts- und Verwaltungshauptamt

Yssel River, 63
Yugoslav Army, 116
Yugoslavia: signs Tripartite pact, 114; invaded by Germans, 115–116; and recruiting for Waffen SS, 150, 169–172, 221

Zeeland, 64, 67
Zeitzler, Kurt, 207
Zhitomir, 217
Zhukov, Georgi, 238
Ziemssen, Dietrich, 253
Zwolle, 63